D0485403

Madame de Pompadour

Also by Christine Pevitt Algrant:

Philippe Duc d'Orléans: Regent of France
(as Christine Pevitt)

CHRISTINE PEVITT ALGRANT

Madame de Pompadour

Mistress of France

Grove Press
New York

Copyright © 2002 by Christine Pevitt Algrant

All rights reserved. No part of this book may be reproduced in any form or by any electronic or mechanical means, including information storage and retrieval systems, without permission in writing from the publisher, except by a reviewer, who may quote brief passages in a review. Any members of educational institutions wishing to photocopy part or all of the work for classroom use, or publishers who would like to obtain permission to include the work in an anthology, should send their inquiries to Grove/Atlantic, Inc., 841 Broadway, New York, NY 10003.

Published simultaneously in Canada
Printed in the United States of America

FIRST GROVE PRESS PAPERBACK EDITION

Library of Congress Cataloging-in-Publication Data
Pevitt, Christine.
    Madame de Pompadour : mistress of France / by Christine Pevitt Algrant.
        p. cm.
    Includes bibliographical references.
    ISBN 0-8021-4035-1 (pbk.)
    1. Pompadour, Jeanne Antoinette Poisson, marquise de, 1721–1764.   2. Louis
XV, King of France, 1710–1774 — Relations with women.   3. Favorites, Royal —
France — Biography.   4. France — Kings and rulers — Mistresses — Biography.
5. France — History — Louis XV, 1715–1774.   I.   Title.
DC135.P8 P48 2002
944'.034'092 — dc21
[B]   2002023202

Design by Laura Hammond Hough

Grove Press
841 Broadway
New York, NY 10003

03 04 05 06 07   10 9 8 7 6 5 4 3 2 1

For my mother

CONTENTS

LIST OF ILLUSTRATIONS

Charles Lenormand de Tournehem, Louis Tocqué (Châteaux
de Versailles et de Trianon, Versailles, France/Réunion des Musées
Nationaux/Art Resource, NY)

Louis XV, Maurice-Quentin de La Tour (Louvre, Paris, France/
Réunion des Musées Nationaux/Art Resource, NY)

Madame de Pompadour in 1748, Jean Marc Nattier (Châteaux
de Versailles et de Trianon, Versailles, France/Réunion des Musées
Nationaux/Art Resource, NY)

Voltaire, Maurice-Quentin de La Tour (Châteaux de Versailles et
de Trianon, Versailles, France/Réunion des Musées Nationaux/Art
Resource, NY)

The Ball of the Yew Trees, February 1745, Charles Nicolas Cochin,
II (Louvre, Paris, France/Réunion des Musées Nationaux/Art
Resource, NY)

Abbé de Bernis, eighteenth-century French School (Châteaux de
Versailles et de Trianon, Versailles, France/Réunion des Musées
Nationaux/Art Resource, NY)

Madame de Pompadour sculpted as the Goddess of Friendship,
Jean Baptiste Pigalle (Louvre, Paris, France/Réunion des Musées
Nationaux/Art Resource, NY)

View of the Château de Bellevue, Brouard (Châteaux de Versailles et
de Trianon, Versailles, France/Réunion des Musées Nationaux/Art
Resource, NY)

PREFACE

On Thursday, February 25, 1745, King Louis XV of France threw a spectacular party at his palace of Versailles to celebrate the wedding of his only son and heir, the Dauphin Louis, to the Infanta Maria-Teresa Raffaella of Spain. This masked ball was the culmination of a series of balls, ballets, banquets, and operas with which the king marked this important event in the life of the house of Bourbon; the future of the dynasty rested on the marriage of the fifteen-year-old heir and his seventeen-year-old bride.

Louis intended to make the occasion as memorable as possible. The ball would be held in the state rooms, and open to all, provided they were properly dressed, the gentlemen wearing swords, and providing that one member of each party unmasked himself and gave his name.

At midnight the public began to flow up the marble staircase and into the state rooms. Ladies in wide skirts struggled through the doorways of the salon de Venus and the salon de Mars; gentlemen tried to prevent their swords from becoming entangled in the same enveloping skirts. In the Hall of Mirrors eight thousand candles were reflected in the glass of the doors and windows; music was played by two orchestras, and there was dancing in the salon d'Hercule and the salons d'Apollon and de Mercure. Buffets were set up at either end of the Hall of Mirrors and near the Staircase of the Ambassadors; as it was Lent, only fish was served.

At the height of the crush, a strange procession entered the Hall of Mirrors; the Dauphin, dressed as a gardener, and the Dauphine, as a flower seller, led the way, while behind them lumbered eight enormous yew trees, made of papier-mâché, and clipped into the formal shapes of the Versailles gardens. It was known that, concealed within one of these trees, was the king himself. Within minutes, every woman in the throng had descended upon the arboreal procession, striving to identify the royal tree. An engraving of the scene shows the crowd—the strangely costumed revelers, and, in the midst of the clump of trees, a young woman in profile, chatting with one of them. The woman was the wife of a Parisian tax farmer, her name Jeanne-Antoinette Poisson, Madame d'Etioles. As the evening wore on, it became clear that Madame d'Etioles had captured the royal yew.

Louis XV was indeed a highly desirable prize. In his prime, thirty-five years old, handsome, and known to have a roving eye, Louis was the object of intense feminine speculation that night. Having fathered seven daughters and one son with his Polish queen, Marie Lecszinska, the king had turned to mistresses, and in particular to three sisters from the Nesle family, Louise de Mailly, Pauline de Vintimille, and Marie-Anne de Châteauroux. At the end of 1744 Madame de Châteauroux had died a sudden and agonizing death, leaving Louis distraught. Everyone knew that he would soon take a new mistress; his temperament demanded it. For this vacant situation, an honored and traditional one at the court of France, every presentable woman was eager to apply.

To most observers, the encounter between the king and the beautiful bourgeoise marked the "beginning of the adventure of Madame d'Etioles," as the Danish envoy, Baron von Bernstorff, noted in his diary. The conquering nymph seemed to have appeared out of nowhere and stolen the king's heart.

The truth was different. The king was already familiar with Jeanne-Antoinette, and she herself was a highly visible member of the Parisian financial elite. Bernstorff gives the strong impression that this was an adventure long prepared. He was right. This is the story of how it began, and how the tax farmer's wife became one of the most influential women of the age, known to history as the Marquise de Pompadour.

PART ONE
1721–1745

"She was born with good sense and a good heart."

Chapter 1

"She charms everyone who sees her . . ."

Jeanne-Antoinette Poisson was born in Paris on December 29, 1721, the first child of Louise-Madeleine de La Motte, wife of François Poisson. Her birth went largely unremarked; the Poissons, living in modest but comfortable circumstances in the rue de Cléry, were simply a middle-class family lost in the anonymity of the great city. And yet, there were powerful forces taking an interest in this child. Things were not quite as they seemed in the Poisson household.

The couple had married in October 1718. The bride was the daughter of Jean de La Motte, an official of the War Ministry responsible for supplying the Invalides with meat and other provisions. The La Mottes lived at the Invalides and were a very respectable family; one of Louise-Madeleine's sisters was a nun, another married to the fruiterer to the royal household. But Louise-Madeleine herself, not yet twenty when she married, was already remarked in Paris not only for her beauty (she was a handsome brunette with dazzling white skin, "one of the most beautiful women in Paris," according to a contemporary), but also for her high spirits ("she was as clever as four devils"). The capricious young woman had found a husband of similar social standing, but considerably less élan. François Poisson was in his forties, recently widowed. A procurement agent for the army, he was not a glamorous prize, a suitable, if not exciting, match.

As the couple settled into married life, the city around them was experiencing a social and economic upheaval. Since 1715, and on the death of the great King Louis XIV, France had been ruled by Philippe d'Orléans, regent for the five-year-old King Louis XV. D'Orléans had immediately moved the court from Versailles to Paris, installing the little king at the Tuileries, and beginning the transformation of the capital. An application of money and energy stimulated the development of an entire new district of the city, the faubourg Saint-Germain, where the nobility, freed from the constraints of life at Versailles, began to build elegant new town houses; Parisian society turned to the pursuit of pleasure, buying beautiful clothes and *objets de luxe*, discovering the delights of fine cuisine and lavish entertaining, and all the joys of *la vie mondaine*. Restaurants and coffee-houses began to appear, art and antique dealers thrived, makers of fine furniture could not keep up with demand. Life took on a joyous, if often riotous, tone.

Regency society was at once licentious and refined; it was characterized not only by an undeniable grossness of morals, but also by the seductive *fêtes galantes* of Antoine Watteau. The Regent d'Orléans himself exemplified the dichotomy; he was a very intelligent, creative man, but dissolute and coarse in his private affairs. Despite his buffoonery and philandering, however, he kept France peaceful and increasingly prosperous. Until, that is, he entrusted the finances of the country to a Scottish adventurer called John Law, in part responsible for the great financial crash known as the "Mississippi," which ruined everything for which d'Orléans had worked.

In 1720 a dizzying series of events threw Paris into uproar. John Law, with the approval of the regent, had started a commercial bank, which became so successful at promoting the idea of the use of credit and paper money—ideas which were revolutionary in France at the time—that the regent made it the "royal" (that is, officially approved) bank. At the same time, Law took over several moribund French trading companies, amalgamated them into the giant Compagnie des Indes, and embarked on a campaign to encourage the public to bring their gold and silver to his bank in exchange for banknotes, and then invest their notes in the soon-to-be-discovered wealth of the faraway and mysterious land of Louisiana, hence the "Mississippi." Share prices rose, an open-air stock market was set up in the rue Quincampoix in the center of Paris, and frenzied scenes of buying and selling took place against a backdrop of petty crime and violence.

Then, inevitably, at the end of 1720, the whole fragile edifice collapsed. John Law fled the country. Those who had invested in the "Mississippi" saw their savings gone, their security vanished, their hopes destroyed. Philippe d'Orléans had failed in his great attempt to modernize the financial system of France. The failure had a devastating effect on the regent. He retreated from new policy initiatives and, in 1722, he retreated from Paris, taking the court back to Versailles, and choosing to focus his time and energy on the education of the eleven-year-old King Louis XV. The unfortunate separation of king and capital would have heavy consequences for the future. The regent himself would die suddenly at the end of 1723, at the age of forty-nine, worn out by his excesses and by the failure of his cherished scheme to make France prosperous.

While all this was taking place, the Poissons must have observed the frantic atmosphere in the city, the crowds of provincials and foreigners possessed with the desire for riches, the violence in the nearby rue Quincampoix. But they did not join the hysteria. They had better advice; François Poisson was employed by some very grand and important people, men who were John Law's most bitter foes, men who would certainly not have advised their employee any participation in his outlandish ventures.

These men were the four Pâris brothers, bankers to the government and much more besides. They were originally from Grenoble, and had made their fortune during the constant wars of Louis XIV by supplying the French armies with food, water, forage, and munitions. This fortune put them at the center of the French financial system, a network of financiers, bankers, and businessmen who lent money to the government, farmed the taxes, and made vast profits along the way. Their power and influence became paramount.

But the brothers were never ministers; they preferred to stay in the background and control events through their protégés. They have been called "black holes in the history of the eighteenth century," because their dealings, personalities, and modus operandi were mysterious at the time and are still so today. But even if one cannot pinpoint exactly how and where they exercised their power, one cannot dispute the fact that it was theirs to exercise.

The two elder brothers died before the events of this book took place. It was the younger brothers, Joseph and Jean, who in 1722 were successfully established in the Parisian financial world. François Pois-

son worked directly for the third brother, Joseph, known as Pâris-
Duverney, whose field of activity was the original family business of
supplying the armies. He was also close to the youngest brother, known
as Pâris de Montmartel, a banker and financier. It was the protection
and advice of these two men which saved the Poissons from the ruin that
awaited many of their friends in the turbulence of the Mississippi.

When Jeanne-Antoinette was born in December 1721, the family
lived in a modest neighborhood close to the church of Saint-Eustache.
From the first days of the marriage, François Poisson was often away
on business; when a brief war broke out between France and Spain in
1719, he was sent south to start to amass the necessary mules, wagons,
foodstuffs, and other *vivres*. His job was made difficult, and his stay extended, because of a disastrous outbreak of bubonic plague which spread
across southern France.

His wife was not one to stay uncomforted. In the corrupt world of
regency Paris, where it was not uncommon for rich men to purchase the
virginity of young girls, and where every man kept a mistress if he could,
Madame Poisson's looks and temperament guaranteed her success. The
gossip of the day attributed many lovers to her, and this gossip became
more widespread and more prurient in later attempts to blacken her
daughter's name. Dozens of men were linked to her, with little or no
evidence; suffice it to say that both her contemporaries and later histo-
rians have mostly refused to accept the fact that a low-born functionary
like François Poisson could have fathered Madame de Pompadour. It is
of course perfectly possible that he did.

One of the most reasonable alternatives to Poisson as the father of
Jeanne-Antoinette is Pâris de Montmartel, who stood as her godfather
at her baptism, and who had known Madame Poisson very well at the
Invalides before her marriage. The most reasonable, however, is a man
called Charles Lenormand de Tournehem, a tax farmer, a director of the
Compagnie des Indes, and a member of the financial élite, although he
was by no means as wealthy as Montmartel. Tournehem was in his mid-
thirties in 1721, a widower with no children. The ties between Tournehem
and Madame Poisson seem to have gone back a long way. In April 1720
he had attempted to rent a house in the rue Vivienne from one of her
relatives. But it is impossible to reconstruct the course of their relation-

ship, or to confirm his paternity. Only from subsequent events can one draw conclusions.

And so, when the baby girl was baptized at Saint-Eustache on December 31, 1721, François Poisson held her proudly in his arms, Pâris de Montmartel stood as godfather, his wife (and cousin) Antoinette-Justine Pâris as godmother, and Tournehem mingled with the congregation. Whatever was in doubt that day, one thing was clear: Jeanne-Antoinette Poisson came into the world with powerful connections.

François Poisson was doing well. The family lived in comfortable circumstances in the rue de Cléry, with servants and a carriage. In 1725 a baby boy, Abel-François, was born. But Poisson, one of Pâris-Duverney's most trusted agents, was rarely at home; he was usually out on the French frontier or in the provinces, scouting supplies and establishing contacts. In his absence, Madame Poisson maintained a close relationship with Tournehem and, with a sound head for business, benefited from his advice to help improve the family finances by shrewd investments.

This settled way of life ended abruptly in 1726 when François Poisson fled the country. He was accused of speculating in wheat and bearing some responsibility for a grievous famine in Paris that year. His employers were also accused of malfeasance; Pâris-Duverney was sent to the Bastille on charges of corruption and embezzlement. After a trial, Duverney was cleared of all charges and soon rose again to become commissioner-general of supplies. And yet François Poisson, Duverney's loyal employee, remained in exile for almost ten years. Here was a mystery: the Pâris brothers could easily have rescued their employee once they themselves regained favor, but they did nothing. Poisson languished in Germany all that time, and arranged his return to France only through his own resources. For whatever reasons, it was deemed prudent that François Poisson not rejoin his wife and children.

At her husband's flight, Madame Poisson was at first left in some embarrassment. She and her two children were forced to move to modest rooms in the rue des Bons-Enfants, near the Palais-Royal. But she was a brave woman with good connections. She kept her head and kept afloat. She might not have had the *ton du monde,* as a contemporary observed, but she had wit and charm, ambition, and courage. She would not be easily defeated, and she would teach her daughter the necessity for ambition and resilience in an unpredictable and perilous world.

Her first concern, however, was to find the five-year-old girl a haven from the uncertainties of the times. Jeanne-Antoinette was a good-natured and amiable child, already known as "Reinette" ("little queen") to her family. Madame Poisson's way of life did not easily accommodate the presence of children; it would be better for all concerned if her daughter were sent to more salubrious surroundings. François Poisson, although far away, was also anxious to see Jeanne-Antoinette safely settled. He made it clear that he wished to play a part in the decisions affecting the girl's future; it was mainly at his prompting that she was sent to the Ursuline convent at Poissy, some miles out of Paris, where she could be supervised by her father's cousin, Sister Elisabeth, and by Sister Perpetua, her mother's sister. She was there for almost three years, spending those impressionable years, from the ages of five to eight, under the benevolent eye of the nuns.

The Ursulines had as their mission the education of the daughters of the bourgeoisie, and brought up their charges to be good and gentle wives and mothers, to respect God, their family, and the king. Theirs was an ordered, secure world for a little girl caught up in a family crisis, and Jeanne-Antoinette seems to have flourished within it. The nuns were the first of many who knew her to find her charming. They also made it a point to keep the distant father, no doubt at his request, informed of his daughter's activities. A letter from the convent to Poisson in Germany paints a pleasing picture of the girl in August 1729: "Your amiable daughter, monsieur, is well and pretty, and feeling altogether at her ease. Monsieur de La Motte sends someone every market day for her news, and has her taken out from time to time with her cousin Deblois to have dinner with him. . . . She is not at all bored with us, quite the contrary. . . . On August 25 there was a fair at Poissy; we sent her there with her cousin and one of our nuns, who showed them all the interesting things; she also took them to the abbey, where they were very well treated and found to be very amiable. . . . On the day of the Assumption of the Holy Virgin, they sang Vespers in their classes, they were the principal soloists . . ."

But she was not a robust child. The nuns were often writing of her delicate health and describing the nourishing food they gave her, the hot soup, fresh eggs, rice, and country butter. In November 1729 she suffered from a cold and was in bed for six weeks. This illness marked the end of her time at Poissy; on her recovery, in January 1730, her mother reclaimed her. The nuns were sad to see her go: "They have told us that she no longer has a fever, that she is better, that she is very pleased to be with her mother. It seems likely that she is going to stay there. And so, monsieur, we no longer have news of her for sure; we leave it to you to keep in touch about her as we take a great deal of interest in her and love her tenderly. She is always very amiable and so pleasing that she charms everyone who sees her."

Madame Poisson's views on child-rearing were rather different from those of the nuns. No sooner was her daughter returned to Paris than she was taken off with her mother to see the famous fortune teller, Madame Lebon. Madame Poisson clearly had more faith in the crystal ball than in divine providence. Mother and daughter were no doubt quite struck by Madame Lebon's prediction, for, in the future Madame de Pompadour's will, we find an entry: "Six hundred livres to Madame Lebon for having told her at the age of nine that she would one day be the mistress of Louis XV." This prediction, she later told Voltaire, struck her with the force of a thunderbolt. From now on "Reinette," and particularly Reinette's mother, would refer regularly to the prophecy, and not altogether in playful fashion. Madame Poisson had had an epiphany; her daughter was destined for greatness, and she must provide the means and opportunities to help her achieve it.

Louis XV, the subject of the fortune teller's prophecy, was a distant and glamorous figure to most Parisians. In 1730 he was twenty years old, married to a Polish princess, Marie Leczinska, and already the father of five children. He spent his time at Versailles, rarely visiting the capital, and allowed his former tutor, the Cardinal de Fleury, to govern France in his name. He was reputed to be the handsomest man in France, faithful to his wife (his senior by seven years), a devoted father, a good and dutiful king. Under these circumstances, the idea of little Jeanne-Antoinette Poisson joining her destiny to that of this august being was absurd. But Madame Poisson was not to be deflected from her grand project.

In an age when girls were married as soon as they reached puberty, nine-year-old Jeanne-Antoinette was quite old enough to commence her education in the ways of the world. All that was needed was the money to finance the enterprise. And for that, all that was needed was Charles Lenormand de Tournehem.

Tournehem was no doubt as captivated by the charms of little Jeanne-Antoinette as the nuns had been. Perhaps, as a childless widower, he warmed to the delightful little girl; perhaps, as her unacknowledged father, he was determined to provide the very best for her. Her mother encouraged his generous instincts. What a great future lies before her, breathed Madame Poisson, she needs only the best that money can buy in the way of education and polish and she will indeed be a *morceau de roi.* Tournehem turned his attention, and his wallet, to the perfection of their dream. It is difficult not to conclude that Tournehem's interest in the young girl was that of a father. All his future actions pointed to this fact.

In 1736 François Poisson returned to Paris to rediscover his daughter, now fifteen. The French authorities had guaranteed that his original sentence would not be imposed and that no further prosecutions would ensue. (Poisson had performed some useful services for French diplomats in Germany and managed to have his case taken up at court.) On his return, the family moved to the rue Neuve des Petits-Champs, the busy street which ran between the place des Victoires and the place Vendôme. Poisson continued to fight for his good name and, finally, in 1741, his sentence was revoked. Meanwhile, he continued to work for Pâris-Duverney, as he had done while in exile, and was often sent back to Germany on business.

One may assume that Poisson was delighted with his promising young daughter, but one wonders how she herself felt. Her memories of him must have been dim; for many years *"oncle"* Tournehem had been the real father of the family. Poisson arrived in Paris trailing an air of disgrace; much less polished than Tournehem, not at home in the sophisticated world to which his wife aspired; he appeared a rather vulgar, if cheerful, presence. He might have been an embarrassment to an ambitious young woman. And yet Jeanne-Antoinette seems to have welcomed him into the bosom of the family with little difficulty. She would always, and unequivocally, refer to him as her dear father, and she would in later years do her best to ensure him a distinguished way of life. But his presence and influence in her future would never match that of Tournehem.

The family fortunes began to improve. On her parents' deaths, and that of her sister, Madame Deblois, in January 1738, Madame Poisson was able to buy a house at 50, rue de Richelieu, with a view on the gardens of the Palais-Royal.

The rue de Richelieu was not far from the bustle of the city's main east-west thoroughfare, the rue Saint-Honoré, not far either from the place Vendôme, home to the wealthiest financiers, the Bibliothèque du Roi, the Opera. Molière had lived close by; Voltaire still did. Round the corner were the offices of the Compagnie des Indes, where Tournehem worked, and the rue Colbert, where he lived. The streets were narrow, noisy, and no doubt smelly, but all around were gardens, not only those of the Palais-Royal, but of the monasteries and convents which were a feature of the neighborhood, the Filles de Saint-Thomas, the Capucins, the Dames de l'Assomption, the Petits Pères. And, just at the northern end of the rue de Richelieu, were the wide, tree-lined boulevards, beyond them the fields and orchards and vineyards of the countryside. The cries of street vendors, the pealing of church bells, carriage wheels on paving stones, perhaps the sound of rehearsals from the Opera filled the air. The grand old church of Saint-Eustache, the church where Jeanne-Antoinette Poisson was baptized and would be married, seemed to stand guard over the parish.

The children of Madame Poisson were being carefully brought up. While Abel was with the Jesuits at the exclusive college of Louis-le-Grand, his sister continued to receive the best education money could buy. The great singer Jelyotte came to give her lessons, the actor Jean-Baptiste Lanoue taught her declamation, she became skilled at the harpsichord and at all the other arts a young woman needed to shine in society; she read widely, embroidered, developed the art of conversation and the talent for entertaining. She leaned to ride and to drive her own carriage. She excelled in everything. She was designed for society. Endowed with great natural gifts, she also learned the importance of discretion, discipline, and self-control.

Jeanne-Antoinette was also exposed to the way of life of some of the richest and most cultivated members of Parisian society. Although her own circumstances were modest, those of her godfather, Pâris de Montmartel, and his brother Pâris-Duverney, were opulent. Montmartel lived in the Marais, in the former hôtel de La Force, his house a master-piece of elegance and comfort, his garden famous for its rare shrubs, his library full of rare books. Montmartel, whose official posts included Guardian of the Royal Treasury and banker to the court, also had an extensive country estate at Brunoy, to the southeast of Paris, where he indulged his passion for horticulture and botany. Pâris-Duverney grew bananas and pineapples in the hothouses of his estate at Plaisance nearby. And *oncle* Tournehem himself was the owner of a country house at Etioles, on the Seine, which he was constantly embellishing.

For the young girl, visiting these splendid houses and glimpsing this leisured way of life, there were no doubt, on the return to the rue de Richelieu, moments of envy, of melancholy. Perhaps it was then that she became determined to rise to a position in society equal and superior to that of her wealthy acquaintances. Perhaps, remembering the fortune teller, she dreamed of the king . . .

As she turned eighteen, she had fulfilled all her early promise. She was of above average height, with soft brown hair and flawless skin. Her face was a perfect oval, her features regular and charming; her eyes, of an indeterminate color between green, blue, and gray, were noted for their depth and brilliance. And she had very fine teeth (rare in those days) with the most dazzling smile. Svelte, poised, and elegant, she was also well-read, cultivated, and amusing. She was indeed a "morsel fit for a king."

Louis XV being, however, unavailable, the young woman had to find a husband. With all her fine qualities, she should have been a prime candidate for a brilliant match, if it were not for her rather disreputable father and mother and her somewhat ambivalent social position. And crucially, she lacked a dowry substantial enough to remove the other problems. As a great heiress, Mademoiselle Poisson could have attracted a duke. As the daughter of François Poisson she was, however gifted and beautiful, of interest to none of the parties to whom she and her mother wished to aspire.

But she must marry. She could not take her place in society until she had done so. Fortunately, *oncle* Tournehem had the perfect husband for her. Doting as he was, Tournehem was no doubt reluctant to be parted from her. And under the circumstances, he could hardly marry her himself. His only nephew, Charles-Guillaume Lenormand, son of Tournehem's unsuccessful brother, was the designated husband. (If we accept the notion that Tournehem was indeed her father, she would be marrying her cousin, a not uncommon occurrence at the time.)

There is evidence that Tournehem had long contemplated this union. He had already seen to his nephew's financial future, making him a junior partner in tax-collecting farms, and supplying the necessary funds to do so. On December 15, 1740, Tournehem made his nephew his sole heir, disinheriting all his other nephews and nieces, the children of his brother, Hervé-Guillaume, and his sister, the comtesse d'Estrades. Perhaps he thought that this handsome treatment would incline the young man's father to view the match with a friendly eye; if so, he was mistaken. Hervé-Guillaume Lenormand regarded Mademoiselle Poisson as an intruder; perhaps he was only too well aware of the implications of the match. Jeanne-Antoinette was not the bride he had hoped for, despite her qualities. He sensed that his son was being used. When the wedding contract was signed on March 4, 1741 at the rue de Richelieu, he refused to attend, and a rift opened between the Lenormand brothers. As for the groom himself, he seems to have been a shy, obliging young man who fell in love with his wife but who was never a match for her in drive, ambition, or strength of will.

The Parisian lawyer, Edmond Barbier, saw the whole affair in its proper perspective. "Madame Poisson got to know Monsieur Le Normand, *fermier général,* with whom she had always been friendly, even up to this day," he wrote in 1745. "It was during this relationship that her daughter was born, whom Monsieur Le Normand regards as his daughter, and to whom he has given an excellent education. Monsieur Le Normand, having no children, forced his nephew to marry Mademoiselle Poisson, aged eighteen and a beautiful woman, and gave them as a wedding present the estate of Etioles. They lodged with the uncle, defrayed of everything and enjoying an income of more than forty thousand livres a year, with the hope of an opulent succession. She was adored by the uncle, absolute mistress of the household."

Thus, on March 9, 1741, at Saint-Eustache, Jeanne-Antoinette Poisson married Charles-Guillaume Lenormand, who now took the name of "d'Etioles" after his uncle's estate. The couple moved in with Tournehem, then all three moved to the rue Croix-des-Petits-Champs, across the gardens of the Palais-Royal from the Poissons in the rue de Richelieu. They started married life on a handsome footing: Tournehem's financial support enabled the young couple to live in style, with servants, a carriage, and horses; and Madame Poisson managed to provide her daughter with thirty thousand livres worth of trousseau.

At about this time, Tournehem commissioned the society painter Jean-Marc Nattier to paint the portrait of his new daughter-in-law; she regards us coolly, in all the freshness of her youth and beauty, graceful and self-possessed, a smile of gentle confidence on her lips.

Chapter 2

"One of the prettiest women I have ever seen . . ."

As Jeanne-Antoinette prepared to take her place in Parisian society, her *"oncle"* Tournehem, together with her godfather Montmartel, his brother Duverney, and all their circle of friends and associates in the world of finance were preoccupied by the approach of another war.

This was a not unusual state of affairs in eighteenth-century Europe. The ruling houses of France, Austria, Great Britain, Prussia, and the rest were continually forging and reforging alliances, looking for opportunities to gain territory or influence, sensing each other's vulnerabilities and assessing each other's strengths. Issues of succession were particularly likely to erupt into conflict. Earlier in the century the War of the Spanish Succession had consolidated the hold of the house of Bourbon on Spain; in 1741 it was the succession to the vast lands of the Habsburgs of Austria, and to the Holy Roman Empire, which caused strife.*

The head of the house of Habsburg, whose title was archduke of Austria and king of Hungary, had also been Holy Roman Emperor for three centuries and feudal lord of a conglomerate of German states, including Saxony, Bavaria, and Brandenburg. It was the rulers of these states—the electors—who cast their votes for their emperor, and, although Voltaire famously said that this conglomeration was "neither Holy, Roman, nor an Empire," it was still a powerful component part of eighteenth-century European politics.

---

*The Habsburg territories included, as well as Austria itself, Hungary, Bohemia, and Moravia [modern Slovakia and the Czech Republic], Slovenia, Serbia, Croatia, Bosnia, the Austrian Netherlands [modern Belgium], and much of northern Italy.

On October 20, 1740, the Emperor Charles VI died unexpectedly, leaving only a twenty-three-year-old daughter, the Archduchess Maria-Theresa. In order to secure her succession to the throne of Hungary and the other Habsburg territories, Charles VI had invoked a new legal doctrine known as the Pragmatic Sanction. But while most of Europe was willing to accept Maria-Theresa as queen of Hungary, it was impossible for her to ascend to the throne of the Holy Roman Empire. Foreseeing this, her father had made it clear that he wished his son-in-law, Maria-Theresa's husband, Francis of Lorraine, to be elected emperor. Not surprisingly, this prospect was unwelcome in Europe. Three powers in particular, France, Prussia (formerly Brandenburg), and Bavaria, raised strenuous objections.

The French saw an opportunity to break the link between Austria and the Empire; Prussia, under its new young king, Frederick II, looked hungrily at the Austrian province of Silesia; and the elector of Bavaria, Maria-Theresa's uncle by marriage, considered himself the rightful heir to her throne, rejecting the Pragmatic Sanction. The conditions for a new European war were in place.

Cardinal de Fleury, who ruled France in the name of Louis XV, was against any French involvement in a war; he had managed to keep France at peace for a decade and was not anxious to subject her to the financial and human suffering a war would entail. By 1740 he was eighty-seven years old, hardly ready to throw himself into military adventures. But the mood at the French court was different; a vocal party of the nobility was eager for battle against Austria, a traditional foe. Their spokesman, the distinguished solder, the maréchal de Belle-Isle, pushed for war. And then, on December 16, 1740, Frederick II of Prussia, to general surprise, invaded Silesia and raised the stakes. Fleury decided to send Belle-Isle to Frankfurt, where the election of the new emperor would take place. His instructions were to ensure the election of Charles Albert of Bavaria, and to block the candidacy of Francis of Lorraine, a man distrusted by the French not only by virtue of his position as Maria-Theresa's husband, but also because they suspected him of harboring designs to retake possession of his ancestral lands on the eastern frontier of France. Belle-Isle set off in March 1741, privately determined to commit France to join Frederick of Prussia in his aggression against Maria-Theresa.

As the great powers maneuvered for position, they also began to prepare for war. In France, war meant new efforts from the financial community. Extra taxes would be levied, and would have to be collected; supplies would have to be produced and their distribution organized. Since any fighting would take place far away from France, in Germany and Bohemia, long supply lines would need to be established.

The Pâris brothers were, respectively, the chief executive and the chief operating officer of France in times of war, Pâris-Duverney directing supply at the war ministry, Montmartel as the chief officer of the treasury. As the historian Michelet put it: "Every spring the army, extended, badly provided for, entered on campaign. Every year she was saved, fed, thanks to the Pâris brothers, by a miracle of money, of energy. The man responsible was Pâris-Duverney, always on the frontier, and often between the armies, disguised to see better." French generals often referred derisively to Duverney as *général des farines*, or general in charge of flour; but it was upon his prodigious activity, and that of his subordinates — resourceful men like François Poisson — that the French armies depended. Duverney's advice on tactics and strategy was often more influential than that of the commanders in the field, and certainly more than the ministers. Of course, the two Pâris, and all the other members of the business élite, would find ways to benefit financially from the war. Indeed, war was in many ways their business, their bread and butter.

A war would have little impact in Paris. The armies were composed of an officer caste of nobles and a mass of peasants and mercenaries. The Parisian middle class needed to pay little attention to their faraway activities. As far as Jeanne-Antoinette was concerned, the fact of war meant primarily that her friends the Pâris brothers were once more at the center of French affairs, the power behind the ministers, with close access to Cardinal de Fleury, and to the king himself.

On her marriage, the new Madame d'Etioles joined a large, extended Lenormand family. Her father-in-law, Hervé-Guillaume Lenormand, remained aloof; he avoided her as much as possible. But the other members of the clan were more welcoming, in particular Tournehem's niece by marriage, the comtesse d'Estrades. Elisabeth-Charlotte d'Estrades was only a little older than Jeanne-Antoinette and the two were already friends. In fact Madame d'Etioles had known all the Lenormands for years, so much so that her marriage must have seemed rather like a reaffirmation of the ties of family, and one in which her new husband seemed almost overlooked.

Devoted *oncle* Tournehem proudly welcomed this exquisite creature into his home. The Poissons lived close by. For the young woman nothing much had changed; she accepted the presence in her life of her husband, but rather casually, as she might have accepted a brother. She did not, it seems, enjoy a sexual awakening; her temperament, as she herself was to admit, was not a passionate one. She was much more interested in captivating the social world than in captivating her husband.

The acquisition of a husband meant that Jeanne-Antoinette could begin to play the part for which she had been so expertly prepared. She could now frequent the salons of Paris, or at least those where the hostess did not fear admitting a young and pretty woman to join the distinguished guests. After her marriage she appeared at Madame Geoffrin's gatherings in the rue Saint-Honoré near the place Vendôme; she was seen more rarely at Madame de Tencin's more established salon along the same street, for Madame de Tencin disliked female rivals. She found many of the same guests at each — the old literary lion Bernard de Fontenelle, the witty magistrate Charles Hénault, the abbé Prévost, author of *Manon Lescaut,* and the sparkling young writer, Charles Duclos. Duclos, who had spent time in London, recorded how surprised he had been to observe that in England, "Women are not as in France the principal object of men's attention, and the soul of society." It was different in Paris.

Wealthy Parisian ladies of the bourgeoisie placed their time and their houses at the disposal of artists and writers. Voltaire's remark that successful salons were always "presided over by a woman who in her declining beauty shines by her awakening wit" is too dismissive; the leadership provided by Madame de Tencin (and before her, Madame de Lambert) was a new force in a society in which women were searching for a cultural role. In the salons they found one which was vital — that of encouraging and protecting writers and artists, and affording them a space in which to converse and communicate, with one another, with pretty women, and with members of the nobility. From these encounters, the men of letters emerged more polite and agreeable, the aristocrats more enlightened.

The salons in the 1740s were, as has been well put, *"un lieu de brassage social intense"* (places of intense social ferment). Gradually, as the classes mingled, it would become more and more evident that there was something wrong with a society in which men of letters would never be as respected, or favored, as men with titles. A growing sense of injustice came into being, which would in the next decade find a voice in the *Encyclopédie;* there the writers who had mixed so agreeably with dukes and counts were able to raise the questions, and the stakes, about the nature of French society.

But before the upheaval of the 1750s, the salons were mainly influential when it came to such matters as who should be elected to the *Académie Française.* There was usually an election going on, as the ranks of the forty "immortals" were constantly in need of replenishment. Literary talents were not always necessary for admission; noble dabblers, sophisticated churchmen, and men about town were often elected if they were agreeable and known to society. Discussion of the relative merits of the candidates was spirited and partisan.

Feelings also ran high over the new productions at the *Comédie-Française.* Voltaire's historical tragedies were always popular, but so also were the light comedies of now-forgotten dramatists like Nivelle de La Chaussée and Boissy, and, at the *Comédie-Italienne,* the polished fun of Marivaux. One of the most successful plays of the time was Gresset's *"Ver-Vert,"* about a too-talkative parrot in a convent. (Madame d'Etioles, judging from her later productions at Versailles, preferred such sentimental dramas and light comedies to the more sophisticated wit of Marivaux; or perhaps she simply knew her audience.)

As a young woman of fashion, Jeanne-Antoinette participated in all these discussions at the salons, meeting the candidates for the Académie and the up-and-coming dramatists, while developing her critical faculties and knowledge of the world. She also attended the opening of the Salon every year, held each August at the Louvre, where new works by the painters of the day were exhibited. There she would have admired portraits by Maurice-Quentin de La Tour and Jean-Marc Nattier, set pieces from mythology by François Lemoyne and Charles-Antoine Coypel, still lifes and hunting scenes by François Desportes and Jean-Baptiste Oudry. La Tour's pastels were the talk of the Salon of 1740: his portrait of President de Rieux was the triumph of the Salon of 1741; his portrait of the Turkish ambassador again in 1742.

An avid reader, Madame d'Etioles savored Prévost's novel *Manon Lescaut,* weeping at Manon's tragic fate in the "burning sands of Biloxi," and she, along with a titillated Parisian public, devoured the roman à clef by Charles Duclos, *Confessions du Comte de.,* which appeared at the end of 1741 and caused a sensation. Duclos lovingly described the amatory habits of various society ladies, lightly disguised in his novel. Living in the circles of high finance as she did, Jeanne-Antoinette would have appreciated Duclos's remark that "it is not surprising that there are, among the financial classes, some very amiable people . . . financiers are absolutely necessary in a State, and it is a profession of which the dignity or the baseness depends uniquely on the fashion in which it is exercised." (Duclos would later receive generous treatment from Madame de Pompadour.)

Jeanne-Antoinette soon became pregnant. Her health, never good, became cause for concern. She wrote to Poisson, away again in Germany, on September 3, 1741. "My very dear father, no longer be anxious about my health, I beg you, I am well at present, I had two bouts of fever but it is now ten days since I had them and I am quite recovered; I took a lot of quinine, was bled twice, and the medicine has entirely cured me. I will tell you that to console myself for these unpleasant drugs I am going today to the Opera . . ." Her first child, a boy, was born in December 1741 but died the following year.

By now she was becoming well-known in the fashionable circles of Paris. In July 1742 the magistrate Hénault, a great man about town, told Madame du Deffand: "I have just met one of the prettiest women I have ever seen. . . . She knows music perfectly, sings with all the taste and gaiety in the world, knows a hundred songs, plays the comedy at Etioles in a theatre as fine as the Opera in Paris."

And yet she had the wit to flatter Madame Geoffrin's daughter, the marquise de La Ferté-Imbault, telling her: "How lucky you are! You are always in the company of that charming duc de Nivernais, that amiable abbé de Bernis and that gentle Bernard, and you see them as much as you want! As for me, I have all the trouble in the world to have one of them for supper with my uncle Tournehem because his company bores them." One feels rather sorry that poor Tournehem, who was so proud of his nephew's wife, and who would do anything for her, should be so casually dismissed. It was an early indication of Jeanne-Antoinette's cool realism and lack of sentimentality.*

Madame d'Etioles saw herself as a rival, not so much to Madame Geoffrin or Madame de Tencin, who catered to a mostly male group of intellectual guests, but rather to another Parisian hostess, Madame de La Popelinière, who entertained her lover, the duc de Richelieu, as well as Voltaire and the artists Van Loo and La Tour, at her house at Passy. The even richer Madame Dupin held court at the beautiful hôtel Lambert on the Ile Saint-Louis. This opulent way of life, cultivated and leisured, was that to which Jeanne-Antoinette aspired. She succeeded in founding such a society, but at Etioles rather than Paris, where she clearly felt that Tournehem and her husband did not contribute to a sparkling salon.

Etioles was a handsome estate, some miles to the southeast of Paris, set on the bank of the Seine, surrounded by the forest of Sénart. Tournehem had expended a great deal of money on this place, adding to the original estate and embellishing it. The sprawling property was comprised of two châteaux linked by a wide gravel walk and surrounded by a vast park planted with rare shrubs and parterres of flowers. There is only one image of it at this time, a painting by Grevenbroek of 1740. It shows a large mansion set in a park extending to the river. In the distance, splendid houses dot the opposite bank of the Seine.

In those days, the area was a retreat for the wealthy bourgeoisie of Paris. Pâris de Montmartel lived nearby at Brunoy, the rich tax farmer Etienne Bouret at Croix-Fontaine; Pâris-Duverney lived a little further away, at Plaisance, in a château decorated with fashionable *chinoiseries* and where he grew all kinds of hothouse fruits. Across the river rose the magnificent château of Petit-Bourg built by the duc d'Antin.

In this milieu there was plenty of money to spend on embellishing one's house and garden. Tournehem lavished care on Etioles; the new châtelaine entered into possession of an estate such as she had dreamt of. Here she could enjoy a luxurious version of country life many years

*Pierre-Joseph Bernard, known as Gentil-Bernard, was a poet whose "Art of Love" was, according to Voltaire, better than that of Ovid.

before Marie-Antoinette built her Hameau at Versailles. Wine was made locally, and many of the proprietors' vineyards had small model farms where cows and chickens provided distraction as well as healthy food. The inhabitants also indulged in the contemporary passion for theatricals, all the richest families having their own private theatres and competing for the services of professional actors and actresses from Paris. One of the finest theatres was at nearby Chantemerle, the estate of Madame de Villemur, where such great nobles as the duc de Nivernais, the duc de Duras, and the duc de Richelieu condescended to come and try their hand at acting. Early in her marriage, Madame d'Etioles was invited there to perform. She had, as we know, received lessons from the leading artists of the day; she also had outstanding natural ability as actress and dancer, and was gifted with a particularly beautiful voice. The sophisticated guests at Chantemerle marveled at her talents and she, socially ambitious as she was, immediately understood the benefits of putting her gifts to good use. She asked Tournehem if she could have her own theatre at Etioles. No sooner said than done. A modern and luxurious theatre sprang up near the château; it must have been a most agreeable stroll from the main house up to the theatre, along the grassy walk beneath the trees hung with lanterns, and to walk back to the house through the sounds of a summer night, torches illuminating the path, the river in the distance.

In the summer a chic Parisian crowd came to Etioles to enjoy the pleasures of the house and grounds. Jeanne-Antoinette extended invitations to young duchesses and elderly writers, to anyone who was entertaining and amusing. In her theatre were performed current successes of the Parisian stage, as well as favorite classics such as Destouches's comedy *Le Glorieux;* naturally, it was always Jeanne-Antoinette who took the leading role. And on fine afternoons guests sat outdoors to read aloud to one another. A guest at Etioles recalls his hostess reading Samuel Richardson's *Pamela,* a novel which dwelt, at length, on the rewards of chastity; for a thousand pages, Richardson's heroine resisted temptation. Madame d'Etioles no doubt entered sympathetically into Pamela's tribulations, but she clearly felt that such lessons were not for her; she felt herself perfectly equal to conquering the perils of wordly life.

An added excitement at Etioles each August was the arrival of the king and the court at the nearby château of Choisy. Louis XV had bought Choisy in 1740 and liked to come to hunt in the forest of Sénart before going on his annual autumn visit to Fontainebleau. No doubt, for "Reinette," his presence in the neighborhood, so near and yet so far, was a source of hope and despair. For Madame d'Etioles might be the toast of Paris, the darling of elderly intellectuals and dashing young blades alike; she might have an adoring husband and devoted family; but she had not forgotten the fortune teller and her prediction.

Years later, she told Voltaire that she "had always had a secret presentiment that she would be loved by the king, and that she had felt a violent inclination for him." "This idea," added Voltaire, "which would have seemed chimerical for one in her position, was based on the fact that they had often taken her to the king's hunts in the forest of Sénart. Tournehem, her mother's lover, had a house in the neighborhood. They took Madame d'Etioles along in a pretty little carriage. The king noticed her, and often sent her presents of roebucks. Her mother never stopped telling her that she was prettier than any of the king's mistresses, and the *bonhomme* Tournehem often exclaimed: 'One must admit that the daughter of Madame Poisson is a morsel fit for a King.' In short, when she finally held the king in her arms, she told me that she had firmly believed in her destiny, and that she had been proved right."

Madame Poisson had done everything in her power to prepare her daughter for what she saw as a glorious destiny, that of *maîtresse déclarée* to the king of France. She had imbued Jeanne-Antoinette with the notion that she was put on earth to accede to this lofty position, and Jeanne-Antoinette, compliant, had dedicated herself to attaining it. The audacity of their ambition was staggering. Kings of France were sacred beings, semidivine to their subjects; many had taken mistresses, and the fortunate women remain celebrated in French history: Diane de Poitiers, Gabrielle d'Estrées, Louise de La Vallière, Athénaïs de Montespan. But never had a king of France taken as his mistress a member of the bourgeoisie. For Madame Poisson this was no drawback. But between her vaulting ambition and the sacred person of Louis XV there was a vast gulf. Madame Poisson trusted her daughter to cross it. And then the fortune of the Poissons and of Tournehem would be made, and that of the Pâris brothers even more firmly established. And so Jeanne-Antoinette drove out in her carriage into the forest, elegantly attired, deliciously pretty, elusively unavailable, the bearer of the hopes and dreams of her family. As her path crossed that of the king, she respectfully waited for the royal party to gallop by. The king noticed her, but rode on ahead. Impossibly near, impossibly distant. Louis XV, the object of so much desire, the focus of so many aspirations, what kind of man was he?

Chapter 3

"The King likes women . . ."

In 1742 Louis XV was thirty-two, in his physical prime. Handsome and manly, with a noble and majestic air, he was also shy, timid, and awkward in society. Given his upbringing, this lack of confidence was perhaps not surprising. In one terrible week at Versailles, in 1712, both his parents and his only brother had died, carried off, probably, by virulent scarlet fever. The two-year-old child became heir to the throne, and prisoner in the iron cage of etiquette imposed by Louis XIV, the child's awe-inspiring great-grandfather.

He had been brought up by obsequious courtiers, subject to tedious and rigid ceremonies. He ate in public, watched in a worshipful silence by those with the privilege of entering his presence. He rose and went to bed accompanied by elaborate ceremonies and disputes among his nobles as to which duke had the right to hold his shirt, which the candlestick. His governor, the old maréchal de Villeroi, treated him with a mixture of bombast and groveling. The boy became silent and withdrawn, increasingly moody and sullen. He grew to hate public appearances, was happy only when out riding and, increasingly, slaughtering deer and stag. His only confidante was the duchesse de Ventadour, his governess, who had saved his life in 1712 when she refused to hand him over to the doctors' murderous ineptitude and gave him a little wine and a biscuit.

"Maman" de Ventadour could not, however, help him in the decisions imposed upon him by virtue of his exalted rank. The boy was taught to bear the heavy and inescapable responsibilities of his position, and trained in the necessity of diligence, by his great-uncle Philippe d'Orléans, of whom he was very fond. Orléans's sudden death in 1723 left the boy

isolated again. He found solace in his benign old tutor, the abbé de Fleury, and in 1726, after a disastrous interlude of rule by one of the king's uncles, the duc de Bourbon, Fleury, made cardinal that same year, formally took control of the government of France. He was already aged seventy-three, expected to be no more than an interim figure, but for almost the next two decades he ruled France with a steady hand. Fleury lived modestly, kept the country at peace, and presided over expanding commerce and foreign trade. Louis XV followed his advice in everything.

The king was happy to leave the task of governing to Fleury. He had discovered the joys of married life, and gave himself enthusiastically to the business of fathering children. When Louis XV was eleven, he had been engaged to a three-year-old Infanta of Spain who was brought to Paris and remained long enough to embarrass him before being sent back home. He was then presented with his new bride-to-be, the pious Polish princess Marie Leczinska, who had been living in penurious exile in Germany. At their marriage in 1725 she was twenty-two, the king fifteen. Louis was faithful to her for ten years, in which time she gave birth to ten children, not all of whom survived infancy. *"Toujours coucher, toujours grosse, toujours accoucher,"* she sighed ("Always in bed, always pregnant, always giving birth"). Unfortunately for her, she produced only one son, and a succession of girls, first twins, Madame Elisabeth and Madame Henriette, then five more who were called Madame Third, Madame Fourth, and so on; after the birth of Madame Seventh in 1737, the king made it clear that she was "Madame Last."

Sometime before this last child was born, the king had started an affair with a lady of the court, Louise-Julie de Mailly-Nesle, comtesse de Mailly. Madame de Mailly was "well-made, young, but ugly, with a large mouth with big teeth, but amusing nonetheless. She has little intelligence and no opinions; and so the cardinal has consented with good grace to this arrangement, seeing that the king needs a mistress." The king enjoyed the excitement of their secret meetings, and he liked the fact that she made him laugh. There were many practical jokes and boisterous parties. It was all rather adolescent.

The king's affair with Madame de Mailly was countenanced by Fleury as a harmless diversion. Louise-Julie was not interested in politics or power. But the austere old man was not so tolerant when it came to the king's own family. He observed the seven little princesses with disapproval; in his mind, they were merely a drain on the royal treasury.

In 1738 the cardinal banished the four youngest girls to the convent of Fontevrault in the Loire valley; Victoire was five, Sophie four, Félicité two, and Louise one. Over the next ten years the children received no family visits of any kind. (Félicité died at the convent in September 1744.) Fleury considered them an unnecessary expense, and the king and queen did not disobey him. Only the Dauphin and his three older sisters, Elisabeth, Henriette, and Adélaïde, were allowed to remain at court, and in 1739 twelve-year-old Elisabeth was married to her cousin, Don Felipe, a younger son of the king of Spain, and left Versailles for Madrid.

Louis seemed insensible to his daughters' departure; he had little understanding of family life. He and Madame de Mailly continued their liaison, often in company with her sister Pauline, the marquise de Vintimille. Pauline was cleverer than Louise-Julie; she talked of more serious things, even showing an interest in affairs of state. In turn, Louis began to show an interest in her; he soon began an affair with the second Mailly sister. But in September 1741 Pauline died, giving birth to the king's child.

Louis was devastated, leaving the court for almost a month. He returned to Madame de Mailly, but then, to general disbelief and consternation, he turned to yet another sister, the youngest of them, Marie-Anne, marquise de La Tournelle, very pretty and recently widowed. People found it rather disturbing that the king's attention should be uniquely directed to members of one family. It seemed somehow incestuous. But Louis XV was a very lonely man, uneasy with new faces, comfortable only with familiar ones. Timid by nature, he sought out people with whom he could be at ease. The sisters afforded him the comfort of habit.

On January 29, 1743, Cardinal de Fleury died, after ruling France for seventeen years. He was almost ninety years old. Louis XV had known no other prime minister, had trusted the old man completely, and went so far as to tell his uncle, King Philip V of Spain, that "having had the misfortune to lose my father and mother before I knew them, I have always regarded him as such, which makes his loss more grievous."

❖   ❖   ❖

But the country was at war; there was no time to grieve. In 1741 the French, in alliance with Prussia, had sent two armies into Germany, one heading north to contain Hanover, the territory of the British King George II, the other south to show support for Charles Albert, the elector of Bavaria, in his quarrel with Maria-Theresa. The latter army, under Belle-Isle, had succeeded in taking Prague and this bold action contributed to the election of Charles Albert as Holy Roman Emperor at Frankfurt on January 24, 1742. But subsequently things had gone badly. In June 1742 Frederick of Prussia deserted his allies to sign a separate peace with Maria-Theresa, under the terms of which he kept Silesia; the Austrians marched into Munich, the capital of Bavaria, and made the new Emperor an exile from his own land; the British then took up arms in support of Maria-Theresa. The Franco-Prussian-Bavarian coalition was in shambles.

Louis had to make crucial decisions on the conduct of the war. He announced that he would henceforth be his own prime minister; but in fact, as a complete novice in the art of governing, he listened carefully to Fleury's team of trusted advisers, particularly the old maréchal de Noailles and the minister of finance, Philibert Orry.

Marie-Anne de La Tournelle was determined to be heard as well. In October 1743 she was created duchesse de Châteauroux; this was an important step for her, for, besides the royal family, only duchesses could sit in the presence of the king (but on a stool, of course) and she was also appointed a lady-in-waiting to the long-suffering queen. Exercising her power, she ordered Louis to banish her sister, Madame de Mailly, from court; he obeyed at once. Madame de Châteauroux was an ambitious woman, strongly pro-Prussian and anti-Austrian, and she was soon cultivated by the Pâris brothers, always eager to help an influential mistress, particularly one who encouraged the war policy from which they benefited so generously. The brothers were well aware of the king's inexperience in governing, his lack of confidence, his timidity. He needed constant bolstering and encouragement in order to pay attention to his duty. Madame de Châteauroux was sure she could keep him in line.

The new duchess was a frequent guest at Pâris-Duverney's luxurious country house at Plaisance. Perhaps she met Madame d'Etioles there, or saw her at the hunt in the forest of Sénart. She was certainly well aware of the seductive young Parisienne; by 1743 she felt obliged to remark to the duchesse de Chevreuse, a friend of Madame d'Etioles: "Do you not know, madame, that they wish to give the little d'Etioles to the king?" She made her displeasure so plain that Madame de Chevreuse, alarmed, warned her friend to keep her distance from the court.

Jeanne-Antoinette, duly warned, must have observed the glamour of the royal house parties at Choisy that year with special wistfulness. Louis XV took a special interest in Choisy; this was his own house, where he could relax etiquette and take pleasure in adding to the buildings and embellishing the gardens. He had greatly enlarged the terrace on the river and was building a new wing for a theatre. He came there primarily to hunt the stag, and the spectacle must have been magnificent. The hunting parties went out by boat across the river and plunged into the forest. On their return, they supped by candlelight on gondolas moored near the ferry at Soisy-sous-Etioles before gliding back with the current to Choisy. One can imagine the longing glances cast at this splendid spectacle by one neighbor in particular.

But even in these idyllic surroundings, Louis XV was often moody and bored. The duc de Luynes, a veteran courtier and dogged diarist, noted that the king was more at ease at Choisy than elsewhere; but he went on to remark that "the king's temperament is not lively nor cheerful; there is rather something black humored about him; violent exercise and dissipation are necessary for his equilibrium . . ." Luynes had correctly perceived Louis XV's intense frustration with the demands of etiquette, his resulting bad temper, and his need to escape into the welcoming arms of the forest, or a mistress.

But duty called. On March 15, 1744, France declared war on Great Britain and, on April 26, on Austria. The government (which meant the king, Noailles, and the new war minister, the comte d'Argenson) had decided that the best defense was a good offense; they would go on the attack, not as auxiliaries of the elector of Bavaria anymore, but to protect their own interests. The French were determined, in alliance with Spain, to launch a campaign against the Austrians in Italy in order to secure the duchy of Parma for Don Felipe, Louis XV's son-in-law; they decided to renew relations with Frederick of Prussia; and they would play a card they had neglected—that of Charles Edward Stuart, the "Pretender" to the throne of England. Stuart, the last member of the former ruling house, had been languishing in exile in France, treated deferentially as the rightful heir to the British throne, but not taken very seriously. Now the French saw a use for him. He could create a diversion in Scotland and thus draw British troops back from mainland Europe. An expedition was prepared.

A further consequence of France's declaring war on her own account was that Louis XV could personally take command of his troops. Louis was not bursting with enthusiasm. He was a reluctant warrior, finding the prospect of going to the front boring and uncomfortable, and the prospect of battle worse. But, on May 1, 1744, propelled by Madame de Châteauroux, who was more avid for his *gloire* than he was himself, Louis departed for the northern frontier, bent on a campaign against the Anglo-Dutch forces in Flanders; for the first time in decades a French king was taking the field. Louis was nominally in command of the main French army, with Noailles as his second; a second army protected the Rhine; and a third, under the command of the brilliant soldier, Maurice de Saxe, followed the king's army closely. Also following close behind came Madame de Châteauroux herself, accompanied by yet another sister, Diane, duchesse de Lauraguais.

After inspecting Calais, Boulogne, and Dunkerque, the king's party departed for the city of Metz to offer support to the French army on the Rhine, arriving there in early August. Madame de Châteauroux lodged across the street from the king and had a wooden passageway built to connect the two houses; the citizens of Metz were horrified at what seemed an unnecessary flaunting of a relationship best carried on with discretion.

And then Louis XV fell seriously ill. The "scenes of Metz" were to be so traumatic for him that he could never recall them without anger and pain. His illness was, at first, considered not to be serious, but after a few days his doctors became concerned. As the king lay in bed, courtiers and clerics rushed about. It was decided that the king must make his confession, send away his mistress, and summon the royal family. Louis did as he was told; when the bishop of Soissons formally demanded the banishment of Madame de Châteauroux, Louis was heard to say from beneath the sheets, "And her sister too!"

But Louis recovered very quickly; when he found his wife and son hovering over his bed, his confession made public, and his mistress gone, he was furious. He felt profoundly humiliated, and he determined to strike back at those whom he considered responsible for his public embarrassment. The queen was rudely sent away; the bishop of Soissons, who had extracted the confession, was exiled, and the officers of his household who had been present at Metz—the ducs de Bouillon and de La Rochefoucauld—were also punished. Louis wrote abjectly to Marie-Anne de Châteauroux, who had been covered with abuse on her journey from Metz and was secluded in Paris. She would have her revenge, he promised her.

He was as good as his word. When the fighting ended for the winter, the king, who had not even come close to an actual battle, made a triumphal entry into Paris on November 13. A week later he was at Versailles, ready to recall Marie-Anne to his side.

Madame de Châteauroux had been confident of victory: "When he returns to his senses, I shall have no more worries; he will miss me madly and will be full of repentance . . ." she had written to her confidant, the duc de Richelieu, "and I can tell you now that we will return more brilliant than ever." She began to make preparations for her glorious return. One of her conditions was that the comte de Maurepas, the minister of the navy, call on her personally in Paris and humbly request her to return to court; Maurepas had been one of her most bitter foes, had constantly intrigued against her, and was now to pay the price.

At Versailles Louis XV ordered Maurepas to leave for Paris at once; he was at Madame de Châteauroux's house in the rue du Bac that same evening, November 26. Marie-Anne could not hide her exultation. But the next day she developed a fever and took to her bed. Her condition quickly deteriorated, she became delirious and tormented. Rumors of poisoning were immediately abroad. Maurepas had the reputation of being a ruthless man, a man who might perhaps have decided to rid himself of his enemy; however, poisoning was the great fear of the age, it was suspected in any sudden death, and it was always impossible to ascertain. All we know is that Madame de Châteauroux sank into delirium, screaming with pain, terrified and incoherent. On December 8, 1744, after days and nights of suffering, she died. She was twenty-seven years old.

Profoundly shocked and saddened, Louis XV shut himself up at the little château of Trianon in the grounds of Versailles with his great-aunt, the old comtesse de Toulouse, and a few other ladies of the court. Then news came of the death of *"Maman"* de Ventadour, his old governess and confidante. The king had lost, over a very short time, Fleury, the only father he had known; Madame de Ventadour, the only mother he had known; and Madame de Châteauroux, the woman he had loved; not to mention his little daughter, poor, abandoned Madame Félicité, dead at the age of eight, far away from her family.

Restless and distraught, more alone than ever, the king left Trianon for his hunting lodge of La Muette in the bois de Boulogne, with very few companions. But a king of France could never really be alone; even on these flights from grief he was accompanied by his captain of the guards and all the others who had the right to accompany the king. On December 26 he welcomed there the duc de Richelieu, just named First Gentleman of the Bedchamber. (The king had four of these, each serving a year on duty. Their duties brought them the inestimable privilege of intimacy with the monarch, and they were important players in court politics.) Richelieu, a noted intriguer and celebrated womanizer, had expected to be enjoying the reflected glory of the favor of his friend Madame de Châteauroux; now everything was uncertain. Except for one thing: Louis XV could not live for long without a mistress. The only question was, who would she be?

The king's grief at the death of Madame de Châteauroux was an opportunity for those who were always looking for ways to influence him. The poor man was being manipulated when he was at his most vulnerable. All those who surrounded him had their own agendas. They knew that he needed a woman for sex, companionship, encouragement, and advice. They all had their candidates for the post. There were two more Mailly sisters, Diane de Lauraguais and Hortense de Flavacourt, there was the pretty comtesse de Forcalquier, even some bourgeoises such as the rich and imperious Madame de La Popelinière . . .

And the outside world did not stand still. After four years of war, the French economy was beginning to hurt; Montmartel and Duverney were making it clear that perhaps a diplomatic opening to Austria might be feasible, and an early end to the war possible. The French commanders, in particular the comte de Saxe, urged that war continue. But Louis XV's council was divided; the king himself was preoccupied and depressed.

There was a new minister of foreign affairs, the marquis d'Argenson (brother of the minister of war), a novice in international affairs; the old maréchal de Noailles had one opinion, the military commanders another. When Charles Albert of Bavaria, the Emperor Charles VII, the man for whom the French had gone to war, died on January 20, 1745, the French government was unsure as to whether this was an opportunity to open negotiations with Maria-Theresa, or to keep fighting. In order for Louis XV to resume an active role in affairs of state, all agreed that he needed a woman to console and distract him, to restore his self-confidence and equilibrium. The moment had come for Madame d'Etioles and her backers to make their move.

Chapter 4

"They say she is madly in love with the king . . ."

The king, sad and preoccupied, remained at Versailles through January and February 1745. There was much for him to consider, apart from the sudden death of his mistress: the wedding of his only son, the fifteen-year-old Dauphin, to a Spanish Infanta, was being prepared for April, a great and festive event; a new military campaign was also being planned and, for the second time, the king would join his armies. A landing in Scotland by the Jacobite "Pretender," Charles Edward Stuart, was to be attempted. His generals and his ministers tried to rally Louis, but morose and surly, lonely and afflicted, the king seemed remote, uninterested.

Madame d'Etioles had, of course, kept up with the events at Versailles and Paris. In the midst of the "scenes of Metz," on August 10, 1744, she had given birth to a daughter, Alexandrine-Jeanne. Now she must have felt that her moment had come. Madame de Châteauroux, her rival, was dead, the king was unattached, she herself was at the height of her youth and beauty. It was time to marshal all her forces.

She was not alone in dreaming of a lofty destiny. In addition to her mother and Tournehem, the Pâris brothers—one her godfather, the other a friend since childhood—saw their opportunity. They had seen their careers greatly helped by the important women of the day. They were fully aware that, in helping the current favorite, whoever she may be, they were helping themselves. They had never neglected an opportunity to stay in favor and inoculate themselves from intrigue; in 1725, under the ministry of the duc de Bourbon, they had had a mutually beneficial relationship with the duc's mistress, the marquise de Prie. They had been discreetly helpful to the queen in her early days. When Madame de

Châteauroux became the king's mistress and showed her determination to remain so by brutally banishing her sister from court, the Pâris brothers had realized that this was another useful connection for them.

The death of Madame de Châteauroux came at an important juncture for the brothers. They had gradually lost enthusiasm for the war, considering it a dangerous drain on the finances of the country. But the French could not make peace from a position of weakness; military victories were the essential precondition for any serious negotiations. Whatever their reservations, the Pâris brothers had to do their utmost to sustain the war. But the success of any new campaign would depend on the king. Louis XV must be reminded of the need for *gloire;* it was imperative that he regain his courage, his vitality. If he did not, the enemy would be given the impression that France had lost its nerve. Someone must give the king the force to go forward, and, knowing Louis as they did, the brothers knew that that someone had to be a woman. They wasted no time. Tournehem, on the alert, saw to it that his nephew, Monsieur d'Etioles, was hastily sent off to the south of France on business.

It is impossible to know exactly how and when the king and Madame d'Etioles first met, still less when they became lovers. Perhaps the Pâris brothers ensured that she was granted an audience with the king, on the pretext of requesting a post for her husband. Perhaps her distant cousin, Gérard Binet, valet de chambre to the dauphin, intervened to help her into the king's presence. Or perhaps the king's cronies, the duc de Nivernais and the duc d'Ayen, recalled the lovely lady in her carriage in the forest of Sénart, and piqued his interest. In whatever circumstances the meeting took place, it seems to have occurred very early in 1745.

As early as February 8, the duc de Luynes, a highly reliable court chronicler, alluded to an intrigue already far advanced; he reported that the king had danced with a *belle inconnue* at a masked ball at Versailles, in the rooms of the king's daughters, seventeen-year-old Henriette and thirteen-year-old Adélaïde. And then he noted that the king went to another masquerade in the town of Versailles: "They even say that they suspect some flirtation took place there, and they believe they noticed that he danced yesterday with the same person of whom they spoke. Yet, it is a slight suspicion, hardly reasonable. The king appeared yesterday to have a great desire not to be recognized . . ." Three nights later, the king left Versailles after the ceremony of his Going to Bed, and went no-one-knew where.

On Monday, February 22, the Dauphin's wedding celebrations began with a ball at the hôtel de Ville in Paris. The next day, at Versailles, after the wedding itself, the court attended the first performance of *La Princesse de Navarre*—music by Rameau, words by Voltaire. The latter, who had not got on well with his collaborator Rameau, said that, although the king seemed very content with the play, the courtiers made even more noise than the theatregoers in Paris. (Perhaps an observer was right when he remarked that the piece was considered "long, boring and bad.") But, in fact that night, the play was not the thing; the château of Versailles, illuminated and glowing, animated and glamorous, temporarily restored to its former glory under the *Roi Soleil*, was the real star.

The day after the wedding, February 24, a grand ball, by invitation only, took place in the Large Stables at Versailles. Madame d'Etioles was there; she told Hénault that her cousin, Binet, was attending to her accommodation. And then, on February 25, at the ball of the yew trees, she first attracted attention and the rumors began.

For the next two months the lovers pursued their idyll, sometimes in the public eye, mostly in discreet intimacy. A few days after the ball of the yew trees, on Sunday, February 28, they were seen at a masked ball at the hôtel de Ville in Paris, one of many given by the city in honor of the royal wedding; an acquaintance saw Madame d'Etioles there, "in a black cloak, in the greatest disorder." The crush was tremendous, and the king gallantly took Jeanne-Antoinette home, returning to Versailles at eight-thirty the next morning. Having heard Mass, the king slept until five.

So far, this seemed no more than a passing dalliance with one of the prettiest women in Paris. But on March 10, the duc de Luynes mentioned Madame d'Etioles for the first time: "All these masked balls have provided the occasion to talk of the king's new love affairs and principally of a Madame d'Etioles, who is young and pretty; her mother is called Poisson. They claim that, for some time, she is almost always here at court and that this is the choice the king has made. If it is true, it would not realistically be more than a flirtation and the lady not a mistress." Luynes simply could not accept that the king would contemplate polluting the sacred precincts of Versailles with a mistress from the bourgeoisie. It could not be.

Gossip was spreading, however. "They are talking about a young woman of Paris called Mme d'Etioles," noted the Parisian lawyer, Barbier; "she is twenty-two and truly one of the prettiest women of Paris. They say that the king saw her at the hunt in the forest of Sénart and that since then she has been at all the balls and all the celebrations at Versailles, which has made one assume that there is something special here, although without anything of note."

There was a rumor that she had been seen at a performance of Rameau's ballet *Platée,* at the court theatre. And then, on April 3, Luynes caught sight of her there "in a box near the stage, very much in view of the king's box, and consequently in that of the queen; she was very well dressed and very pretty."

As Luynes and the other courtiers watched this unfolding drama with fascination, Jeanne-Antoinette had installed herself at Versailles in the tiny suite in which Madame de Mailly had lived in 1742; there she had a small bedroom, a sitting room with two windows, and a reception room at the corner of the Marble Courtyard. Nearby were the king's *petits cabinets,* the little rooms which served as libraries, dining rooms, and studies for Louis and his intimates. Here she began to meet the king's inner circle at little supper parties; the duc de Richelieu, the duc d'Ayen, the duc de Boufflers, and the duc de Luxembourg were all presented.

Finally, on April 27, the duc de Luynes, had to acknowledge the unthinkable: "That which seemed doubtful a little while ago is almost a constant truth; they say that she is madly in love with the King and that this passion is reciprocated." One can almost hear him sigh.

Such are the outlines of the developing relationship between Louis XV and Madame d'Etioles. In the mystery of intimacy they had clearly found in each other compatibility, sympathy, harmony. One may be sure that Jeanne-Antoinette, her moment having come, well knew how to make the most of it. One may also assume that Louis responded ardently to the charms of an elegant, accomplished, entertaining woman, a woman who made no secret of the fact that she herself was madly in love. After three months of acquaintanceship, he was ready to make her his *maîtresse déclarée.*

Barbier, the Parisian, added what he knew: "This Madame d'Etioles is well made and extremely pretty, sings perfectly and knows a hundred amusing little songs, rides marvelously and has had all the education possible. . . . Her husband is associated with his uncle in the place of farmer general, and, in that function, has been sent to do a tour in Provence. This distance from Paris has the air of lasting for a long time."

In fact, poor Monsieur d'Etioles returned to Paris that April, completely unaware of the dramatic change of circumstances. Tournehem broke the news, telling his nephew that "he could no longer count on his wife, that she had such a violent predilection for the King that she could not resist, and that there was no other part for him than to separate from her. Monsieur d'Etioles fell in a faint at this news. He has since then been obliged to agree to the separation." But he did find the strength to write a letter to his wife begging her to return; Jeanne-Antoinette, perhaps hoping to attract the king's sympathy, showed him the letter. Deeply embarrassed, Louis remarked only that her husband seemed a very decent man.

Monsieur d'Etioles received no reply from his wife; he was advised to make the best of the situation and, to help him in doing so, Tournehem offered him his own lucrative place as farmer-general. He was also advised to leave immediately for a year-long tour of inspection in his new area of responsibility; he remained in Grenoble for the next eighteen months, discreetly watched by the governor of the province, Monsieur de Marcieu, who was authorized to persuade him to accept the post of ambassador to Constantinople. Lenormand refused the bait, and eventually returned to Paris to take up his work as a farmer-general, and to sow some wild oats. (Over the years he remained extremely discreet, and his wife was grateful. She was always anxious to mollify him, intervening several times to help him when he requested legal or financial aid.)

The day was approaching when the king had to join his armies at the front and when the lovers had to part. But not before practical matters were attended to. The king's decision was taken—that Madame d'Etioles, bourgeoise or not, Poisson or not, would come to Versailles as his declared mistress. It was an extraordinary *prise de position* by this timid man, a tribute to the hold she already possessed over him.

The king's decision had many ramifications. She must be presented at court, and for that she must be given a title. There must have been thrilling discussions as to which title she might bear and how to acquire it. As early as April 5 the king's cousin, the prince de Conti, was asking his lawyer to investigate the marquisate of Pompadour, an estate in the Limousin with a tangled ownership. Jeanne-Antoinette must have immediately appreciated the beauty of the name. It was a distinguished one; a recent marquise de Pompadour had been governess to the children of Louis XV's uncle, the duc de Berry. (And she might have come across the name already; one of the last of the Pompadours, the widowed marquise de Courcillon, still lived at Soisy-sous-Etioles.) Intensive legal work began, and Pâris de Montmartel agreed to advance the necessary funds. Louis XV left Versailles for Flanders on May 6; the next day lawyers for Madame d'Etioles were demanding her dowry back and a formal separation from her husband.

Jeanne-Antoinette was to spend the summer at Etioles, learning of the strange customs of Versailles, writing to the king, being gently coached in etiquette. She must learn court ways, and acquire that polish and refinement indispensable to her success. The court prided itself on being a different country to the rest of France; it had its own language, its own code of conduct; it was a world in which ridicule was death. She began to study the rules of Versailles and the names and family histories of those with whom she would be living. She knew that the court ladies would be lying in wait for the *"petite bourgeoise"* to make her first mistake. But she was nothing if not sure of herself, she had never met a man she could not conquer, she felt herself destined for her glorious calling. She never betrayed a moment of self-doubt.

All those aware of the astonishing turn of events, and anxious to profit from them, rushed to Etioles that summer. Jeanne-Antoinette's cousin by marriage, Elisabeth-Charlotte d'Estrades, whose husband, Tournehem's nephew, had been killed in 1743 at the battle of Dettingen, was determined to associate herself as closely as she could with the rising star. She suggested that her dear friend could learn much about the court from the abbé de Bernis, a plump, pink-cheeked little abbé about town, known more for his pretty verses than his religious convictions. Voltaire called him *"la belle Babet* with his garlands and his bouquets of flowers,"* and thus Bernis came to be known in society as Babet the flowergirl (*Babet la bouquetière*).

Bernis was well-born, but heavily in debt; even so, according to his memoirs, he had to struggle mightily to convince himself to condescend to enlighten this little bourgeoise about the ways of the truly noble. His friend, Madame de La Ferté-Imbault, the daughter of Madame Geoffrin, thought that he could only benefit from becoming a confidant of the king and his mistress. She added, tellingly, "No one, at the time, had any notion of the role which Madame d'Etioles would play at the court, and I fell into a fury when someone told me that she would play a great role."

Bernis allowed himself to be convinced, and before long he was discovering that it was no disagreeable thing to spend time with Jeanne-Antoinette, mere bourgeoise though she was. "Madame d'Etioles had all the graces, all the freshness and all the gaiety of youth: she danced, sang, played comedy; she lacked no agreeable talent. She liked literature and the arts. She had a lofty soul, sensitive and generous; it is true that in order to make good use of the credit she had, she lacked knowledge of men and affairs . . ." Bernis felt confident that he could supply her with such knowledge. Seeing himself as the right hand of the favorite, he envisaged dazzling vistas opening before him.

Another frequent visitor to Etioles that summer was Voltaire, who had met Jeanne-Antoinette in Paris, and was a friend and business associate of Pâris-Duverney. Already rich and famous, Voltaire was, even so, always eager to insinuate himself with any new luminary. He never had any difficulty in flattering outrageously; it was indeed part of his charm. He bounded to Etioles, a poem at the ready, a deft reference to Louis's appearance as a yew tree at the ball at Versailles:

> This hero of lovers as well as warriors
> Has joined the myrtle to the laurel;
> But today it is the yew which I revere . . .

He accompanied this ode with a note: "I interest myself in your happiness more than you think, perhaps there is no one in Paris who takes a more lively interest. It is not as an old flatterer of beautiful women that I speak, but as a good citizen, and I ask permission to come and tell you a little something at Etioles or Brunoy. Have the goodness to let me know when and where. I am with respect, madame, of your eyes, your figure, and your wit a very humble and obedient servant."

The omens for the lovers seemed particularly auspicious when the king's army won a great victory at Fontenoy, near Tournai, on May 11. The battle of Fontenoy was the zenith of the glory of Louis XV. The maréchal de Saxe, in command of the French troops—suffering so from gout that he had to be carried around in a wicker chair—won the day against the Duke of Cumberland and his Anglo-Dutch-German army with a furious infantry charge; the Irish soldiers fighting for France were particularly bold against the old enemy. The king remained near the heaviest fighting throughout the battle, encouraging his men and rejoicing at their victory.

The marquis d'Argenson, minister of foreign affairs, who had been with the king, told Voltaire that "it is the King himself who has won this battle, by his will, by his firmness." But d'Argenson could not help reflecting on the cost of victory: "Triumph is the finest thing in the world . . . but the cost of all this is human flesh and blood." There had indeed been significant casualties; the Anglo-German army suffered 9,000 dead or wounded, the French about 6,000. We are told that Louis XV, despite his high spirits, was deeply affected by the suffering and carnage he had witnessed, and told his son, "Behold the cost of victory. The blood of our enemies is still the blood of men, and the real glory is to spare it."

Voltaire had no such qualms. Having been appointed historiographer to the king in April, he was ecstatic at the prospects for new odes, new eulogies, new tributes. "Ah! What fine work for our historiographer!" he told d'Argenson. "It is three hundred years since a King of France has done anything as glorious. I am mad with joy." He immediately dashed off an immensely long ode, *La Bataille de Fontenoy*, which was rushed into print in June. Unfortunately it received poor reviews, indeed much derision. Jeanne-Antoinette wrote to him consolingly: "I do not know why they attack your poem. It seems to me the most unjust thing in the world. It must not afflict you in any way. It is the lot of great men to be envied." Voltaire and Jeanne-Antoinette quickly established a mutually beneficial relationship. She would do her best to support him in the king's favor, and he would sing her praises, as a sort of public relations man. They were both living on their wits, both outsiders in the stratified world of the court, both gifted with an exceptional ability to survive.

The king, victorious in love and war, wrote frequently to Jeanne-Antoinette, more than eighty letters between May and September, sending them to Pâris de Montmartel at Brunoy for forwarding to Etioles. Finally, on July 9, Louis XV could send his mistress confirmation of her new title, addressing his letter to "Madame la marquise de Pompadour," instead of to "Madame d'Etioles." Jeanne-Antoinette immediately adopted the title, and the Pompadour arms, three silver towers on an azure ground. Having thus, at the instance of the king, been instantly ennobled, she could now be presented at court, a privilege normally extended only to those who could prove their noble ancestors back to 1400.

Voltaire stood ready to celebrate:

> Sincere and tender Pompadour,
> For I can give you in advance
> This name which rhymes with Amour . . .

Bernis also picked up his pen to celebrate the occasion:

> Just like Hebe, the young Pompadour
> Has two pretty dimples on her cheek,
> Two charming dimples where pleasure plays,
> Made by the hand of Love . . .

Such overheated and undistinguished effusions were the precursors of a chorus of flattery and adulation to which the new favorite would quickly become accustomed.

On August 10 Pâris de Montmartel gave a reception for his goddaughter at Brunoy. There she was congratulated by a distinguished crowd, including the minister of finance, Philibert Orry; Orry, secure in the long occupation of his post, smiled benignly on the newcomer, seemingly unconcerned about her intimate relationship with the Pâris brothers, with whom he himself was often at odds. All eyes were on the new marquise.

Voltaire continued his eulogies, informing all his curious Parisian friends that Madame de Pompadour was "well brought up, sensible, amiable, graceful and talented, born with good sense and a good heart"; and to the writer and magistrate, Charles Hénault, he confided, somewhat patronizingly, "I was talking a few days ago to Mme de Pompadour about your charming, your immortal Précis of the History of France; she has read more at her age than any old lady in the place where she is going to reign and where it is most desirable that she reign . . ."

Voltaire helped her with her literary education, and perhaps with her letters to the king, but he could not help her with the arcane rituals of court life. Bernis was too busy with his own grand visions: "I advised her to patronize men of letters; it was they who had given the name Great to Louis XIV. I had no advice to give her on the subject of cherishing and seeking out honorable people; I found this principle established in her soul." For the practical details of life at court, Madame de Pompadour turned to an aristocratic acquaintance, Charles-Antoine de Gontaut.

According to Bernis, the marquis de Gontaut played only a secondary role in this sequel to Pygmalion. "With the exception of M. de Gontaut, who stayed there for a few days," he wrote, "I was the only man of the world with whom the marquise de Pompadour had relations . . ." But Gontaut made a lasting impression on the new marquise. Charming, kind, and amusing, he was perfect company, self-effacing and disinterested; he was known in society as the "white eunuch" and as "an excellent piece of furniture for a favorite; he cannot excite jealousy, and does not interfere in anything." He would be a faithful friend to Jeanne-Antoinette all her life.*

Gontaut could help the new marquise learn the titles and family histories of the nobles who made up the court. She needed to know how to distinguish between a duchess and a mere countess, how to recognize the right of one lady to be seated in the royal presence, another not, how to use the court vocabulary, how to walk and sit and speak. (Court language and pronunciation were quite different from that of Paris; courtiers said "*roue*" for "*roi*," "*chev soi*" for "*chez soi*"; certain words and phrases were never used, "*cadeau*" should be "*présent*," "*louis d'or*" should be "*louis en or*," and so on.)

All summer long, Voltaire, Bernis, and Gontaut attended to the lovely young woman on the brink of such a dizzying future. They found her a most receptive pupil. Judging from her subsequent actions, Ma-

---

*Gontaut, born in 1707, had married a wealthy heiress, Antoinette-Eustachie Crozat du Châtel, who died in 1747 after giving birth to a son, the duc de Lauzun, who was probably the son of the duc de Choiseul.

dame de Pompadour had every intention of using her place for far more than mere entertainment, and from the very beginning.

On September 7, after four months at the front, Louis XV made his entry into Paris. The royal family assembled at the Tuileries to greet him. Two days later, on September 9, there was a reception and dinner at the hôtel de Ville. Jeanne-Antoinette, still unpresented at court, and therefore unofficial, dined upstairs with her brother, Tournehem, and the comtesse d'Estrades. The duc de Gesvres, governor of Paris, the duc de Bouillon (Great Chamberlain), and the duc de Richelieu (First Gentleman of the Chamber) all came to pay their respects. A few days later the court returned to Versailles and the new marquise put the finishing touches to her preparations for her new life.

On Sunday, September 12, the comtesse d'Estrades was presented at Versailles. Her late husband's family had the necessary noble credentials for this presentation to seem acceptable, even though the comtesse herself, born Elisabeth Huguet de Semonville, was also a bourgeoise. Madame d'Estrades hoped to share to the full in her friend's elevation. Bold and self-confident, without being pretty—"rather plump, short, with very fat cheeks," according to Luynes—she had declared herself the indispensable confidante. And Jeanne-Antoinette, realizing that she would need the comfort of at least one familiar face in her new life, was glad to be able to hear from her friend an account of the elaborate ceremonial she herself would be obliged to undergo in the coming days.

As in all areas, the court way of dressing, and even of walking, was different from that of Paris. Ladies of the court wore very low-cut, tightly laced bodices which showed off their busts and waists against billowing, paniered skirts. At Versailles they walked very fast with tiny steps on high-heeled mules. Coiffures were elegant chignons. Faces were powdered and highly rouged, beauty spots carefully placed. (The question of rouge was so important that the Spanish Infanta, who had just married the Dauphin, almost caused a diplomatic incident by refusing to wear it at first. A pale face looked sad and court ladies must sparkle.)

The new marquise de Pompadour made her entrance into the salon of the Oeil-de-Boeuf on Tuesday, September 14, after Vespers, at six o'clock in the evening, preceded by the dowager princesse de Conti, a member of the royal family, and followed by Madame d'Estrades. Arrayed in the obligatory black *robe de cour*, jeweled, rouged, and powdered, she was in full bloom. "Very well-made . . . a magnificent skin, superb hands and arms, her eyes more pretty than large but of a fire, a spirituality, a brilliancy I have never seen in any other woman," according to one contemporary. And another observer noted that "she seemed to capture the nuance between the last degree of elegance and the first of nobility . . . her eyes had a particular charm, which they perhaps owed to the uncertainty of their color; they had none of the sparkle of black eyes, the tender languor of blue, the particular finesse of gray; their indeterminate color seemed to render them ready for all kinds of seduction and to express in succession all the impressions of a very mobile soul."

A large crowd watched in silence as the little procession made its way into the cabinet du Conseil, where the king, very embarrassed, was waiting. After performing three more curtsies, the marquise murmured a few words. Louis XV remained mute, merely nodding in acknowledgment; then the marquise executed the requisite three curtsies while slowly walking backward, carefully kicking her train out of the way as she went. Back through the Oeil-de-Boeuf she went, finding another large crowd awaiting her in the queen's rooms.

The duc de Luynes, naturally, was an eyewitness to the scene. "All Paris was very curious to know what the Queen would say to Mme de Pompadour. They concluded that she would speak of her dress, a very common topic among women when there is nothing to say. The Queen, knowing that Paris had already arranged their conversation, decided to talk of other things. She knew that Mme de Pompadour knew Mme de Saissac.* The Queen told her that she had met Mme de Saissac in Paris and was very pleased to have made her acquaintance. I do not know if Madame de Pompadour heard what she said, as the Queen speaks very softly; but she used the moment to assure the Queen of her respect and her desire to please her. The Queen seemed content with this speech and

---

*The marquise de Saissac lived in a mansion on the rue de Varenne in Paris; her brother, the comte de Grimberghen, was one of Madame Poisson's reputed lovers.

the audience, attentive to the least detail of this meeting, claimed that it had been very long and comprised twelve sentences."

As the courtiers buzzed, Parisian society was, or pretended to be, shocked. "At that time such a presentation appeared monstrous," noted the future duc de Choiseul, "for it seemed that all the rules of polite society, of justice and of etiquette were being violated by carrying off the wife of a farmer-general in the middle of Paris and, after had her change her name, making her a woman of rank fit to be presented."

Some at court were not so much astonished as they were horrified. The comte de Maurepas, the witty, rather sinister minister of the navy, nemesis of Madame de Châteauroux, noted in his journal: "she is excessively common, a bourgeoise out of her place who will displace all the world if one cannot manage to displace her." But Jeanne-Antoinette Poisson, marquise de Pompadour, having successfully arrived at the destination she had so ardently desired, was not to allow gossip and malice to spoil her joy.

PART TWO
1745–1751

"Sincere and tender Pompadour."

Chapter 5

*"It seems that everyone finds
Madame de Pompadour extremely polite . . ."*

When Jeanne-Antoinette arrived at Versailles in September 1745, she had had time to reflect on her future life. She had observed the court and become familiar with its customs. But she was about to enter here for the first time as an actor, rather than a spectator. And although protected by the king's passion, she was, even so, an object of intense and unkind curiosity. She was confident that she would, with her charm and grace, be able to defuse the hostility around her. She was, above all, determined to forge a good relationship with the royal family.

The queen, Marie Leczinska, was a long-suffering wife. She was used to her husband's infidelities, taking refuge in her religion and the company of a few trusted friends. He rarely acknowledged her. She never complained. She indulged in endless games of cards, painted a little, ate rather a lot, and, very occasionally, allowed herself to show a flash of a sharp wit. She played her part at court with dignity and made herself respected; but she was completely without influence, and consequently isolated. Even her own ladies frequently failed to hide their eagerness to escape their duties with her and flee elsewhere. After being too often humiliated by the imperious Madame de Châteauroux, she was, initially, in no mood to accommodate the new favorite's proclaimed desire to please.

The dauphin was also pious, but of a sarcastic disposition. But he was newly married and paid the new marquise little attention. Uxorious and lethargic, he spent his time in his pretty rooms at Versailles, criticizing all the world, too timid to speak in his father's presence, preferring solitary dissidence. He called the marquise *"maman putain"* (mama whore) and tried to ignore her. His two sisters, Madame Henriette and Madame

Adélaïde, were as yet too young to take notice. (Three other sisters remained forgotten at the convent of Fontevrault.)

The only other member of the royal family who could provide the marquise with opposition was the king's cousin, Louis-François de Bourbon, prince de Conti, a clever man with great ambitions and a desire to play a role. Conti was a brave soldier and had been away from court with the army when Jeanne-Antoinette was presented. To his chagrin, it was his own mother who had made the presentation (she had done so, they said, in return for the payment of her debts). When Conti returned to court at the end of 1745, he and the newcomer regarded each other warily.

Apart from the personalities with whom she would have to deal, the marquise would have to master the great château of Versailles itself and its hierarchy of spaces. The king and queen lived in rooms on the first floor around the central Marble Courtyard, the king on the north side, the queen on the south. Members of the royal family lived in rooms in the adjoining wings; privileged courtiers a little further away. Everyone else lived in uncomfortable attics and entresols, far away from the scenes of royal life. Being present at the King's Rising, Mass, Dinner, and Going to Bed meant wearisome hours of standing in drafty halls, dressed to the teeth, and a very long walk home at the end of it. And the château itself was outmoded, old-fashioned. What had been acceptable for the *Roi Soleil* was less so fifty years later. Versailles was inadequately heated, lacking in modern sanitation, ill-ventilated, and none too clean. Parts of it were close to collapse. The grounds were neglected, the fountains rarely played.

The king himself was uncomfortable in this magnificent prison. He preferred warm rooms and modern bathrooms to grand chambers inlaid with freezing marble, cozy settings to majestic ones. But he dutifully maintained Versailles as a shrine to his formidable great-grandfather, a shrine to be treated with respect, but not loved. And in this shrine, he felt himself unable to end the public ceremonies bequeathed to him by Louis XIV. This unwillingness to undo what his great-grandfather had done led to absurd situations. Every morning he would get out of bed in his private bedroom, put on a dressing gown, and scurry through two rooms to lie down in his official bed, where a long ceremonial accompanied every move of his Rising, with a crowd of courtiers being permitted to enter at various stages of the ceremony. Every night he would endure the same ceremonial in reverse, before hurrying back in his dressing gown to his own bed. The poor man complained that the rooms were freezing, that he wanted a stove to heat the official bedroom; his architect told him that a stove would spoil the magnificent symmetry of the room. He asked for a second fireplace; it took six years to arrive, having to be made to the highest artistic standards.

He and Madame de Châteauroux had spent their time in the "*petits cabinets*," a warren of little rooms on the floors above the king's bedroom. Here were libraries and dining rooms and bathrooms, a workshop for Louis's lathe (he was an amateur woodworker), a distillery where he made perfumes, and kitchens where he made pastries. Here the king was happiest. Low ceilings, mirrors, and a décor of light, bright colors provided the king with a warm and intimate setting for suppers, reading, and the luxury of simply being alone. Louis XV was constantly experimenting with new locations for these private rooms; his bathroom, with two tubs, one for soaping, one for rinsing, was moved four times, as was his little workshop. *Cabinets de chaise*, equipped with the most modern plumbing — that is, flushing toilets — multiplied. At roof level there were extensive terraces with trellises, dovecotes, birdcages, and even a chicken coop. Staircases — spiral, semicircular, inside and outside — were constantly added to serve the increasing demands of the kitchens. When the king disappeared into the *petits cabinets*, the great rooms of Versailles lost the sparkle conferred by the presence of royalty. For the courtiers who milled around hoping for a chance to approach the king, it was increasingly difficult to find him.

Madame de Pompadour's first rooms were on the attic floor, above the king's *petits cabinets*, with a panoramic view of the parterre du Nord, the bassin de Neptune, and the hills beyond. Today one can still see the paneling, the view is largely unchanged and a portrait of Tournehem hangs in the salon. These few rooms had been those of Madame de Châteauroux, empty for over a year. The marquise reached them by means of a *chaise volante*, kept exclusively for her use. This "flying chair" was a kind of primitive lift, controlled by a set of ropes and pulleys, decorated with mirrors and carved paneling. It saved the marquise a long climb; all those who came to wait on her had, however, to make that climb themselves.

The marquise had no sooner moved in than the king took her off to his beloved Choisy for a few days. As she walked on the wide new terrace there and looked down the river toward Etioles, did she give a thought to her past, to her husband, her one-year-old child? One doubts it. She was completely focused on the present, the unimaginably exciting and glamorous present. One senses that she felt herself equal to whatever lay ahead, fortified by the king's passion, eager to make her mark.

She boldly invited to Choisy some of her Parisian intellectual friends; Duclos, Voltaire, the abbé Prévost, among others, came to dinner, although they supped in a different room from the king's, but the experiment seems not to have repeated. It was rather an awkward visit altogether. Madame de Châteauroux's sister, the duchesse de Lauraguais, was in the party, accompanied by the duc de Richelieu, the late duchess's intimate friend, and the king's cronies, the duc de Duras and the marquis de Meuse, politely on the lookout for faux pas. The king developed a fever. And when the queen came to visit with her father, they were disconcerted to find the marquise in riding habit playing quadrille in the king's bedroom. Marie soon left, having been made to feel unwelcome. Everyone was having to come to terms with a new regime.

Soon it was time for the yearly trip to Fontainebleau. Every autumn the court descended on the little town for six weeks or more and took possession of the splendid, rambling old palace. Louis XV was always trying to make it more orderly, more regular. He and his favorite architect, Ange-Jacques Gabriel, were constantly poring over plans to see how to increase the space for the courtiers and make the private suites lighter and prettier. The palace remained, however, its intractable, charming, medieval and Renaissance self. Once again Madame de Pompadour moved into the rooms of her predecessor, Madame de Châteauroux, on the ground floor with a view of the jardin de Diane.

The six-week-long visit to Fontainebleau was a prolonged idyll for the couple. The king spent every minute he could with Jeanne-Antoinette. "As soon as the King is dressed, he goes down to Mme de Pompadour and stays until time for Mass; he returns and eats some soup and a cutlet, for he never eats at midday, and remains with her until five or six o'clock when it is time for work. On council days he goes down to her before and after."

She herself hardly appeared in public, except to attend the queen. She had an extremely good cook and gave *"petits soupers, mais excellents"* to the king and very few others. She attended the court theatre, sitting in a private box with Louis. Sometimes she rode out to the hunt dressed *en amazone* with him and his daughters. The golden autumn days at beautiful Fontainebleau, where etiquette was not as severe as at Versailles, and where she could make her first steps in court life with less surveillance, passed as in a dream.

But reality intruded. While the court was at Fontainebleau, Philibert Orry, the minister of finance, was dismissed. This caused a stir. He had been in the job for many years and was generally considered a model of probity. The king had never before dismissed a minister so abruptly. The influence of the favorite and that of the Pâris brothers was detected. Orry had been recently uncooperative with the brothers; they had often found him difficult about paying their bills; he now found their most recent expenses excessive. The Pâris brothers took their opportunity; they accused Orry of suggesting that the state of finances would not permit the war to go on much longer. This was, in fact, their own position, but they took great care not to be vocal about it. Orry was sacrificed for stating too openly what many knew to be the case. This was the first indication of the increased influence the brothers would enjoy in the new scheme of things at Versailles. Every minister was on notice that his policies would have to be attuned to those of the formidable brothers. Jeanne-Antoinette had also for the first time proved that she could successfully present the Pâris' point of view to the king and that she could persuade him to act. Attention was paid.

The marquise may well have played a part in Orry's fall, on behalf of her patrons the Pâris, but she had nothing to do with the choice of his successor. Orry himself, who was in fact suffering from some fatigue in his post, recommended Jean-Baptiste Machault d'Arnouville, the king's representative at Valenciennes, and worked with him when he arrived.

The real significance of Orry's fall, as far as Madame de Pompadour was concerned, lay in the fact that his departure meant that the post of director of the King's Building Works (the *Bâtiments*), also held by Orry, became vacant. This was a post to which Orry had not paid much

attention, rightly regarding the finances of France as being more important. But the marquise saw possibilities in the *Bâtiments*. The department
was responsible for the upkeep of all the royal palaces — Versailles and
Fontainebleau, Choisy and Compiègne, Trianon, Marly, and La Muette,
and so on. The king's architect, Ange-Jacques Gabriel, worked for the
Bâtiments, and all new building projects were financed and approved
there. In 1745 the department's budget was small, for the country was
still at war, and very few projects were on hand. But when peace came,
the marquise had her own plans for the amusement of the king, plans
which involved his love of building.

With her "*oncle*" Tournehem, at court, she would not only have the
pleasure of his company, but she would be able to rely on his support for
her future projects. In short order she introduced Tournehem to the king
and persuaded him to make the appointment, which was announced in
December. Not announced just yet was the fact that Abel Poisson would
be Tournehem's designated successor. It was the first indication of the
marquise's priorities, and of her extraordinary self-assurance.

But all was not cloudless. Madame Poisson, having fallen ill during the latter part of 1745, had been unable to witness her daughter's
triumph, unable to come to court. All the rich rewards of which she had
dreamed for so many years would not be hers. On Christmas Eve she
died, at the age of forty-six, and was buried at Saint-Eustache two days
later. In Paris, her passing was greeted with derision;

> Here lies one who, coming from muck,
> In order to make a proper fortune,
> Sold her honor to the farmer
> And her daughter to the owner.

Some might have thought that the marquise would feel a certain relief;
her mother, after all, would always have been a potential source of
embarrassment. But Madame de Pompadour thought nothing of the kind;
deeply grieved, she went into seclusion, mourning the brave and
ambitious woman who had taken her to the fortune teller and called her
"Reinette." But this being the court, she was obliged to appear at Marly
a few days later. (The exquisite gold snuffbox, with a watch inside, ordered by the king for Madame Poisson's Christmas present, was given

to the queen who, unaware of its origin, expressed herself very touched by her husband's thoughtfulness.)

It was in the *petits cabinets* that Madame de Pompadour could forget her grief, and the hostility of the court; there were held the *"petits soupers"* two or three times a week, at which a few intimates could enjoy the privilege of dining in relaxed fashion with the king and his favorite.

The marquise realized very early the importance of the *petits cabinets* for her own ends. She understood that the king liked this intimate, comfortable, pleasant, and cheerful setting—very bourgeoise; she came to comprehend that, by establishing an ambience at once cozy and royal, relaxed and refined, she would become essential to his life. After becoming accustomed to such congenial society, after a tedious council or exhausting ceremony, Louis would not be able to do without it. And if it were she, and she alone, who was responsible for the good cheer, the discreet friends, the voluptuousness of it all, then without her, he would enjoy none of this. The marquise set about establishing this *"petit club très chic, très amusant et très fermé"* (a little club, very chic, very amusing, very exclusive).

The *petits soupers* took place in the king's private dining room, which was decorated with two jolly paintings of gourmands, De Troy's *Lunch with Oysters* and Lancret's *Lunch with Ham*. Next door was the *"petite galerie,"* where guests assembled before supper and played cards afterward. It was adorned with eight large paintings of exotic hunts, including Carle Van Loo's bear hunt, Lancret's leopard hunt, De Troy's lion hunt, Boucher's tiger hunt, and Parrocel's elephant hunt. One can still see the delicate carving of the window embrasures and imagine the refinement of the décor, the bright light tones of the painted and varnished wood.* Next door was a little room where Louis XV sometimes made coffee for his guests. He delighted in the warmth of these gatherings; his passion for the woman who had created them increased. He could not do without her.

Knowing that she was loved, Madame de Pomapdour could forget the storm of abuse which fell on her head since the day she arrived at court. Parisian comment was merciless:

*The king's *"vernisseur,"* Etienne Martin, was in the process of inventing a special varnish named after him, which necessitated the application of as many as forty-three coats of varnish. The colors most commonly employed were *"petit vert"* or *"vert d'eau,"* *"gris perle,"* *"bleu de Prusse,"* and *"ton jonquille."*

A little bourgeoise
Raised to be a slut
Brings everything down to her level
And makes the court a slum.

But the hostility of the populace could be trumped by the deference of others. Whatever the reservations of the royal family, most courtiers went to the opposite extreme. When, in mid-January 1746, the court went to the little château of Marly in order to view Coustou's newly installed statues, the Horses of Marly, the twenty-six-year-old future duc de Choiseul, at that time comte de Stainville, was there and wrote: "I found Mme de Pompadour the appointed mistress of the kingdom . . . One was presented to her as to the Queen. I found her etiquette much more exalted than had been that of Mme de Châteauroux, who had preserved social politeness and equality . . . people paid her the basest respects and homage."

Stainville moved in the circle of many of Pompadour's friends—Gontaut, Bernstorff, Bernis—but he was a proud young man, unwilling to acknowledge that a Madame d'Etioles might be an important figure in France. His pride conflicted in this instance with his intelligence, which told him that Madame de Pompadour might be a good influence. It would take some years, and a dramatic development, for these two gifted people to come to terms.

Chapter 6

"Madame de Pompadour has been very useful to us . . ."

Madame de Pompadour began to settle into the predictable rhythm of court life. After the visit to Fontainebleau in the autumn, it was back to Versailles for the celebration of Christmas and the New Year of 1746, followed by the winter carnival season leading up to Lent. The king's year revolved around the festivals of the church—Christmas, Easter, Pentecost, and so on—but also around the hunt, for which he had a passion verging on obsession. He hunted every day he could, finding pleasure in the fresh air and the exercise, and in the luxury of the comparative solitude of the forest. His passion often took him away from Versailles to hunting lodges such as La Muette, in the bois de Boulogne, to Choisy, to Rambouillet, or Marly. These *"petits voyages"* lasted several days and a small group of friends were invited to join the house party. Once again the marquise saw possibilities; in taking the king away from the tedious rituals of court to agreeable little châteaux where congenial faces greeted him, where there were cards and conversation, good food and fine wine, she could extend the charm of the *petits cabinets.*

The marquise realized that Louis was happiest in small groups, with familiar faces, free from representation and ceremony. She did not understand, however, that for the king to abandon such duties would be to give up part of his claim to the affection and loyalty of his subjects. Louis XV himself considered that, if he continued the daily rituals of the Rising and Going to Bed, the public suppers and the regular attendance at Mass, he could then withdraw into his private rooms for rest and relaxation. Yet the fact that by so doing, he deprived Versailles and the court of much of the prestige and éclat with which it had always been associated, was one consequence. More importantly, by withdrawing from some of the public rites of kingship, he compromised the sacred role the king played in the life of the kingdom. Since 1738 Louis XV, acknowledging his adultery, had found it impossible to confess and take communion at Easter; he then discontinued the age-old rite of touching those affected by scrofula, as his ancestors had done; he considered himself a sinner living in adultery, and he would not be dishonest. But there was no denying the scandal this had caused, and was still causing.

In May 1746 it was time for the king to join his armies in Flanders. The French found themselves in a difficult situation; in October 1745 Francis of Lorraine, Maria-Theresa's husband, had been elected Holy Roman Emperor, the very outcome which the French had striven to avoid. Furthermore, in December 1745, their feckless ally, Frederick of Prussia, had made a separate peace with Maria-Theresa, leaving Louis XV and his armies to continue the fight with the Austrians and British alone. By now, the French were fighting simply to establish an honorable position from which to make their own peace.

Madame de Pompadour had to face the king's departure once again; this time, however, Louis did what he could to make her solitude comfortable and dignified. He bought for her the château of Crécy, near Dreux, some miles to the southwest of Versailles. The king wished his mistress to spend the months of his absence in her own house with her friends, away from the court. Jeanne-Antoinette was pregnant this spring; peace and rest were absolutely necessary for her. But at Crécy, she plunged into one of her favorite activities—interior decorating.

Crécy was the first of the houses in which she could indulge her talent for creating an elegant and refined *cadre de vie*. Luynes noted that the château was "very handsome, well furnished, with a terrace they say has cost one hundred thousand *écus* . . . the King is buying it in the event that the place and the neighborhood suit her: she seems extremely happy with it, and is already making arrangements for the King's person, counting on him coming to visit."

The château at Crécy needed work, even though it was relatively new; the wings had to be rebuilt, the central block enlarged. It was a long,

low house, with a terrace overlooking the valley of the river Blaise. Over
the years it was transformed at vast expense. To beautify the facing hill,
which was thought too bare, a vast lawn was created—a grassy slope
forming an amphitheatre between two woods. To widen the view still
further, the nearby estates of Aulnay and Magenville were appropriated.
Today, one is astonished that whole villages could be thus acquired, re-
ordered to make a view, and the inhabitants sent elsewhere. There was
no brutality about it, it was simply accepted by all concerned that *les grands*
could do such things. The voice of the *petit peuple* was as yet unheard.

The indispensable Pâris de Montmartel advanced the funds to purchase the estate. Louis XV arranged to reimburse him with funds outside the finances of the State, by creating a second post of Treasurer of
the King's Stables. Whoever bought the post (for almost all positions in
the Ancien Régime were bought and sold) would be paying the price to
Montmartel. This would become a pattern for the financial dealings of
the king and his mistress; the idea was to avoid large expenditures being
made public. Over the years, this mingling of public and private funds
would become habitual.

On May 1, 1746, the king took his leave of the marquise at Choisy;
the dauphin did not join his father on campaign but remained at court to
be with his pregnant wife. As the king bade farewell to his family, there
came sad news from Scotland, where the remnants of "Bonny Prince
Charlie's" army had been slaughtered at Culloden. The Stuart Pretender,
having landed in Scotland, had marched as far south as Derby, but received
little support from the populace. Forced to retreat, his exhausted and
demoralized army had met with a brutal end, and the Pretender had barely
escaped with his life. It was the end of France's attempts to depose the
Hanoverian monarchy in the United Kingdom. The grim news did not seem
to augur well for Louis's own campaign; and, six weeks after these tearful
farewells, having achieved very little at the front, his dislike for campaigning
confirmed, Louis returned to court for the dauphine's confinement, and
to comfort Jeanne-Antoinette, who had just miscarried.

The long and anxious watch over the young dauphine had a tragic
end. On July 22, the girl, whose marriage had been celebrated with so
much pomp only eighteen months earlier, died, having given birth to a
baby girl. The king and the royal family fled Versailles for Choisy; the

dauphin was overcome with grief, his sisters wept, the queen prayed, and the atmosphere soon became deeply morose. Activities were restricted, with card playing forbidden, and the king was soon in a bad humor. Abruptly, he left with the marquise for Crécy, taking a few ladies and his cronies, the ducs de Richelieu, d'Ayen, d'Aumont, de Villeroi, and others. Louis XV found his solace, as always, in the hunt; but now he also found comfort in the company of Jeanne-Antoinette.

Even before the mourning for the dauphine was over, the court turned its attention to the question of a second wife for the grief-stricken young man. There were several candidates, including a princess of Savoy, and another infanta of Spain; there was also the daughter of the king of Saxony, a niece of the maréchal de Saxe. The marquise lost no time in lending her support to the Saxon princess; not only did she want to gratify the maréchal, a man she admired, but she found an irresistible opportunity to display her influence. It also afforded her the chance to play a part in the great feud between Saxe and the prince de Conti, the one her "*cher ami*," the other her enemy.

Louis XV took the opportunity of his bereavement not to return to the front that year, leaving the conduct of the war to his commanders, the maréchal de Saxe and the prince de Conti. These two men found it hard to work together; both were proud and inflexible, neither tolerated opposition or contradiction. Saxe, the bastard son of the elector of Saxony, and Conti, Prince of the Blood and cousin of the king, quarrelled constantly. Each wanted the supreme command. Conti was an intelligent young man, ambitious and influential with the king; but Saxe had an asset that Conti lacked—the support of Madame de Pompadour. Saxe made it his business to amuse and flatter the marquise, whereas Conti made no secret of his disdain for the parvenue. That summer the comedy was played out.

On August 4 the comte de Stainville, one of Conti's lieutenants, arrived at Versailles with news of the fall of Charleroi. He made his report to the king, then to the foreign minister, the marquis d'Argenson, and then, as was becoming obligatory, to Madame de Pompadour; after which he wrote, "I was very coldly received by this last." The marquise knew that Conti was demanding the supreme command of French armies

in Flanders and she made clear to Stainville, who had brought the matter up, that she was against the idea. "I was not unaware that Madame
de Pompadour infinitely favored the maréchal de Saxe," Stainville noted,
before returning to the front to report his lack of progress to Conti.

On hearing the bad news, Conti abruptly left the army; he was at
Versailles three days later. It seemed as though the prince had given in to
a fit of petulance. But he was received warmly at court, invited to Choisy
and Crécy. The king showed no sign of displeasure; in fact the two men
were closeted together for a considerable time, for Conti had a connection
with the king of which very few people were aware; they both were secretly
working to place Conti on the throne of Poland, in direct opposition to the
official policy of the French government, which was to make Augustus III
of Saxony king of Poland. These dealings with Conti were the beginnings
of a project which became known as the "*secret du roi*," a project which would
complicate French diplomacy in Europe for years to come.

Louis had a taste for intrigue. He adored secrets and codes and
disinformation, and delighted in instructing the few with knowledge of
the "secret" to pursue policies opposed to that of his official ministers
and then witnessing the ensuing confusion; it never seemed to have occurred to him that this was not the most effective way of pursuing foreign policy. He prided himself on the fact that this was one of the few
areas in which he managed to preserve some privacy and freedom of
action. The marquise, at this stage, knew nothing about it, but she no
doubt suspected something. There was a great deal of comment at court
about the king's relationship with Conti. "People are always astonished
by the intervention of the prince de Conti in the affairs of state," noted
d'Argenson, and the duc de Luynes was among those most astonished.
"This prince often carries great portfolios to the King's quarters and
works with His Majesty, but one has difficulty understanding what can
be the nature of their work."

It was complications from this odd state of affairs that brought Conti
so suddenly to court; he urgently needed to countermand instructions
given to the French ambassador to Saxony. Madame de Pompadour
watched these goings-on with frustration; she could not charm or flatter
Conti, and her dislike for him increased. When, at Choisy, Louis XV
granted Conti the rank of supreme general, she wrote at once to Saxe to

reassure him: "Between ourselves, this promotion has satisfied Monsieur the prince de Conti and has repaired his reputation, which he believed was lost. That is what he thinks; as for myself, I believe that it is an embarrassment for the King, and that it will prevent M. the prince de Conti from being employed as much as he believes it will. In any case, this has nothing to do with you, and one will always put you ahead of all this. Adieu, my dear maréchal, I like you as much as I admire you. That is saying a lot."(The marquise was right; later in the year Saxe was made maréchal-général, outranking the mere supreme general.)

In October Saxe was victorious at the battle of Rocoux, near Liège, the largest battle of the century in terms of the number of troops on the field — 120,000 French and 80,000 Anglo-Dutch. It was also one of the few infantry engagements in which the French defeated the British. The young and handsome marquis de Valfons brought the news of Rocoux to Fontainebleau. Madame de Pompadour had met him in Paris when she was still Madame d'Etioles. Now at Versailles she invited him to chat with her, allowing him to sit in an armchair. "She asked me a thousand questions, above all about the maréchal de Saxe, whom she likes as much as she hates M. d'Argenson [the foreign minister] . . . She offered to be of service to me, and asked if they had promoted me. 'No, Madame.' 'Oh! that will happen . . . come tomorrow to my toilette at ten o'clock; my door will not be open to the public until eleven; I still have many questions to ask. My maréchal is then content! How handsome he must be at the head of an army, on the field of battle!'" Flirtatious and coy, the marquise was at the same time very serious about insinuating herself into army affairs on the side of her favorites. Conti had underestimated her influence, to his cost.

When the armies returned, the matter of the dauphin's marriage became the chief topic at court. It seemed as though the young man himself was inclined to his late wife's sister, the Infanta Antonia of Spain, but as Stainville maliciously noted, "The same man [Louis XV] who very illicitly had had all the sisters of one family was not willing to allow his son to have in marriage two Infantas . . . all of a sudden the maréchal de Saxe persuaded Madame de Pompadour that it would be infinitely more suitable that the dauphin should marry a Saxon princess . . ." This princess, Saxe's niece, was the fifteen-year-old Marie-Josèphe, daughter of

King Augustus III. By the end of October Saxe was telling Augustus, his half-brother, that "Madame de Pompadour has been very useful to us . . . ," adding smugly that he was "not unpopular in the cabinets." Saxe also noted that "the Pâris brothers have helped me a great deal in this whole affair; they are friends of the favorite . . . two personages who do not wish to appear at court, because they make the machine move." Duverney, in particular, made it his business to get to know and evaluate the commanders of the French armies. He was very influential in selecting those he liked for high command and dispensing with others. He admired Saxe and supported him on many issues.

Poor Queen Marie Leczinska, whose father was driven out of Poland by Augustus III, was now required to accept his daughter as her daughter-in-law; her opinion, of course, had not been asked. The marriage was announced on November 26 at Fontainebleau, and ten days later the duc de Richelieu left for Dresden with a large entourage to escort the princess back to France. The dauphin was glum about the prospect of another wedding, another bride, Madame de Pompadour was elated at the thought of a marriage in the royal family, a family she now firmly considered her own. The court took note of another example of the importance of having the marquise on one's side.

We are perhaps afforded a glimpse of the marquise at this stage in her life, in a portrait by Boucher, dated 1746, but known as that of Madame Bergeret.* The painting shows a young woman in a pose strikingly similar to that of the otherwise earliest known Boucher portrait of the marquise of 1750; she is standing in a rose garden, a straw hat in her hand, her dress, her hair, and her throat embellished with flowers. On her left wrist is a four-strand pearl bracelet with a cameo, seemingly the same bracelet she wears in many other portraits. One recognizes the direct gaze, the lustrous eyes, the calm assurance. One senses the strength of will beneath the dazzling appearance. If the portrait is indeed that of Madame de Pompadour, it depicts her at the moment in which she is about to embark on a new project, a project brilliantly conceived and executed, designed to enchant the king.

*This painting is now in the National Gallery of Art in Washington, D.C.

Chapter 7

"There was almost no favor done without her participation."

When the minister of foreign affairs, the marquis d'Argenson, was abruptly dismissed on January 10, 1747, many at court thought they detected the influence of the marquise. D'Argenson himself certainly did. But she was not directly involved. D'Argenson had been a disappointment, erratic and muddled in his thinking, not able to extricate France from the war, as the king now desired. The venerable maréchal de Noailles, who carried a great deal of weight with the king, had criticized the minister in a long memorandum which he sent to Louis XV in December 1746. From this point on, d'Argenson and the snubbed prince de Conti would be implacable enemies of the marquise; each clearly felt that she had somehow conspired against them. D'Argenson's journal became dedicated to insulting her and ruining her reputation; Conti, who remained close to the king in their dealings over the *secret du roi*, began a guerilla war against her.

The marquise, however, had powerful friends who were winning the argument with the king. The Pâris brothers were anxious to put an end to the war; they were also in favor of an accommodation with Austria. It was their candidate, the marquis de Puysieulx, who replaced d'Argenson at the office of foreign affairs. It is therefore not surprising that d'Argenson describes him thus: "of commonplace ideas which he made use of beneath an exterior of wisdom and reserve; nourished in the seraglio, he knew its folds and windings perfectly."* And "he confided everything to the

---

*D'Argenson's reference to seraglio was an instance of the fashionable use of Turkish words and phrases, first employed by Montesquieu in "The Persian

Pâris brothers, who had recruited him as the adviser and friend of Madame de Pompadour."

The king remained in love. But the marquise knew that Louis was restless, easily bored, and needed distraction. If she did not provide it, he would find it elsewhere. At the beginning of 1747, in the dark days of winter when the hunt was often impossible, and time slowed, she had an idea for amusing this difficult man. She recalled her successes in her theatre at Etioles, the fun of amateur theatricals, rehearsals, laughter, complicity, and an opportunity to dazzle her lover anew. She had heard of the plays performed at the house of the comtesse de La Marck in Versailles, where such great nobles as the duc d'Ayen and the duc d'Antin had performed. Why could she not have her own company of courtiers to entertain the king?

The great new undertaking got under way in January. The marquise and a few intimate friends would perform some comedies in a little theatre set up in the *petits cabinets,* for the private amusement of the king. Once Louis gave his consent, Jeanne-Antoinette drew up a set of rules for her troupe, some of which read as follows:

> To be admitted into the troupe one must prove that this is not the first time one has acted.
> No player may refuse a part under the pretext that the part is not right or that he or she is too tired.
> Only the actresses shall have the right to choose the plays the troupe shall present.
> The actresses shall also have the right to indicate the day of the performance, to fix the number of performances, to designate the day and time.
> Each actor will be expected to arrive at the exact time designated for performance on pain of a fine which only the actresses can designate.

Letters." D'Argenson meant to depict Versailles as the King's harem, Madame de Pompadour as a concubine, and Puysieulx as a sort of grand vizier.

The actresses are accorded a half-hour grace period, beyond which a fine will be levied, the amount to be decided by the other actresses.

The marquise selected the players from the intimate group surrounding the king, calling upon the duc d'Ayen, the duc de La Vallière, and the marquis de Gontaut; and she invited from Paris the duc de Nivernais and the duchesse de Brancas, who played on a private stage at the hôtel de Brancas in the rue de Tournon and were considered to be as talented as any professional actors. The prince de Dombes, a cousin of the king, was asked to play the bassoon in the orchestra. Perfectionist as she was, Madame de Pompadour invited the leading actors and musicians from the *Comédie-Française* to instruct the actors and to play in the orchestra. One can imagine that no one could refuse such an invitation.

On January 16, 1747, in a space improvised behind the landing of the Ambassadors' Staircase, Madame de Pompadour and her troupe inaugurated the *théâtre des petits cabinets* with a performance of Molière's *Tartuffe*. A week later, La Chaussée's *Le Préjugé à la Mode* and Dufresny's *L'Esprit de Contradiction* were performed; the marquise had the leading role in each production, of course.

At first, the audience was very select; there was room for only fourteen spectators. The king, Tournehem, Abel Poisson, the maréchal de Saxe, Madame d'Estrades, and Madame du Roure, the sister of the marquis de Gontaut, were among the first invited. The little theatre was clearly seen as a family affair, intimate and unofficial. In these private amusements, the marquise had found a brilliant way of keeping the king's attention focused firmly upon her, while also adding a little spice to the relationship. His Majesty was amused. Admission to the theatre being so restricted, courtiers who sought to be on intimate terms with the king and his mistress could only hope for an invitation to a *petit souper*. But these too were hard to obtain.

The importance of gaining entry into Madame de Pompadour's little society, and the difficulties which lay in the way, are vividly described by a visitor to Versailles that winter. Emmanuel, duc de Croÿ, was a young man of noble birth, the owner of great estates in northern France. Every year he came to court for a few weeks, hunting with the king, seeing the ministers, reassuring himself that his credit was intact. On his arrival in 1747, he observed the state of affairs at the court and saw that the king "abandoned himself completely to his love for madame la marquise de Pompadour (formerly Mme d'Etioles), and that she had a great deal of credit and that every one paid court to her, in such a way that I arranged to be presented to her in an attempt to get on good terms with her. . . . I did not know her at all: she seemed to me charming in looks and character. She was at her toilette and one could not be prettier. In addition, she was very amusing and entertaining, and the king seemed to love her more than all the others, and he was right: as a mistress, she was the most pleasant. And so there she was, in a very declared position. . . ."

Croÿ was determined to obtain an invitation to a *petit souper*. "After I had worked at this for some time," he recorded, "Pâris de Montmartel spoke of me today to madame la marquise de Pompadour. He and his brother are the men in whom, rightly, she has the most confidence, and even, I believe, who direct her conduct in general, which could not be better for the place she occupies."

A few days after Montmartel's intervention, Croÿ received the prized privilege of an invitation. He has left a detailed and fascinating description:

One went up to the *petits cabinets* by the staircase behind the salon de la Guerre and gathered before supper in the little gallery. The dining room was charming and the supper most agreeable, without constraint. One was served by two or three servants who retired after having given one what one needed. The King was cheerful, at ease, but always with an air of grandeur which one could not ignore. He seemed very much in love with Mme de Pompadour . . . It seemed to me that this "intimacy of the cabinets" was not so intimate, it only consisted of supper and an hour or two of cards after supper, and that the real intimacy was in the other little cabinets, where very few old and established courtiers may go . . . We were eighteen at table, commencing on my right with M. de Luynes, then Mme de Pompadour, Mme la comtesse d'Estrades, the great friend of Mme de Pompadour, the duc d'Ayen, the tall Mme de Brancas, the comte de Noailles and so on. . . . The maréchal de Saxe was there, but did not sit at table, preferring to stand

and take little bites of everything, being extremely gourmand. The King, who always called him comte de Saxe, seemed to like and esteem him and replied to him with an admirable frankness and clarity. Mme de Pompadour was very much attached to him.

We were two hours at table, eighteen of us, all most relaxed with no excess. At last the King went into the "petit salon"; he heated and made the coffee himself, for there were no servants, one served oneself. He played cards for small stakes; the King likes cards, but Mme de Pompadour hates them and seemed to be trying to make him stop playing. The rest of the company made up two parties, also for small stakes. The King ordered everyone to sit, even those who were not playing; I remained leaning on the fire screen to watch him play, and Mme de Pompadour pressing him to retire and falling asleep; he got up at one o'clock and said to her quietly and cheerfully; "*Allons!* Let us go to bed." . . . We all went down Mme de Pompadour's little staircase, returning by the state rooms for the King's public Going to Bed, which took place at once.

There was no doubt that, after eighteen months at court, the influence of Madame de Pompadour was already dominant. At the wedding of the dauphin and Marie-Josèphe of Saxony, which took place at Versailles on February 9, the ceremonies and celebrations were similar to those of the dauphin's first marriage, two years earlier. But this time it was Madame de Pompadour who was in charge. When the duc de Gesvres, the First Gentleman of the Bedchamber, gave the king the list of names of those to be invited to the wedding ball, he was told, "You have rather forgotten the ladies of Paris; give me your list: madame de Pompadour knows them and she will make the arrangements." It was the marquise who made decisions on everything, from décor to guest lists. And although Croÿ said she managed everything with gaiety, a light touch, and infinite charm, there were many, not least among the ladies of Paris, who were most unhappy about her highly visible role. Grumble about the court as they might, most Parisians could not resist an invitation to go there.

The dauphin was a reluctant bridegroom. Still grieving for his late wife, he was in no mood for parties, and in addition, he found the marquise officious and presumptuous: "M. le Dauphin increases in boorishness, apathy, and hatred for the mistress," noted d'Argenson. "As soon as he sees her, his mood darkens." And the queen was still distressed at the thought of the daughter of the Saxon king as her daughter-in-law. But Jeanne-Antoinette was insouciant; when it came to inviting only the wives of the great officers of state to the festivities, she insisted on the inclusion of her sister-in-law, the comtesse de Baschi, who had just been presented. "I can be counted as one of the great officers," she proclaimed, "and so my sister-in-law can be put on the list."*

At the ball following the wedding, Croÿ saw the king, "masked, at the feet of Madame de Pompadour, who was charming. I only recognized the King due to the anxiety that escaped her when she saw him pass by the benches where Madame de Forcalquier sat; I compared her to Madame de Pompadour and found her prettier but less graceful. As for a mistress, the King could not have chosen better; and he seems to be madly in love."

The new dauphine did not have an easy introduction to the French court. Although there were the usual tactful remarks about her appearance and charm, there were also comments on her large nose and clumsy German ways. In addition, she found her husband cold and distant. But Marie-Josèphe was not unintelligent and she persevered in winning over her new family. She had received explicit instructions as to the course of conduct she should adopt with regard to the favorite. The Saxon envoy at Versailles, Loss, had reported back to Dresden that "Madame de Pompadour is playing a great part at the court. The friendship with which the King honors her, the interest she has shown in the Dauphin's alliance with the house of Saxony, the suggestions she has made to the King in order to fix his choice, all this will oblige the Dauphine to pay attention to her and get on well with her. The marquise has an excellent character; she exerts herself to be agreeable to the Dauphine, who will pay her court to the King by showing friendship to the lady whom the Queen

---

*Charlotte Lenormand, comtesse de Baschi, the sister of Monsieur d'Etioles, saw no difficulty in coming to court and benefiting from Jeanne-Antoinette's position. Her husband, despite being extremely incompetent, would be given important diplomatic postings; and she herself would act as Tournehem's official hostess.

herself overwhelms with politeness." Marie-Josèphe, unlike Marie-Antoinette twenty years later, and despite a grumpy husband, listened to these wise words of advice.

The marquise was gathering a staff. At the beginning of 1747 Nicole Collesson, widow of Monsieur du Hausset, an acquaintance from the Invalides, joined her as *femme de chambre*. She moved into rooms at Versailles in the attics under the dome of the salon de la Guerre, just above her mistress, and remained with her until the end.*

In addition to a staff of personal maids and valets de chambre, Madame de Pompadour had her own librarian, the abbé Bridard de La Garde, author and theatre critic; it was his job to catalogue and care for the hundreds of books she would acquire over the years, all bound in the finest Morocco leather, in red, blue, or yellow, and stamped with her coat of arms in gold. The marquise could recruit the nobility to serve her needs. To the scandal of the court, the chevalier d'Hénin, member of a noble family from Alsace, became her equerry, following her sedan chair and carrying her cloak. Her entourage was dressed in yellow livery. Her carriages were stabled in the rue d'Orangerie, near the château. Hers was becoming a royal household in miniature.

Even in her grandeur, the marquise did not neglect her family. François Poisson was ennobled and rose in rank for "important services rendered to the State with as much disinterest as zeal." He became seigneur de Vandières (Vandières was a small property he owned near Château-Thierry) and adopted a coat of arms with two golden fish in the shape of back-to-back mullets. Poisson's way of life did not change; he continued to live companionably in Paris with Tournehem (at the hôtel de Conti,

---

*Madame du Hausset's memoirs were published in 1809. The circumstances of their publication have led to doubts about their authenticity. After the death of the marquise, so the story goes, Sénac de Meilhan, one of Louis XV's doctors, found her brother attempting to burn a manuscript and persuaded him to hand it over to him. Sénac later sold it to a man called Quintin Crawfurd, a Scottish émigré, who had it published. The general view is that Sénac embellished the genuine memoirs of Madame du Hausset. Juicy as they are, they should be treated with a prudent reserve.

rented to them by the duc de La Vallière), and it was his son Abel who became Monsieur de Vandières, or "Monsieur d'avant-hier" ("Monsieur of the day before yesterday," as the courtiers had it).

At the end of March 1747, the first season of the theatre of the *petits cabinets* came to a close. The queen came to the last performance, and everyone agreed that another season should commence next winter. Madame de Pompadour, although gratified at the success of her project, was exhausted. She was suffering from severe migraines (a malady which would afflict her throughout her life), possibly suffering from the after-effects of another miscarriage.

She also had to endure the king's absence once more; another summer of military campaigning loomed. The marquise felt, as did most of the ministers, that the war had gone on long enough. Louis XV himself had come to dislike the whole business. The original goals of the war had always been uncertain: now they were unrealizable. Francis of Lorraine was emperor, the Pretender was back in France, and Frederick of Prussia had taken his spoils and retired from the fray. Nonetheless, the French decided that they must make one last aggressive push north to teach the Dutch a lesson, and leave themselves with a decent negotiating position. The Pâris brothers had already made clear their view that the war should be ended on honorable terms. Madame de Pompadour, their loyal ally, saw Louis depart in May and was determined that this would be the last time.

On July 2 Louis XV was present at the battle of Lawfeldt, near Maastricht, as was the Duke of Cumberland, on the opposite side, in command of the Anglo-Dutch army. Even more so than most of these ghastly, blood-soaked, pointless affairs, it was virtual carnage. "Four desperate hours of killing," reported an observer. Louis no doubt recoiled from the horror, no doubt redoubled his determination to try for an honorable peace. He had never liked war; now he hated it.

The marquise never stayed at court when the king was away. She retreated to Crécy or Choisy, where she could see her family, in particular François Poisson and her daughter Alexandrine. It was an opportunity for her to catch her breath. She amused herself by engraving precious stones, instructed by the artist Jacques Guay; after Lawfeldt, she engraved a sardonyx with an image of Victory, personified by herself, standing on ground strewn with cannons and flags, and had it made into a bracelet. She carried on an extensive correspondence, writing not only to the king and her friends at the front, but also to old friends like the comtesse de Lutzelbourg, who lived in Alsace. The letters exchanged between the two women had an intimate, domestic tone. The marquise, busy with the decoration of Crécy, directed Madame de Lutzelbourg to help her: "I do not require printed cotton," she wrote, "but if you can find grosgrain of a suitable color to make linings for the furniture, be it yellow and white, crimson, green or blue, that would have more resistance than taffeta. If you can still find cotton damask, I would not be displeased to have two or three yards of it for the beds in the dressing room . . ."*

She also kept up a correspondence with the comte de Clermont, the king's uncle, who was away at the front. "I am bored to tears here," she wrote in August. "I tell you kindly that you are naughty when you tell me that the king looks handsome and well, I am delighted, but it is not charitable to tell such things to a miserable woman exiled ten leagues away . . ."

According to Count von Kaunitz, who would become the Austrian ambassador to France a few years later, "She received her courier from the army every day when she lived at Choisy in the absence of the king. Nothing was concluded without her. Her decision upon everything was awaited. She spent whole nights in replying. Her conduct was in charge of the marquis de Gontaut, who was derisively called her chief eunuch. She saw hardly anyone. This life very quickly bored her. A royal lover causes double anxiety; another could steal his heart. These considerations contributed not a little to the promotion of peace. Besides, she was piqued at not having followed the King to the war, whereas Madame de Châteauroux had done so." Kaunitz was not in France in 1747, and his comments must be treated with a certain reserve; yet he was a highly perceptive man and had very good sources. One may doubt that "her decision upon everything was awaited," but not her anxiety over the

---

*Madame de Lutzelbourg was born Marie-Ursule Klinglin. She was the daughter of a Strasbourg magistrate, considerably older than Madame de Pompadour, a widow, and a friend of Voltaire. How the two women met is unknown. To Madame de Pompadour, Madame de Lutzelbourg was *grand'femme.*

king's prolonged absence and her desire to bring him home for good, thus accomplishing not only her own objective, but that of the Pâris brothers as well.

As the armies began to disperse for the winter, efforts to find a way toward peace intensified. On September 11 the Earl of Sandwich and the marquis de Puysieulx met in a convent at Liège to discuss the issues. A congress to meet at Aix-la-Chapelle was proposed. But on the night of September 15 the French general Lowendahl launched an attack on the Dutch port of Bergen-op-Zoom, an attack which became "a charnel house of pillage." Lowendahl was made a maréchal de France. The French had proven that they were still capable of delivering mighty blows on Dutch territory, but peace seemed even further away.

Toward the end of September the armies were ready to return. "On Monday," the marquise told the comte de Clermont, "I shall be in a position to tell Your Highness how handsome I find the King, for His Majesty has wished that I go to Compiègne to join him again. The place is so beautiful, they say, and the ladies so curious, that I have determined to go there without difficulty."

Louis XV loved hunting in the vast forest of Compiègne, and the glorified hunting lodge in which he stayed. But the marquise, on arrival, thought the château old-fashioned and uncomfortable. Why should the king not build a suitably grand house here, and thus indulge his twin passions for building and for hunting? All that was required for this and her other ambitious projects to materialize was a lasting peace.

The Pâris brothers encouraged the thought. They, better than anyone, knew how debilitating the war was becoming for French finances. And what they thought mattered. "It is the Pâris brothers who govern everything, principally Duverney," noted d'Argenson. "M. de Puysieulx is only his assistant and go-between. The whole policy, like the military strategy, is the work of Duverney. The ascendance of the Pâris brothers on the determinations of the King is very great. . . . Duverney is very careful not to appear in public. He puts before him [the King] his brother Montmartel, such a good fellow to all appearances. . . . And now he has a mistress in his hand, and everything a favorite brings along with her."

At Compiègne, the marquise turned to another initiative. Eager to attach herself to the royal family and win their approval, she had had the painter Nattier sent in secret to Fontevrault to paint the king and queen's three youngest daughters, Victoire, Sophie, and Louise. In October the portraits were shown to the queen. Marie was much moved at the sight of these forgotten daughters, now in their teens, practically grown-up, not seen since they were little children. Plans began to bring the eldest princess back to court. Madame de Pompadour—that promoter of family values—was enthusiastic. By now she felt herself an integral part of the royal family; she wanted Louis XV to experience some of the joys of family life that he had never known, and she wanted to be recognized as the beneficent force which brought this about.

When the duc de Croÿ returned to court in December, he reported that Madame de Pompadour's toilette was now "a kind of ceremony." Croÿ attended, standing respectfully with the others as the marquise applied her rouge and powder, condescending to single someone out with a word or gesture. The perfume of adulation could be overwhelming; Croÿ watched the duc de Bouillon arrive to thank the marquise for helping obtain a favor for his son, groveling before her "in the most base manner," and could not help finding himself embarrassed by the fact that he himself was also in attendance on the marquise in order to win preferment. "This was the subject of fine reflections which did not escape me, since I was rather in the same case and very occupied on my own account."

Croÿ thought that the marquise "mingled in many things, without seeming to do so or appearing occupied: on the contrary, whether naturally or politically, she seemed more occupied with her little comedies or other trifles than the rest. She was very teasing with the King and employed the most delicate flirtatiousness to seduce him. From the beginning, she sought to please everyone, in order to provide herself with creatures, above all people of importance; then, established and knowing her world, she was a little more decided and less forthcoming, but always very polite and seeking to please, or at least to seem to do so." He also made the point that "there was almost no favor done without her participation, which brought the whole court to her as if she were Prime Minister: but, in great matters, it is unclear if the King trusted her with everything, as he was born reserved."

As the king was the fount of all honors, courtiers had no other recourse than to solicit his favor. Louis XIV had used this fact to his advantage, granting and withholding favors in order to keep his nobility obedient; but Louis XV had neither the interest nor the talent to do as his great-grandfather had done. He gladly allowed Madame de Pompadour to assume the role of listening to endless requests and entreaties, reserving for himself the ultimate decision. But, while thus unburdening himself of responsibilities he considered tiresome, Louis XV allowed the perception to arise that it was indeed the marquise who controled everything, a perception which would be very damaging for his prestige, and that of the monarchy.

One of those who benefited from Madame de Pompadour's attention was Voltaire, who came to Fontainebleau that fall in his new position as Gentleman of the Chamber, an honor he found hard to take as seriously as he should have: "Here I am at Fontainebleau," he wrote, "and every night I make the firm resolution to go to the King's Rising, but every morning I remain in my dressing gown working on *Semiramis* . . ."

Voltaire, as usual, was ill at ease in these rarified surroundings. He watched with alarm as his mistress, Madame du Châtelet, lost large sums playing cards at the queen's table; as her losses increased, Voltaire murmured to her in English: "You do not see that you are playing with crooks?" But he was overheard. To speak thus of the men and women at the queen's table! The couple fled the court in some disarray. Voltaire's only reference to the fiasco is a cryptic note to his niece, this time in Italian: "*Cara, siamo stati rapiti in differenti vortici, non ho potuto veder vi a Versailles.*" ("Darling, we have been caught up in different vortices, I could not see you at Versailles.") It was evident that Voltaire's days as a courtier were numbered. Madame de Pompadour did not look kindly on such embarrassing episodes.

Chapter 8

"Pompadour, you embellish the court . . ."

Throughout January, February, and March 1748 the performances in the *théâtre des petits cabinets* continued. More rows of seats, boxes, and a balcony were added to accommodate the growing audience. On the first night there was a performance of Dufresny's *Le Mariage Fait et Rompu*, followed by *Ismène*, a ballet with music by Rebel. Madame de Pompadour danced Ismène, wearing a blue taffeta dress, the sleeves of gold brocaded gauze, knots of blue ribbon embroidered in gold around her neck and wrists, and a straw hat lined with white taffeta and crowned with flowers. Luynes had to concede that "it is not possible to be more graceful or talented than she."

The marquise excelled on stage, dazzling her audience with her acting, singing, and dancing, not to mention her spectacularly glamorous costumes. For her dancing role in *Almasis*, she wore "a low-cut bodice of rose taffeta decorated with a pattern of silver, the skirt in the same, open onto a underskirt of white taffeta embroidered in rose and silver; her cloak was of white taffeta trimmed with silver, embroidered in flowers of pastel colors." On February 27 she appeared for the first time *en travesti* as Colin in Destouches's *Ragonde*. (Luynes noted that her costume was indeed that of a man, but "as ladies are when they ride on horseback: it was very decent.") After the performance, the king kissed the marquise in public, calling her the most delicious woman in France. D'Argenson was sour. "The court is occupied solely with pleasures. The King appears in public with reluctance, but on the other hand cherishes his private pleasures. They think only of the comedies of the *cabinets*, where the marquise de Pompadour deploys her talents and her graces for the theatre."

Voltaire was ironic. Still in some disgrace after his remark about "*fripons*" at the queen's gaming table, he was nevertheless invited to the marquise's theatre. Unfortunately Voltaire, being Voltaire, could not leave well alone. He tried some poetic flattery:

> Pompadour you embellish
> The court . . .
> Now that Louis has returned
> May you both enjoy peace
> And both keep your conquests.

The royal family took offense. Yet again Voltaire had overstepped the mark. "These verses, presented to the King, seemed at first charming. Madame de Pompadour was the ornament of the court. But on reflection they seemed very presumptuous and inappropriate."

Then Voltaire tried teasing; he attempted a verse making gentle fun of the marquise and her penchant for bourgeois expressions:

> Between ourselves, it seems to me that "little fatty"
> Is really rather a common word, beautiful Pompadouretty.

But now Madame de Pompadour was offended. Voltaire, despairing of ever learning how to be a good courtier, left Versailles with Madame du Châtelet for Lunéville, and the more welcoming court of Stanislas Leczinski, the queen's father, installed as Duke of Lorraine. Rather sadly, he told the distinguished Benedictine abbot Dom Calmet that he would like to come and stay in his monastery, needing only "a warm cell, a little mutton and some eggs. I would prefer this sane and sensible frugality to any royal meals."

Madame de Pompadour saw Voltaire go with some relief. Life at court was difficult enough without his indiscretions. She was unwell that spring, exhausted by her theatrical activities. When the marquis de Coigny, one of her leading men and an intimate of the king, was killed in a duel with the prince de Dombes—a member of the orchestra and cousin of the King—she abruptly canceled the scheduled performance of Voltaire's *L'Enfant Prodigue* to comfort Louis XV, who was distraught at Coigny's death. The marquise, accustomed to her lover's morbid sensibility, did not fail to console him. And a week later the performances started again at the little theatre, the marquise shining in the title role of Almasis with the prince des Dombes playing his bassoon as though nothing had happened.

It had been a shock though; a few days later the marquise was too unwell to appear in *Le Méchant,* and then she was struck with a violent migraine and could not sing Erigone. A week after that she had a bad cold which prevented her from singing. It took her almost a month to recover her health. Even though she had completely conquered the reticent duc de Luynes ("one can add nothing to the perfection of acting, taste and voice of Madame de Pompadour"), she was not sorry to see the season end.

For once, d'Argenson was right when he remarked that "she cannot stand up to the life she is leading, with its late nights, occupations, spectacles, continual expenses to amuse the King; whereas she herself, moreover, is, without cease, occupied with activities, and in the middle of a continual whirlwind of people."

The marquise admitted none of this to her friend Madame de Lutzelbourg. "The misfortune of poor Coigny has left us in despair. The King has been so affected as to frighten me, he has given evidence of his good heart, but I feared the consequences for his health. Happily reason has taken charge . . ." She then characteristically moved on to happier topics. "I have abandoned Trétou [a house near Saint-Cloud which she had had for only a few months] and have bought in its place La Celle . . ." (The château of La Celle was not far from Versailles. It had belonged to Bachelier, one of the king's valets de chambre, who sold it for quarter of a million livres. Her plan was to come here for short stays in the summer. La Celle, or *"petit château,"* as she called it, was not as grand as Crécy, but, even so, from 1749 to 1751 she had work done at a cost of almost 70,000 livres and there were seventeen suites for guests.)

The gloom over the death of Coigny was increased when the little daughter of the dauphin and his first wife died "from her tooth." But this loss was quickly forgotten with the arrival at court of fourteen-year-old Madame Victoire, tenderly welcomed by her parents, who had not seen her for more than ten years. The king rode out to Sceaux to meet his daughter and their interview was *"vive et tendre."* When Madame Victoire came to Versailles, Luynes noted that she had "a fine brown complexion, eyes quite large and very handsome, a resemblance to the late Regent . . . a little plump. They say that her character is charming."

But not everyone was pleased. D'Argenson found another way to criticize the marquise, deploring the expenses Madame Victoire's return would entail. And when it became known that the king had not only bought for Madame de Pompadour the sumptuous Hotel d'Evreux in Paris (the present day palais de l'Elysée), but had also acquired land near Sèvres for a new country house for her, d'Argenson and many others were outraged. Even though the bills would be paid partly from government funds, partly from private stratagems, all mingled together in a creative and undetectable way by Tournehem and Pâris de Montmartel, it seemed to many that the marquise was conducting herself in an unnecessarily ostentatious manner.

Madame de Pompadour herself believed that it was her mission to keep Louis XV diverted, cheered, and amused, and that the best way to do so was to interest him in building projects of all kinds. She scoffed at the notion that the costs of these projects were a burden on the state. She was entirely concentrated on the king's pleasure, enduring his frequent ill humor, exerting herself to provide him with congenial company, never for a moment allowing her own exhaustion or indisposition to manifest itself, always seemingly delighted to put aside her own concerns the instant he appeared. D'Argenson, of course, saw a darker side. "She besieges the king constantly, shakes him, agitates him, never leaves him by himself for an instant. Before, he used to work for several hours in his office; today he has not a quarter of an hour to himself."

The marquise truly believed that Louis was happier when he was distracted from the cares of office. But, in fact, the more the king sought diversion, the more melancholy and bored he became. Their way of life became exhausting, not to mention ruinously expensive, but neither one was able to stop the constant movement from one place to another, even though neither one enjoyed it. It became, in the end, a hellish way to live.

This self-imposed but unrelenting regime led to a gradual breakdown of her health. She began to suffer from migraines, palpitations, infections of the eye and ear. She required a doctor in constant attendance and, from the end of 1748, she relied on François Quesnay to take care of her ailments, physical and psychological.

Quesnay was in his fifties and highly intelligent, his cheerful disposition a great help to his patient. The marquise lodged him near her at all the royal châteaux. She also encouraged him to publish his progressive views on economics, and to maintain his contacts with the Parisian intelligentsia. From now on Quesnay, ensconced in luxury, was able to entertain his friends of liberal thinking, among them Duclos, Diderot, Buffon, and Helvétius, and to work on his books.

Madame de Pompadour also invited into her household that year, as her personal lawyer and business manager, Charles Collin, who had worked for her mother in Paris. Collin, like Quesnay, was cheerful and amusing; the marquise trusted him completely. She told him bluntly that he was taking a risk in giving up his practice in Paris, that she could not guarantee her favor would last; Collin accepted her proposal and remained in her service until her death.

Much of Europe was looking forward to peace. Finally the draft of the peace treaty, which would end the war, was unveiled at Aix-la-Chapelle on September 23, 1748 and signed by the French, British, and Dutch on October 17; the Austrians signed a week later. The French public, unaware of the terms of the treaty, was overjoyed: Those terms, when published, would come as a shock. A precursor of the shocks to come was the arrest of the Young Pretender as he left the Opera in Paris on the night of December 10. Charles Edward had returned to his accustomed life in Paris after his defeat at Culloden; but under the terms of the treaty, the French government had agreed to expel him from their country, in deference to British demands, and had discreetly asked him to leave for Fribourg in Switzerland, where he was promised an honorable retirement. Stuart refused to go, preferring the acclamation which greeted him at every turn in Paris. Finally the French government felt it impossible to tolerate this state of affairs any longer and moved to arrest him. After five days of comfortable imprisonment in the fortress of Vincennes, he allowed himself to be escorted to Switzerland.

The arrest of Charles Edward was seen by the Parisians and the French in general as nothing less than the kidnapping of a prince whose family had been supported and lodged by the French king for decades. It was thought to be a shameful betrayal of France's support for the legitimate king of England, an act of obeisance to the British. The public began to murmur negatively about the peace. They began to wonder what they had been fighting for.

A happier consequence of the peace was the arrival at Versailles of Louis XV's eldest daughter, Louise-Elisabeth; she had been living unhappily at the court of Madrid, yearning to return home. Now she and her husband, Don Felipe, had been created Duke and Duchess of Parma, and she had immediately taken the opportunity to make her way to France, "on her way" to Italy. She had not seen her father, mother, or sisters for almost ten years, and their reunion was emotional. Madame Infante, as she was called, was so delighted to be back at Versailles, and so reluctant to join her husband again, that she announced her intention of staying for a year while her new residence in Parma was prepared. Madame de Pompadour smiled benignly. But she mistrusted the twenty-two-year-old princess—a fat, rather coarse young woman who liked to dabble in politics. She would be a threat, a rival for the king's time and attention. Madame de Pompadour resolved to give her as little opportunity as possible.

The seemingly happy arrangement between his family and his mistress led Louis XV to believe that he might look forward to placid times. The end of the war, he hoped, guaranteed a period of peace and prosperity for the nation. At the beginning of 1749 this normally pessimistic man could be forgiven for indulging in a little optimism.

Chapter 9

*"The life I lead is terrible; I have scarcely
a minute to myself."*

On January 14, 1749, the terms of the Treaty of Aix-la-Chapelle were published; they were proclaimed in the streets of Paris in February. All French conquests in the Austrian Netherlands were returned to Austria; Bergen-op-Zoom, gained at such a cost, was returned to the Dutch; nothing was gained for France—for all that bloodshed—except that Don Felipe of Spain, Louis XV's son-in-law, received the territories of Parma, Piacenza, and Guastalla in Italy. Louis XV was well aware that the peace treaty gave France little reason to cheer; he wrote to his cousin, King Ferdinand of Spain: "The restitutions I am making and the little advantage I am gaining from this peace will make it sufficiently known to Your Majesty that it was pity for my peoples and religion, which have had more influence on me on this occasion than the spirit of aggrandizement." The real victor was King Frederick of Prussia, who kept Silesia.

Louis XV hoped he could avoid further wars. If it had been up to him, France would have entered a lasting peace. Unfortunately the Prussians, Austrians, and British were not so pacifically minded. For the next several years these nations would joust diplomatically, each eyeing the others' particular prizes. The Prussians wanted protection from Austria, the Austrians wanted revenge on Prussia, the British wanted the French colonies in America. It was naive of the French king to hope to stay out of such quarrels. But in 1749 he was determined to enjoy all the advantages of peace for as long as he could.

A torrent of insulting verses flowed through Paris. A young man called Jean-Baptiste Desforges, a lawyer's clerk, was arrested for writing and distributing verses in which allusion is made to the arrest of the Pretender:

People once so proud, now so servile,
You are no longer a refuge for unhappy princes.
The enemies you defeated on the field of Fontenoy
Have on their own conquerors imposed the law . . .

Desforges was sent to the Bastille for nine months, then imprisoned in an iron cage at the abbey of Mont-Saint-Michel for three years. After that ordeal, he was released into the abbey itself. "I believe it most essential to punish, and most severely, the authors of such verses," Madame de Pompadour would write to the comte d'Argenson. "It is necessary to make examples of these infamous people." She never hesitated from demanding punishment for those who wrote and disseminated unflattering opinions. We never detect any softening in her resolve nor any understanding of the cruelty involved.

The terms of peace were decidedly unpopular. When they were officially proclaimed in Paris in awful weather on February 12, the response to "*Vive le roi*" was thin. Matters were made worse the next day when the king was unexpectedly absent from the Te Deum at Notre-Dame. That night Madame de Pompadour played Europa at Versailles in *Jupiter et Europe.* The king clearly preferred these diversions to a journey to cold and unwelcoming Paris. A few days later "there was carnage on the quai Pelletier where there were fireworks for the peace," according to Barbier. "There are two hundred people dead or wounded; there is no joy among the people. . . . They attribute every evil, every fatality, to the faults of the government."

"They say that, in the markets, the fishwives, when they argue, say, 'You are as stupid as the peace,'" Barbier went on to recall. "The people are partly right. The adventure of Prince Edward has caused displeasure: besides, everyone knows that we have neither won nor kept any town."

Madame de Pompadour was not insensitive to the complaints she heard from Paris, much as she pretended to be. But she had more immediate concerns at Versailles. Madame Infante had settled into rooms at Versailles on the ground floor overlooking the parterre du Nord, one floor down from her father. Madame de Pompadour was one floor above. There was rather a struggle over the king. The marquise, according to the duc de Luynes, was particularly alarmed when the king took to going downstairs for long conversations with his eldest daughter, and quickly came to the conclusion that it would be much easier if she too had rooms on the ground floor, giving Louis XV no opportunity to hesitate on the landing. The marquise began to make her plans.

Another inimical presence to Madame de Pompadour was that of the duc de Richelieu, back to perform his year of duties as First Gentleman of the Chamber, and ready for a fight with the marquise over her theatre. Richelieu, very proud of his lineage, regarded the marquise as a presumptuous upstart whose bourgeoise ways were bringing the court into disrepute. He made it clear that he meant to take an active part in running the theatre of the *cabinets*, the entertainments in the king's rooms being traditionally in the purview of the First Gentleman. The marquise was having none of it. "You say that we will have some quarrels about our theatre," she had written to him before his arrival. "I do not believe a word of it, and do not doubt that you will listen to reason. However it turns out, awaiting a discussion or not, I compliment you with all my heart." A delicate warning had been delivered.

D'Argenson was pinning his hopes on the newcomer: "The maréchal de Richelieu on arrival at the Court has taken the grandest tone, which promises more in the future. He makes himself feared by the Court and loved by the master. For myself, I think that, since he has so much power, it would be desirable if he were to become Prime Minister, as his uncle was. He would put things back in order."

Richelieu immediately quarreled with Madame de Pompadour's stage manager, the duc de La Vallière, and made himself a great nuisance, counting on the king, who hated to change the rules in such matters, to support him. The king did not; one day he casually asked Richelieu how many times he had been to the Bastille. "Three times, Sire." Nothing more was said. In a rage, Richelieu jumped up and down above the marquise's room at La Muette. "The maréchal de Richelieu has conducted himself like a schoolboy since his return to Court," reported d'Argenson despondently. "And so all doors are closed against him. This is not the way for him to succeed."

The marquise herself was showing signs of strain. She was probably pregnant again and feeling unwell. "I hope and flatter myself, *grand' femme*," she wrote to Madame de Lutzelbourg, "that my silence has made no impression on you; in any case, you would be very wrong if it had. The life I lead is terrible; I have scarcely a minute to myself. Rehearsals and performances, travel twice a week, to Petit-Château [La Celle], La Muette, etc. Duties considerable and indispensable. Queen, Dauphin, Dauphine, happily keeping to her chaise longue, three daughters, two Infantas [Madame Infante had brought her little daughter, the Infanta Isabella, to Versailles]; judge, if it is possible, to breathe; pity me and do not accuse me."

Despite Richelieu's attempts to disrupt things, the marquise was as dazzling in her theatre, as usual, playing the part of the nymph Pomona in two performances of La Terre, from the ballet *Les Eléments* with music by Lalande. Wearing a white taffeta dress embroidered with flowers and fruits and a cloak of white and silver taffeta lined in cherry-red satin, Pompadour/Pomona was a vision of ardent love. The marquise was so pleased with her performance that she commissioned her favourite painter, François Boucher, to paint *Vertumus and Pomona* for the château of La Muette.

But outside court circles, such performances seemed to many an unseemly celebration of adultery. (And one wonders what the queen, graciously invited to be present at the marquise's triumphs, really thought.) When Madame de Pompadour sang the great aria from Lully's *Armide:* "*Enfin, il est en ma puissance . . .*" ("At last, he is in my power"), she gave ammunition to those who accused her of ruling the king, body and soul. The damaging image of the king as a weakling, dominated by a woman, began to take hold; the more conspicuous her role, the more dazzling her theatrical triumphs, the more compelling that impression became.

Madame de Pompadour and the king retreated as often as possible to the little pavilion in the park of Versailles she called her Hermitage. She told Madame de Lutzelbourg that she spent half her life there. "It is sixteen yards by ten, so you can judge how grand it must be; but I can be alone there, or with the king and a few others, so I am happy. They will have told you that it is a palace, like Bellevue,* which has nine bays on the front by seven; but it is the fashion nowadays in Paris to talk nonsense, and about everything. Bonjour, *ma très grand' femme*, I shall pre-

---

*The château being built for the marquise near Sèvres.

pare a room for you at Bellevue, and I wish that you would promise me that you would come."

The Hermitage at Versailles was the first of several exquisite little pavilions which Madame de Pompadour was having built near all the royal châteaux. Here she could take the king's desire for intimacy to a new level. Here she, and only she, could divert, entertain, and comfort him. Together they formed a new interest in gardening and animal husbandry. The dovecotes and chicken coops of the Versailles roof were transplanted to the Hermitage; cows were added, and, in the summer, the house was bowered in a profusion of scented flowers and shrubs — lilacs, oleanders, myrtle, olives, and roses.

Luynes testified to the very exclusive nature of the place: "The King supped yesterday at the pretty new garden of the marquise's, near the gate to Trianon. He was there *en tête-à-tête* with MM. de Tournehem and de Vandières. He enjoyed himself a great deal." But Luynes added that "one talks only of the melancholy into which he falls at every moment."

The king was preoccupied with the agonizing question of the dismissal of another minister. Madame de Pompadour had mentioned to him her irritation with the comte de Maurepas, the minister of the navy, and clearly expected Louis to do something about him. Maurepas had held the post for many years and had an extensive network of powerful relations at court. But he was a malicious, rather dangerous little man; Madame de Châteauroux had hated him, and his presence in her house shortly before her agonizing death had caused many to suspect him of poisoning her. Now it was Madame de Pompadour's turn to complain about him.

The marquise had already exchanged words with the minister about the insulting songs and pamphlets which rained down upon her. She had tried to ignore them, but the abuse was becoming more frequent and more vile. When scurrilous pamphlets began to appear at Versailles, Madame de Pompadour decided to take action. In April she went with Madame d'Estrades to pay a visit on Maurepas, announcing that "they will not say that I summon ministers, but that I go to them." "When will you find out who is writing these songs?" she demanded. "When I do so, madame," replied Maurepas, "I shall tell the king." The marquise recognized the snub: "Monsieur, you show very little respect for the king's mistresses." Maurepas smiled. "On the contrary, madame, I have always respected them, whatever kind of people they may be." With that they went their separate ways. It seemed that Maurepas was almost daring the king to make a choice between himself and the favorite. His insouciance was astounding.

That night at supper, in front of thirty people, Maurepas was asked about the marquise's visit. "It will bring her bad luck," he remarked. "I recall Madame de Mailly coming to see me two days before she was sent away by Madame de Châteauroux. I bring them all bad luck."

Events came to a conclusion when the marquise was made aware of a verse widely distributed at Versailles, in which an allusion to a certain gynecological complaint was thinly veiled:

> By your manners noble and frank,
> Iris, you enchant our hearts;
> On our path you spread flowers,
> But they are only flowers of white.

The poem appeared at the time when the court believed that the marquise had just suffered a miscarriage (at least her third, noted the very discreet Luynes). There were immediate suspicions that Maurepas himself was the author; he had been present at a supper during which the marquise had carried a bouquet of white hyacinth. Jeanne-Antoinette, already in a rather fragile state, was further alarmed when ill-intentioned courtiers spread the word that Maurepas was trying to poison her, as, they said, he had poisoned Madame de Châteauroux. There was talk of a plot to bring back Madame de Mailly, a plot orchestrated by Maurepas.

Whether Madame de Pompadour was really in fear for her life, or simply out of patience, she decided to act. She repeated her grievances against Maurepas, and she begged Louis XV to act. The king consented. Maurepas received the following letter from La Celle: "I told you, Monsieur, that I would let you know when your services were no longer necessary to me. I keep my word. Make arrangements to go to Bourges as soon as you can. While you wait, see few people, even those of your own family. I would have allowed you to go to your house at Pontchartrain, if it were not too near Versailles and Paris. No reply is necessary. Louis."

Perhaps Maurepas was not completely surprised. He had bet against the marquise and lost. But his friends and contemporaries were stunned.

"What sadness, for these people, accustomed to the fracas of the court, to the pleasures of Paris," lamented Barbier, "to find themselves transplanted to Bourges, where . . . one must content oneself with such new acquaintance as one can find, in order not to bore oneself to death."* The dismissal of Maurepas, coming shortly after the unpopular peace and the expulsion of the Pretender, was perceived in Paris as the action of a king in thrall to a devious, upstart mistress. Mud continued to be thrown.

> The great lords abase themselves,
> The financiers enrich themselves,
> All the Poissons are aggrandized,
> It is the reign of scoundrels . . .

The King handed responsibility for Paris to the comte d'Argenson, already minister of war, and for the navy to Antoine Rouillé, a man of outstanding mediocrity. After this burst of energy, Louis sank once more into melancholy, retreating for hours every day into his usual distraction of the hunt.

But Louis XV could not escape his responsibilities altogether. And it would not be accurate to say that he paid no attention to affairs of state. He was a studious reader of official documents, annotating and replying in ways which showed his understanding of issues. But he lacked the confidence and will to impose his view. The most he allowed himself was tacit support of a minister who had a decisive course of action. After the dismissal of Maurepas, Louis threw his weight behind his controller of finances, Machault, in a crucial initiative to modernize the French taxation system.

In the France of the Ancien Régime, there was only one direct tax — the *taille*, which was not paid by nobles nor by the clergy. Every year the King's Council fixed the amount of the *taille* and divided it up among

---

*Maurepas and his wife were allowed to return to their much more luxurious château of Pontchartrain, after an exile of three years, but were forbidden to appear at Versailles, or even to go to Paris, except when the court was away at Compiègne or Fontainebleau. In the oddest twist to the tale, Maurepas was called out of retirement twenty-five years later to serve, disastrously, as a minister for Louis XVI.

the various provinces, taking for a base the amounts of the previous year and the advice of local administrators, the *Intendants*. Although somewhat crude, this system worked; the *Intendants* were experienced men and their evaluations were usually impartial.

But when it was time to collect the tax, abuses set in. At the end of the day, the amount collected fell short of the goal. Gradually the government began to rely on contracts with middlemen, tax farmers, who assured them of a certain amount, probably rather less than the sums theoretically due, but indubitably a better bet than continuing to fall short. Machault, with the king's approval, was now determined to use the opportunity of peace to push through a new and more equitable taxation system. He aimed to establish the *"vingtième,"* or the twentieth, a tax designed to fall on all subjects in proportion to their goods and means.

The new tax was a levy of 5 percent on the revenues from land, property, industrial and commercial enterprises, and from those who held government posts and offices. Everyone, including dukes, bishops, and chief magistrates, would be audited. For all those who had considered themselves beyond the reach of taxation, those who believed that only the little people should pay, this was a rude and mighty shock.

It was the constitutional role of the French *"parlements"*—the assemblies of magistrates and lawyers which sat in Paris and other provincial capitals—to register, or approve, the king's edicts. It was also their right to "remonstrate," or protest, if the edict displeased them. Not surprisingly, when the edict was sent to *parlement* on May 5, 1749, it met with a hostile reception. The magistrates refused to register it, voting instead to adjourn and address *remonstrances* to the king, as was their right. In return, Louis XV ordered registration *pur et simple,* which was done on May 19 and, five days later, to underline his support for the tax, he named Machault a minister of State. The scene was set for a long, drawnout conflict between *parlements* and the crown. And at the same time, other controversial issues between the king, *parlements,* and Church were coming to a head.

In June, the Archbishop of Paris, Christophe de Beaumont, ordered the strict application of a church rule demanding that a dying person procure a *"billet de confession"* before the last rites could be given. This *billet,* or document, showed that the dying man or woman had confessed to a priest who had accepted a papal proclamation known as "*Unigenitus*." By so doing, such priests had signified their adherance to the pope and their rejection of a doctrine known as Jansenism, a doctrine to which most of the senior members of *parlement* subscribed. Jansenists, named after an archbishop of the last century, considered themselves good Catholics; but their austere interpretation of the means of attaining salvation and grace did not find favor with the "established" Church, the Jesuits in particular. *Unigenitus* had appeared in 1715 and had strongly condemned Jansenism, but the fracture in the French church remained. By insisting upon the rigourous application of the *billets de confession*, the archbishop de Beaumont was dangerously raising tensions with *parlement*.

Louis XV suddenly found himself in the middle of a financial fight with *parlement* over the *vingtième*, as well as in a religious fight over the *billets de confession*. The first summer of peace was turning into a summer of domestic strife.

But neither refractory magistrates nor admonitory archbishops could disrupt the court's summer visit to Compiègne. At Compiègne, the summer sojourn was treated like a large picnic. Luynes describes the king's wooden house in the forest as a cabin, but a cabin with parquet floors, gold and porcelain dishes, silver coffeepots, and tablecloths of the finest linen. The garden was planted in the shape of a star, with sinuous pathways and unexpected detours. A belvedere was suspended in a tree. Here Madame de Pompadour entertained the king and his friends in countrified elegance, thirty years before Marie-Antoinette had the same idea.

At Compiègne, the marquise continued receiving distinguished foreign visitors at her toilette. There was by now an established etiquette for this ritual. On Tuesdays she received the ambassadors, on other days the ceremony was attended by all those who wished to obtain a favor by shameless flattery and adulation. Everyone, from princes of the blood to the newest arrival at court, was required to stand respectfully at a distance while the marquise regarded them and herself in her dressing table mirror, applying her rouge and powder, her hair loose, her body swathed in a dressing gown. Those to whom she addressed a word were the object of unfeigned envy. For supremely favored individuals, there was an

invitation to her *toilette secrète*, at which she gave audience in her boudoir, before the arrival of the multitude. Her manner was always gracious and dignified; she was always interested in meeting people of all
kinds. That summer a young British naval officer, Augustus Hervey, was
presented to her, describing her as "a rock of diamonds, and the handsomest woman I ever saw." At the height of her splendor, she caused her
satellite, the comtesse d'Estrades, to be promoted to *"dame d'atours,"* the
second most important post in the household of Mesdames Henriette,
Adélaïde, and Victoire. The princesses, who found Madame d'Estrades
vulgar, could only acquiesce.

But beyond the enchanted forest of Compiègne, attacks against the
throne continued and the tumult claimed a distinguished victim in July
when Denis Diderot was arrested and sent to the fortress of Vincennes,
accused of disturbing the peace of the kingdom. He had shocked the
authorities by delivering a passionate defense of agnosticism in his new
book *Lettre sur les Aveugles à l'Usage de Ceux Qui Voient (Letter on the Blind
for the Use of Those Who See)*, and was arrested on July 23, 1749. He remained in solitary confinement until August 20, and was finally released
on November 3, after three and a half months in jail. His imprisonment
had been loudly protested by his well-connected friends; Voltaire had
written in support from Lorraine, d'Alembert and Rousseau had visited
him in prison. Diderot had received a scare; but he was still eager to go
forward with his embryonic project, the *Encyclopédie*. The authorities kept
up a mild surveillance; the project gathered strength.

More and more, the tenor of the pamphlets flooding Paris, and the
conversation in the cafés and salons, was critical of royal expenditures. The
Menus Plaisirs, the department which was responsible for entertainments
at court, and which paid the bills for many of Madame de Pompadour's
expenses, were said to be costing an annual two and a half million livres,
as against four hundred thousand under Louis XIV. The royal household
was absorbing twenty-five million livres a year, nearly a tenth of the total
revenue, and more than all of the expenses of the entire navy.

In the autumn of 1749, building work was going on at all the royal
palaces. Hermitages, menageries, and pavilions were springing up everywhere. Complaints centered on the fact that these projects were not grand
and magnificent testimonies to the glory of France; rather they were very

private, very exclusive little establishments. When Louis XV turned to more grandiose projects at Fontainebleau, Choisy, and Compiègne, the complaints only increased. The king constantly had the impression that he could do nothing right.

One of the reasons given for the fall of Maurepas was that he had failed to modernize the navy. Perhaps with this in mind, in late 1749 the king decided to make a visit to Le Havre to inspect his fleet and show his support. One senses the influence of Madame de Pompadour behind the plan; Louis hated changes in his routine, disliked meeting new people, and loathed the ceremonial. He would not have made this trip without being persuaded into it. D'Argenson, naturally, sniffed at the whole idea. "We have had news today that the King is going to make an outing which is still secret. That is, to go to Havre and to Dieppe, to show the marquise the sea, and to eat fish. A party, they say, of real rubbernecking, which makes His Majesty a little giddy. A King should only propel himself for the public good, and for some object serious and worthy. What will the public say about these gadabouts giving themselves indigestion!"

The royal party left Crécy on September 17. There were four women in the party — Madame de Pompadour, Madame d'Estrades, the duchesse de Brancas, and the comtesse de Livry — and twenty men; among others, three royal princes, several ministers, officers of the Household, intimates like Gontaut and Soubise, as well as Abel Poisson. The party traveled via Rouen, stopping only to see the maneuvering of the bridge on the Seine and the passage of a ship before pressing on. After almost twenty-four hours on the road, the king arrived at Le Havre at six in the evening, to the noise of canons of the port and citadel. He entered the hôtel de Ville, where he was rather badly lodged, but where, one assumes, the exhausted party slept soundly.

The next morning, after an audience of the *parlement* of Rouen, they visited the interior basin, where the king inspected a new warship equipped with thirty-six cannons, and they saw three other vessels launched. Madame de Pompadour laid the first plank of a ship to be called *Le Gracieux*.

The party then left the port for the roadstead, where they witnessed a mock naval battle involving two hundred ships.

A handsome album of engravings was published to commemorate the journey, and the marquise wrote to the duc de Nivernais: "You cannot imagine to what point the adoration for the King, and even for those who were with him, was carried . . . the Normans have only followed their hearts." But whether the presence of Madame de Pompadour at the king's side in such a public way caused comment, or because the costs of such a trip were prohibitive, or perhaps because the experience was simply too exhausting for everyone, no such trip was ever taken again.

The end of 1749 brought some significant changes at court. On October 6 Madame Infante left court for Parma, where she would rejoin her husband, and where she would be expected to produce a son and heir to her new Italian estates. She went with a heavy heart. Madame de Pompadour, on the other hand, was visibly cheered by the departure of a woman she considered a bad influence—and a rival. She hastened to press on the king her new idea of she moving into new rooms at Versailles, on the ground floor, where she would no longer be so far from him, and where she could do away with the tiresome "flying chair" and the inconvenience of the many stairs for her visitors.

On December 28 the duc de Luynes felt able to announce that the move was imminent. This was a major move in the hierarchical system of lodgings at Versailles. So far, only members of the royal family and, many years earlier, the declared mistresses of Louis XIV, had lived in this sacred central part of the château. The king was making Madame de Pompadour's position as clear as he could. She was the established, declared favorite with an honorable and important position at court, and one she would most likely hold for a long time to come.

Madame de Pompadour felt that she could look to the future with confidence. And at the same time as she was embarking on new plans and projects, she saw her brother Abel also set off on a new stage in his life. On December 20 he left for Italy, bound for a grand tour of Italian art and architecture. Now twenty-four, he was destined to take over the *Bâtiments* from Tournehem in due course. It was necessary that his artistic knowledge be broadened in the usual way, by a prolonged visit to Italy in the company of knowledgeable guides. Abel was scheduled to see Rome, Turin, Bologna, and Naples, among other cities, and was expected to take note of all he saw. He was to travel with three companions: Charles-Nicolas Cochin, a talented engraver and draftsman, already working for the *Bâtiments;* the abbé Leblanc, a writer on the arts; and Jacques-Germain Soufflot, an architect who had been making a name for himself in Lyons. Soufflot had studied in Rome and spoke fluent Italian. All three men were approved by Tournehem; they would all—particularly Soufflot—use this journey with the favorite's young brother to ensure long and successful careers.

Thirty-one letters exist today from the marquise to her brother, undated but with the date received. Here is one which arrived at Lyon on December 28: "You did well, *frérot* [little brother], not to bid me adieu; for, despite the usefulness of this journey for you and my desire for your welfare, I would have had trouble seeing you go. . . . Do not lose sight of our conversations; and do not think that because I am young I cannot give good advice. I have seen so many things since I came here four and a half years ago that I know more than a woman of forty."

Madame de Pompadour liked to complain of the rigors of her existence. And there is no doubt that Louis XV was a difficult man to please, that the court was a nest of vipers, that the public lost no opportunity to insult her. But the unimaginable opulence in which she lived, the adulation with which she was surrounded, the addictive nature of absolute power and influence, were more intoxicating than perhaps she herself knew. After almost five years at court, she was harder and more cynical, wary and suspicious of those who surrounded her, ready to use the weapons at hand to remove a foe, as she had shown in the case of the comte de Maurepas, absolutely determined to maintain her position.

Chapter 10

*"Excepting the happiness of being with the King,
which assuredly consoles me for everything, the rest is
nothing but a tissue of wickedness, platitudes, in short,
all the miseries of which poor humans are capable."*

Grave problems were developing in Paris. As a result of poor harvests in the previous few years, many hungry peasants had come to the capital in search of employment and, finding none, had ended on the streets, a menace to the citizens. On November 12, 1749, a royal *ordonnance* had been issued calling for the arrest of vagabonds and undesirables. Berryer, the chief of the Paris police, executed it with rigor, not hesitating to pick up and arrest even small children to keep them off the streets. The public began to complain.

Louis XV kept himself informed of events in Paris through his preferred method of reading private letters, intercepted by the *"cabinet noir,"* a group of men employed to open the mail and reseal it in an undetectable way. "My brother," reported d'Argenson, referring to his brother, the minister of war, "is killing himself with work spying on Paris, which the King has much at heart. He wants to know everything that is said and done. What unhappy work! Espionage through the mail!"

As he pored over the salacious gossip he enjoyed, Louis XV became uncomfortably aware of a sinister undercurrent to the disturbances surrounding the arrests of the homeless children. Riots had broken out in several districts, caused by the spread of bizarre rumors that the children were being kidnapped and killed so that their blood could be used for the baths of a royal prince, in order to cure his leprosy.

"One does not know what such stories are founded on," worried Barbier. "This remedy was proposed to the Emperor Constantine, who did not wish to make use of it. But here we have no such prince, and, even if one existed, he would never employ such cruelty as a remedy." But the stories grew wilder; the king was clearly implicated, although never by name. Somehow, Louis XV had come to be perceived as a king "given over to caprice and anger, unable to restrain his sexual appetite." He had been transformed from Louis the Well-Beloved to Louis the Bloodsucker.

Louis XV was deeply shocked by these heinous slanders. He did not understand that his refusal to confess or take communion, his abandonment of the religious rites of kingship (such as the touching of those with scrofula) might have jeopardized the perception of him as Eldest Son of the Church and helped to inflame the Paris mobs. Louis refused to submit to the charade of taking the sacraments or performing religious functions when he knew himself to be a sinner, and a sinner with no intention of changing his sinful ways. This attitude, however admirable in a private citizen, contributed to an impression that the king had tarnished the monarchy, and was an unfit ruler. In the overheated atmosphere of 1750 he found himself held up to ridicule and abuse.

It is ironic that, at the very time such irrational and macabre scenes were being played out, elsewhere in Paris, in the salons of Madame Geoffrin, Madame du Deffand and others, the first seminal publications of the great intellectual awakening known as the Enlightenment, the vaunted triumph of reason, were coming into being.

Diderot and d'Alembert were launching their ambitious project for a universal *Encyclopédie*, a "Manifesto of the Modern Mind." Jean-Jacques Rousseau was beginning his improbable career, winning first prize from the Dijon Academy for his *Discours sur les Arts et les Sciences*, in which he outlined his life's belief: "Man is by nature good, only our institutions have made him bad!" Also at this time, Montesquieu's *L'Esprit des Lois* was examining the ways men governed themselves.

In the salons, men and women were being swept along in an exciting and unpredictable quest to extend the boundaries of human knowledge, and thus create a perfect society. But in the poor quarters of Paris, life was not changing very much; there, the concern was chiefly that of having enough to eat. The gulf between the unlettered poor, uncertain of their livelihoods, their security, their very lives, and the well-born, the educated, and the fortunate was a very wide one in Paris in the mid-eighteenth century.

Louis XV found himself precariously placed between those who were attacking him for neglecting his religious duties and those who would ridicule him if he attempted to play the religious role. In sophisticated circles, the idea of the king performing his religious duties caused skepticism, even amusement. But to the conservative clergy and their parishioners, the king was in a state of mortal sin and not only he, but all of them, would be punished for it. Louis XV was caught in the crossfire of the clash between new ideas and old values, which would animate the rest of the century. The regime would need an energetic and coherent response to challenges from both sides. But Louis XV, prey to depression and melancholy, reluctant to lead, unwilling to make hard decisions, found the conflict distressing and insoluble. He fled from it.

For her part, Madame de Pompadour, well aware of the volatile situation in Paris, could only brood. "The more I advance in age," she told her brother, "the more philosophical are my reflections. . . . Excepting the happiness of being with the King, which assuredly consoles me for everything, the rest is nothing but a tissue of wickedness, platitudes, in short, all the miseries of which poor humans are capable."

She was becoming increasingly introspective. After a liaison of five years, her relationship with the king was changing. She had never enjoyed the sexual activities which were such an essential part of any mistress's life. ("He thinks me very cold," she once confided in Madame du Hausset.) She had always trusted more her power to amuse, entertain, and soothe the king, rather than her prowess in the bedroom. Gradually, the physical ties were loosening, while the emotional ties were becoming stronger. She started to consider how to preserve her place at court, a place usually accorded to a woman on the basis of her powers of seduction, not on her powers of mind and heart. She referred more frequently to the force of friendship, rather than that of love, and started to prepare for a transition in her life.

Her preoccupation with her own problems prevented her from taking seriously Voltaire's latest complaints. At the end of 1749 he had experienced a great loss. His mistress, Madame du Châtelet, who had allowed herself to indulge in a brief affair with the marquis de Saint-

Lambert, and had become pregnant as a result, died six days after giving birth to a baby girl. Voltaire was distraught: "To have seen her die, and in such circumstances! She herself knew nothing of the horror of her death. It was only her friends who felt it."

In his grief, Voltaire's thoughts turned to flight—away from France, away from sadness and humiliation. For some time he had corresponded with the king of Prussia, Frederick II, a ruler at once ferociously militaristic and effusively poetic. Frederick had frequently attempted to woo the most celebrated writer in Europe to his court at Potsdam, thus far without success. But now Voltaire's thoughts turned to new faces and fresh territories. He had already told Frederick, "If you wish to perfect yourself, it would be necessary for you to have the goodness to work with me each day for six weeks or a month."

Voltaire tried to tell Madame de Pompadour that he felt unappreciated at court. We have her response, truly noble in tone: "I see that you are afflicted by the gossip, and by the spiteful things said about you. Should you not be used to this, considering it the lot of great men to be calumnied during their lives and admired after their deaths? Remember what happened to the Corneilles, the Racines, and so on, and you will see that you are no more poorly treated than they were. . . . You are right in saying that they also direct their insults at me; I treat all these horrors with the most complete disdain, and I am in fact very serene, knowing that it is my work for peace, my contribution to the happiness of humankind, which inspires their wrath. . . . Adieu, keep well; do not dream of going to find the King of Prussia; however great a King he is, one should not have any desire to leave our master [Louis XV] when one knows his admirable qualities. In particular, I myself would never forgive you." But Voltaire continued to brood on his misfortunes.

A further predicament was the developing tension between the government and the Church. In the spring of 1750, clergy from all over France were gathering in Paris for their quinquennial assembly. Feelings were running high, due to Machault's demand that, unprecedentedly, the Church should pay the *vingtième* along with everyone else. The clergy were not accustomed to paying taxes; instead, they awarded to the government an annual "*don gratuit*," the amount calculated by themselves. Machault estimated that the Church's contributions to public funds through the *don gratuit* worked out to about 3 percent of her taxable revenue, estimated to be 250 million livres. He thought, not unrealistically, that they could afford more. But far from agreeing with that way of thinking, the majority of the clergy assembling in Paris were against any idea of paying taxes, and were threatening not even to pay the *don gratuit*.

Outside Paris, other *parlements* were also refusing to impose the *vingtième*. On January 29 the annual meeting of the assembly of Languedoc had convened in Montpellier and immediately protested the *vingtième*, voting to postpone payment of their taxes. The duc de Richelieu, who was presiding over the assembly in his office of governor of Languedoc, was having difficulty in bringing the magistrates to order. Madame de Pompadour could not resist sending him a gentle rebuke: "Women are not made, Monsieur le Maréchal, to discuss politics. And so I do not interfere. All I know, and reason dictates, is that, the King being justice and goodwill incarnate, those who do not obey him must be regarded by all the universe as very bad subjects of their master. I do not doubt that you have done your best and that you are very upset at what has happened. And so I most strongly desire . . . that all this ends to the satisfaction of the King, whose goodwill, wisdom, and firmness will assuredly never fail. I thank you for the herbs you sent. I hope they will perfume my greenhouse at the Hermitage . . ."

The marquise never trusted Richelieu. In all her correspondence with him, there is a note of menace, little jabs and allusions designed to unsettle him. Richelieu never knew what she might say about him at court; but he must have sometimes felt that whatever he did, he would somehow be blamed. As she herself remarked, if one was not completely loyal to her, one could expect no support from her. Richelieu was one of many who could not bring himself to pay obeisance to the marquise, and one of many who would suffer for it.

But she lavished concern on her brother, Abel Poisson. In contrast to her disingenuous letters to Richelieu, the tone of Madame de Pompadour's letters to her brother was affectionate and warm, full of practical advice. She warned him to be very careful about what he wrote back to her, "for you can easily imagine that the letters of Madame de Pompadour's brother will be opened at Turin . . . anything private that you wish to tell me should be kept until there is a courier. It is silly of me to have forgotten to warn you of such an essential thing. I have had a little cold, but am recovered." She goes on to applaud his initiatives in the world at large: "You have done well to make the acquaintance of comte Alfieri: always follow this course, you will find it useful. A conversation with a learned man is often worth more than one's own point of view, for one has not the time to learn a thousand things as one can in a conversation." She worried about his wardrobe: "Find out what clothes you need for these fêtes, and let me know; I will look after them for you, as I wish that you may be suitably dressed in all regards. Let me know also if you have lace suitable for a party." And she imparted her own conclusions about life at Versailles: "As for courtiers, I am obliged to enlighten you about them; you do not judge them as they are. . . . I have seen a lot and thought a lot since I came here; I have at least gained an understanding of human beings, and I assure you that they are the same in Paris, in a provincial town, as they are at Court. The difference in objects makes things more or less interesting, and makes vices appear in a clearer light . . ."

Madame de Pompadour's interest in and solicitude for her brother were only part of the activity in which she engaged on behalf of her family. There was no cousin too removed whom she was not eager to marry well, no relative too distant to promote. She looked forward with particular anticipation to making a fine marriage for Abel on his return from Italy.

As for François Poisson, he was happily established on his new estate at Marigny, some distance to the northeast of Paris (and a very long way from Versailles). The estate had been purchased for him by the king, in a characteristic attempt to deceive those who might wish to discover the source of the funds. The king "recollected" that he had, since 1744, owed Poisson the amount of 200,000 livres, as recompense for the unjust accusations made against him. With this money, the estate of Marigny could be acquired from the duc de Gesvres.

Poisson made no effort to disguise his pride of ownership. He told his son that the formalities and paperwork were exhausting, but that, after it was all done, "I defy the King, and all the powers in the world united, to be able to throw us out of Marigny after this." (Poisson refused, however, to call himself marquis de Marigny. "You should take the name," he told Abel, "for, as for me, my name is François Poisson.")

But Poisson's appetite for family aggrandizement was not assuaged by his new property. He approached Jeanne-Antoinette about having Abel promoted to superintendent of the *Bâtiments* on his return. This would be an entirely new post, and the marquise did not hesitate to disabuse him. "I believe I have already told you, my dear father, that superintendent [for Abel] is not right, and you must never think of it." She went on to administer a skillful refusal to invite Poisson to court. "You are quite right not to wish to come here. If you knew this place as I do, you would loathe it even more. But your presence at the Court is of no usefulness; the King is always creating estates to comtés, marquisates, etc., and the possessors never come here."

Poisson did however, make frequent visits to Crécy and Fontainebleau. Unabashed by the tremendous change in his fortunes, he remained very much his own man; he and Tournehem lived amicably together in Paris, and the question of the paternity of Jeanne-Antoinette remained, presumably, unspoken. He wrote often to Abel in Italy, keeping him abreast of family news: "Your sister has just sent me the prettiest writing table. She also wants to send her decorator, against my wishes, so that he can take measurements of the rooms which she wishes to furnish for me. One must put up with what one can't stop!"

Poisson doted on little Alexandrine, his grandchild, known in the family as *"Fanfan,"* now almost six years old, and about to enter the aristocratic convent of the Assumption in Paris. Before she was sent off to Paris and her new life, she spent a week with her mother at Marly. "She is in good health, although very thin," Jeanne-Antoinette informed Poisson, before she informed him of another *petit voyage:* "we leave tomorrow for Crécy, and stay until Saturday, and again on Wednesday until Saturday following. I know that you are aware of how much I enjoy these voyages to Crécy; my only regret is that they are so short, I should like to spend my life there." Perhaps responding to his concern, she went on to tell him "not to worry about my health, it is very good; everything going on will not derange it, because my principle is to do the best I can, and not to trouble myself about these attacks, when I have nothing to reproach myself with. I am, in consequence, very serene . . ."

The marquise was referring to the turbulent conditions in Paris, about which she was more worried than she said. She was somewhat anxious about Alexandrine's safety in the city, but resolved to see her settled there. Her own memories of convent life were clearly happy ones, and she wished her daughter to experience some of that calm and ordered world. She also wished her to acquire the necessary polish for a glittering future. Alexandrine was being brought up as a royal princess, addressed as "Madame Alexandrine," and destined, already, for a grand marriage. Only a duke would do for a husband, and the question of which duke was beginning to occupy her mother's thoughts. The little girl herself had no such concerns. "Dear Papa," she told Poisson, "I am going to learn to write very quickly so that you can have my letters every day."

The only worry in the Poisson menage was the health of "*oncle*" Tournehem, whose unceasing work at the *Bâtiments* was taking its toll. "I have been to see M. de Tournehem at Etioles, which gave him great pleasure," she wrote. "I found it charming . . ." Tournehem escaped to Etioles whenever he could. He had never ceased to love the place, even after Jeanne-Antoinette, mistress and inspiration of it all, had left for her glorious destiny. Charles-Guillaume Lenormand, the abandoned husband, had ceased to call himself "d'Etioles" and was not inclined, nor invited, to visit his former home. Thus, the marquise de Pompadour could safely pay a call on "*oncle*" and share with him the joys of improvements to the property. "What a pretty new grove of trees!" "How the lilacs have grown!" "Do you remember when we read *Pamela* in their shade?"

The riots in Paris continued. "A propos of folly, you have heard that of the Parisians," she wrote to Abel. "I do not believe there is anything more stupid than to believe that one wishes to take blood from children in order that a leprous prince might bathe in it. I admit, to my shame, that I thought people less imbecile. The *Parlement* has issued an edict and all is over."

The riots had two very different consequences. Pâris-Duverney, observing the seditious scenes in Paris at close hand, thought it time to resurrect one of his pet projects. He persuaded the marquise that this would be an excellent opportunity to press to the king his idea for the establishment of the *Ecole Militaire*, where five hundred "young and poor gentlemen" could be trained in the military skills. The idea had been gathering dust in various ministerial offices. Now came the impulsion of the powerful favorite and her highly placed friends. Her first letter to Duverney (her "dear Blockhead") on the subject of the *Ecole* is dated April 4: "I have asked the little Saint [M. de Saint-Florentin, the relevant official], my dear Blockhead, for the papers relating to the establishment for gentlemen; he told me that he was sure he had given them to the big Pâris [Pâris de Montmartel] . . . the King is very eager to accomplish this project; he wishes to find out first what funds are needed to ensure its viability as His Majesty does not wish any extraordinary funds for it. . . . Arrange matters in consequence, dear Blockhead, and be very sure of my tender friendship for you."

Duverney replied by return courier, expressing his delight that the king had been persuaded to take an interest, and assuring the marquise that he would find the funds. He noted sadly that the disturbances in Paris were "not conducive to the love which the master expects and desires from his subjects, nor to the love he has for them." But the events convinced him that it was more important than ever to go forward, since "it is in the nobility and the military where the State finds its defense and its firmest support, and thus it seems to me, Madame, that one cannot excite the zeal and fidelity of these two bodies too much at a time when one could perhaps complain of that of others . . ."

Pâris-Duverney was very enthusiastic about the *Ecole Militaire*. He realized full well how important it would be for the French army to have available a professionally trained group of officers, and he threw all his weight behind the idea. It was not easy to persuade Louis XV to devote his attention to the project, but Duverney and the marquise persevered.

The other consequence of the riots was less happy. The king, his feelings wounded at the strange uproar in Paris over the "disappearance of children," and understandably hurt at being compared to King Herod, was uncharacteristically decisive. Pondering on his summer visit to Compiègne, and the necessity to pass through Paris, he gave orders to build a new road which would bypass the city. He would use it for the first time that summer.

The day before he was to leave for Compiègne, Louis XV made a tour of inspection of his domain near Versailles. He went at noon to walk to the Hermitage and Trianon; there he saw the mirrors being installed in the little *pavillon Français,* an elegant new retreat for summer entertaining and gambling. With its inlaid marble floor and white and gold décor—including a gilded frieze of hens and chickens and other farmyard animals, with a small room at each corner for a kitchen, a "café," and an English-style lavoratory—it was the apotheosis of luxury and sophistication. Having expressed his satisfaction, the king returned to Versailles to visit the pregnant dauphine, drove over to Bellevue to see the new château being built there for the marquise, and then went to sup and sleep at La Muette.

Having drawn attention to five of the expensive little follies that were attracting so much criticism, Louis left the next morning for Compiègne, driving through the bois de Boulogne to Saint-Denis on the new road, avoiding the usual route along the ramparts of Paris, where representatives of the citizenry would have awaited him. The Parisians lost no time in dubbing the king's road *"la route de la Révolte"*; Louis XV had shortened the distance between Versailles and Compiègne, but widened the gulf between court and capital.

Madame de Pompadour regarded Paris as a hotbed of sedition. Loftily, she told her brother that "neither the King nor anyone in his family has been to Paris, to punish the inhabitants for their stupidity . . . ," demonstrating the distorting effects of several years' existence in the rarified air of the court. In her mind, the Parisians were being punished by withdrawal of the king's presence. These unruly subjects simply did not deserve to glimpse the master's countenance. The attitude in the capital was different; the king's decision to avoid his capital was deplored, and even the lawyer Barbier, who was a sensible man, found reason to blame the marquise. "All this has an air of flight about it, which desolates all good Frenchmen. Behold the hate inspired in the King against the Parisians, greater than that of Louis XIV. It is only women of low birth, they say, who could give such advice."

There was little more good news that summer. On June 30, 1750, the clerical assembly began to debate the *vingtième.* Six weeks later, they rejected any cooperation over the new tax. Louis XV was dismayed. The bishops loftily informed the crown that conscience prevented them from consenting to the sacrilegious despoiling of revenues consecrated to God for the maintenance of public worship and the relief of the poor. The new tax, they stated, "threatened the social order of the kingdom as a whole by

reducing the Church to the condition of the rest of the King's subjects."
Barbier was not alone in finding the bishops' attitude "insolent for subjects."

Determined to maintain his authority, encouraged by Machault,
Louis XV dismissed the assembly. The clergy were sent back to their
dioceses with orders to come up with a plan for some kind of taxable
amount in six months' time, the king having proposed that they make a
registry of all their goods and revenues. Here was an uneasy standoff
between the king and his bishops.

The insolence of the clergy was a major annoyance, the decision by
Voltaire to leave France a minor one. The marquise had failed to persuade him to remain and was now resigned to see him go. He presented
himself before her, hoping, perhaps, for a plea from her that he should
stay; but she simply asked him to give her respects to King Frederick of
Prussia. "One cannot offer a more agreeable commission, nor give it more
gracefully. She did it with all modesty, with 'If I dared,' and so on . . . ,"
but then she turned away. Voltaire never saw her or Versailles again.
Louis XV remarked that now there would be one more madman at the
court of Prussia, and one less at that of France.*

Voltaire's departure could not have mattered less to the court; there,
the concern was with the dauphine's forthcoming *accouchement* [confine-
ment]. But, on August 27, d'Argenson reported: "Bad news: madame la
Dauphine gave birth yesterday at six o'clock in the evening to a princess, and not to a prince, as one wished for so much."

Madame de Pompadour regarded the birth of a girl as "a real misfortune." But, she told her brother, "as madame la Dauphine is in very
good health on her eleventh day, she will give us a prince next year. One
must take this as an object of consolation. . . . I saw little Madame yesterday for the first time, I could not resolve myself to do so until that
moment. She is indeed delicate, I do not know if she will live."**

The general disappointment felt at the birth of a girl was due, partly,
to the fact that, under French law, only males could inherit the throne.

---

*When Voltaire presented Madame de Pompadour's compliments to
Frederick II, the king of Prussia responded drily, "I do not know her. . . ." "Nevertheless," Voltaire told his niece, "I have told Mme de Pompadour that Mars received, as he should, the compliments of Venus."

**The baby was named Marie-Zéphirine. She died at the age of five.

Even though Maria-Theresa ruled in Vienna, even though Elizabeth I and Anne had sat on the throne of England, even though Catherine the Great would become ruler of Russia in 1762, the French court would never consider a princess the equal of a prince. Madame de Pompadour, by now more royalist than the king, accepted this as immutable wisdom.

But the exclusion of women from succession to the throne, and, in society at large, their exclusion from any important office, meant that the only way a woman could wield power and influence was through a man. In this sense, Madame de Pompadour played a very traditional role. But she also chose, and cherished, the image of a *"femme savante,"* as when she had herself painted with all the attributes of culture and learning. Having acquired her position at the king's whim, she very early signaled her intention of keeping it by her own talents. Studying the examples of the mistresses of Louis XIV, the voluptuous marquise de Montespan and the pious marquise de Maintenon, she had arrived at a conception of her own role; from dazzling beauty, actress, and seductress, she would transform herself into valued friend and adviser. The emphasis she placed on her accomplishments and seriousness of mind would prepare the ground for such a metamorphosis. Her plan was not to become prime minister; it was to keep her place at court and her hold on the king. It was the course of events which would lead her into a more political role.

In 1750 she was painted by François Boucher, a portrait known today only from an oil sketch in the Louvre. In it she is shown touching a harpsichord, roses at her feet, a bound volume nearby, stamped with her arms, together with a globe and some architectural plans. She is wearing a dress of green and gold silk, draped in the Spanish fashion. The impression given is that of a cultivated woman familiar with the arts and sciences, a woman worthy to be the mistress of the king of France. This would become her signature iconography over the years, these attributes of art, architecture, music, and literature; in this portrait she makes her first appearance in her self-designated image, her first step into her new role.

After the birth of *"la petite Madame,"* there were more family reunions at Fontainebleau that autumn. The great event was the arrival from Fontevrault of the king's two youngest daughters, Madame Sophie and

Madame Louise, twelve years after they had been sent away. Sophie was now sixteen and Louise thirteen, both still timid children completely unprepared for the outside world. The girls, plucked from the convent and thrown into the equally enclosed and rigorous world of Versailles, had merely to exchange one set of rules for another. They joined their sisters in the sad and restricted life to which etiquette condemned royal princesses, passing idle hours in desultory conversation and assorted artistic dabblings, the highlight of each day a short and ceremonious visit to their father. (It is, therefore, hardly surprising that *Mesdames* "kept in their cupboards hams, sausages, stews, Spanish wine, and shut themselves up all the time to eat at every hour." None of them ever married; they all remained rather childlike, treated as such by their father who called them by nicknames, *Torche* (Torch) for Adélaïde, *Coche* (Pig) for Victoire, *Graille* (Snot) for Sophie, and *Chiffe* (Rag) for Louise.)

Madame de Pompadour, who liked to claim credit for inspiring Louis XV with the idea of uniting his family, tenderly observed the king's tearful reunion with his daughters, and then proceeded to dissect their appearance: "In truth, nothing is more touching than these meetings. The king's affection for his children is touching, and they respond with all their heart. Madame Sophie is almost as tall as I, very attractive if rather plump, with a fine complexion; in profile she looks as like the king as two drops of water, but from the front, she is not nearly so like him, as she has an ugly mouth. Madame Louise is very small, not at all mature, her features bad rather than otherwise, but with an expression which pleases much more than if she were beautiful. We were all presented today. . . ."

Another new arrival at court that autumn was of greater significance. The new Austrian Ambassador, Count von Kaunitz-Rietberg, arrived at Fontainebleau on a delicate mission. His instructions were to develop a sympathetic audience for the Empress Maria-Theresa's desire to recover Silesia (lost to Prussia under the terms of the Peace of Aix-la-Chapelle in 1748) and, somehow, to persuade the French to withdraw from their alliance with Frederick of Prussia. Kaunitz, a clever, sophisticated man, set out to be charming, to warm the relationship between France and Austria. On November 2 he had his first audience with Louis XV.

From the beginning of his stay in France, Kaunitz was interested in the king's favorite; his instructions from Vienna were to take note of any possible inclination toward Austria, and he had indications that the marquise might be sympathetic to his cause. The Pâris brothers had already discreetly indicated that they were not uninterested in an alliance with the empress. Kaunitz made a careful study of Madame de Pompadour: "Her eyes are blue, set well apart, her expression charming. Her face is oval with a small mouth, pretty forehead, an especially nice nose. She has a good complexion, and it would be much more so without the quantity of rouge she puts on. Her ash-blond hair falls in profusion to her waist. The care she takes to hide her hands and bosom prove that they are not up to the rest. Her favorite attire is a sort of Greek dress which buttons up to the neck, with sleeves to the wrist. For the rest, she is tall rather than short, thin rather than fat; her carriage is noble, her graces touching. . . . Her figure has something distinguished about it, so uncommon that even other women find in her what they call the air of a nymph."

Kaunitz thought the French court to be inhabited by unimpressive specimens of male and female beauty. But another visitor at Fontainebleau that fall, the young Venetian adventurer Giacomo Casanova, was dazzled, and, as is the way with adventurers, helped himself on the way to fame and fortune with a chance encounter. Seated near the box of Madame de Pompadour at the court theatre, Casanova could not help bursting out laughing at the theatrics of the actress Le Maur; for this he was reprimanded by the maréchal de Richelieu, who was with the marquise. As the conversation proceeded, Richelieu asked Casanova which of the actresses pleased him most. "That one." "But she has ugly legs." "In the examination of a woman's beauty," said Casanova, "the legs are the first things I lay aside." "My retort became famous, and I was given a gracious welcome."

Casanova, like Kaunitz, found the court ladies very ugly, the king's daughters particularly so, but he thought Louis XV extraordinarily handsome when he saw him pass by with his arm round the shoulders of the comte d'Argenson. Casanova found court customs incomprehensible, but cause for amusement. He attended the queen's public dinner, standing with everyone else in a reverent silence as the queen ate, the silence broken only when she commented graciously to Monsieur de Lowendal that she "thought the best stew of all is a fricassée of chicken."

*　　*　　*

Madame de Pompadour always liked to meet interesting foreigners; she was much more curious and openminded in this regard than the king. But she made sure to distill such encounters into stories which would entertain Louis XV. Like Sheherazade she relied on her ability to distract, amuse, and soothe her lover in order to keep him enthralled.

The marquise was preparing herself for another stage in her life with Louis XV. When the court returned from Fontainebleau she expected to move into her palatial suite of rooms at Versailles, rooms which were, by virtue of their size, splendor, and location, a declaration of her preeminent position; and she was also anxiously supervising the final touches being applied to Bellevue, the château she had designed as a testament to the glories of French art, and to herself. Neither project succeeded as she would have wished.

At Versailles the sculptor Verberckt was working furiously on the paneling brought from Paris, but was threatening to stop work because he had not been paid. The marquise harassed Tournehem; when could Martin do his many coats of varnish? It must be done as quickly as possible because of the smell "which could incommode her if the varnish were freshly painted." Marble chimneypieces and tabletops, and many mirrors, had to arrive from Paris before the furniture could be delivered. Orders were placed with Lazare Duvaux, her favorite dealer, for candelabras of polished copper decorated with porcelain flowers, for Bohemian crystal, for hangings of silk and cotton, for "little panels of Chinese tissue paper printed with flowers and birds" for her dressing room.

The last delivery of woodwork arrived during the night of November 6, 1750. Tournehem was telling his subordinates: "Think on it that Friday is November 14, and that the King is arriving on November 19 and so one must do the impossible to make everything ready." One easily detects the note of alarm, almost panic, over the consequences of a delay. And in fact the rooms were not completely ready until the spring. Not everything was possible, even for Madame de Pompadour.

But the great event at the end of 1750 was the inauguration of Bellevue, the place in which Madame de Pompadour had invested so much effort. The marquis d'Argenson was already spreading the rumor that it had cost "almost seven millions, while they affect to say that it will not cost more than seven hundred thousand livres." He also reported that "they are working at Vincennes to make one hundred thousand livres worth of porcelain flowers for the parterres of Bellevue." Neither of these statements was true; but d'Argenson found many in Paris who believed him. (It is true that more than two and a half million livres were spent there, not including the furnishings.)

But the first visit to Bellevue, on November 22, was not an unqualified success. The marquise had presented her male guests with a new Bellevue uniform—suits of purple velvet embroidered with gold—but the colors were unflattering, all the men looked tired. The chimneys smoked to such an extent that the supper had to be transported to Brimborion, the little pavilion at the bottom of the garden near the river, and the marquise developed a prodigious migraine. François Poisson remarked that the house was "the most beautiful thing created, but not at this time of year, when there are cold winds from the early morning."

While courtiers who were excluded from Bellevue gloated over the unfortunate events there, Parisians devoured some new verses:

> Daughter of a leech, and leech herself,
> Poisson, with an extreme arrogance,
> Displays in this château, without shame and without dread,
> The substance of the people and the shame of the King.

But solid Barbier begged to differ: "In good faith, what does this mean? This château is only costing more than the others because of the work needed to cut through the hill below Meudon, which has given work to a great many people . . . as for the rest, one criticizes this château for being too small: a tax farmer would have built a bigger one." And Barbier felt compelled to defend the king from accusations of immorality: "With regard to shame, what does the public mean? Is it because the King has a mistress? But who has not? . . . Of the twenty seigneurs of the court, there are fifteen who never live with their wives and who have mistresses. Nothing is so common in Paris, among private individuals. It is thus ridiculous that the King, who is indeed the master, should be in a worse condition than his subjects and than that of all his royal predecessors . . ."

To this bourgeois citizen, the threats and insults being leveled at the king were out of proportion and misconceived. Unfortunately, however, Barbier and those who thought like him were not the voices most heard. As usual, the angriest had the advantage.

At the end of 1750 Madame de Pompadour had cause for reflection. She knew the first fine, careless rapture of her love affair with the king was over. Perhaps she shivered at the thought of the irrational hatred unleashed in the streets of Paris. As a practical woman, and a perfectionist, she was certainly irked by the distressing faux pas at Bellevue, and by the fact that her new rooms at Versailles, rooms designed to make a grand statement about her position at court, remained unfinished. The first whispers that she and Louis had ceased their physical relationship were beginning to circulate.

"They say on all sides, those who know her best, that there is hardly any *plaisir d'amour* between her and her Royal lover anymore," noted d'Argenson, ever on the lookout for indications of the marquise's imminent fall from grace. But he found little reason for cheer. "Let us assume that passion is no longer the knot of her ascendancy over him. There remains only: habit, which is very powerful in men as gentle and honorable as the King; the superintendence of his amusements and the careful attention to forestall his moments of boredom; and trust, the habit of soothing his heart and soul. It is by these means that she has arrived at governing the affairs of the State . . ."

D'Argenson thought the king needed "a new mistress, more suitable and more dignified, new amusements, a male friend of the heart in whom the King would confide his troubles, his difficulties and his plans."

Madame de Pompadour had no intention of following such a prescription. She had her own ideas. At the end of 1750 she commissioned the sculptor Pigalle to fashion two allegorical statues reflecting the metamorphosis of her relationship with the king. In *Friendship*, dressed in a sort of tunic fitted at the waist leaving the chest half bare, she offers her heart to an unseen Louis XV, her left arm advanced, in sign of welcome, her right arm placed on her heart. A new stage was beginning.

PART THREE

1751–1756

"Louis XV is letting himself be guided by her advice."

Chapter 11

"The mistress is Prime Minister, and is becoming more and more despotic, such as a favorite has never been in France."

At the beginning of 1751 Madame de Pompadour was letting it be known that she was now the friend, and not the lover, of the king. Not by coincidence, 1751 was Holy Year (or the "Jubilee") in France, the year during which Catholics could gain forgiveness for their sins in exchange for contributions to the Church, penitence, and the taking of the sacraments. The marquise wished to pave the way for her new role as *"amie nécessaire"* by heading off the dangers inherent in Holy Year. If the king repented for his sin of adultery, specifically if he took communion at Easter, he would feel intense pressure from the Church to lead a reformed way of life, a new life in which the marquise would have no part. That must be avoided at all costs.

"Madame de Pompadour has had some fits of fever," reported d'Argenson sardonically. "This is what they call Jubilee fever, because the proximity of the Jubilee puts her into a great state of anxiety. . . . If the King decided to return to sincere religious practice, a strict confessor could demand that the marquise be considered as complicit in his adultery and should be publicly sent away." That, of course, was what d'Argenson and many others devoutly wished.

Fully aware of the peril, and perhaps to keep the king distracted, his mind off the critical times ahead, the marquise multiplied the voyages, the plays at Bellevue, all sorts of building projects. During the year, only nine weeks would be spent at Versailles. The king moved from place to place almost three times a week.

Bellevue was brand-new. And imprudent, for more than one reason. The king was pouring money into Choisy, Trianon, Compiègne,

Fontainebleau; the marquise had already spent a fortune at Crécy; now
came Bellevue, so close to Paris that it became the focus of hostility
against her, and, by extension, the king and his court.

The marquise was at pains to downplay Bellevue's grandeur. "It is
not very large," she told Madame de Lutzelbourg, "but comfortable and
charming, without any magnificence. We shall play some comedies there.
The king wishes to diminish his expenses in every way, since the cost of
this house is not considerable, although the public believes it is, I have
wished to take account of public opinion and set an example." Even to
her brother, she felt she must stress that Bellevue "is the prettiest place
in the world, with the greatest simplicity." She also argued that she meant
Bellevue as a showplace for French art and craftsmanship; but it was a
very exclusive place, and very few were exposed to its marvels.

Today, even though Bellevue has completely disappeared, the only
poignant memory of its wonders a fragment of a wrought-iron balus-
trade, one can reconstruct it in detail from plans and drawings. It is
worth giving a full description of a place which exemplified Madame
de Pompadour's perfectionism, taste, and personal impulsion. The most
distinguished artists of the day—the painters Boucher, Van Loo, and
Oudry, the sculptors Pigalle and Falconet, the fresco artists the Brunetti
brothers, the landscaper Garnier l'Ile—all produced masterpieces for this
place.

Bellevue was unusually sited, for the road from Meudon to Sèvres
ran right in front of it, separating the house from the gardens on the
entrance side. It was the vista from the back of the house that made its
situation striking and desirable; beyond terraced gardens descending to
the river Seine, the domes and spires of Paris were visible, close enough
so that one could examine each church and monument in detail, while
being far from the noise and smell of the city.

One entered the house through an imposing vestibule, the floor of
black and white marble, statues in niches on either side; one of these
depicted the marquise as Music, holding the score of *Issé*, the other presented her as Poetry. To the right, the grand staircase curved upward,
its walls frescoed with trompe-l'oeil depictions of Mars and Venus,
Bacchus and Ariadne, Zephyr and Flora. An elegant wrought-iron bal-
ustrade was highlighted in gilded bronze, a glass lantern with six gilded

branches hung above. This staircase led to the king's suite, the council chamber, and chapel; the marquise's rooms were on the ground floor.

From this vestibule, one entered the grand salon straight ahead, its windows overlooking the wide terrace and the distant view of Paris. This room was decorated in the grand style, with paneling carved with hunting and fishing motifs, two marble fireplaces surmounted by large mirrors in elaborate frames. Porcelain vases mounted in gilt bronze were displayed on tables topped with violet marble; the chandeliers and candleholders were decorated with porcelain flowers from Vincennes; over the doors hung still life paintings of hunting dogs, waterfowl, and game by Oudry.

Madame de Pompadour's bedroom was to the left of the salon. This room was known as the *"chambre à la turque"* because of its vaguely Oriental décor. (Turkey and the Far East were often indistinguishable to eighteenth-century minds.) The walls were hung with panels of Chinese silk, the furniture was inlaid with lacquer and veneered in exotic woods, the porcelain vases were of Oriental origin, and the portraits of the marquise, painted by Carle Van Loo, depicted her in Turkish costume. Next door was her boudoir, decorated with Boucher's Chinese landscapes, and containing her bidet and "chaise d'affaires." In the mezzanine were rooms for her maids, "cabinets" painted in light, bright colors.

On the floor above were the king's rooms, directly above those of the marquise and connected to them by secret staircases, as well as a council chamber and salon. The latter also served as a chapel, where Boucher's painting *The Light of the World* was kept in a kind of cupboard that turned into an altar when needed. In the attic were a few guest rooms, in the basement a vast kitchen and wine cellar.*

This "simple little house" was accompanied by two wings around the courtyard, one which held the theatre, decorated "à la Chinoise," and one which held a luxurious bathing suite for the king and the marquise, where Boucher's ravishing nudes, the *Toilet of Venus* and the *Bath of Venus*, were placed.

---

*Madame de Pompadour kept wines from Burgundy, Champagne, and the Rhône in her cellar, as well as Tokai and Spanish and Portuguese wines, but no Bordeaux.

Across the road from the courtyard were extensive gardens and a long grassy walk leading to a pool, with groves on either side, including one with a statue of the marquise as the Goddess of Love. In summer, jasmine and lilac scented the grounds; in winter dense stands of evergreens framed the vista.

In Paris, rumors of the cost of this exquisite place multiplied. "The Parisians are telling such lies," the marquise complained to her brother. "You know without doubt that Bellevue has fallen to the ground, that all the mirrors and chimneypieces are in smithereens . . . that I have sold it to the King for eight hundred thousand livres. These scavengers would be quite startled to know that I despise them royally, and that they cause me not the slightest pain . . . *Bonsoir, mon cher bonhomme,* we have at Bellevue a little bauble of a theatre ["*brimborion de théâtre*"] which is charming; we shall perform a comedy there for the first time on the 26th of this month; it will only be a comedy. I love you and embrace you with all my heart."

The Bellevue theatre was inaugurated with a performance of *L'Amour Architecte,* in which a mountain burst open to reveal a miniature Bellevue, complete with dancing gardeners. The choice of subject provoked more sarcasm in Paris. But the marquise hoped that such negative reaction could be overcome by the publication of an edict with which she was closely associated—the proclamation of the establishment of the *Ecole Militaire.*

Madame de Pompadour was delighted. Earlier she had told Duverney that she had been "in the enchantment of seeing the King enter into the detail . . . I am burning to see the thing made public, because, after that, it will not be possible to draw back. I count on your eloquence to seduce Monsieur de Machault, although I believe him too attached to the King to oppose himself to his glory. In short, my dear Duverney, I count on your vigilance that the universe shall soon be instructed."

The marquise congratulated herself upon successfully persuading the king. She believed that it was her tenacity and enthusiasm which had won the day for Duverney's pet project, over the initial objections of the king's ministers, Machault and the comte d'Argenson. She expected a public acknowledgment of her role.

Emphasizing the importance she attached to the *Ecole Militaire,* she informed her brother in Rome that "Monsieur de Tournehem is up to his neck in the plans for the *Ecole Royale Militaire.* I am sending you a half-dozen proclamations; you should give them to Monsieur de Nivernais if he does not have any." And to Nivernais himself, the French ambassador in Rome (who was known to her as "little husband," in reference to a role he played in her theatre at Versailles) she wrote: "I am very sure, knowing your attachment to the King, that you will be enchanted, above all when you know that it is His Majesty himself who has been occupied for more than a year with this project, the corrections and generally every detail; in truth, there are few monarchs who employ their moments of leisure in doing such fine things. The day after tomorrow we are performing comedy at Bellevue for the first time. The theatre is as big as a hand, but charming; I hope to see you shine there before too many years go by . . ."*

The Parisian reaction to the *Ecole Militaire* was positive. "This establishment is admirable and greatly pleases the whole public," noted Barbier, making an elegant reference to the nearby Invalides. "One will see two neighboring hôtels—one the cradle, the other the tomb of the army." But to Madame de Pompadour's irritation, she received no public credit for her role in bringing it about. She had wanted her name mentioned in the edict and was disappointed that it was not. (In 1752, in a letter to Duverney, she would refer with some bitterness to "*le chagrin affreux et irréparable*," the deep lasting bitterness, which the project had caused her. Increasingly conscious of her public image, she came to feel that an opportunity to burnish it had been missed.)

Meanwhile, criticism of her expensive passion for building persisted. On January 13, 1751, the king took his hunting party to the marquise's Hermitage in the park of Versailles to inspect the hothouses for rare plants, the henhouse, the flower beds, the herb and vegetable gardens. "All this is arranged with good taste," noted the duc de Croÿ, who was present, "and executed at great cost, all the more unfortunate as they are doing almost

---

*The wording of the royal edict proclaiming the creation of the school was as follows: "The King is founding an institution in which to lodge, feed, maintain, and instruct in the military art, and all the exercises and sciences which are related to it, five hundred young and poor gentlemen, from the ages of nine to eighteen, when they will leave the school to join the army, according to the dispositions and talents they have displayed, with two hundred livres of pension to help them sustain themselves in the first posts they are given." To be admitted one had to prove four generations of nobility.

as much at all the King's houses, as well as those of the Marquise; this unfortunate taste for little buildings and these little accoutrements is immensely expensive, without anything fine remaining."

When the king moved on to Choisy, Croÿ again commented on the money being spent, in this case on a new road from Versailles: "This has cost a great deal, there having been extensive earth-moving with a lot of land lost." "There she was," he went on to muse, "at Choisy, five leagues from Etioles where she had never dreamt of playing such a role. The King seems more charmed than ever, and she conducts herself with him with much art, attention, and respect."

Others were less charmed. "One constantly mentions bourgeois and ridiculous remarks of the marquise," carped d'Argenson, "who affects full power and the prime ministership, as did the cardinal prime minister [Fleury]. She said to an ambassador taking leave: 'Continue, I am pleased with you, you know I have been a friend of yours for a long time.' She settles everything, she decides."

Madame de Pompadour was, of course, not prime minister, nor as influential as d'Argenson liked to think. But she was beginning to take an interest in political and diplomatic matters; she saw an opportunity to form a new bond between her and the king, a bond based on trust and discretion rather than on sex.

At the beginning of 1751 the Prussian envoy Le Chambrier told Frederick II that the marquise was not interested in diplomacy. "The marquise de Pompadour is all powerful for what they call graces, and for benefits of money and jobs. . . . She has no influence in political affairs, except in placing a minister in foreign Courts in which she takes an interest, in concert with the marquis de Puisieulx; but, as for things regarding negotiations with foreign powers, the marquise de Pompadour does not interfere. She has no liking for these kinds of matters; she does not understand them. She would have to be educated by someone if she wished to influence political affairs. If I had ever believed that one could make some use of this woman for important matters, I would have indicated it to Your Majesty a long time ago."

Le Chambrier was wrong. In March he was obliged to tell his master that Madame de Pompadour was indeed working with Puisieulx and the king. "The marquise must be delighted at being able to impress the King by developing talents he had not thought her capable of until now. Behold her thus brought to take cognizance of the most important matters . . ."

Madame de Pompadour had no doubt calculated that her position would be more secure if she developed a working relationship with the king; but she had also had the opportunity to see that Louis XV was uncomfortable in his role as absolute monarch, too timid and indecisive to regard his supreme power as anything but a crushing burden, and one from which he fled. She, who never doubted her own abilities, was probably sincere in her belief that she could be an asset and a support to the king, as adviser, confidante, and ally. As always, her actions could be interpreted as those of an overweeningly ambitious woman, or those of a sincere and disinterested friend, or both.

The political atmosphere was tense. A confrontation between church and state was preparing. February 17, 1751 was the date by which the clergy were supposed to have furnished a declaration of their goods and revenues, preparatory to being assessed for the *vingtième*. They had not done so. But Louis XV was anxious to avoid an open rupture, particularly as Holy Year was about to open, and, in Paris, there were extraordinary displays of religious fervor. "One has never seen such devotion," marveled Barbier. "It seems that people of quality are making a comparison to the circumstances in which the master finds himself."

Louis XV's circumstances were, indeed, scandalous; but he himself seemed unaffected by the danger to his immortal soul. In a man so timid and impressionable, this was odd. But according to the later testimony of the duc de Choiseul, Louis believed himself sure of salvation. He had been told, as a child, that no one of the race of kings of France could be damned, provided they committed no injustice toward their subjects, nor harshness to the poor. King Louis IX, Saint Louis, protected his descendants. Choiseul was amazed at the king's naïveté; but, as far as Louis XV was concerned, if he continued to be kind to his servants, he would be protected from the wrath of God, whatever sins he committed. Such a view certainly made life easier for him. But public scandal could not be wished away.

As religious fervor increased during Holy Year, the king's former mistress, the comtesse de Mailly, died in saintly fashion in Paris. For several years she had lived a pious and charitable life. If Madame de Pompadour feared any invidious comparisons, she seemed not to show it. "Poor madame de Mailly is dead," she told her brother. "I am truly grieved, she was unfortunate, the King is touched by it," before adding, inconsequentially, "I forgot to ask you for white masks from Venice, they cost seven sols each, and so I believe that for a louis I could have them to resell. Bonsoir . . ." On the same day she told Madame de Lutzelbourg: "It is true, *grand'femme*, that it is a long time since I wrote to you. We have been constantly on the run before Lent, and since then, laziness has taken over. . . . The death of Madame de Mailly has caused the King pain; I was also distressed by it, I have always pitied her, she was unfortunate."

But d'Argenson claimed, of course, that Madame de Mailly was "regretted by all Paris, as a very good woman . . . this affection comes as much from the extreme hatred for her who replaced her as from her personal attributes . . ."

Would the king take communion at Easter? Would he be influenced by the death of Madame de Mailly? The answer soon came; Louis stayed at Versailles throughout Lent, but did not perform his Easter duties. The pious sighed, the enemies of the marquise gloomed, most of Parisian society shrugged, the court went on its way. But there was a more interesting development than the king's salvation; a wedding was to be held at Bellevue, a wedding which held some promising possibilities.

On April 25 eighteen-year-old Charlotte-Rosalie de Romanet was married to the comte de Choiseul-Beaupré, in a ceremony attended by all the ministers. The bride was the great-niece of Tournehem, and the niece by marriage of Madame d'Estrades. (Her mother, Marie-Charlotte d'Estrades, was the daughter of Tournehem's sister.) Such connections merited a splendid wedding, and a slew of rewards and preferments. The groom received a position of gentleman-in-waiting to the dauphin, and soon after, the very lucrative post of inspector general of the Infantry. The bride was named a lady-in-waiting to Madame Henriette.

Madame de Pompadour was delighted to be of service to Charlotte-Rosalie, who was pretty and high-spirited. The marquise's enemies immediately began to speculate as to whether the young comtesse had what it took to replace the favorite, but one astute observer, the comte de Stainville, the future duc de Choiseul and a distant relative of the bridegroom, thought her lacking in class: "She was fairly well-made with a common face and the air of a kept woman who has plenty of experience in the world. I have never seen such bold, one might even say loose, manners . . . I noticed the marked flirting in which she indulged with M. de Beauvau."

Stainville was very ambitious; but he had not yet succeeded in attracting the favor of the marquise. If he had thought that the new Madame de Choiseul-Beaupré had the necessary intelligence and toughness to capture the king, he would, no doubt, have allied himself with her. But he observed Madame de Pompadour closely, and, although at this stage he did not like her, he recognized her qualities of heart and mind. By comparison, Madame de Choiseul was a lightweight. As events unfolded, and Madame de Choiseul was pushed forward by others, he never doubted that she would fail.

D'Argenson, on the other hand, increasingly desperate to see the marquise fall from grace, found reason to hope: "She is young and pretty, and succeeds a great deal, above all with the king. One anticipates that the king could have some penchant for this young person, and that the marquise could perhaps be the dupe, however skillful she may be in the art of governing our monarch."

D'Argenson was not the only one to pin his hopes on the little countess. Madame d'Estrades also saw an opportunity. Despite all her obligations to Madame de Pompadour for bringing her to court, establishing her in the intimate circle of the king, promoting her to high office in the royal household, Madame d'Estrades's ambition was not satisfied. She sat every night on the king's left hand at supper, seemingly delighted to be there, content to bask in her friend's reflected glory, loyal and discreet. But in fact she ached to supplant the marquise, not in the king's bed, but as the power behind the throne. She began an affair with the comte d'Argenson, the minister of war and enemy of the marquise. They each believed that their alliance could topple the favorite and replace her with a more pliant mistress. Madame de Choiseul seemed perfect for the part they wished her to play. It is very difficult, even for those who disapprove of Madame de Pompadour, not to find Madame d'Estrades's conduct despicable.

If the excitement at court was centered on Madame de Choiseul, cultivated Parisians were much more moved by two publishing events that

were not only dazzling to their contemporary audience, but have remained so to this day. Montesquieu's *L'Esprit des Lois* was finally permitted to be published in France, after its original publication in Geneva in
1748 in two unsigned volumes. The French clergy had condemned it and
the government had forbidden its distribution in France. But in 1750 the
new director of the royal library, or chief censor, Chrétien-Guillaume
Lamoignon de Malesherbes, removed the prohibition, and twenty-two
editions were printed in fifteen months.*

L'Esprit des Lois advocated the separation of powers into legislative,
executive, and judicial branches, fairer land distribution, the end of farm-
ing tax collection out to private individuals, and of slavery. It made the
use of the term of *"despotisme"* fashionable ("in despotism one man alone,
without law and without rules, takes over everything by his will and caprices"), and was used by the *parlements* as a reference point, not always
accurately, in the years to come. It ignited a debate on what was the right
form of government, and this was to have far-reaching consequences.

The success of *L'Esprit des Lois* ("we find this work in the libraries of our scholars and on the dressing tables of our ladies," noted the
abbé Raynal) was followed in June by the appearance of Volume I of
the *Encyclopédie*, a handsome nine-hundred-page book embellished with
Cochin's frontispiece *"avec approbation et privilège du Roi,"* dedicated to the
comte d'Argenson, and prefaced by d'Alembert's luminous "Discours
préliminaire." The first entries in this groundbreaking alphabetical store-
house of knowledge set the tone; Diderot's article on authority talked of
the "power which comes from the consent of the people," and suggested
that the duty of obedience ceases with regard to a sovereign who breaks
this implicit contract.

Naturally, conservative clerics denounced the work. But Malesherbes
defended it, and Diderot, d'Alembert, and the other contributors to the

---

*Malesherbes was in charge of the book trade from 1750 to 1763, and
steadily refused to suppress modern, which was virtually the same thing as illegal,
literature. He opened loopholes to leave room for unofficial but inoffensive works
to circulate without receiving legal recognition by the state. In 1788 he wrote that
"a man who had read only books that originally appeared with the formal approval
of the government would be behind his contemporaries by nearly a century."

Encyclopédie joined Montesquieu as required reading for educated Frenchmen and women.

In May the marquise was finally able to move into her new rooms at
Versailles. The new apartment was of regal proportions. One entered
by way of the *cour royale,* through a vaulted passageway connecting the
courtyard to the gardens; two large antechambers led to the reception
room, or salon, its three windows overlooking the parterre du Nord.
Beyond the salon was the bedroom, with the bed in an alcove facing the
windows, a bathroom and boudoir en suite. And beyond the bedroom
were the marquise's private study, in which she gave audience to favored
courtiers, and, next door, the even more private *"cabinet-intérieur,"* a room
with red lacquered walls, where the marquise would often seclude herself
with the king. On the floor above were a warrant of rooms for her maids
and her wardrobe, as well as apartments for her doctor, Quesnay, and her
femme de chambre, Madame du Hausset.

Her rooms today are empty, and stripped of everything that might
bring to mind the memory of the marquise. The walls are painted white,
not paneled in delicate pastel colors, there are no silk upholstered arm-
chairs and chaise-longues, no porcelain figurines, no bouquets of flowers, no laughter or whispers, no life. But in the spring of 1751 these rooms
were about to become for Louis XV a sanctuary, and for the marquise a
headquarters.

The spring of that year was cold and wet. "I have rather a bad cold
which has given me a fever for twenty-four hours," the marquise told her
brother from Marly, "but I'm getting a little better. I am going down to
the salon this evening, which, by the way, is diabolical for colds; it is enor-
mously hot, then cold as you leave, and so one hears more coughing than
at Christmas. I count on going to Crécy on Monday until the day before
Pentecost, and to return there on the fourth until the ninth. I shall be in
despair if the weather is like today, that is, like February at its worst . . ."

In the same letter to Abel, she obliquely addresses the worrying state
of Tournehem's health. ". . . Monsieur de Tournehem still has a cold, his
health worries me, and his mood still more, for he has become terribly
gloomy. Be very friendly to him when you write, he is sensitive; that will

not be a burden for you, since you surely love him as much as he loves you." But she could not help looking to the future: "Monsieur de Tournehem awaits, they say, your return before he steps down; I hope that this is not so, but if it is, I would prevent it with all my power, firstly because it would kill him, and secondly because you are not ready. Although you have acquired knowledge, you are not yet twenty-five; if you can get to be twenty-eight or thirty before you take on this job, that would be better . . ."

Madame de Pompadour had been worried about her "*oncle*" for some time. Tournehem's workload at the *Bâtiments* was crushing, and increasing. He was responsible for new building at all the royal châteaux, and building was now almost a mania for the king. Tournehem was a conscientious man; but he was finding it hard to keep up the pace. In addition, he and the marquise were on poorer terms than formerly; she had become more demanding, more difficult. And the thought so coldly expressed in the previous letter, namely that Tournehem was required to live long enough to ensure that Abel was fully ready to take his job, had presumably crossed "*oncle*'s" mind as well, and contributed to his black moods.

Besides the worries about Tournehem, the marquise was concerned about her daughter, Alexandrine, who was convalescing at court after an illness. "I do not know when she will return to the convent," she told Abel. "Her nurse is dying of the same malady as your mother; it will be a dreadful loss for my daughter." But there was no time to grieve; "We are going to Compiègne for six weeks. We leave behind madame la Dauphine in very good health, and a very restless baby in her womb. God grant that all goes off well and that the child is a boy. I assure you, and you can believe it without difficulty, that I am tired of seeing only girls."

The marquise was in constant motion, always "*en fuite en avant*" (running here and there without being able to stop). She arrived exhausted at Compiègne after brief visits to La Muette and Crécy. Tournehem gave news of her to François Poisson: "Madame your daughter arrived here the day before yesterday at about eight thirty in the morning. She went straight to bed and stayed there until she took her bath. The King arrived, so I could not see her; but I learnt she was well recovered from her fatigue. Yesterday I saw her for a moment, when she left for the *maison de bois*; she looked wonderful. The King is very cheerful here and seems content. . . . Madame your daughter looks better than I have ever seen her."

Poor Tournehem. One wonders at his emotions, as he tenderly regarded this dazzling but vulnerable creature and shared his thoughts about "madame your daughter" with Poisson. The marquise, for her part, was just as concerned about him: "Monsieur de Tournehem is rather ill; it makes me tremble, they have bled him twice yesterday; he is however better today, the fever and the cough are much better . . ."

It probably did not help Tournehem's ailments that the marquise had demanded that, while the court was at Compiègne, the floor over her new bedroom at Versailles be taken up because the noise from above had disturbed her. She also required that all the mirrors be taken down and repolished, and two oval skylights be pierced above her bed to give more light to the interior corridor.

Madame de Pompadour's anxieties were compounded by the obvious attention the king was paying to Charlotte-Rosalie de Choiseul, who was now present at all the *petits soupers*. Although the perceptive Croÿ found her only "fairly pretty with a giddy air," others considered her "as beautiful as an angel, tender, discreet, faithful, a dish fit for a King." For Madame de Pompadour, trying to establish her relationship with the king on a new footing of friendship and companionship, this was an unwelcome, and unexpected, challenge.

On September 13 the dauphine gave birth to a male heir, the duc de Bourgogne. The birth took everyone by surprise, none of the great officers of state were present, and the dauphin had to rush around to find some guards and a porter to sign a document witnessing the august event. The king and the marquise were at Trianon, but returned to Versailles at once. "You can judge of my joy from my attachment to the King," the marquise wrote to Madame de Lutzelbourg. "I was so overcome that I fainted in the antechamber of Mme la Dauphine. Fortunately, they pushed me behind a curtain and I was seen only by Mme de Villars and Mme d'Estrades. Mme la Dauphine is doing wonderfully well, M. le duc de Bourgogne also. I saw him yesterday; he has his grandfather's eyes; that is not maladroit of him . . . This is as long a note as I can write, for we are eternally on the high road, in truth we are."

A week later the king, queen, dauphin, and Mesdames went in procession to Notre-Dame de Paris to celebrate a Te Deum; this royal procession traveled along the Champs-Elysées and the quays, but the crowd was thin, and there were very few cries of "*Vive le roi!*" Barbier thought that Louis XV seemed sad and serious . . . "Perhaps he was not content with his people." Croÿ recorded a "sad silence," and added that "perhaps there never was a public celebration which appeared to be done with less good heart . . . the consequence of the *vingtième,* the other impositions, the affairs of the Clergy and the *Parlement,* and many other equally unfortunate. If the King was aware of all this, it was matter for him to make serious reflections."

The marquise was said to be upset about the cool reception, and at the fact that she herself had not been included in the procession. (One assumes the reception would have been even colder had she been.) She was in ill-humor for another reason; ardently desiring a fine marriage for little Alexandrine, she had approached the duc de Richelieu for his son, the duc de Fronsac. "M. de Richelieu had responded that he was of course honored, but that "the mother of his son being from the house of Lorraine, he must first consult the Emperor, so as to know if he would approve this marriage or not." This was a snub. Mme de Pompadour had never liked Richelieu. From now on they would be at each others' throats, but in the most exquisitely polite way.*

In the meantime, Abel Poisson returned from Italy at the end of September. He had seen Turin, Genoa, Bologna, Rome, and Naples, had studied designs for a possible court theatre at Versailles, and had sent back to France examples of the work of the students at the French Academy in Rome, as well as specimens of Italian fruits, vegetables, and sausages.

His journey was considered a success, and his companions were thanked and would be soon rewarded.**

---

*Madame de Pompadour was not to be deterred from finding a suitably grand husband for Alexandrine. It was finally arranged that Alexandrine would marry the duc de Picquigny, son of the duc de Chaulnes, when she became twelve.

**Soufflot went back to Lyon and worked on the Grand Theatre there, but was soon recalled to Paris and made controller of the *Bâtiments* at the Louvre and at Sainte-Geneviève (now the Pantheon). Cochin became secretary of the Académie Royale de Peinture et de Sculpture.

However, Abel's homecoming was marred by the death of Tournehem's brother, and Madame de Pompadour's father-in-law, Hervé-
Guillaume Lenormand. And then came a greater sorrow. On November
17 Tournehem was taken ill at Etioles; he died there in the early morning of Friday, November 19, at the age of sixty-seven. The marquise permitted herself only this, to Madame de Lutzelbourg: "I feel only too much,
grand'femme, the misfortune of having a sensitive soul; my health has been
a little upset from the death of monsieur de Tournehem. I have been a
little better the last four days . . ."

It was an uneasy time for Madame de Pompadour. The king had
been morose for most of the year, anxious about the state of his soul, upset
with both his bishops and his *parlements*, agitated by the youthful charms
of Charlotte-Rosalie de Choiseul. The marquise had to endure not only
the presence of this giddy little flirt, but could also plainly see the hand
Madame d'Estrades was playing to push her niece forward. The base
ingratitude of this former bosom friend must have been a bitter blow.
But the *petits soupers* continued without any overt signs of strain, the king
seated each night between the marquise and Madame d'Estrades, everyone smiling agreeably.

Madame de Pompadour was sad and anxious. Tournehem was
gone, the king was distant, Madame d'Estrades disloyal. In her agitation, she turned to a man who would play an important, and sinister, role
in her life. Nicolas-René Berryer was the head of the Paris police, privy
to all the secrets and intrigues monitored by his spies and agents in the
capital. Berryer and the marquise made an alliance; he would keep her
informed of anything he might discover of an alarming or threatening
nature and together they would take the necessary steps to deal with it.
In practice, this meant the imprisonment of writers of *mauvais propos* or
even mere spreaders of gossip. "Nothing is as dangerous as the use she
makes of M. Berryer, *lieutenant de police*, who gives an account to this lady
of all that happens and is said in Paris: for all women, and above all this
one, are vindictive, dominated by passions, short on sense and probity."

Jeanne-Antoinette was constantly worried about her own safety.
In March she had written to the comte d'Argenson, the minister of the
interior, thus: "A priest just came here, Monsieur le Comte, who asked
for my maid. He gave her a bottle, saying that he took an interest in my

health, that it was an excellent potion, and that she should give me some without telling me. She had the prudence to refuse; he offered her ten thousand livres, but she wanted no part of it. When he saw her stubbornness, he asked her to keep quiet and went on his way. This has only just happened; I believe him gone, but in case he is not, one must have someone sent to all the inns in Versailles. Manon described him wonderfully despite the fear she felt."

The comte d'Argenson was the recipient of a steady stream of notes from the marquise, mostly on the subject of favors for her friends and relatives, but also often on the need to take action against those who spread malicious gossip through pamphlets and songs. "I believe it very essential to punish, and very severely, the authors of such mischief," she complained. "If M. Berryer cannot find these people, one must at least punish those one can find, for one must make an example of these infamous villains." She was taken at her word; those convicted of writing or distributing material considered seditious (a category covering a multitude of offenses) were savagely treated, often put in the Bastille for life. In one case, a certain chevalier de la Rochegreault, accused of writing a libel on Madame de Pompadour, was arrested in Holland, extradited to France, and Bastilled. He was still in prison thirty years later.

Madame de Pompadour may have thought she was thus protecting herself from danger; but in fact, such espionage served to increase her fears, making her even more ready to see plots and enemies everywhere. She was often manipulated by Berryer, who used her insecurities to follow his own agenda. He was one of the few in whom she placed complete confidence, and he would rise to high offices in the state because of her favor.

The opening of the mail by government bureaucrats was an acknowledged fact. Most prudent people did not entrust their secrets to the *Postes*. The office in charge of steaming open letters and resealing them inconspicuously—the *cabinet noir*—worked in secret. Neither the names of its members nor the whereabouts of its office were revealed, but they were feared. Louis XV had always been fascinated with the dirty laundry their work uncovered, especially the sexual peccadillos of seemingly respectable people, particularly the clergy. He pored over his weekly packets of extracts with furtive pleasure. Now Madame de Pompadour,

nervous and suspicious, began to make use of the same unsavory information. The department of the *Postes* became one in which she liked to
place her own people at every level, and, in due course, she would be as
well informed as the king, and perhaps better.

A more beneficent impulse caused her to act on behalf of one of her
oldest friends. She used her influence to have the abbé de Bernis named
ambassador to the Venetian Republic. The marquise had told Pâris-
Duverney that she had "not yet been able to do anything for the abbé de
Bernis, he is the only one of my friends of whom this is true." And Bernis
himself had been disappointed at his failure to obtain preferment. He had
begun to wonder if all his assiduous courting of the royal mistress had been
in vain. "I do not wish to remain the complaisant confidant of the marquise," he complained to Madame de La Ferté-Imbault, before proceeding to a delicate critique of his former pupil. "She is very ardent and very
ambitious, but she believes everything they tell her, and she has not the
experience of the world to separate friends from courtiers." Bernis was
ready for an opportunity to show his worth. "I wish to enter the department of Foreign Affairs; if I do well, I shall deserve a reward for my work,
and if I succeed, it will be my own fault if I do not make a little money."

Now his prayers had been answered. The posting to Venice was not
the most senior embassy, far from it, but it had many advantages, one of
which being the renowned city's famously free and easy social life. Bernis
was gratified, but others did not take his appointment as seriously. The
writer Jean-François Marmontel wondered if Bernis would cut a swathe
through the Venetian beauties. D'Argenson was sarcastic about "this *bel
esprit* of the Académie, this languorous abbé, who writes some pretty verses.
. . . But madame de Pompadour will help him, as will the Pâris brothers.
These are the powers who have brought him to prominence."

As 1751, Holy Year, drew to an end, Louis XV made an abrupt and
surprising decision. Having negotiated secretly with his bishops over the
vingtième, and waited patiently for them to show some cooperation, he
came to the conclusion that the whole matter must be dropped. On December 23 an edict of the council suspended the tax on the Church. (At
the quinquennial assembly of the clergy in 1755 this suspension was tac-
itly transformed into a definitive exemption.) Opinion in Paris was predictably hostile. "Behold a good idea gone awry," lamented Barbier, "one

will not easily recover. They say that M. de Machault has been ill these past days. Perhaps chagrin has played a part."

Louis XV, who respected Machault, named him Keeper of the Seals and tried to make it clear that he did not regard the failure of the attempt to tax the church as the fault of his minister. In fact, it was the king who wanted to abandon the effort, knowing himself to be in a state of sin and unable to end it, trying to make amends by appeasing the Church and in so doing, please his family. But he seemed not to be anxious to publicize his change of heart; the suspension of the plan was revealed in a document with a very limited circulation. The consequences were heavy; without the clergy's contribution, the revenues expected from the *vingtième* would not be enough to reduce the deficit, or achieve a real modernization of the system.

This year cost France dearly. The level of spending on the King's *petits voyages* and building reached new heights. The finances, poised to recover after the years of war, were ruined anew. The failure of the tax on the clergy at the end of the year was another heavy blow.

The king's appeasement of the clergy was significant. D'Argenson, however, was more interested in the gossip that Madame de Pompadour was about to be banished, her place taken by Madame de Choiseul. "What a triumph for Madame d'Estrades!" But d'Argenson could not quite convince himself that the days of the marquise were numbered: "She is more beautiful than ever, and has a contented air," he noted dolefully.

There was better news for d'Argenson at the party held at Versailles to celebrate the birth of the duc de Bourgogne, at which he claimed that "what one remarked principally was the change and gloomy sadness in Madame de Pompadour. One saw there, they say, something funereal. The King looked at her with difficulty, and turned his back on her as soon as he saw her. The grande parure she wore augmented these appearances of change and disgrace, of which one does not know the cause."

The party was a rather depressing affair. A cold wind destroyed part of the illuminations; the candles in the Hall of Mirrors were placed too high, which made the women look old. Madame de Pompadour did not need such unflattering shadows to remind her that, in comparison to her youthful rival, she was no longer at the height of her beauty. She was fully aware that she had to find new ways to retain her sway over the king. But, as d'Argenson himself was compelled to remark, "she made fun of the credulity of those who believed in the King leaving her, and she was very sure of herself." The marquise would rather die than give her enemies the satisfaction of seeing her downcast. Whatever the effort, and it was considerable, she would present herself as the serene and untouchable, if uncrowned, Queen of France.

Chapter 12

"The marquise swears by all that's Holy that there is nothing physical between her and the King."

On February 2, 1752, Madame Henriette fell ill at Trianon. Obliged to ask her father's permission to return to Versailles, she requested an audience, but, feverish and unwell, had to wait for a long time while the king worked with the prince de Conti. At Versailles, her condition did not improve; on February 7 the king spent a long time at her bedside, and came out of her room in very black humor. He hunted for a short time, but was clearly very worried. Henriette was Louis XV's favorite daughter, a gentle, shy young woman, delicately pretty, with a love of music. Louis could not hide his anxiety. A trip to Bellevue was canceled. And then, on February 10, Madame Henriette died. She was twenty-four years old.

In the awful aftermath of this death, as, according to royal precedent, the body was opened and the heart removed, Louis fled to Trianon, so devastated that he left no orders about who should follow him, overcome by grief. Croÿ noted that "his natural tenderness, and the particular affection he felt for this daughter, whom he cherished above all, petrified him."

Everyone was left to make their own arrangements. Madame de Pompadour, scenting danger, wasted no time: "Madame la marquise went to Trianon alone, on her own account, two hours after the King, and went into seclusion. She was right to fear the King's black mood, that being afflicted as he was, he might let himself become remorseful." And d'Argenson noted: "Since she shows great courage in the office she fills for the monarch, she suddenly made her decision like a great captain; she left for Trianon, had the King informed that she was there: was shown in: took possession of the principal apartment, even though the Queen was there; the latter lodged where she could." As usual, the queen, even though in her own torment of anguish, was completely ignored.

Louis remained at Trianon while the pomp and circumstance of the royal funeral unrolled in Paris. On February 17, at seven in the evening, his daughter's body, which had been lying in state at the Tuileries, was taken to Saint-Denis. Along the rue Saint-Honoré, out by the rue de la Ferronnerie went the casket, preceded by sixty paupers marching, two by two, followed by troops of the black and grey musketeers, light horse, household troops, the hearse draped in white and silver, covered with ermine.

Louis XV was, as Croÿ had perceived, petrified with grief. Stoically, he hunted at Saint-Germain, taking some soup with his entourage, saying not a word; in silence, he drove back to Versailles; mute, he supped with his intimates. No one could divert him.

All through Lent, the King remained melancholy and sad, keeping himself in seclusion, supping only *en petit particulier;* the court saw him only on Sundays. He continued his flight from himself, even more restless than usual, going from place to place in search of distraction; he was absent from Versailles every week from Tuesday to Friday, spending a week at Trianon, another at Bellevue, then Choisy, and another week at Bellevue.

Louis also had to deal with the anguish of his daughter Adélaïde. She had been sharing a suite of rooms at Versailles with her late sister; now she refused to return to those rooms where Henriette had died. Sympathetic to her grief, unable, as always, to stand up to a woman in tears, Louis made a decision which has been much deplored. In order to provide Madame Adélaïde with rooms befitting her rank, the Ambassadors' Staircase, the grandiose marble triumph of the art of Le Vau and Lebrun, was to be demolished. The monumental staircase was rarely used and had become an impediment to creating new living space in the vast but cramped château, but the planned destruction was badly received. Croÿ was sad: "And so they are beginning to demolish the beautiful marble staircase and to erase the beautiful paintings by Lebrun, so that, without losing any time, they can make four suites so that in two years the King can have, so to speak, his four daughters under his hand." Luynes shook his head: "They are completely destroying that beautiful staircase."

In the meantime, Adélaïde moved next door to the marquise as an interim solution. Court gossip, always eager to speculate on the favorite's imminent downfall, found reason to hope that the king might turn to his daughter for company, rather than the marquise. Adélaïde, now twenty, was a high-spirited, passionate young woman, very attached to her father, and very concerned to detach him from *"maman putain"* and return him to the bosom of his family. She was the unquestioned leader of her sisters, and more energetic by far than her brother, the dauphin. But she never managed to become a credible threat to Madame de Pompadour; the marquise, who had more dangerous enemies, always tried to treat Adélaïde and her sisters with kindness.

Madame de Pompadour kept the king under a close watch. With great difficulty, she persuaded him that plays should start again at the theatre at Bellevue after Easter. But gradually, "the court, which has been very much afflicted, and the mistress very anxious, resumed its ordinary course. Her influence remains as strong as it has ever been." The marquise had succeeded in restoring the king's morale; her ascendancy over his spirit remained intact. But, on the wider front, she could not extricate him from the seemingly insoluble disputes between church and *parlement*, which grew more virulent that spring.

The archbishop of Paris was still refusing to allow his clergy to give absolution to those who were dying without a *billet de confession*. Infuriated, the Paris *parlement* drew up an edict claiming for itself the right to assure citizens the opportunity to take the sacraments, whether they were Jansenist or not. This edict was printed in large numbers and sent round the kingdom. On April 29 the king rebuked the *parlement* for meddling in spiritual matters and required them to refer cases involving such matters to ecclesiastical courts; but he also reminded the clergy that they must abide by the canons recognized in the kingdom. He then announced his intention to appoint a commission of prelates and magistrates to investigate "the new problems."

"This is serious," noted the excellent Barbier. "The greatest part of Paris hates and despises the Archbishop, who is a troublemaker, and who has caused all this trouble. Liberty is dear to all men, and one does not like at all this constraint of the *billets de confession*. People are extremely outraged that the clergy pays nothing at all of the taxes with which other subjects are charged; but *parlement* is profiting from these circumstances to speak with boldness and to attribute to itself a power which, in reality, it has never had."

At the same time, another dispute broke out when volume two of the *Encyclopédie* was published and deemed by the bishops to contain a heretical article. At the request of the archbishop of Paris, the king's council banned the book, and it remained banned until May, when Malesherbes, the chief censor, prevailed upon the king and his ministers to allow the book to reappear with "tacit permission." According to d'Argenson, "Madame de Pompadour and some ministers asked d'Alembert and Diderot to resume work, while observing a necessary reserve on everything concerning religion and authority." The marquise took an interest in this great work, albeit at a distance, and at this stage tried to be as supportive as she could. Her views would harden over time, when she began to think of the *encyclopédistes* as a threat to stability, but she would never completely lose sympathy for the cause.

In May 1752 the king went to Marly, trying to forget the quarrels of his church and his magistrates, and the troublesome *encyclopédistes*. But it was rather a cheerless voyage. The marquise was unwell and had to be bled twice for a sore throat and fever. The comte de Stainville was there and recorded the king's furious passion for faro (he lost 3,000 louis to the marquis de Livry, a record) and for wine. "Madame de Pompadour, who was the King's sincere friend, did everything she could to divert him from his passion for gambling but could not manage to. It was the same as regards champagne, which Louis XV drank beyond measure so that his royal majesty was sometimes compromised upon leaving table. It followed that the King, who was still used to listening to what was said in the council, and sometimes joining in the discussion, lost all concern for the affairs of the kingdom." Choiseul wrote this in the bitterness of exile; Louis XV never entirely lost his sense of duty, however sporadic and fleeting it was.

Apart from gambling and drinking, the king was also ogling Charlotte-Rosalie de Choiseul, but Croÿ detected no sign that the young woman was "giving madame la marquise umbrage, as they have said." On the contrary, Madame de Pompadour dissimulated all her concern, presiding every evening in the *petits cabinets* with her accustomed poise and seeming serenity.

In July a young man called Jean-Nicolas Dufort de Cheverny arrived at Compiègne. He had been named to the post of *introducteur des ambassadeurs*, which involved escorting foreign envoys to and from audiences with the royal family, and which gave him a privileged position at court. Dufort was only twenty-one, an attractive young man, fancying himself a connoisseur of women, and very eager to record his impressions of the favorite. "Mademoiselle Poisson, madame Lenormand, marquise d'Etiolles de Pompadour, whom every man would have wished to have for his mistress, was tall for a woman, without being too tall. A round face, all her features regular, a superb skin, very well-made, superb hands and arms, her eyes were more pretty than large, but of a fire, a spirituality, a brilliancy I have seen in no other woman . . . she effaced all the prettiest women at court."

Another young man, the up-and-coming writer Jean-François Marmontel, saw Madame de Pompadour at about this time, and has left an amusing account of her toilette and its rituals: "A little poem I wrote on the establishment of the *Ecole Militaire*, a monument raised to the glory of the King by the Pâris brothers, intimate friends of Mme de Pompadour; this little poem, I say, caught her attention and placed me in a favorable light. The abbé de Bernis and Duclos used to go together to see her every Sunday, and as they were both friends of mine, I went along with them. This woman to whom the greatest in the Kingdom and the Princes of the Blood themselves paid court at her toilette, a simple bourgeoise who had had the weakness to wish to please the King and the misfortune to succeed, was in her elevation the best woman in the world. She received the three of us familiarly, although with very delicate nuances of distinction. To one she said with a light air and crisply: 'Bonjour, Duclos'; to the other, with a friendlier air and tone: 'Bonjour, abbé,' sometimes giving him a little tap on the cheek; and to me, more seriously and in a lower voice: 'Bonjour, Marmontel.'"

Marmontel was angling for a "regular and undemanding" job, aware that his talents as poet and playwright might not be enough to guarantee him a carefree existence. Madame de Pompadour did not take his hint. "She told me that I was born to be a man of letters: that my distaste for poetry was merely a lack of courage: that instead of leaving the field,

I must make my comeback as Voltaire had done more than once, and pick myself up from failure with a success."

And so Marmontel started his play *Sesostris:* "She often asked where my new play was; she wished to read it when it was finished, and did so with so much attention that she made detailed criticisms. But the whole seemed good to her. When the manuscript was in her hands, I presented myself one Sunday at her toilette in the salon, crowded with courtiers come from the King's Rising. She was surrounded, and either because there was someone there whom she disliked, or because she wished to take a diversion from the boredom which all this caused her, she said as soon as she saw me: 'I have something to say to you,' and leaving her toilette went into her cabinet with me following her. It was simply to give me back my manuscript, on which she had penciled notes. It took five or six minutes for her to show me the notes and explain her criticisms. The circle of courtiers had remained standing round her dressing table and waiting. She returned, and I, hiding my manuscript, went modestly to my place. I thought I knew the effect such a singular incident would have, but the impression it made on the minds of those present went far beyond my expectation. All eyes were fixed on me, on all sides people gave me little imperceptible salutes, gentle smiles of friendship. And before I left the salon I had been invited to dinner for every night of the coming week and beyond. A titled man with whom I had dined sometimes at Mme de La Popelinière's, le M. D. S., finding himself next to me, took my hand and said softly: 'You do not wish then to recognize your old friends?' I bowed, confused at his servility, and said to myself: 'Oh! What is favor then, if it's mere shadow gives me such a singular importance?'"

At the end of July 1752 the dauphin left Compiègne for Versailles; on arrival there, after a journey of almost twelve hours, he became feverish, and took to his bed. Almost at once smallpox was diagnosed. The king and court returned in haste and kept an anxious vigil over the dauphin until his recovery was announced on August 17. There followed an outburst of organized rejoicing, including fireworks at Versailles and in Paris, and at Crécy, where the marquise dowered the marriages of eight girls of the village. She also gave a party with fireworks at Bellevue, and another at Brimborion, a little villa in the gardens there.

Madame de Pompadour declared that she had been "very frightened by the danger to Monsieur le Dauphin." "One does not doubt it," remarked the duc de Croÿ, "for speculation had it that, if he had followed his sister in less than a year, that would have given the king many things to reflect upon." It was always the hope of the devout, and of those opposed to the marquise, that Louis XV would in the end turn to his family for solace and company. It never happened.

Nothing, it seemed, was allowed to interfere with the stately progress of the court to Fontainebleau where, after the five-hour journey from Choisy, they arrived on September 26. Madame Infante joined the court from Parma, Crébillon's *Pyrrhus* was performed, the hunting and shooting were *très considérable.* Everything seemed as usual.

On October 12 the king made a surprise announcement; he was awarding to Madame de Pompadour the rank and title of duchess, "wishing to give marks of his particular consideration to her person, according her a rank which distinguishes her from the other ladies of the court."

The honor was a great one; the details centered, as was usual at the French court, on matters of seating. As a duchess, Madame de Pompadour could now sit (but only on a stool, or *tabouret*) at the public supper of the king and queen, in the presence of the dauphin and Mesdames, and at all public ceremonies. More importantly, it signified her continuing favor with the king. (Madame de Pompadour never used the title of *duchesse*, but assumed all the privileges of the rank, including the ducal coronet on her coat-of-arms and on her carriages.)

In the evening of October 17 the ceremony of the *prise de tabouret* by Madame de Pompadour took place in the king's study. The duchesse-marquise was followed by Madame d'Estrades and Madame de Choiseul. It was, or should have been, a moment of triumph. And yet there were many questions in the air. The conspicuous presence of Madame de Choiseul, the young contender, and of Madame d'Estrades, her aunt, raised some eyebrows. Was the ceremony the prelude to disgrace, a sham designed to send Madame de Pompadour away with a measure of dignity? Or had something occurred in the intimacy of the king's rooms which propelled him to act so suddenly to appease his friend?

A plot was hatching that autumn at Fontainebleau. The ascension of Madame de Choiseul was about to be consummated. According to an account furnished to Marmontel by an eyewitness, the young woman came breathlessly to find her aunt, Madame d'Estrades, in the rooms of the comte d'Argenson, where Madame de Pompadour's doctor, François Quesnay, also happened find himself. "It is done, I am loved, she is going to be sent away; he has given me his word," she cried. In the rejoicing, Quesnay remained silent. "Monsieur," said Madame d'Estrades, "nothing changes for you, and we hope that you will stay with us." "But, Madame!" replied Quesnay, "I have been attached to Madame de Pompadour in her prosperity, I shall continue to be so in her disgrace." Quesnay left; the conspirators were discomfited. "I know him, he is not a man who will betray us," said Madame d'Estrades. And Quesnay, although deeply disturbed, kept his peace.

While this was going on, the court was awaiting the première of a new opera, Jean-Jacques Rousseau's *Le Devin du Village*. This charming pastoral music drama of true love had been given its first rehearsal at the Paris Opera in June, and from the first note of the first rehearsal, when the soprano sings,

> *"J'ai perdu tout mon bonheur,*
> *J'ai perdu mon serviteur . . ."*
> ("I have lost all my happiness,
> I have lost my young lover . . .")

it was clear that the work was destined to be a prodigious success. The head of the *Menus-Plaisirs*, the department of the government responsible for court entertainments, demanded that the piece have its premiere at Fontainebleau, not in Paris, and all concerned had to yield to the royal command. October 18 was the date selected for the first performance.

On the day of the dress rehearsal (and of Madame de Pompadour's *prise de tabouret*), Rousseau traveled to Fontainebleau with the great actress Marie Fel, who was to play Colette. (The leading French tenor of his generation, Pierre Jelyotte, played Colin, despite being much too old for the part.) Rousseau recorded his impressions of the première the next day.

He was seated in a box facing that of the king and Madame de Pompadour and was very nervous and uncomfortable, feeling extremely out of place. "But, whether it was the effect of the master's presence, or the natural disposition of hearts, I noticed nothing but kindness and good nature in the curiosity of which I was the object. . . . I trembled like a child as the program began. The piece was very badly performed by the actors, but very well sung and executed by the musicians. From the first scene, which truly is of a touching naivety, I heard rising from the boxes a murmur of surprise and applause almost unheard of in this kind of piece. . . . One does not clap in the presence of the king: that meant that one heard the whole piece, to its advantage and that of the author. . . . I heard around me the murmuring of women who seemed to me as beautiful as angels, and who were saying to each other in whispers: 'This is charming, this is ravishing, there is not a sound which does not speak to the heart' . . . I have seen plays which excite more lively transports of admiration, but never an intoxication so complete, so sweet, so touching, reigning throughout a spectacle, and above all at Court on its first representation. Those who have seen such a thing should remember; for the effect is unique."

That evening Rousseau received a message from the duc d'Aumont to the effect that he should come to the château of Fontainebleau at eleven the next morning to be presented to the king. "There would be a pension for me and the King wished to tell me of it himself."

But Rousseau, with that often infuriating mix of pride and obstinacy, was too shy to appear before the king and, after a night of anguish and perplexity, fled early the next day. Jelyotte wrote reproachfully: "You were wrong, Monsieur, to have left in the midst of your triumphs. . . . The King, who, as you know, does not like music, has been singing all day with the worst voice in the Kingdom, "*J'ai perdu mon serviteur, j'ai perdu tout mon bonheur*,' and he has asked for a second performance of your opera within a week."

As Madame de Pompadour listened to Rousseau's haunting melodies, was she aware of the coming triumph of Madame de Choiseul, and perhaps resigned to it, to the end of the struggle? Had the honor of being created a duchess been her last? Would Louis XV, in his usual fashion, overwhelm her with attentions before delivering the coup de grâce?

The answer is no. The comte de Stainville has left a compelling account of what happened next. He relates that, in the latter part of

October at Fontainebleau, Madame de Choiseul showed him some compromising letters from the king; alarmed and, he claims, concerned at
the dishonor to the family name, Stainville persuaded the young woman
to leave court to avoid a scandal; she was three months pregnant, and he
advised her to stay in Paris until her confinement. The young woman
seemed to agree.

A few days later, Stainville was present when the marquis de Gontaut,
his brother-in-law, and a close friend of the marquise, was deploring the
distress the Choiseul affair was causing her. Stainville could not resist
claiming that he could set everyone's mind at rest with one word (that
is, that the troublemaker was to leave court). That evening he was summoned to see Madame de Pompadour. The marquise wept, beseeching
him to tell her what he knew. He did so, and, once again, unable to resist
the opportunity to show how much he knew, added that he had seen a
letter from the king, even quoting part of it to her. The king was heard
returning from Evensong, Stainville effaced himself. "I felt uneasy about
what I had just done. . . . The sight of Madame de Pompadour in tears
had excited my head a little."

The marquise knew her man. She immediately confronted Louis
with the fact that she knew the contents of a letter he had written to
Madame de Choiseul, demanded that he explain himself, drew on all her
theatrical instincts to play the part of the woman wronged. Louis was
reduced to stammering an apology and begging forgiveness. That night
he saw Madame de Choiseul; he reproached her with her indiscretion
and told her she must leave . . . "perhaps you will be able to return later."
But Madame de Choiseul realized that the game was up and took the
only revenge she could: She told the king that it was Stainville who had
betrayed her trust. Louis, humiliated and frustrated, bore to the comte a
secret, strong, and lasting dislike.

Madame de Choiseul was not banished completely; she still came
to court for her week of duty with Mesdames. But she and her husband
were placed under surveillance in Paris, no doubt on the orders of Madame de Pompadour to her creature, Berryer.*

---

*Madame de Choiseul died following childbirth on June 2, 1753, five days
after delivering a daughter. She was twenty-one years old.

One need not accept Stainville's account completely in order to trust its broad outlines. One might be skeptical, for instance, that he saw no opportunity for advancement in betraying his cousin, that his only concern was the family's good name. He was an ambitious man: in 1752 he badly wanted an ambassadorship; he had thought of Madrid and of Stockholm; he had even discussed Warsaw with the marquise. He was not one of her intimates, as she thought him too sarcastic and cutting to be a success at the *petits soupers* and did not invite him. But they each recognized in the other intelligence, subtlety, and willpower. If the means of their reconciliation were sordid, its fruits would be significant.

With the plot of Madame d'Estrades and the comte d'Argenson a failure, the atmosphere in the *petits cabinets* was tense. But nothing changed, on the surface. Madame d'Estrades maintained her place in the king's intimate circle; she and the marquise were polite, even friendly. But each watched the other for the next move in the game. Madame d'Estrades remained determined to gain the upper hand; Madame de Pompadour dissimulated her feelings with the ease of a gifted actress. The score remained unsettled.

Judging from Madame de Pompadour's letters to Poisson later in October nothing serious had happened at Fontainebleau that autumn. "It is not nice of you, my dear father, not to have given a sign of life for a century. I have had a fever for ten days, the King has given me the honors of a duchess, all these events mean nothing to you. . . . I see that little Alexandrine has chased Reinette from your heart. I am sending back her letters, for it appears that you make a great fuss of them. . . . Bonsoir, my very dear father, I am overwhelmed with visits and I still have about sixty letters to write."

A few weeks later, from Bellevue: "I have had your Alexandrine come to La Muette yesterday, my dear father, she was in good health. However you have to reproach yourself with having caused her indigestion. Why must grandpapas always spoil their grandchildren? I find that she has become much plainer, but as long as she is not shocking, I will be satisfied, for I am very far from wishing for her any extraordinary beauty. That only serves to make enemies of the whole female sex which, with the friends of the said ladies, makes up two thirds of the world. . . . Bonjour, my dear father, I am well, be calm, and above all never believe what you hear . . ."

None of the court diarists breathed a word of the affair of Madame de Choiseul. The marquise had survived a brush with disaster; but only the abrupt disappearance of Madame de Choiseul from the *petits soupers* told the story. The marquis d'Argenson, however, knew the details from his brother. "Madame de Pompadour has chased from *chez elle* the little Choiseul, like a little whore who behaved badly and flirted with the King . . ." D'Argenson was losing hope that the marquise would ever be vanquished; and now he had cause to worry about his brother, who had been part of the conspiracy, and upon whom the vengeance of the marquise would surely fall.

If the comte d'Argenson and Madame d'Estrades were the great losers of the events at Fontainebleau, the comte de Stainville was the great winner. Very soon the marquise was on easy terms with Stainville, joking with him about her constant, but always unavailing, plans to find a wife for Abel. Her choice had fallen upon a Mademoiselle de Chimay, another distant relative of Stainville's; "I have been paid back for taking care of your little cousins; in spite of that, of all the girls of quality offered to me, she is the one who tempts me the most because of the good qualities she shows. . . . Tell me what you know of this young girl, of whom everyone agrees to speak well. It being understood that I shall never hear talk of the rest of the family."*

The marquise, having surmounted the crisis at Fontainebleau, sounded confident and energized. Louis XV, on the other hand, now that his pathetic attempts to escape the psychological domination of his mistress had failed, ceded to her even more of his authority. His self-confidence wavering, his taste for work and duty soured, he began to rely more and more on Madame de Pompadour's judgment and willingness to help him shoulder the burden. Although there was no overt change, the comte d'Argenson was despondent, telling his brother, with some exaggeration, that "the mistress is Prime Minister, and is becoming more and more despotic, such as a favorite has never been in France." He recognized that he had lost a significant battle, and that Madame de Pom-

---

*The marquise never succeeded in finding a wife for her brother. He stubbornly refused all the enticing candidates offered and married only after his sister's death.

padour had won a significant victory. "She believes herself Queen," he remarked bitterly, "having dreamt one night that it was so."

Madame de Pompadour might have been the influential friend and adviser of the king, but she was no longer the triumphant beauty of 1745. She had to face a new stage in her life, to decide if she wanted to keep her powerful position at court and, if so, whether she wanted to dedicate to the maintenance of it all the efforts which would be necessary. She told herself that the king needed her, that he would sink into depression if she left; possibly so, but in her heart and despite all her protestations to the contrary, she gave short shrift to any thought of abandoning her post. Her decision was made; she would defend herself without pity and without scruples. From now on, her life would be, as she was to say, "a perpetual combat."

Madame de Pompadour's complaints about court life must be taken with a pinch of salt. She chose this way of life, remained in it, and tenaciously clung to it at cost to her health and, in the end, to her life. Every day she had the exquisite pleasure of bestowing favors on the greatest in the land who prostrated themselves before her—and every day the even more exquisite pleasure of refusing her gracious help to others. Those who did not absolutely accept her primacy and grovel were pursued with a rancor which never lessened. Even those who performed the obligatory obeisances at her toilette could lose her good will in an instant if she suspected them of making use of any other channel but her.

The duc de Croÿ, for example, was a most assiduous courtier; but when he once approached the comte d'Argenson for help, instead of the marquise, he found himself later treated by her with icy coldness. It took all his protestations of fidelity and adoration to regain her good graces, and he never repeated his mistake. There were many others in his case, and, in the end, all other avenues to the king were closed off.

Chapter 13

"It is his heart I want! All these little girls with no education will not take it from me. I would not be so calm, if I saw some pretty woman of the court or the capital trying to conquer it."

On New Year's Day 1753 Count von Kaunitz, the Austrian ambassador, left for Vienna. He had been successful in establishing a warm personal relationship with the king, but particularly with the marquise, and he had made a point of seeking an audience with her to say farewell. They agreed to continue to write to each other. The court of Vienna would now have access to those at the highest levels at the court of France. "If Madame de Pompadour mixed in foreign affairs," Kaunitz wrote, "I have reason to believe that she would not render us bad services; she has a great deal of good will, and some confidence in me." There was also reason to believe that the marquise had listened to the Pâris brothers, still very much at her side, and accepted their conviction that a rapprochement with Austria would be a good thing. The Pâris brothers, the leading members of the *"clan Pompadour,"* were still fully engaged in making sure that their ideas controlled French policy. Madame de Pompadour herself was their most potent weapon.

Kaunitz delivered a few perceptive observations as he left France. He noted that the marquise was "killing herself" trying to amuse the King, inviting more and more people to the *petits soupers* to stave off his ever-threatening ennui, putting up with his frequent rudeness in return. *"Quel vieux conte du marais fait-elle là?"* ("What boring old wives' tale is she telling now?"), Louis remarked one evening to the company at large. Kaunitz's conclusion was that the marquise had to work very hard to preserve her position: "It requires more skill than one might think to feign being madly in love without making oneself ill." It is a grim picture.

At court, word had spread about the intrigue of Madame de Choiseul. "I found the Marquise at her toilette, more influential than ever, and still very pretty indeed," noted Croÿ. "When one spoke of the King's infidelity, everyone took her [the marquise's] part, for, since there must be a mistress, one is more content with this one than others of whom one fears worse. The most there is to reproach her with is the considerable expenses for trifles, and the embarrassment that seems to have caused the finances. All the rest speaks in her favor. She is a patron of the arts, and in general does good and no evil. . . . One never speaks at Court of the great affairs of the Archbishop and *parlement,* which are causing so much stir elsewhere."

The reason for the newest strife was, of course, the dispute over the *billets de confession.* When a nun in a Jansenist community in Paris was refused the sacraments, *parlement* enjoined the archbishop to have this scandal stopped; the archbishop replied that this was a spiritual issue, and that he owed an account of his actions only to God; *parlement* started to draw up *"grandes remonstrances"* against what they saw as abuses of ecclesiastical and royal authority. They went to work on them with enthusiasm. There was a whiff of sedition in the air. (But perhaps the discord between Church and *parlement* was not making such a stir, even in Paris. There, the talk was of the visiting Italian opera troupe who were performing Pergolesi's *La Serva Padrona* and igniting a quarrel—known as the "Affair of the Buffoons"—over the relative merits of French and Italian music.)

The king seemed sublimely indifferent to clergy, *parlement,* and Buffoons. The *petits voyages* took him to La Muette in January; this was the closest he ever came to Paris, but it never occurred to the king to go there to see his subjects. Madame de Pompadour also seemed unaffected by Parisian turmoil. "I have had your Fanfan come today to La Muette," she told François Poisson. "I have even dined with her, her health is good." Poisson had raised the question of money with her: "I have nothing to add to what I have told you on more than one occasion; I am much less rich than I was when I was in Paris. I still have funds in the hands of Monsieur de Montmartel; they are not very much, because I have lent almost all my money for the *Ecole Militaire;* but I can only offer what I have. I am worried about a writing desk and a

large goblet from Vincennes, which left more than a fortnight ago by
the wagon for Marigny; I cannot conceive what can have happened to
them . . ."

François Poisson never ceased to importune the marquise on behalf of any and all their relatives. He was particularly persistent for
Abel. The last known letter from Madame de Pompadour to Poisson
sounds a familiar note: "There has never been a question of the post of
Provost of Paris for my brother, neither he nor I have the funds required; this post is very expensive, brings in little, and does not make
him a greater seigneur than he is; but it is very true that the public will
have every post which becomes vacant given to him; they have been
used to insatiable people. I would be very annoyed to have that infamous character, or that my brother had it . . ."

The clear-headed marquise was, of course, perfectly aware that she
was regarded as an "infamous character," that she was perceived as a
leech, a spendthrift, and worse. She gave the impression, however, of
being unaffected by such insults, just as she seemed impervious to the
king's infidelities, Madame d'Estrades's plotting, the dangers she saw
everywhere. But the constant strain under which she lived, the dissimu-
lation and self-control necessary for her survival, worked insidiously upon
her. Frequent migraines continued to plague her. One night at La Muette,
while she kept to her room, Croÿ saw the dauphin and Mesdames, one
after the other, send their servants for news of her. The next day, however, she left for Bellevue. The relentless schedule she and the king had
inflicted upon themselves continued relentlessly. She never allowed her
indisposition to get in the way of the king's pleasure.

At Bellevue, she had the opportunity to do what she loved most,
to exert her influence on behalf of a friend in distress. Jean-François
Marmontel, whom she had encouraged to pursue a literary career, had
dutifully finished his play *Seostris;* unfortunately it was a resounding
flop at its first performance on February 5, 1753. "I wrote at once to
Mme de Pompadour to tell her of my misfortune and urgently renew my
request that she help me obtain useful employment. She was at table with
the king when she received my letter, and after the king gave her permission to open it, she exclaimed, 'The new play is a failure. And do you
know, sire, who tells me this? The author himself. The unhappy young

man! I should like to have a position to offer him at this moment to console him.' Her brother, who was at this supper, told her that he had a
position of secretary at the *Bâtiments* if she wished it for him. 'Ah! Write
to him tomorrow, I beg you.' And the king seemed satisfied that she was
granting me this consolation."

Marmontel had landed his sinecure; but he would not be completely
free from stress. Abel Poisson was a difficult man to work for. He had,
according to Marmontel, "an unstable sense of self-esteem, was easily
offended, excessively susceptible to mistrust and suspicions. A decent
man, enlightened, upright, of rare probity, but his moods spoiled everything and made him often rude and brusque." Abel knew that the courtiers made fun of him behind his back, that he was regarded as a low-born
interloper, attending the king's suppers only through his sister's influence. It was not surprising that he was moody and sarcastic; even with
his formidable sister he remained intractable, refusing time and again
the desirable marriages she placed before him. He preferred to concentrate on his work at the *Bâtiments*, for which he had real talent, and to
preserve as much independence as he could.

It was only a short time before Louis XV, deprived of Madame de
Choiseul's presence in his bed, turned to other distractions. Disturbed
by his own sexual appetites, intimidated by Madame de Pompadour, he
proposed an arrangement. (Or perhaps it was proposed for him.) He
would take his pleasure with young girls (young, so that they would be
virgins and thus free of the curse of venereal disease), but discreetly, and
in such a way as to preserve the marquise's position by his side. Madame
de Pompadour agreed. She would tolerate Louis's escapades on the understanding that these girls would be no threat to her. "It is his heart I want!
All these little girls with no education will not take it from me. I would
not be so calm, if I saw some pretty woman of the court or the capital
trying to conquer it."

At the beginning of 1753 Mademoiselle Trusson was whispered of;
her mother, one of the dauphine's maids, had been a talented singer in
the theatre of the *petits cabinets*, and d'Argenson was certain that "Madame de Pompadour has consented to it, and has given her [Mlle
Trusson] to him herself, wishing to keep her position as good friend."
There was also talk of Mademoiselle Niquet, daughter of a magistrate

from Toulouse. Perhaps the reason the king now rented the little house in the Parc-aux-Cerfs in the town of Versailles was for his girls, a place which would be transformed, through rumor, into a veritable harem, but which was in fact a modest house in a side street near the château. Barbier mentioned it for the first time in March when he made note of a pretty young girl of fifteen or sixteen who was lodged there. From the Parc-aux-Cerfs the girls were taken to the rooms of Lebel, the king's valet de chambre, "with the knowledge of the marquise. This room is called the Birdcage because one takes young birds there."

Louis gave himself to these clandestine adventures with abandon and relief, continuing to attend the marquise's *petits soupers* before slipping away. Presumably he established the equivalent of the Parc-aux-Cerfs at his other residences. Croÿ, at Choisy, noticed no change. But he sensed that the king was in low spirits, "never actually showing ill-humor, or anger, just generally indifferent, not enjoying himself, but not really bored, preferring gambling to anything else, never talking of affairs, in short, showing many good qualities, but not the energy to make use of them."

Louis was becoming more secretive, more opaque. He pursued his "young birds" in secret, he brooded on the secrets of the mail, and he continued his mysterious conferences with the prince de Conti. Conti was still operating the king's secret diplomacy, working to place himself on the throne of Poland and form alliances against a perceived Russian threat. "The most knowledgeable people are completely in the dark as to what they discuss," wrote the duc de Luynes. "M. le prince de Conti arrives now and then with a briefcase, sometimes thick, sometimes not, and on several occasions their work lasted quite a long time. It is rather singular that, with this close relationship with the King, on unknown topics, very far from being in close liaison with Madame de Pompadour, he never goes to call on her; it is only a year ago at the most that he began to call, but, so to speak, in spite of himself . . ." Conti was an irritant to Madame de Pompadour, a person beyond her control; now there appeared another, but of a rather different sort.

Marie-Louise O'Murphy was brought at first to the two little rooms of the Birdcage, then, from March 1753, she was installed in the Parc-aux-Cerfs. She was "well-made, quite tall, brunette, a rather long, delicate face, very pretty indeed. She has a bosom and is very formed for her age. She became nubile only three or four months ago." Marie-Louise was sixteen-and-a-half years old.

Her origins are obscure. Her mother, according to d'Argenson, dealt in secondhand clothes and had a small shop near the Palais-Royal; she had four daughters, all available to those who could pay. D'Argenson reported that the king sent his valet Lebel to Paris "to shop for a new maidenhead . . . he saw the little Murphy girl, and found her just right."

Perhaps she is the young girl whom Boucher depicted in his *Blonde Odalisque*, lying langourously on her stomach, a vision of innocent lust. But contemporary accounts are confusing; d'Argenson seems to imply that the king did in fact sleep with a young girl who posed for Boucher, but that she was not O'Murphy. Meusnier, the inspector of the Paris police, repeated what he had heard: "It was through the copy painted by Boucher for M. de Vandières [Abel Poisson] that the king became desirous of seeing the original." But he added, "It is not possible to adopt this opinion, or at least one would have to presume a singular lack of judgment on M. de Vandières' part." (It is true, however, that Abel possessed a painting by Boucher of a young girl lying on her stomach; he had commissioned it for his *cabinet des nudités* and had requested "very little, if any, drapery.")

And so, the young girl in the painting may or may not be Marie-Louise O'Murphy (or "Morphise," as she became known at court); but she might very well have been the king's bed partner, after he had seen the painting, either through Abel Poisson or someone else in the chain of procurement for Louis XV. What is certain is that, by April, the name of Morphise was everywhere.

Madame de Pompadour concealed any embarrassment she might have felt and, once again, summoned up all her forces to appear serene and dignified. In her new role as friend and adviser, she let it be known that she was striving for a reconciliation with the Church, following, as Croÿ noticed, "her plan, which I have anticipated for some years, to win over the king's mind and spirit, and, following to the letter Mme de Maintenon, to end by being pious with him." But Croÿ wondered if she would have the time to put her plan into practice. "They say she is in danger," he recorded. "Perhaps so — but the truth of such matters is not easy to ascertain."

The marquise did not feel she was in danger; she had taken the measure of her man, she had constructed her defenses, she had made herself an indispensable part of the king's life. But Croÿ was correct in observing that she now wanted the Church's blessing. She felt that she had a strong claim on its sympathy. The fact that she no longer enjoyed a sexual relationship with the king surely meant that she could stay at court with the full approval of the king's confessor. She could point to the king's decision to suspend the *vingtième* as evidence that she was working to influence him on the Church's side. And as the conflict between *parlement* and bishops over the *refus des sacrements* escalated, she made it clear that she took the bishops' part.

This dispute reached new heights that spring. At the end of March, a commission appointed by the king to find a compromise failed to come to a conclusion. Then, on April 5, 1753, the *parlement* of Paris issued its *grandes remonstrances*, in which the magistrates staked their claim to adjudicate in ecclesiastical matters as well as secular ones. The king demanded that all matters relative to the *refus des sacrements* be referred to his council; *parlement* retorted that these were precisely the matters they themselves wished to deal with. Impasse.

On May 5 *parlement* halted its work, "given the impossibility of making the truth reach the throne." Here was rebellion. The old maréchal de Noailles advized the king to take prompt measures, complaining that the French people no longer seemed to recognize the rules of propriety and subordination. After a meeting of the king's council at Bellevue, on the night of May 8, musketeers moved into Paris to arrest four of the *parlement*'s troublemakers, and nearly two hundred lawyers were sent into exile throughout France. On May 10 the senior body, the *Grand' Chambre*, was banished to Pontoise. A third of France was left without its higher court.

The king's decisive action was greeted with joy at court. "The Dauphin ran to his father and embraced him," recorded d'Argenson. "His Majesty supped at Bellevue with the marquise, and never more gaily. She sang and whistled tunes all evening." Madame de Pompadour was far from sympathizing with the zealous archbishop of Paris, but she was indignant at the *parlement*'s insubordination. She firmly believed that subjects should obey their master. And her desire to regularize her own position meant that she had an interest in supporting the Church's stand. As for Louis XV, he believed that his clergy *au fond* was attached to him and loyal and that *parlement* would like to "place me under supervision! They and their *remonstrances* will end by ruining the State . . . they are an assembly of republicans! Yet enough of this; things as they are will last as long as I do."

And there one has Louis XV's philosophy. The king of France, in theory an absolute monarch, felt himself unable to control the fractious opponents of the state. Despite his exiling of *parlement* that spring, the thought of radical, decisive action was abhorrent to him, particularly as he had no idea what radical, decisive action to take. And so he hesitated and changed course, not receiving coherent advice from his divided council, where the comte d'Argenson and Machault rarely agreed on anything, unable to proceed from any convictions of his own.

The court moved on to Compiègne. But the voyage was not as carefree as in the past. There were building works everywhere, for king's great plan for the renovation and expansion of the château had begun; the weather was extremely hot, making it impossible to walk outdoors because of the stink of stagnant water. And there was the absence of dashing military officers that summer; armed training camps had been set up in France, and many assiduous courtiers, including many of the marquise's friends, were away. Although Europe was at peace, there were worries in the French war ministry about readiness. Pâris-Duverney, as influential as ever, reminded the ministers that many issues from the last war remained unresolved. It was prudent to stay alert.

Madame de Pompadour turned to the matter of helping the comte de Stainville, with whom she had become friends after the dramatic events at Fontainebleau the previous autumn. She invited him to one of her suppers at Compiègne, a much sought-after honor. She was eager to help him advance in his chosen career of diplomacy (he was hoping for the embassy to Rome) and wanted the king to take a liking to him. Unfortunately, Louis XV had conceived a deep dislike for Stainville since the affair of Madame de Choiseul, and the comte was made perfectly aware of the king's feelings. "As soon as he saw me, I noticed that his face changed to such an extent that it was thought in the room that he had fallen ill. Mme de Pompadour hurried over to him; she asked him what was the matter; he said that his stomach was not working well, and sat down to cards. I played with him; chance would have it that I made impossible wins for him which consoled me infinitely for his sour look."

Neither Madame de Pompadour nor Stainville knew that Louis XV had found out about their activities at Fontainebleau; neither was aware that the king had interrogated Madame de Choiseul and discovered Stainville's betrayal. But the marquise did know that she might have implicated the comte by revealing her knowledge of the king's letters. She nevertheless invited into her intimate circle a man she knew the king would find distasteful. Clearly, she felt able to deal with Louis's sulkiness. And indeed, despite Louis's show of ill-temper, she proceeded to push Stainville along.

At Fontainebleau, Stainville formally requested the Rome ambassadorship and was formally turned down. The minister of foreign affairs, Saint-Contest, dutifully reported the king's refusal to the marquise. But eventually, on November 16 Stainville wrote: "I received a note from Madame de Pompadour proposing that I should go to her room. There I found M. de Saint-Contest who informed me that the King had sent for him before going hunting to tell him that he was nominating me for the post at Rome. I thanked him, saying I had not expected it. I then remained with Madame de Pompadour."

The marquise had asked Louis why he hated Stainville, and he told her that he knew of Stainville's role in the affair of Madame de Choiseul: "If he had lived on intimate terms with me," said the king, "I would have punished him for having played such a perfidious trick, but as I did not spend time with him, I simply showed him my displeasure and refused him any preferment."

Mme de Pompadour drew herself up. "If you do not nominate Stainville today, I shall take your refusal as my own dismissal and shall go to Paris, never to return to Court." Louis XV, once again intimidated, hastened to send word of Stainville's nomination. Madame de Pompadour had once more succeeded in imposing her will on her feeble lover. She always claimed in cases like this that she was acting for the good of the state; for once, in this case, she was right. Stainville was a remarkable man, and, by pushing him into the political arena, the marquise was properly acknowledging his qualities. However sordid the beginnings were, their friendship would mature into a partnership which would stand France in good stead.

But in Rome, under the tension of constitutional conflict between the *parlements* and the crown, Stainville's job would not be easy. Nor would he receive a warm welcome from the pope. Benedict XIV told Cardinal de Tencin that Stainville's appointment "stabs us to the heart with grief, because Rome in its present state has no need of any more libertines." Stainville, however, like the marquise, was supremely confident in his own abilities and looked forward to this next step in his career with relish.

In July 1753 the delicate negotiations to return the Paris *parlement* to work — conducted by the prince de Conti — had collapsed. *Parlement* was insisting on wresting authority from the archbishop and the ecclesiastical courts, and the provincial *parlements* of Rouen, Aix, Bordeaux, Toulouse, and Rennes were taking up the cause.

Louis XV was advised to take a radical step — to establish a new body of his own creation in order to take over the Paris *parlement*'s duties. And so, in November, he called into being a *chambre royale* and invested it with all the attributions of *parlement*. It received a predictable cold shoulder from the dissenting magistrates. Louis XV, caught between his pugnacious archbishop and his insolent magistrates, could think of no solution. Lord Chesterfield, writing at the end of 1753, was alarmed enough at the political situation in Paris to note that "all the symptoms which I have ever met with in history previous to great changes and revolutions in government, now exist, and daily increase, in France."

Louis XV, in his usual gloomy state, consoled himself with Morphise. Relations between him and Madame de Pompadour were uneasy. The papal Nuncio, Durini, recorded in his journal that "the reign of Mme de Pompadour is over . . . at Crécy before the court went to Fontainebleau, there were such scenes that everyone believed that the favorite would have chosen to leave of her own accord without waiting to be dismissed. . . . The new Irish star is going to Fontainebleau where they have prepared rooms for her; she has received diamonds and magnificent dresses."

At Fontainebleau, the marquise preferred to occupy herself with Boucher's spectacular new decoration for the council chamber, the wall panels painted in delicate colors, representing the seasons, all tinted in pinks and blues. Boucher had also finished his depictions of the Rising and the Setting of the Sun (now at the Wallace Collection in London) which were much admired and both acquired by the marquise for Bellevue. These large paintings are the apotheosis of Boucher's love affair with the nude, and of his role in creating the image of Madame de Pompadour as the beloved of Apollo, the beauteous nymph who had stolen the god's heart.

But the nymph was rearranging her persona. Boucher would never paint her again as Tethys or Issé or Pomona; from now on he, and the other artists employed to create, and elevate, her image, would depict her attributes as a cultivated and discerning woman, still a vision of beauty, still Venus, but a Venus transformed from the goddess of Love to the goddess of Friendship. Setting the tone for the future, she had her favorite sculptor, Jean-Baptiste Pigalle, deliver to Bellevue his statue of Friendship, in which the features of the marquise can be perceived.

Artists and writers were fully aware that Madame de Pompadour controlled access to all court commissions, all official patronage. She was, consequently, bathed in flattery to such an extent that it is hard to imagine how she kept any equilibrium. That autumn her personal doctor, François Quesnay, published his *Treatise on Fevers*, dedicated to the marquise. And then Voltaire sent her the manuscript of his *History of the War of 1741*, in which she found the following paragraph: "One must admit that Europe can date its happiness from the date of the peace of Aix-la-Chapelle. One will learn with surprise that it was the fruit of the urgent advice of a young woman of the highest rank, celebrated for her charms, her singular talents, her intelligence, and her envied position . . ." Madame de Pompadour showed the manuscript to Duclos "with some complacency; she had no doubt that this article would be printed one day."

The marquise was already very concerned about her place in history. She wanted to be remembered as the protector of the arts in France, the supreme patron and muse. In this spirit she began her sustained support of the manufacture of French porcelain, in particular of the factory at Vincennes. Having been persuaded of the importance of establishing French porcelain as a rival to that of Saxony, she began to investigate the possibilities of bringing the Vincennes factory closer to Versailles. She had already given Vincennes lavish commissions for the décor of

Bellevue. A beautiful new blue, white, and gold dinner service was being created there for the king, and a series of brilliant ground colors had been introduced: lapis blue, sky blue, and daffodil yellow had already appeared; soon would come apple green, violet, rose, and royal blue. The marquise intended to make her passion for the porcelain flowers, bowls, and potpourris of Vincennes a national treasure.

D'Argenson, of course, found the marquise's enthusiasm overdone: "At the King's suppers, the marquise says that it is unpatriotic not to buy it, as long as one has the money." But most of the French people only wished they did have the money. "The porcelain from Vincennes continues to perfect itself," sighed the duc de Luynes. "But the prices are still excessive."

It would be wrong to say that Madame de Pompadour was a pioneer in the arts, or even a maker of taste. She was a generous patron interested in new things, with exquisite taste and, of course, limitless money. But she was a customer, rather than an innovator. She listened carefully to her advisers—first Tournehem, then her brother—as to which artists to patronize; she employed those artists mainly for decorative reasons, but also included them as participants in her program of self-glorification. Her personal preferences were for bibelots, porcelain, and paintings of flowers, birds, and dogs. Her passion for porcelain was certainly responsible for the creation of the factory at Sèvres; her admiration for the sculptors Bouchardon, Falconet, and Pigalle, and for her favorite painter, Boucher, ensured their careers. Her intervention on behalf of writers such as Crébillon, Marmontel, Duclos, and, of course, Voltaire, was decisive. Even clever artisans like Beaumarchais, a watchmaker, benefited from her patronage. Her brother told the young Greuze that if he was successful in his designs for the marquise, "they will be seen by all the court, and great advantages can follow." What she most loved to do was to provide the setting and the opportunity for the court to see new things and thus be helpful to artists and writers. She was, in short, a marvelous shop window and a tireless promoter.

Chapter 14

"One could hope for no opportunity to be near the King other than through her, and he no longer talked at all to any others."

At the beginning of 1754 Madame de Pompadour was gathering her strength, determined to survive in an increasingly difficult environment. She had made a decision; despite the king's infidelities, despite her uncertain health, she would not leave the court unless forced to do so. She told herself that Louis still needed her, that she must stay for the good of France; her egotistical soul easily convinced itself of this.

From the beginning she had complained about the miseries of court life, but she was disingenuous in complaining; she had quickly become accustomed to opulence and adulation. She assessed not only ministers and advisers, but also Louis XV himself. By all her calculations, she felt herself superior to them all. She rarely expressed self-doubt, rarely made any admission of mistakes. In her firm belief that she was right, that she was serving the master better than anyone, that she knew best, she expended her energy and will on creating for herself an impregnable position.

She took stock of those on whom she thought she could rely, and of those whom she distrusted. The prince de Conti was a particularly irritating presence, slipping in and out of the king's rooms at all hours, self-important and maddeningly mysterious. The alliance of the comte d'Argenson and Madame d'Estrades was also of concern; Morphise, on the other hand, was merely an embarrassment, not a serious threat. Madame de Pompadour, believing herself to be at risk from shadowy plots and intrigues, exerted herself to forge a relationship, create an obligation, multiplied her efforts to name ambassadors, and positions at every level of government, in the arts, and in the military. She busied herself with a plethora of favors, preferments, benefits. It was a kind of greediness, perhaps a substitution for the loss of the king's love.

When the duc de Croÿ returned for his winter visit in January, he had, as usual, a favor to ask. This time he wanted the assurance that the governorship of Condé-en-Hainault, which had been in his family, would remain his. His odyssey took him first, of course, to the marquise, where he was admitted to attend her *toilette secrète*. She took him into her red lacquer *cabinet* and listened to him for three-quarters of an hour, before the king appeared, "like an apparition." Their conversation concerned Voltaire, who had now left Prussia after a quarrel with Frederick, and was languishing in Alsace, awaiting permission to return to France. Croÿ thought her sad and apprehensive. She lamented to him "how few people one could trust, how few honest men there are at court, what a terrible place it is, most people are so despicable." She talked, he thought, as though she feared for herself.

Croÿ doggedly trailed after the king and the marquise as they walked round the gardens, the hothouses, and the menagerie at Trianon. He seized the opportunity to talk to Louis XV about his own building project for a salon in the middle of the forest, and the king immediately took him into the new *pavillon Français* in the gardens, saying, "This is the way in which one should build." Louis asked his architect, Gabriel, who was in attendance, to give the duc two plans he had done in this style, and, asking for paper and a crayon, Croÿ drew a sketch of what he wanted. The three men spent more than an hour over this. And then, having seen all the hens and collected the fresh eggs, they went through the hothouses to see the fruit trees, peaches, plums, cherries, and apricots, all flowering in January.

After lunch Louis XV went on foot through the gardens to the Hermitage to find the marquise. "There is nothing so pretty as the taste she has employed in this little spot. I admired above all the flowers; there were hyacinths and a kind of pheasant the color of fire and yellow gold . . . I admired a clock with a canary whistling several airs, most skillfully made . . . I have never spent a more agreeable and intimate day at Court."

The exhausting assiduity of Croÿ's resulted in success. He obtained the promise he wanted and went in high spirits to La Muette for a hunting luncheon. There he noticed "the new buildings where they are creating, for five hundred thousand francs, pretty rats' nests and beautiful gardens." For the rest of his stay, Croÿ was invited to all the suppers; he was now one of those whom "the King, who was very much a man of habit, always accepted," and Louis now called himself Croÿ's architect. One night, at the king's Going to Bed, Croÿ was given the supreme honor of holding the candlestick.

During Lent, the marquise was seen in public only on Tuesdays, when the ambassadors attended her toilette, together with *toute la France.* Croÿ continued to pay his tributes, wishing now for the privilege of staying overnight on the *petits voyages,* "one of the final steps of courtier which I wished to take."

At the end of his stay at court, Croÿ summarized his impressions of Madame de Pompadour: "It was most agreeable to have to deal with such a pretty Prime Minister, whose laugh is enchanting, and who listens very well. But when she is opposed to something, as I have seen her, that is a very different thing!" (Of course, Madame de Pompadour was not Prime Minister; Croÿ was employing a figure of speech. But the words were often bandied around, and contributed to the perception of the marquise as a presumptuous and ambitious intruder.)

Croÿ gives us a glimpse of a seemingly carefree, self-indulgent life at court. But Louis XV was somber. Morphise was six months pregnant. The royal chamber, his alternative to the exiled *parlement,* was not a success. The government was in need of funds only the *parlements* could provide. It seemed to the king that he had to open negotiations with the disaffected parlementaries at Soissons; he took no pleasure in it.

Louis turned to his confidant, the prince de Conti, for advice. Conti had good relations with *parlement;* he had made something of a study of their claim to be a body which represented the people — on the model of the English parliament — and had positioned himself as a go-between through whom the king could enter into a dialogue with his magistrates. (Conti was advised by a man called Adrien Le Paige, who in 1754 published "Historical Letters on the Essential Functions of Parlement," which was a radical interpretation of the primacy of the *parlements*.)

Conti managed to persuade Louis XV to invite the chief magistrate, René de Maupeou, to Versailles and try to find a way out of the impasse. The king, profoundly bored with the situation, agreed and, without the knowledge of his council, summoned Maupeou to the château. The two men met together in secret for over an hour.

When news of the meeting came out, the lawyer, Edmond Barbier, rejoiced: "This meeting with M. de Maupeou puts an end to all the gossip and reinstates the honor of the King." Barbier had been shocked by "the rumors which people have spread indecently in Paris on the reliability of the King: that he applies himself to nothing and that all he does is run about; that when they hold a council, he is bored, dissipated, comes and goes from his cabinets; that he knows nothing of this business, nor of the misery of the people of Paris, nor of the uselessness of the Royal Chamber; that he does nothing, that the Chancellor and his ministers hide everything from him; that he has allowed himself to be hounded by the clergy; that he does not wish that they even mention *parlement* to him."

These were, of course, extremely damaging impressions to take hold. Louis XV should, in these times of peace and prosperity, have been a very popular king. But his withdrawal from Paris, his refusal to take the sacraments, his visible and extraordinary expenses, had soured the mood of the times. Now the *parlements*, in their assault on royal authority, were bolstered by the king's unpopularity.

The duc de Luynes was a very discreet diarist. Even in his private remarks, his *Extraordinaires*, he rarely allowed himself to utter a criticism of the monarch. But he was concerned enough that April to make a detailed, and very perceptive, analysis: "The better one knows the King, the more one is troubled that he does not listen to arguments on each side of an issue, and then declare his will. He has qualities rare and amiable in a sovereign: he is easy to serve; he respects virtue and probity; he recognizes those who are truly attached to him and is touched by their sentiments and their zeal for his service; he even puts his trust in them." But Louis XV was too timid to impose himself on his ministers, and the government was never as unified or as determined as its opposition.

Louis XV was now unable to do without his "young birds." The pregnancy of Morphise led him further astray. "The King is plunged more than ever into *l'amour volage.*" The girls were brought from the Parc-aux-Cerfs in a sedan chair with closed windows. "I have seen several arrive under a little vault where one opened a secret door which led by a hidden staircase to a room next to the King's suite," noted the comte de Saint-Priest. "This little room had a window from which the lady could see the King get out of his carriage."

Madame de Pompadour's anxiety over Louis's little girls was now overtaken in the saddest way by anguish over her own daughter. On Friday, June 14, Alexandrine was taken ill at her convent in Paris. The nuns sent word to both parents; her father came immediately, but Madame de Pompadour was away at Choisy. When news arrived there, the king sent his own doctors, Sénac and La Martinière, but when they arrived in Paris the next day the little girl was dead. She had succumbed to an attack of acute peritonitis at the age of ten. Her father had been with her at the end.*

The marquise retired to Bellevue "very afflicted and unwell; she has been bled from the foot." The queen sent a page with her condolences. It was there at Bellevue that she learnt of the death of François Poisson on June 25, 1754. He had not been able to overcome his grief at the death of his little Fanfan.

For Madame de Pompadour her daughter's fate was cruel. She had built great hopes on Alexandrine, all dashed. Her brother Abel was now the only family she had. And as she struggled to surmount her sorrow, she received the news that Morphise had given birth to a baby girl, Agathe-Louise Saint-Antoine de Saint-André, who was baptized at the church of Saint Paul in Paris days after Poisson's death. The loss of her own daughter was compounded by the birth of a daughter to Louis XV by another. It was a bitter moment for her. She had need of all her powers of self-control.

But she could not seclude herself for more than a few days. She must join the court at Compiègne, whether she felt strong enough to or not. The king made her the concession of supping quietly with her, suspending the *petits soupers*, but only for a week or so. After that, she reinstated

---

*Later in 1754 Lenormand d'Etioles, now a reformed rake, would make his mistress Marie-Anne Raime pregnant and start a family with her.

her suppers, which were "more *recherchés* [more exclusive] than those *chez le Roi*, because there was less of a crowd and the guests better chosen, no one but intimates." The king's suppers, as Count von Kaunitz noted, all too often became occasions of excruciating boredom, with the guests who had all hunted with the King that day, tired out, the conversation sluggish, the host taciturn. The marquise now rarely attended these affairs, preferring a smaller group of familiar faces, men and women, where the king could come and go, and where conversation turned on matters other than the number of stags killed.

The duc de Croÿ was at Compiègne, six weeks after the death of Alexandrine, and went to the marquise's toilette. "I saw her for the first time since the death of her daughter, a terrible blow from which I thought she would be devastated. But as too much grief would have done harm to her looks and perhaps even weakened her position at court, I found her neither changed nor downcast, and, by one of those miracles at the Court which are frequent of this kind, I found her no less dashing, nor affecting any more serious air. And yet she has been deeply shaken, and she was in all likelihood as unhappy inside as she seemed happy without." Madame de Pompadour's acting talents were still equal to the task.

Croÿ was perturbed to find the king morose and distant. He seemed more cautious and indecisive than ever, sunk in lethargy. But he was more conscientious than one thought. After Maupeou's visit to Compiègne, Louis had listened carefully to the advice of the prince de Conti on coming to an agreement with *parlement*. When Conti started to draw up the critical documents to enact a compromise solution and sent drafts to the king, Louis wrote from Bellevue: "I have told you what troubled me in the drafts. I am returning them to you with some notes I have made. I am also sending you another one, very imperfect, but it will prove to you that my mind is busy. I have gathered fragments right and left, and they are very badly stitched. Make your observations and give them to me in writing, for long audiences with you might make too much of a stir, and I confess that it never stays in my mind as does what I read and think over either by day or by night when I do not sleep." Here is poignant testimony to Louis XV's lonely vigils and attempts to do the right thing.

While the delicate negotiations between king and *parlement* were under way, the minister for foreign affairs, the comte de Saint-Contest,

died suddenly at Versailles. Louis XV decided on a reshuffle of his council. Antoine Rouillé, the navy minister, was named as minister for foreign affairs and was replaced at navy by Machault, who in turn gave up
control of the finances, while remaining on the council of state. Jean
Moreau de Séchelles became controller of the finances.

At first sight this was surprising. Rouillé was generally considered
incompetent: "He was seventy years old, had no ideas, and was too old
to acquire any . . . it was to the last degree absurd and grossly ridiculous
to have made him Minister of Foreign Affairs." Machault was highly
regarded at finance, and was thought necessary to work for the *vingtième*,
his project. His experience with naval matters was nil.

But in fact Machault, having failed to impose his taxation on the
clergy, was feeling somewhat bruised. The quinquennial assembly of the
clergy was approaching in 1755; neither he nor the bishops relished another confrontation. Machault would remain on the council of state and
would retain the king's trust, but he would hand over the financial headaches to Séchelles. And to accommodate his move, the agreeable but limited Rouillé would be handed the crucial post at foreign affairs.

Madame de Pompadour had intervened in favor of Machault. She
trusted his judgment and knew him to be a faithful ally of hers. By now,
Louis XV not only consulted her on every ministerial change; he almost
always found himself in agreement with her views. "She had the courage
to take a part in political affairs and was soon well informed in them because she had a lively and accurate mind," wrote the comte de Stainville.
"She gave the King advice and it was rare that it was not judicious.
Louis XV acquired the habit of letting himself be guided by her advice . . ."

Her acumen was also applauded by Kaunitz, who noted that she
had "excellent qualities of mind and heart. The ministers inform her of
everything they have to say to the King. It is the King himself who
requires it. . . . She has one quality which renders her fit for great affairs, that of impenetrable discretion. That is how she has gained the
King's confidence."

Recovering from the death of Alexandrine, Madame de Pompadour
had the pleasure of seeing her brother, now marquis de Marigny, permitted to ride in the king's carriage, a great and rare distinction. But of
course, malicious tongues wagged. "The King cannot, they say, make the

son of a lackey called Poisson all of a sudden spring from the ancient nobility," complained d'Argenson. "One only sees that in China, where the Emperor ennobles, all of a sudden, five or six of his dead ancestors." Marigny expressed his own reaction in his characteristically sardonic way: "The King has cleaned me up."

Nothing seemed impossible for Madame de Pompadour. She herself now assumed an air of grandeur and gravitas, thinking it her duty to speak for the king in matters great and small. Just before the court departure for Fontainebleau, Luynes recorded that "du Barailh, vice-admiral, was in the gallery at Versailles. Madame de Pompadour had been at the Queen's toilette and followed her to Mass. On the way back, she called du Barailh over and told him that the King was extremely pleased with his services. Barailh was very old; he paid court assiduously to the King and Queen, but did not get out much in the world. He had no idea who Madame de Pompadour was, and asked his friends who that lady was who had spoken to him. He related this story to several people." What amusement must have been caused by the old man's lack of savoir-faire. How could one not know that Madame de Pompadour was the de facto queen of Versailles?

She continued to receive artists and inventors of every kind. At the end of 1754 a young watchmaker appeared at Versailles to show off the new timing mechanism he had invented. He presented a watch to the king, and offered Madame de Pompadour a ring with a watch within it. The young man's name was Pierre-Auguste Caron, and he was rewarded for his invention with a post in the royal household. He was given the honor, for one week each month, of escorting the king's meat from kitchen to table when His Majesty ate in public. Upon receiving his new position, Caron married the widow of the king's *contrôleur de la bouche*. The lady brought with her the estate of Beaumarchais, and from this time on Caron became known simply as Beaumarchais. His next invention, a mechanism to make playing the harp easier, brought him to the attention of Mesdames de France, to whom he was appointed music teacher. Beaumarchais was beginning his ascent, observing all the while the foibles of social life which would illuminate his tale of *The Barber of Seville*.

The marquise graciously received the artist Joseph-Marie Vien, whom she had commissioned to paint an altarpiece of the Virgin for the

church at Crécy. Vien's painting was liked, and put on display in the
marquise's rooms. But then she heard whispers that Vien had used for
his model the features of Morphise! Madame de Pompadour took another look at the painting, declared herself displeased, and had it banished from her rooms, and from the church. (A sketch of it is today at
the Musée des Beaux-Arts, Rouen.)

Morphise was still very much on view at court, her relationship with
the king reestablished after the birth of her daughter. Madame de Pompadour could not help but be jealous. Sensing the king's drifting into dissipation, she took more and more upon herself, interviewing the ministers,
writing to the king's attendants, generals, and officials, sparing herself
nothing. "The King felt no gratitude to her," wrote Stainville, "because
egotism is the basis of his nature, and the cause of all the stupidities he
commits." But this was written many years later, after Stainville (then duc
de Choiseul) had been abruptly dismissed from office by Louis XV. His
bitter feelings led him to write unfairly of the king, who, as has been seen,
tried to do his duty as a ruler, albeit sporadically and with no overriding
vision.

In November 1754 the comte de Stainville left for Rome. He had a difficult job ahead of him, and there were many, including the king, who
were skeptical of his ability. But Madame de Pompadour was not only
his strongest supporter; she was, by now, a close and intimate friend. They
had formed a bond, a bond which had been strengthened by the death of
Alexandrine. The marquise rarely allowed herself to allude to her loss,
but she wrote to Stainville that November to say, "I often fall back into
the sadness in which you have seen me—and how can I forget that unfortunate child. But I must not bore you any longer . . ."

The departure of Stainville left her lonelier. And the king's struggle
with *parlement* caused her pain. Louis XV, acting on the advice of the
prince de Conti, decided to dissolve the royal chamber, the ill-fated and
short-lived alternative to the exiled *parlement,* and to recall the magistrates
to Paris. When they returned, on September 4, there were acclamations
from a great crowd of people, a rebuke to the king. Louis XV had insisted, as a condition of their return, that the *parlement* register a royal

declaration imposing silence on matters of religion, and enjoining them "to hold their tongues, so that nothing which could be contrary to this silence and the peace be done, attempted or innovated." Louis XV regarded this declaration as his handiwork, a signal of his wish for peace. But the magistrates were balky. They spent two days discussing the registration of the royal declaration, and in the end, the vote was close, ninety-two to seventy-two for registration. The king, who had hoped for a clear-cut and resounding vote in favor, was disappointed. But he had at least brought the *parlement* back to work and could now go forward with the raising of monies for the next financial year.

Madame de Pompadour found the settlement with *parlement* unsatisfactory. "My nerves have been in a very bad state for ten days," she told Richelieu. "You have learnt all that went on since the return of *parlement*. You will easily believe that it is this which has made me suffer so much. In truth, one's mind has too much power over one's body and makes one ill." She could not resist adding her familiar jab: "I repeat, Maréchal, that the more you know me, the more you will like me and the more you will desire to have a friend as unique as I am for my friends."

At the end of 1754, with the conflict in France between *parlement* and Church barely contained, events in the outside world were starting to become threatening.

The Treaty of Aix-la-Chapelle of 1748 had left most of Europe anxious and unhappy. Almost from the moment of the declaration of peace, a search for new alliances began, in secret and in a hurry. Austria, Prussia, and Great Britain had unachieved objectives; Austria wanted the return of Silesia, Prussia wanted more security from her neighbors, Great Britain wanted more opportunities for commerce; Louis XV was alone in wanting peace.

But it was not in Europe where the spark was lit that led to war. It was in North America, in the remote back country of Ohio. The French and British had long had conflicting interests in this part of the world; the French wanted unfettered access from Canada to Louisiana by way of the string of forts they had constructed along the Mississippi; the

British wanted to expand their colonies on the eastern seaboard to the west. It was clear that these two objectives would collide.

During 1754 the French became anxious that the British might attempt to seize control of the Ohio territory in their westward march; in response, they started to construct fortified settlements to bar the way. In May the British sent an emissary, twenty-one-year-old Major George Washington, to find out what the French were up to; when he returned with evidence of military activity, he was ordered back with 160 men to attempt to prevent the French from further building of settlements. In their turn, the French sent Ensign Joseph de Jumonville to the territory; his task was to engage Washington in a dialogue, and he took only thirty-five men. But in a confused and bloody encounter, Washington and his men set upon and killed Jumonville and most of his small band.

This news caused furious indignation at Versailles. And when, in October, the French court learned that the British cabinet had decided to send two regiments of Irish infantry to America, with the mission to occupy the French forts of the Ohio Country and Lake Erie, they knew they had to plan for war. In order to buy time, they opened negotiations with the British to create a neutral zone in America, while they were fitting out ships and men for the defense of their Canadian and American settlements the following spring. At the same time, Louis XV began to consider a radical shift in French foreign policy, a rapprochement with Austria, France's enemy for generations. In this he was encouraged by Madame de Pompadour and the Pâris brothers, particularly Duverney, who had for a long time held the view that France should enlist Austria as an ally against British influence on mainland Europe, thus enabling the French to concentrate on protecting their maritime commerce from British aggression. Kaunitz, whose mission to Paris had been to accomplish exactly this, counted on the marquise and her friends to help him fulfil his objective.

By the end of 1754 the French court and that of Vienna had made considerable progress toward rapprochement; stealthily and inexorably, Europe was heading for conflict. On December 28 the duc de Croÿ, newly arrived at court, was told that war was "close and inevitable."

Chapter 15

*"I do not like war, but now is not the moment
to think about that."*

While the clouds of war gathered, the French government was still concerned with the paralyzing dispute over the *refus des sacrements*. The silence which Louis XV so ardently desired was not forthcoming. The uncompromising, and decidedly unsilent, archbishop of Paris was exiled in February 1755 to Lagny-sur-Marne, because of his insistence that the Church, and only the Church, could decide on sacramental matters. Once again, the archbishop had infuriated *parlement* and deepened the rift in French society.

The marquise badly wanted a satisfactory agreement with the church, for reasons personal as well as political. "Do not lose courage," she exhorted Stainville, who was endeavoring to enlist the pope's aid. "Don't give in to boredom." But even to Stainville, she could not resist extending a little *coup de patte* (cutting remark). "Give me the arms to make them forget what they said when you were nominated, and you can be sure I shall use them effectively." "The King is content with your private letter," she added, "and with the conduct you have followed on the subject of the Archbishop."

The marquise had moved comfortably into the mode of speaking for the king, and adding her own views, not just to Stainville, but also to other ambassadors. But she was not the king's chief adviser, much as the words "Prime Minister" were bandied about. Louis XV still relied on his own advisers, particularly Machault and d'Argenson, as well as on the prince de Conti.

Croÿ was right in saying that the marquise "still had the greatest influence in the awarding of favors. It seems that she influences great affairs less, since she has not been able to lessen the credit of M. le prince de Conti and M. d'Argenson, the only two who are against her. All the other ministers were on good terms with the Marquise and handled her carefully."

Croÿ reported that the comte d'Argenson had complained about the open hatred the marquise showed him and asked the king to come to his aid. For once, in her constant sniping at d'Argenson, Madame de Pompadour had gone too far; the king was displeased. And yet Louis lacked the courage to tell her so to her face. Characteristically, he had her friend, the prince de Soubise, tell her that the comte d'Argenson was a trusted minister whom he respected and that she should desist from her attacks. "Being a woman, and able to hide her feelings through a long familiarity with the court, she became more reserved since that warning," wrote the baron de Besenval. "She no longer dared attack M. d'Argenson so openly, and contented herself with stabbing him in the back whenever she could. This was not a new tactic; she was patient in her hatred, and she almost always triumphed in the end."

Besenval was right. The marquise now restrained herself on the subject of d'Argenson, but she maintained her implacable hostility toward him. She carefully observed his close liaison with her former friend, Madame d'Estrades, instructed inspector Berryer to keep her informed, and watched and waited.

During early 1755 the nations of Europe began to search for allies in the event of war. The French were making military preparations in North America, and beginning tentative contacts with Austria. They hoped to prevent a war in Europe by making alliances to isolate Hanover and make it impossible for the British to defend it. The Austrians, eager to retake Silesia from Frederick of Prussia, were looking to detach France from her former Prussian ally. The British were looking to make gains in North America, but concerned about the possible fate of Hanover in a European conflict. Envoys were dispatched from London to Saint Petersburg and Vienna, from Vienna to Paris and Saint Petersburg, from Berlin to London. Negotiations were conducted in the style of an elaborate minuet.

The French moved very tentatively in this minuet. Despite their reservations about Frederick of Prussia's reliability, despite clear evidence that the British were preparing themselves for war in America, Versailles hesitated to cement an alliance with Austria. There were inexperienced men at the head of the important ministries at this critical time; Rouillé, at the foreign ministry, was old and lacking in energy, and Machault, at the navy, was new to his department.

But even as diplomats stepped up their search for reliable allies in the event of war, the naval forces advanced. In April, Admiral Edward Boscawen, with eleven warships and twelve hundred soldiers, was sent to patrol the Gulf of St. Lawrence and prevent French reinforcements from reaching Canada. He had secret orders to attack French ships without warning. At the same time, a French fleet of twenty-seven ships under Dubois de La Motte left Brest for Canada, six regiments aboard.

The abbé de La Ville, chief assistant to Rouillé, told Croÿ that the king felt honor-bound to answer the British actions in America: "Once we have shown our teeth," he boasted, "all England will back down." (Croÿ thought that if they were to show their teeth, it would be better to have some!) The mood at the French court was hardening. On April 21 the marquise told Stainville that nothing was yet decided about the war: "If anything were to happen, it would not be before next year." But three weeks later, on May 12, she felt differently: "I fear war only for the evil it does to the kingdom, and I would fight with all my forces, if that could be of any use."

In June the abbé de Bernis arrived back at Versailles from his embassy to Venice. He had done well there and had made valuable contacts, including the ubiquitous Casanova, whom he employed as spy and procurer. He had also, it was whispered, enjoyed an intimate relationship with Louis XV's eldest daughter, Madame Infante, to whom he had made several visits in Parma, where she and her husband had established residence as duke and duchess. (Bernis, Choiseul later wrote, "liked to caress the generous breasts of the eldest daughter of Louis XV.")

Madame de Pompadour received her old friend with *la plus vive joie*. "I found her in a very different situation from the one in which I had left her," Bernis wrote, "she was no longer the woman surrounded by all the amiable and talented people, who governed France from the heart of pleasures. The king had for some years had no more passion for her; there remained only friendship, trust, and that habit which with princes is the strongest tie of all. Madame de Pompadour had need of consolations."

(To the marquise's chagrin, Morphise was once more established at Versailles, and more *en vue* than ever.)

The marquise told Bernis that she had written to the king to obtain his permission to retire from court ("this persuaded me only that she was tired and in a bad humor") and also showed him memoranda she had written on political affairs ("I would never have believed that she could speak to the King with so much force and eloquence").

Bernis encouraged her to continue to offer the king advice, and also advised her to reconcile with the comte d'Argenson, sacrificing her personal resentments for the good of state affairs. "She gave herself to my advice with difficulty; but, in the end, she gave me responsibility for this negotiation, in which M. d'Argenson always refused to participate." The comte d'Argenson and the marquise de Pompadour were both too wary of each other to make the first move toward reconciliation. Bitter feelings ran too deep.

Bernis's solicitude for the marquise would earn him a major promotion that summer. When the court moved to Compiègne for a two-month summer stay, he was named ambassador to Spain. This was an important post; France would need Spain as an ally in the event of war, and the previous Ambassador, the duc de Duras, had completely failed to persuade the king, Ferdinand VI, or his pro-British wife, to join in an alliance with France. The abbé de Bernis was entrusted with a delicate and important negotiation. Croÿ, who had very much wanted the Madrid posting, and who had spent so many hours at the marquise's toilette and suffered so many little humiliations, was deeply disappointed.

At Compiègne there was a new wing to the château, and Gabriel, the king's architect, had begun to have the gardens planted and the kitchen gardens arranged. The building was sufficiently advanced for Marigny to place orders for tapestries for the new council chamber and gaming room. The marquise had a new Hermitage *à l'italienne*, facing the royal windows, where she gave supper to the king after the hunt. (She had a little dairy there, a forerunner of Marie-Antoinette's *hameau*.)

But on July 17, in the evening, a courier arrived from the French ambassador in London, the duc de Mirepoix. "You know that it is at

Court where one talks the least about interesting things," the duchesse
de Luynes told her husband, "but I know that M. de Mirepoix's courier
brought no agreeable news."

The news was that the British fleet under Admiral Boscawen had
attacked part of the French convoy from Brest on its way to North
America and captured two vessels, the *Alcide* and the *Lys*, and ten companies of men. The French claimed that, upon signaling, "Are we at peace
or at war?" they received the answer "Peace! Peace!" immediately followed by "Fire!" The court was outraged. Although most of the French
fleet reached safe harbor at Louisbourg, on Cape Breton Island, this was
an insult which had to be avenged.

The French thought that the British were hell-bent on war. In fact,
the British wanted freedom of action in America, but no European war.
But now they had, by this clumsy action, given the French court "occasion and motive to declare war." On their part, the French were equally
opposed to a war in Europe. But if France and Britain were to come to
blows in America, conflict in Europe could not easily be avoided. The
French would cast their eyes on Hanover; the British would be compelled to defend it. Madame de Pompadour summed up the mood at
court: "Never talk to me of war, little animal that you are," she wrote
to Stainville, in the habitually jolly tone she now used with him, "it
grieves me. That does not prevent me from thinking with all the hauteur
suitable to a good Frenchwoman."

At Versailles the struggle between Madame de Pompadour and the
prince de Conti was approaching a critical phase. Conti had been instru-
mental in helping to bring the Paris parliamentaries back from exile. But
the king had been disappointed with their continuing lack of cooperation; the marquise, who thought Conti's influence had been troublesome,
took the opportunity to voice her criticisms of the prince. This time the
king listened. He began to cool toward "my cousin, the lawyer," as he
called Conti somewhat derisively.

By now, Conti himself was swimming in dangerous waters. He had
met with pastor Paul Rabaut, the leader of the Protestants in southern
France. Since the revocation of the Edict of Nantes in 1685, French
Protestants had been unable to practise their religion freely, and were
often savagely persecuted and hunted down. Rabaut hoped and believed

that Conti could help alleviate their lot and bring changes to their legal status. The two men kept up a correspondence in the spring of 1755, and in July, Rabaut came to Paris to attend two secret meetings with the prince. But there was a more sinister backdrop.

Conti was ambitious. He knew Louis XV well enough to see how disengaged he was in affairs of state, how easily influenced, how weak-willed; he believed that by cultivating those who had political differences with the king, he could become the leader of the opposition, the man with whom Louis would have to deal in important affairs, the power behind the throne. Having established himself as an advocate for *parlement* in its struggles with royal authority, he was now trying to show the Protestants how helpful he could be. Realizing that one major obstacle to his plans was Madame de Pompadour, he redoubled his efforts to unseat her, producing a candidate of his own for the position of *maîtresse déclarée*, the vicomtesse de Cambis. The marquise took note; she sent instructions to Berryer, her spy, to keep the prince under surveillance. (Madame de Cambis did not get very far; d'Argenson instantly dismissed her as "well-made, but only ordinarily pretty.")

Rumors of war meant that the country would require an infusion of funds. The clergy had obliged by voting a *don gratuit* [free donation] of sixteen million livres at their assembly. *Parlement* had also voted for appropriations. The king's court could hardly refuse to contribute, and long discussions were held about ways to cut royal expenses. "It is certain that the King retrenches his extraordinary expenses, outings, cooks in the country houses, horses," wrote Luynes. "This comes to more than ten million. All spendings on building are being suspended, except for the Louvre, for which two hundred thousand livres a year is granted . . ."*

The king announced that, in the spirit of economy, he would no longer go to Crécy. Outings there had always been highly expensive.

---

*The Louvre was in perilous condition. In 1754 part of the colonnade collapsed, and the generally decrepit state of the building had become a scandal. Abel Poisson's former traveling companion, the architect Soufflot, had been summoned to Paris to supervise the renovations. He embarked on major works there, but in 1758 money ran out, and in 1770 he gave up hope of finishing this important project.

Sadly, the marquise agreed; her ambitious plan for a triumphal arch designed after that of Septimius Severus was abandoned. "His Majesty proposes to make great cuts in his expenses," she told Stainville. "I thought I should set an example . . . I only regret my poor Crécy, but I only admit it because I am sure of overcoming my weakness. And so do not reproach me for my liking of this house; never was there a more unhappy passion."

Two days after writing this letter, Madame de Pompadour succeeded in toppling Madame d'Estrades, the woman who had betrayed her two and a half years before, the woman with whom she had lived since then in a relationship based on deception and lies. It is hard not to think that the timing of the banishment was linked to the marquise's wish to strike a new blow at the comte d'Argenson, having been forbidden from attacking him overtly. "The marquise pushed the King to it, as she knows how to," wrote d'Argenson. "She is a very good actress; she weeps with grace and plays despair. She knows how to insist and carry the day without displeasing the King, and this is how she has attained her objectives."

The comtesse d'Estrades dined at La Muette on August 5, sitting to the left of the king as usual. "They behaved to her normally, and she seemed very sought after by the courtiers. She had no suspicions." The next day the comtesse left for Paris, planning to rejoin the king at Saint-Ouen, where he was going to dine and spend the night with the prince de Soubise. On her way into Paris, near Chaillot, her carriage was stopped by a courier bearing a letter from the king. It was her order of banishment. As Madame d'Estrades digested the awful news, a black carriage was said to have passed by, the curtains at the windows pulled back. If Madame de Pompadour were, as was alleged, the occupant of the carriage, she must have savored her revenge. Here was mortification for one old friend, and triumph for the other.

The marquise resumed her "official" duties with renewed enthusiasm. There was a serious shortage of funds for the *Ecole Militaire*. "No, assuredly, my dear Blockhead," she told Duverney. "I shall not let perish in port an establishment which must immortalize the King, make his nobility happy, and let it be known to posterity my attachment to the State, and for the person of His Majesty. I told Gabriel today to see to it that there be the necessary workers at Grenelle to finish the job. My income for this year has not come to me yet, I shall use the whole of it to pay the dozens of day-workers . . ."

After the nomination of Bernis to the embassy of Madrid, another of the marquise's friends, the duc de Nivernais (her "little husband") was named for a mission to Berlin, to sound out Frederick II on his commitment to the alliance with France and negotiate a new treaty. As the pace of events quickened, Bernis rushed from Paris to Versailles, constantly in touch with Pâris-Duverney, the man who continued to pull so many strings. Bernis told Duverney that "Madame de Pompadour does not want M. de Maillebois at all for the post in Holland; she has thought of M. d'Affry. She was most impatient to know if you had converted M. de Séchelles. Behold the state of affairs, which proves to me that she must have seen in the King a more pronounced inclination for vigorous resolutions." In other words, the likelihood of war was increasing.

At the Salon held at the Louvre in August, there was a further powerful statement about the relationship between the royal family and the Poisson family, and the vast patronage the latter now commanded. The place of honor in the exhibition was given to Nattier's portrait of the late Madame Henriette playing her *basse de viole;* but on either side of this painting were portraits of Madame de Pompadour and her brother, Marigny.

La Tour's portrait of the marquise shows her as she wished to be perceived: elegant, dignified, regal, a cultivated and discerning woman with modern tastes, "marvellous in finesse, grace, poise and exquisite beauty," as Sainte-Beuve wrote.*

But contemporary reaction to the portrait was muted. Another artist, the young Jean-Baptiste Greuze, took the salon by storm with his depictions of simple country people in *The Father Reading the Bible to his Family* and other works. In fact, the stir caused by Greuze was such that

---

*La Tour's preparation for this portrait produced the following reaction from other nineteenth-century critics, the Goncourt brothers: "If you should seek the authentic Pompadour, you may study her here, her eyes of porcelain blue set wide apart, the down on her upper lip, her complexion no longer young, rather blotchy and mottled, a faded rose upon her cheeks and a pale vermilion on her lips."

Marigny immediately sent him to Italy, to the French Academy in Rome, to extend his knowledge. (Marigny thought that he would be able to put the young talent to work for the crown; but Greuze's style never suited court taste. Instead, he had opened the way for an outpouring of sentimental art, "moral art" as Diderot called it, which would in the end help to undermine not only court art, but the court itself.)

In the ongoing dance of the European nations for new alliances in the event of war, the Austrians finally played their card. Maria-Theresa and her cabinet had decided in August 1755 to declare war on Prussia; in order to give them a free hand, France must be detached from Frederick. Kaunitz was authorized to activate his contacts with Versailles.

Kaunitz sent a courier to his envoy in Paris, Count von Starhemberg. The courier brought a personal letter from the Empress Maria-Theresa to Louis XV; Kaunitz wanted this letter delivered to the king by someone whom Louis trusted, a person who would thereby establish themself as the intermediary between the Austrian court and the king of France. Kaunitz himself had first thought of the prince de Conti; but perhaps Madame de Pompadour would be more persuasive. He left it to Starhemberg to make the choice. If Starhemberg opted for Madame de Pompadour, Kaunitz would enclose a letter for her. (This is Kaunitz's own version; it seems more likely that he himself selected the marquise. He had had the opportunity to observe her closely at Versailles, and had come away impressed with her qualities of discretion and resolution. But he preferred not to take public responsibility for involving the mistress of the king.)

On August 30 Starhemberg had an audience with the marquise and gave her the empress's letter to pass on to Louis XV in confidence, and the note from Kaunitz. "Madame, I have often desired to recall myself to your memory; an opportunity presents itself which, if I am correct in knowing your sentiments should not be disagreeable to you. . . . Monsieur le comte de Starhemberg has matters of the greatest importance to propose to the king, and they are of a kind that can only be treated through the canal of someone whom His Most Christian Majesty honors with his entire confidence . . ."

Charles Lenormand de Tournehem, a member of the Parisian financial élite, and possibly the father of Madame de Pompadour.

Louis XV, the handsomest man in France, depicted at the time he met Jeanne-Antoinette Poisson, Madame d'Etioles.

Madame de Pompadour in 1748, in all the freshness of her youth and beauty, depicted as Diana, Goddess of the Hunt.

Voltaire, an early friend and admirer of the marquise. He held her in affectionate regard even after he deserted the French court for Prussia in 1750. For him, she was "a soul born sincere."

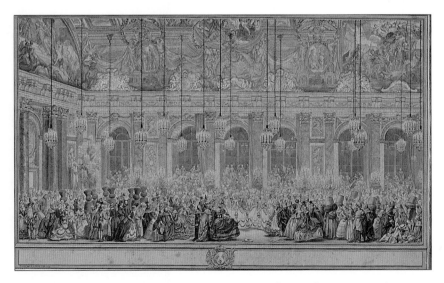

The Ball of the Yew Trees, February 1745. Louis XV, disguised as a tree, can be seen in conversation with a charming young woman, probably Madame d'Etioles.

The abbé de Bernis enjoyed a swift rise to power
with the backing of Madame de Pompadour,
becoming in succession ambassador, minister for
foreign affairs, and cardinal. His fall was equally
swift; the marquise engineered his dismissal at the
end of 1758.

Madame de Pompadour sculpted
as the Goddess of Friendship, the role
in which she wished to be recognized
after her affair with Louis XV was over.

Bellevue, the château built by Madame de Pompadour on the banks of the Seine, designed as a showcase for French decorative arts, and for herself as patroness.

Ménars, the château on the banks of the Loire where Madame de Pompadour intended to live in retirement.

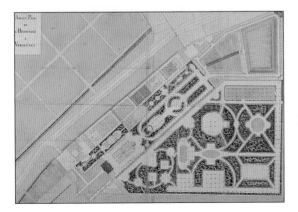

The Hermitage at Versailles, an elegant little retreat created by Madame de Pompadour for herself and the king, one of several such retreats she had built near the royal palaces of Versailles, Fontainebleau, and Compiègne.

Madame de Pompadour at the height of her ascendancy in 1757, painted in her "coronation robes."

Madame Infante, the eldest daughter of Louis XV, ready for the hunt.

"The Blonde Odalisque," Boucher's painting is possibly a portrait of Marie-Louise O'Murphy, one of Louis XV's "young birds," or that of some other young girl painted to arouse the king's desire.

The duc de Choiseul, one of Madame de Pompadour's favorites, was by far the most talented of her protégés. Able and ambitious, he rose to become the de facto prime minister of France in 1759.

Madame de Pompadour in the haunting sketch made by the artist La Tour. She seems surrounded by a "mist of sadness."

Madame de Pompadour received this note with some excitement. Here was a chance to make her mark on history! She immediately turned to the person she trusted most, the abbé de Bernis; she told him of the contents of Kaunitz's letter. Bernis claims in his memoirs that he immediately saw "a trap set for the King, and a very dangerous risk to my own fortune and repose," and that he "pointed out to Madame de Pompadour everything there was to be feared in entering into a negotiation with the court of Vienna, whether it was sincere or if they wished to amuse us . . ." In the midst of the abbé's reply, the king arrived suddenly by way of his private staircase. On hearing Bernis's objections, Louis said almost angrily, "'You are like the others, the enemy of the Queen of Hungary . . . we must thank M. de Starhemberg and tell him we do not wish to listen to him.' 'That is not my view, Sire. Your Majesty has everything to gain from learning the intentions of the court of Vienna, but one must be on one's guard with the response one makes.' The king's expression became more serene, he then ordered me to hear Monsieur de Starhemberg in company with the Madame de Pompadour, who would only assist at the first meeting . . ."

Louis XV had responded positively to Maria-Theresa's letter. The marquise told Bernis that the king had always admired the empress, that he liked the idea of allying with another Catholic monarch, and that he distrusted his nominal ally, the king of Prussia. In fact, contacts between the courts of Vienna and Versailles had been maintained in great secrecy for some time. Now the empress's démarche had quickened the pace. And thus was the abbé de Bernis designated to act for the king in these most sensitive and crucial of negotiations. Bernis, although indubitably upright and intelligent, had limited experience at this level of diplomacy, and was anything but the cautious and prudent personality one might have desired.

As for Madame de Pompadour, "she was not insensible to the idea of playing a nobler role than those she had played in her theatre in the *petits cabinets*. She saw herself a *personnage d'état* and put into play all her talents." Duclos was right; the marquise did perhaps see her role as a high diplomat as her most important so far. But he was also correct in saying that "it was by chance that the marquise found herself in this position, without having planned it. It was Kaunitz who made her mistress of France." The marquise was ready and willing to take on an international political role; but had it not been for Kaunitz, she might not have become so prominent a player in foreign affairs.

Writing later, Stainville, when duc de Choiseul, agreed that the marquise had become "the arbitress of the destinies of the Kingdom," adding "it was a role she had scarcely dreamt of, and one which she was obliged to assume in spite of herself. It became the cause of unworthy slanders against her, and of terrible vexations, which poisoned the rest of her life."

On September 22, 1755, the protagonists met at Brimborion, the pavilion on the grounds of Bellevue. Starhemberg presented the propositions of the court of Vienna, as Bernis and Madame de Pompadour sat in silence, having agreed beforehand not to reveal any reactions. The empress proposed handing the Austrian Netherlands over to Louis's son-in-law, Don Felipe, and the throne of Poland to Conti. All the king had to do in return, Starhemberg announced, was renounce his alliance with Prussia. France would not be involved in a war; the armies of Russia, Saxony, Austria, and Sweden would do the fighting; France would simply make financial contributions.

Louis XV found these proposals attractive. He welcomed an alliance with a Catholic nation, rather than with Protestant Prussia. But he considered himself bound to Prussia by a treaty that would not expire until June 5, 1756. (Frederick's principles were rather more flexible; when the British and the Russians signed a treaty on September 30, 1755, he became convinced that he was in danger from this coalition of Russians, Austrians, and the British, and quickly decided to start his own negotiation with London, without informing France.) Louis XV, in ignorance of Frederick's *volte-face*, believed he must act toward the Austrians with the greatest caution.

The marquise, on the other hand, having served as intermediary in these secret talks, felt herself an active participant in international affairs. She also worked toward a reconciliation between Church and *parlement*, inclining to support the position of the bishops on the *billets de confession*, not so much out of any great sympathy with either position, but because she saw a chance to receive support from the Church in the future. She was preparing herself for a religious conversion, a return to piety, in order to secure a more open, dignified, and honorable place at court.

To her confessor, the gentle père de Sacy, a protégé of her close friend, the prince de Soubise, she expressed a desire to repent. He advised her to write to her husband and ask him to take her back. One can imagine the reaction of Lenormand, living peacefully with his mistress and young family, when the letter arrived. He wasted no time in replying: "I received, Madame, the letter in which you inform me of the plan you have made to give yourself to God. I can only applaud such a resolution. . . . I wish I could forget the harm you have done me; your presence would only bring back the memory more sharply. And so the only course we can take is to live apart. Whatever cause for discontent you have given me, I would hope that you consider my sense of honor, and I would regard it as compromised if I received you *chez moi* and lived with you as my wife . . ." (It was said that Soubise and Machault were both sent to see Lenormand and make sure that his letter was written with tact and was not embarrassing.)

The marquise reasoned that, if her husband refused to take her back, and her sexual relations with the king were over, then père de Sacy could now absolve her and she could take a position at court which was officially sanctioned by the Church. She expressed her new piety in characteristic fashion—telling Stainville in Rome that she was sending the pope a holy-water basin of Vincennes porcelain: "Ask him in payment for a little piece of the True Cross. Send it to me by the first extraordinary courier . . ."

Stainville was making progress with the pope, and Madame de Pompadour was appreciative. "What the Pope has written on the subject of the *billets de confession* is worthy of a shepherd who wishes for peace. One feels very strongly here that it is out of the friendship he feels for you that one owes the prompt expedition of this business. . . . The King seems satisfied with your services." She burned to see Stainville do well, partly as validation for her struggle to have him appointed, and partly because she felt him a soul mate. His cheerfulness, optimism, and energy greatly appealed to her; and on his part, he never failed to flatter and praise her with his natural subtlety and tact.

She continued to hope that the pope "will feel the necessity of bringing peace to the Church and not leaving any pretext for the madmen who wish to annhiliate religion and put the kingdom to the torch. The same motives will animate you, monsieur, and give me good hope." The marquise now regarded the parliamentarians as "madmen who wish to put the kingdom to the torch"; she clearly saw the disobedient and unaccommodating magistrates, associated in her mind with the seditious Conti, as a much greater threat to stability than the recalcitrant bishops. And her personal interest in forging an alliance with the Church led her to view *parlement* as the real foe.

But Madame de Pompadour was, in general, much less tolerant of dissent than she had been in the past. She had fallen out with her former protégés at the *Encyclopédie*, considering them too outspoken and impertinent. She had, after so many years at court, become a supporter of authoritarian solutions, less disposed to speak up for those who believed in making society more liberal. The maintenance of the king's prestige meant more to her now than such novel ideas as freedom of expression or the voice of the people. Her character was not one given to compromise; she seethed at *parlement*'s presumption, and at the *encyclopédistes'* audacity.

From then until the end of the year, the twin troubles of internal strife and external threat would dominate the discussions at court, overshadowing even the disaster of the Lisbon earthquake on November 20. By the end of November 1755 the British had taken, worldwide, almost three hundred French merchant ships and six thousand officers and men. And as the British were audaciously capturing French ships, rumors of Prussia's negotiations with London began to leak. Bernis, alarmed at being solely responsible for the preliminary talks with Austria, asked the king to brief his ministers of the state of events. Louis XV did so reluctantly; at the end of October Machault, Moreau de Séchelles, Rouillé, and Saint-Florentin were summoned as a "secret committee" and told of the communications with Vienna. It is significant that the comte d'Argenson (minister of war) was excluded, as was the prince de Conti. One cannot help but suppose that Madame de Pompadour, jealous of her political handiwork, refused to share it with her arch foes. Thus the two men most experienced in diplomacy were shut out of the most significant negotiations France had held for decades.

These enemies of the marquise might languish, but her friend Bernis was riding high. "They talk a great deal of the abbé de Bernis for foreign affairs," wrote d'Argenson, "that is why they are keeping him here until January." The marquise de Pompadour no doubt influenced this choice. "She has all the air of the prime minister of France. The king wishes it so. . . . Certainly, it is better to see a beautiful nymph at the helm than an ugly monkey, as was the late cardinal de Fleury. But these fine ladies have the caprice of white cats, who caress you first of all, then bite you and scratch you."

The marquis d'Argenson tried to warn his brother, the comte d'Argenson that, having banished Madame d'Estrades, the marquise and Machault would redouble their attacks on him. He felt that his brother was stooping to the same sordid intrigues of which he accused the marquise. "My brother has named the sieur Janel director of the *cabinet de la poste.* He has already worked with the King, that is to say, discovering the secrets of human weaknesses. . . . This Janel is a great knave and traitor; he has already deceived two or three ministers under whom he has served. I hope that my brother finds him of use. But who would make use of these evil souls, treacherous and perverse? He who loves danger will perish by it."

The marquis d'Argenson was right. The sinister Robert Janel was already responsible for unsealing the mail of those whose names were given to him by the king personally; Louis XV would read the letters and pass them onto the marquise, "for he hid from her neither his own secrets, nor those of his subjects." It was, increasingly, Madame de Pompadour who gave Janel his orders, and it was to her, not to the comte d'Argenson, to whom he would soon owe allegiance.

To mark her ascendancy further, the marquise discharged Morphise, the king's young mistress. She had had enough of Marie-Louise O'Murphy's continuing favor with the king, her young child, and her lodgings near Versailles. It was said that O'Murphy was banished because she asked the king how he was getting on with his "*vieille coquette*" (old flirt); when word reached the marquise, she demanded the girl's banishment. Once again Louis XV bowed to Madame de Pompadour's wishes; he was probably already bored with the young Irish girl. On November 27 Morphise was married off to Monsieur Beaufranchet d'Ayat, a poor but noble army officer, and protégé of Soubise. The king gave her an enormous dowry of 200,000 livres, and a magnificent trousseau. Then the couple set off for Ayat, far away in the Auvergne.

On November 25, the same day Morphise's marriage contract was signed, another contract was signed, that of the sale of a house in Versailles, 4 rue Saint-Médéric, to a proxy of the king. This was the famous Parc-aux-Cerfs; the king, addicted to his "young birds," had decided to acquire the house for their future residence. From there they would be brought to Versailles, would entertain the king, and promptly return. Madame de Pompadour thought this prudent; she had tired of the risks represented by the presence of a *petite maîtresse* on the premises, and preferring that Louis take his pleasures with these girls than find a more dangerous rival mistress at court, she acquiesced to the permanent establishment of the Parc-aux-Cerfs. In this, she was not so much a procuress as an enabler.

This satisfactory year — 1755 — for the marquise ended in yet a higher key, when she succeeded in persuading the king to award Stainville the coveted order of the Holy Ghost. This was the loftiest order of chivalry in France, and those named to it were entitled to wear the *cordon bleu,* the blue silk sash. She broke the news in the characteristically flirtatious way she had adopted with him: "Whatever difficulties you might find, I do not doubt of your success. You will make use of your gift of persuasion, your friendship with the Holy Father, the finesse and charm of your character, and even more, your sentiments for the King, his repose and the good of the State. Among such great names I dare not place myself! It is however very true that you are contributing a great deal to my tranquility. I cannot aspire to it as long as the King is tormented and his kingdom is in turmoil. . . . I hope to send you a little blue courier [the sash] on New Year's Day. Agree that it is a pretty color."

For Madame de Pompadour the exercise of such power was very pleasurable. And beneath the surface, there were other reasons for cheer. Madame de Pompadour's intelligence network was recording the meeting between the prince de Conti and the Protestants of southern France. It seemed that Conti was stirring up subversion. The marquise would well know how to use this ammunition.

PART FOUR

1756–1759

"The marquise is Prime Minister."

Chapter 16

*"It is true that, if I had given in to my taste for ease
and tranquility, I would have left this place long
ago, where one lives in slavery..."*

On February 8, 1756, the marquise de Pompadour was named a lady in
waiting (*dame du palais*) to the queen. The queen had twelve such ladies;
the position was the most prestigious at court, given only to ladies of the
highest rank and reputation. Unprecedentedly, the marquise was named
as the thirteenth *dame du palais*, a supernumerary position which accorded
her the honors, but not all the duties, of the position. The announcement
was stunning; Madame de Pompadour had suddenly achieved the highest
of court honors, had moved into a new and seemingly untouchable position. The duties of the post were not the issue; it was a question of what
the post represented. The nomination implied that not only the king, but
also the Church, found the marquise morally acceptable. The court, on
the other hand, immediately concluded that the marquise's recent mani-
festations of piety had been a charade; she had, it was said, disguised her
real aims under the cover of a feigned penitence.

The queen, of course, was among the last to hear of her new lady in
waiting. Louis XV dealt with the tricky business of informing her in a
typically circuitous way. He had been with his wife during the morning
of February 7, but had said nothing. Later in the day, Marie was handed
a letter from the marquise herself, which broke the news of her appointment. (One imagines that Louis had meant to tell his wife and had not
found the courage; characteristically, the marquise had taken matters into
her own hands.) The queen icily sent back a reply by way of a servant.
Of course she had no choice but to accede to the king's desire.

After lunch that day, Madame de Pompadour paid a visit to the queen's senior ladies in waiting, the duchesse de Luynes and the duchesse de Villars. "The Marquise told Mme de Luynes that she had neither asked for nor desired this place, that they had urged her to take it, and that she had only done so in agreement with her Confessor," reported the duc de Luynes cautiously. "They say that Mme de Pompadour wishes to fulfil all her duties and to live in a Christian fashion. They are going to separate her rooms from those in which the King eats, so that there will be no contact . . ."

The court was curious about the pious arrangements of the marquise. "She has stopped eating meat. . . . She is limiting her public toilette and, next Tuesday, is receiving the ambassadors while at her needlework instead. They say that she is going to give up rouge, but she was, on the contrary, extremely made-up today, and she performed her service with the Queen as if she had never done anything else. The Queen distinguishes herself in this business, as in all others, by her dignity and her tact. . . . One has learned that, for some time, madame la marquise has been reading pious books and goes to Mass every day . . . she is wearing her hair more modestly and shows the greatest signs of fervor."

Most people thought the marquise was insincere. If she could not find religion upon the death of her daughter, they argued, she was incapable of doing so now, except as an act of *bonne politique* (clever policy). There were so many advantages to be gained by her "conversion" that she was accused, and found guilty, of hypocrisy.

Madame de Pompadour's sincerity was further questioned when she asked none other than Voltaire to translate for her the Psalms of David. Their mutual friend, the duc de La Vallière, informed the incredulous philosopher of the marquise's new way of life. "She no longer goes to the theatre, she eats meat only three times a week during Lent, but on condition that she is not inconvenienced. The moments she gives to reading are to all appearances used for elevating books. As for the rest, the same life, the same friends, and I flatter myself that I am of that number; as amiable as she has ever been and with more influence than ever." La Vallière tried to persuade Voltaire that he had always been destined for this uplifting work, but the *philosophe* could not bring much conviction to his task. He contented himself with an ironic reflection: "All is well in

France, Madame de Pompadour is pious, and has taken a Jesuit for her Confessor." No more was heard of the Psalms of Voltaire. The marquise had to make do with commissioning Boucher to do eight drawings for her prayer book, pretty confections of young and seductive cupids surrounding a soulful virgin.

The marquise gave her own explanation to the comte de Stainville, on the day after the announcement: "I have made myself much talked of these eight days, Monsieur, particularly over my decision to reform my life, a decision I made after very mature reflection. They accuse me of finesse, of cunning, of plotting, even of falsity. I am, however, only a poor woman who has sought happiness for twenty years and who believes she has found it."

The court was fascinated by this new, non-meat eating, lace-capped, needleworking (if not rougeless) marquise. She herself began to take a loftier tone in her correspondence with Stainville: "Consider at present what a great service you will render to the State, and to me in particular, if you can reestablish peace in the Church. . . . I hope that at last the King will open his eyes, that he will see to what extent the *parlements* have abused his confidence and that he revoke his authority which he would never have lost, if he would only believe the honest people who are devoted to him."

She modestly asserted that "she has not yet acquired the interest or taste for devotion which she would like to have, and that it is a grace she hopes to obtain by her fervent prayers," according to the duc de Luynes, who wanted to believe her: "It is to be hoped that these happy stirrings of piety continue with the same fervor and that they make a real impression on the king . . ."

But Louis XV was far from giving up the pleasures of the flesh. His girls now included one who "paints very well and has painted the King," and one called Mademoiselle Robert, "an extremely pretty girl, intelligent and very well educated." The marquise closed her eyes. It was not a dignified situation, but she saw no threat to her own position in these escapades. She resigned herself to the fact that Louis would not change his ways.

After the brouhaha of her "conversion," the marquise settled in to her religious practices; but she and her confessor remained at cross-purposes.

Père de Sacy, while accepting that her conversion was real, was nevertheless enjoined by his superiors to offer her the choice of leaving the
court, reconciled with God, or remaining without absolution. Madame
de Pompadour thought she had gone far enough in her efforts; she failed
to understand why the Church was still insisting on her departure from
court. She and père de Sacy continued their conversations, but somewhat sporadically.

The marquise was now thirty-five and her health was not good. But
she was an intermediary with the empress of Austria, a political force, a
lady in waiting to the queen. She commissioned Boucher to paint her
official portrait, exactly as one would as a member of the royal family;
this portrait, when finished, would depict her, as the Goncourt brothers
wrote, "in her ceremonial robes." It was at this time that her maid, Mme
du Hausset, described her mistress as "the most content." When Croÿ
saw her at her needlework now, not at her toilette, she was "glittering
with diamonds as usual, still very pretty indeed, and a little plumper. She
seemed cheerful and teased me a great deal." She was at her apogée.

But the marquise would have little time to enjoy her magnificence.
Disconcerting words came from Berlin, where Frederick II had thrown
French diplomacy into confusion. The duc de Nivernais had arrived there
on January 12, having made a leisurely journey from France, confident
in the solidity of the Franco-Prussian alliance. He was about to receive
a rude shock.

After almost a fortnight of equivocal talks, the king of Prussia revealed that he had signed a treaty with Great Britain, the Convention of
Westminster. Under the terms of this convention, Frederick agreed to
defend Hanover and the other German possessions of his uncle, George II,
against his ally, France; in return, the British promised to come to the
aid of Prussia if it were attacked. King George wanted protection for
Hanover, King Frederick wanted protection from Russia and Austria.
France had not been consulted.

Frederick was well aware that the French would react with fury to
his treaty with Great Britain, and his cavalier treatment of Nivernais.
Frederick was particularly interested in the reaction of Madame de Pompadour, asking Knyphausen, his envoy at the French court, to try to flatter her into revealing something of the French attitude to a new war.

Frederick completely misjudged Madame de Pompadour in this; she was extremely discreet, and much too careful and experienced to give the king of Prussia any information. She had never trusted him, and had indeed been very offended by the insults he bandied about (he called her "Petticoat III," Maria-Theresa being "Petticoat I" and the Empress Elizabeth of Russia "Petticoat II"). When Knyphausen requested an interview, she asked him to go through the maréchal de Belle-Isle.

The Convention of Westminster left Louis XV at a great disadvantage. He had not responded definitively to Maria-Theresa's *démarche* on the grounds that he had an alliance with Frederick. Now that Frederick had betrayed France, Louis had no other choice than to come to terms with Austria, or risk being isolated in Europe. But the French negotiating position was much weaker than it had been.

In early February the government repudiated the alliance with Prussia, clearing the way for formal rapprochement with Austria (even though the comte d'Argenson, the minister of war, was still unaware of the full extent of the most recent contacts with Vienna).

As Louis XV and his ministers tried to come to terms with the new European landscape—and an almost inevitable colonial war with Great Britain—they decided to take the military initiative. Pâris-Duverney came up with a plan to launch a surprise attack on the Mediterranean island of Minorca, which had been awarded to Great Britain from Spain in 1715. If the French took Minorca, they could use it to entice Spain into an alliance with them, or simply keep it for use in any future exchange of territories. Duverney's protégé, the duc de Richelieu, was appointed to command the expedition. Richelieu was congratulated by the marquise; but his old friend, the duchesse de Lauraguais (sister of the duchesse de Châteauroux) warned him about how things stood at court. "I must warn you that you are sometimes mistaken in your conjectures. You told me that Madame de Pompadour was flattering you; but I know beyond all question that even though she may treat you well in your presence, it is far different when you are absent. They were discussing with her whether the siege should be undertaken and, if so, who should be chosen for it. You were named among several others and she exclaimed sarcastically, 'Monsieur de Richelieu! He is braggart enough to want to be given the task. He would be as irresponsible in taking a town as in seducing a woman; that would be most amusing! He needs a few good disgraces to teach him not to be so confident.'

"It would perhaps not be a bad thing to let the marquise know, through you-know-who [Bernis]," continued Madame de Lauraguais, "that if you are given the expedition you will fail. If she is badly disposed toward you, that might help . . . take Mahon [the main city of Minorca] and return covered with glory so as to make them burst with rage. What a prospect! What a beautiful dream, my dear duke! If only we can realize it!"

In mid-April Richelieu, close to his sixtieth birthday, went aboard the flagship *Foudroyant* at Toulon, in command of 25 battalions of infantry with supporting artillery and engineers, escorted and transported by a fleet of 17 warships and 198 transport vessels, commanded by the marquis de la Galissonnière. After a disastrous first attempt at departure, when one ship sank and others went aground, the fleet sailed away for Minorca.

Madame de Pompadour adopted a fervent patriotic attitude. One evening at a supper in the *petits cabinets*, Croÿ saw her "as sparkling as ever, though she was eating no meat. In fact, her piety is proceeding slowly, they say that it is only a quarter of a conversion . . ." She spoke in glowing terms of the king's navy and its ability to protect France from the British. "She spoke with much power and dignity and more nobility of soul than one might expect."

At Versailles, the *petits soupers* were now held in a new dining room near the king's bedroom, on the first floor of the château. Guests stayed for gaming and coffee in the salon de la Pendule, next door to Louis's private study, his *cabinet intérieur*. One evening Croÿ peeked into this study and saw "his [Louis's] desk covered with all his documents and catalogues, the room filled with books and instruments and beautiful flowers. I would very much have liked to poke around here for some hours." At supper, he and the marquise talked of "shrubs, which were my folly *du jour*; she sat as usual next to the King, very elegant and, as usual, very lively. I observed no change in outward appearances except that since it was Saturday she was not eating meat."

Rapprochement with Austria was proving difficult. The abbé de Bernis was finding his committee of ministers—Machault, Saint-

Florentin, Rouillé, and Séchelles—reluctant to become too involved with the empress. Old habits died hard. Vienna watched with frustration as the French seemed unable to come to a decision.

Bernis, alarmed at the confrontational atmosphere, asked the king to widen the circle of those who knew of the talks with Austria to include the comte d'Argenson and the marquis de Puysieulx. "I did not wish to be accused of having concluded a treaty of alliance with our former foes without the cooperation of the whole Council of His Majesty." The council met on April 19. D'Argenson, in a sour mood, spoke about his reservations, and matters dragged on. Then Starhemberg had a message delivered to the marquise, who had it sent in to the meeting; it said that the British ambassador in Vienna had just asked Maria-Theresa for an unexpected audience. The implication was that the empress was losing patience. In some disarray, the Council of State immediately and unanimously decided to sign a treaty with Austria. One can imagine the stupefaction of the comte d'Argenson, minister of war, who had learned of the full extent of the discussions with Austria only a matter of hours before finding himself in alliance with her.

Madame de Pompadour, who considered this alliance a result of her work, had the impression of playing a high diplomatic role. At court, although suffering from palpitations and her usual migraines, she was increasingly frenetic. Luynes describes her summoning the duc de Gesvres, the First Gentleman of the Chamber, and keeping two ministers waiting while she spoke to him. She wrote several letters while giving Gesvres her orders, and then rushed away, very pressed because she had a rendezvous at the Hermitage, telling the ministers, who were still cooling their heels, that she would return.

Busy and unwell as she was, she did not neglect her duties to the queen. "She very often comes at midday," noted Luynes, "and continually brings the Queen little presents of flowers. The Queen is not much pleased about this overattention, but thinks it inappropriate to show any displeasure. It would be better if Mme de Pompadour put a little moderation in her zeal; but any mention of this would be dangerous . . ." To incur the marquise's displeasure was by now an act of considerable folly. Even the queen—especially the queen—dared not say a word.

It was 1756 to which Voltaire was referring when he wrote in his memoirs that "Mademoiselle Poisson, dame Le Normand, marquise de Pompadour, was in fact the Prime Minister of the state." With a little reflection, the marquise might have recognized that, being at the zenith of her supremacy, her only way forward was decline.

The Treaty of Versailles was signed on May 1, 1756 at Jouy-en-Josas, the home of Rouillé. France and Austria were obliged to come to each other's aid against any other alliance, except in a war between France and Great Britain. In a secret convention, the empress declared herself ready to come to France's aid if any power invaded her, and France made the same promise.

The pact was strictly for defensive purposes, or that was what the French chose to believe. They did not anticipate that they would become involved in a European war; they believed that the Prussians would be too intimidated to move, and that Maria-Theresa would not move either. As history would prove, they were wrong; as soon as the treaty was signed, Maria-Theresa sent her troops to the Bohemian frontier, facing Silesia. It was obvious that the Austrian objective was to regain Silesia, with French support. Apparently no one realized this at the French court.

When news of the treaty became public in France, informed opinion was hostile. "The principles of the cardinal de Richelieu, and even before him, were our supremacy over the house of Austria," noted the duc de Luynes. "The alliance with the king of Prussia seemed to us a necessary counterbalance to Austria; such were the maxims of our government in the last war; it appears that we have changed these principles. Events will decide."

Bernis, on the other hand, chose to believe that everyone "regarded the treaty as a masterpiece of prudence and politics. One desired peace and one believed that this alliance would bring it and affirm it." And indeed Voltaire wrote to Madame de Lutzelbourg: "You did not expect, madame, that one day France and Austria would be friends. Alone as I am, dead to the world, I dare say I am very pleased with this Treaty. I sometimes receive letters from Vienna; the Queen of Hungary is adored: it was right that the *Bien-Aimé* (Louis XV) and the *Bien-Aimée* (Maria-Theresa) be friends."

The Parisians were more direct:

> Let us spill for the Queen of Hungary
> All our blood
> Let us give her for Silesia
> All our money
> For she has pleased Pompadour.

The marquise was, according to Starhemberg, "delighted with the results of what she considers to be her own work. . . . It is certain that it is to her we owe everything and that it is from her that we must expect everything in the future. She wishes that one esteem her, and she deserves it in fact. I shall see her more often and more particularly when our alliance is not such a mystery, and I should like by then to have things to tell her which will flatter her personally." On June 9, 1756, Kaunitz wrote to the marquise: "One owes absolutely to your zeal and your wisdom, Madame, everything which has been done between the two courts."

Madame de Pompadour, naturally, thought the treaty a work of genius. "I do not hide from you the pleasure which the treaties with the Empress have given me," she told Stainville. "The public, although they do not yet know how beneficial [the treaties] are, have shown considerable joy." She had an onyx engraved depicting France and Austria together laying their hands on the altar of Fidelity and trampling underfoot the mask of Hypocrisy and the torch of Discord. She had Bernis rewarded for his efforts by seeing to it that he was given the very lucrative abbey of Saint-Médard de Soissons, a magnificent prize which included the château of Vic-sur-Aisne. Bernis was rapidly rising.

Richelieu had landed at Minorca on April 17, 1756; five days later he entered Port Mahon and laid siege to the fort of Saint-Philip. In order to divert the attention of the British, the French, under Belle-Isle, had built up their army strength in the Channel ports to 100,000 men; when the British realized what was happening, they immediately dispatched Admiral Byng and ten warships from the Rock of Gibraltar, although they had only just arrived there and were in need of repairs. Byng's orders were to hurry on. When the British fleet hove into view off Minorca on May 20, La Galissonnière engaged him. After a four-hour action, half of Byng's ships were heavily damaged, and no appreciable loss had been inflicted on the French. Instead of standing off at Minorca and awaiting reinforcements on their way from Gibraltar, Byng returned to the Rock. When news of Byng's retreat came to Versailles, the French were naturally pleased.* But the pleasure was tempered by the sober realization that they were now officially at war with Great Britain.

The news of the fall of Port Mahon, which capitulated on June 28, came to Compiègne with the duc de Fronsac, Richelieu's son. On July 11 the marquise wrote to Richelieu: "I believe that you are aware that it is with great sincerity that I call you my *Minorquin*. We are all overcome with joy, above all at the way in which the place was captured. Nothing is so heartening for the nation and for the commander! Admit that your star has risen and that it shall never be dimmed."

On July 20 the marquise invited the court and the foreign ministers to her Hermitage at Compiègne where she threw a party with fireworks and distributed ribbons to the ladies and silken knots for the gentlemens' swords "à la Mahon."

Richelieu arrived back in Toulon on July 16. But instead of returning to Versailles in triumph, he was ordered to remain on the coast in case of British naval attacks. "Madame de Pompadour, who seems to be delighted with you at the moment," wrote Madame de Lauraguais, "may change by tomorrow. . . . You know from experience that she only likes you as the mood takes her: your friend today, she may be against you tomorrow. . . . I can see that on the whole they are annoyed to see you victorious. . . . Burn my letter." It was true that Madame de Pompadour felt some ambivalence about the victories of Richelieu, a man she disliked. She never been able to separate her personal feelings from the needs of the state. If she liked and trusted someone, she believed him fit for high office; if not, however successful he was, she never gave him her wholehearted support. It was one of her gravest faults.

---

*Admiral Byng was arrested at Portsmouth at the end of July and accused of dereliction of duty. After a court-martial, he was shot in March 1757, a rare and shocking decision, one carried out, as Voltaire famously put it, "to encourage the others."

These military triumphs of France were very pleasing. But there were lesser victories to celebrate. The first kiln at the new porcelain factory at Sèvres was installed in August 1756. Etienne Falconet was named head of the sculpture studio. A new color, apple green, was unveiled. Now that the factory was so close, the marquise could make frequent visits with her friends, and encourage the king and the royal family to go as well. As always with her, when she adopted a project, she spared no effort to make it succeed. She supported Sèvres and its work as long as she lived.

And at Choisy, a new retreat for the king and the marquise was completed; the *petit château* was a one-story pavilion separated from the main château by a graveled walk lined with trellised groves. The little house was dedicated to the joys of nature: Madame de Pompadour's rooms were decorated with still-life paintings by Oudry and Desportes, Bachelier's flower paintings and depictions of themes from La Fontaine's fables. In the dining room a "flying table" for twelve, accompanied by four smaller ones, rose through the floor from the kitchen below at the sound of a bell. The marquise and her guests found everything they required on the tables, and the presence of servants was thus rendered unnecessary. The salon was furnished with chairs and sofas upholstered in lilac silk embroidered with a design of parakeets, owls, and monkeys; vivid paintings of exotic birds decorated the walls, and all the marquetry of the furniture depicted birds, flowers, and fruits. This pastoral yet sophisticated retreat would be the marquise's haven in her last days in 1764.

Even in these delightful surroundings, however, the marquise could not escape her usual anxiety. She was now focused on disgracing the prince de Conti, the man she suspected of stirring up *parlement,* encouraging subversion, and plotting nothing less than a *coup d'état.* She would concentrate on Conti's relationship with the Protestants; Conti had already met with their leader, Pastor Rabaut, and had offered to approach the king about a more tolerant policy. Having been rebuffed by Louis XV, Conti had made a radical move. He sent a memorandum to the National Synod of the Protestants asking them to determine how many of their men could bear arms; he seemed to propose nothing less than armed revolt. At a private session of the Synod in the Cévennes on May 10, 1756, Rabaut discussed Conti's proposals. These were not welcomed; the Protestant pastors, already persecuted, did not wish further confrontation.*

While these explosive issues were being discussed, one of those present at the Synod was secretly recording all that was said, sending his information back to Versailles, and specifically to Berryer and Madame de Pompadour. This man was Jean-Frédéric Herrenschwand, a Swiss, a shadowy, rather sinister figure whose past history is unknown, but who was a zealous agent for the marquise. His reports were so alarming to her that in September she demanded the arrest of Pastor Rabaut. She clearly thought that the prince de Conti was playing such a dangerous game that all efforts must be made to stop him. Louis XV could not bring himself to believe that his cousin and old colleague could be flirting with treason. He refused to act. The marquise, Berryer, and Herrenschwand continued their espionage. And a new ally was recruited to the marquise's team of spies: Robert Janel, the man whom the comte d'Argenson had put in charge of his private office, secretly defected to the marquise.

Conti's mysterious activities with the Protestants were only one discomfiting factor that autumn. Another was the *parlement*'s insubordination. On July 7, 1756, Louis XV imposed a second levy of the *vingtième*. *Parlements* all over France refused to cooperate. The magistrates adopted a threatening tone. Their argument, going beyond taxation, was now that no law should be enacted before *parlement* had examined it and approved it. The *parlements* were proposing themselves as arbiters between the people and the king; this was nothing short of a revolutionary proposal, undermining the absolute power of the monarch.

The members of the *parlements*, all of whom had paid for their offices and were representative of the interests of the *haute bourgeoisie*, were unlikely champions of democracy. As a class, they were intolerant and incompetent. But they were also popular with Parisians for standing up to an increasingly unpopular king. Louis XV seemed out of touch, remote, and uninterested in his subjects, acting at the behest of his mis-

*I am indebted to John D. Woodbridge's book *Revolt in Prerevolutionary France: The Prince de Conti's Conspiracy against Louis XV* for the information concerning Conti and the Protestants.

tress. It was her greed, her tyranny, her caprices, they thought, which were ruining the country.

On August 13 the *parlement* of Paris was summoned to Versailles to receive the king's orders and to register his fiscal edicts. This was done at an imposing ceremony called a *lit-de-justice*, at which the king, in person, enforced his authority on his recalcitrant *parlement*. A *lit-de-justice* was rarely convoked; but at times when king and *parlements* were at an impasse, the ceremony was traditionally regarded as the final word. In 1756, however, the king's prestige was not enough to silence the parlements; in Rouen and Languedoc, in the Dauphiné and in the Franche-Comté, there was disobedience and almost rebellion. The *parlements*, posing as the champions of lower taxes, continued to gain popularity.

The prince de Conti was active in this parliamentary power play. Although he continued to have long conferences with the king, his sympathies and ambitions were elsewhere. Madame de Pompadour watched with anger as, in her opinion, he blatantly went against the king. Many others shared her alarm. "What ought to be said is that the principles which he entertains are the same as those of the *Parlement;* that the authority of a sovereign ought to be restricted by the laws of the Kingdom, and that it is the *Parlement* of Paris which is the depository of these laws." Thus wrote the duc de Luynes.

Against this background of internal insubordination, astonishing news arrived from abroad. Frederick of Prussia, having considered the powers allied against him, had taken a breathtaking gamble. He decided that he could not afford to wait until Russia and Austria attacked him. He would be the first one to attack, and try to keep the strategic initiative. "I am innocent of this war," he told his brother. "I have done what I could to avoid it." And then he marched on Saxony, and its capital, Dresden. The king fled, leaving the queen of Saxony—the dauphine's mother—behind; her palace was sacked, she herself maltreated. The city capitulated on October 16 and, within a few weeks, Frederick was master of the country and threatening Bohemia. Frederick's plan was to crush Austria before the Russians could come to her aid, and before the French contingent, which was mandated under the terms of the Treaty of Versailles, could arrive. After pillaging Saxony, he would be able to face Maria-Theresa directly. The Seven Years War had begun.

This was a mighty shock to the French court. Louis XV could not believe that Prussia had decided to take on all of Europe. Now he was obliged to come to the aid of the empress; now he must fight a war not only in America and on the high seas, but also on the European mainland. On September 8 Bernis told Starhemberg that Louis was ready to furnish the help required under the terms of the Treaty of Versailles, leaving the empress to choose between an immediate subsidy, or 24,000 men. Maria-Theresa decided on the troops.

On September 7, 1756, before she knew of Frederick's aggression, the marquise had written to Kaunitz to express her pleasure at the alliance, and to tell him that she was sending him a copy of her portrait by La Tour, as he had requested. (Kaunitz's request was typical of the exaggerated politesse of the times: "Do not doubt, Madame, that it is with the most cruel impatience that I await that charming portrait for which that cruel monsieur de La Tour has made me languish for so long. End my pain, I beg you, and do me the grace of sending it as soon as possible. I kiss your hands with the most profound respect.")

This stately exchange was stopped in its tracks by news of the king of Prussia's precipitous assault on Saxony. Ten days later, Madame de Pompadour was full of righteous indignation. "What do you call the Solomon of the North now, *grand' femme*?" she wrote to Madame de Lutzelbourg. "Let us say Tyrant and you would be right. I thank you for the little map; they tell me that at Strasbourg you can find another of the whole of Germany, similar to the one you have sent me. I would very much like to have three copies of it; of course I shall pay you for them. My spell of fever has not had any consequences, and I am as well as I can be with my poor little ear."

And as if it were not enough to have war erupt on land and on sea, Louis XV and Madame de Pompadour were also worried about the possibility of a British invasion of the west coast of France, possibly in collaboration with the dissident Protestants—the very Protestants with whom the prince de Conti was so intimately associated.

On top of that, the ever zealous archbishop of Paris published a "Mandate on the Authority of the Church," in which he refused in advance to listen to the pope on the question of the *refus de sacrements*.

Parlement, in turn infuriated, forbade any priest to publish the archbishop's mandate, or any printer to print it.

Madame de Pompadour was deeply irritated. "You have heard
about the latest folly of the Archbishop," she wrote to Stainville. "*Parlement* is no longer reasonable. Everyone wishes to be the master: the King
finds that acceptable, apparently. I myself do not believe that this state
of affairs can last. . . . In all of this I try, a difficult thing, not to lose my
objectivity, not to exhaust myself, to do good, to prevent some of the
evil . . ." She had convinced herself that she alone had the interests of
France at heart, that she alone was completely devoted to the king and
working in his best interests.

When the marquise touched on her anxieties to Stainville, he advised her to relax, to give herself respite from her self-imposed responsibilities. She might well have taken such advice as a veiled hint that it
was time for her to retire, but she trusted Stainville and took him at his
word. She replied in touching, if not completely convincing, tones. "Your
sermon would be admirable, if it were not based on a false text. It is true
that, if I had given in to my taste for ease and tranquility, I would have
left this place long ago, where one lives in slavery . . . but I feel that I
owe the King the sacrifice of my cherished ease. . . . I am working with
all my strength to become less sensitive, and I am using all honorable
means to forestall the troubles which are disturbing the Kingdom."

She was far from the exultant woman of six months earlier. The
euphoria of her appointment to *dame du palais,* her responsibility for the
treaty with Austria, the success of Minorca, had dissipated. Having expressed her own determination to stay at her post, she chastised Stainville
for hinting that he had completed his job at Rome and would like to return. He had succeeded in extracting a papal document from Pope
Benedict XIV which he hoped would put an end to the interminable dispute over the *refus de sacrements.* So did the marquise: "I have the greatest impatience, monsieur, to see the Holy Father's letter arrive. I hope
that it will bring the Kingdom peace, for in truth, it is time to finish this
internecine war . . ." But the marquise was not sympathetic to his wish
to return: "Would you wish to expose the fragile health of your wife to a
journey during the month of December? Be guided by your good sense,

not your desire to return to France. . . . You must not be open to reproach for not having finished this business . . ." The marquise's tone to Stainville was always one of playfulness and tact; but there is no mistaking the note of authority, the firm and unquestioning self-confidence.

The encyclical, *Ex Omnibus,* signed in Rome by Pope Benedict XIV on October 16, 1756, did not reach Versailles until October 27. The pope attempted to carve out a middle path: priests were to warn the dying that if they were Jansenists, they would be damned; yet priests, at their own discretion, could give the last rites to the dying, even if they *were* Jansenists. Louis XV sent the encyclical to his bishops, but advised them to do nothing publicly for the time being.

The king was concentrating not on the encyclical, but on the insubordinate *parlements* and their refusal to register his fiscal edicts. He suddenly announced a *lit-de-justice* (the second one of the year) in Paris for December 13, 1756. The Council of State was told of the king's decision only the day before the ceremony. Louis had decided, with the encouragement of Machault, his most trusted minister, to deliver a firm statement of the royal will to the *parlements*. It was a grave mistake.

When news of the nature of the king's intention began to circulate, the atmosphere in Paris became tense. There was a great deployment of troops in the streets; when the king's procession traversed the streets, the crowd was silent. In the Palais de Justice, Louis XV spoke briefly and to the point: "Messieurs, you have heard my wishes. I shall make my authority respected by all those of my subjects who wish to dispute it." But, as the king departed, there were no shouts of "*Vive le roi.*" Louis XV went to La Muette, where the marquise awaited him. "You know me well enough to be sure," she wrote to Stainville that night, "that I shall dedicate myself with all my power to the execution of the King's wishes. One must have courage, I have more than is necessary. It remains to be seen if my wretched body will hold up."

But even as Madame de Pompadour was writing this, a crisis was erupting. That evening, having concluded that "it was totally impossible for them to be of any use in the future for the King's service and the good of his Kingdom," the magistrates resigned en masse. The king's attempt at force had failed. The royal presence had been unable to guarantee obedience; royal authority was now severely compromised. D'Argenson wrote of the "silent wrath" of the *parlement*, and went on: "Here we are then, completely at loggerheads with the king, and a chief [Conti] completely ready to participate in an act of defiance and revolt which could follow. . . . All the people have become partisans of the *parlements*; they see in them the only remedy for their vexations; they have a hatred for priests."

On December 22, 1756, in the midst of the crisis, the duc de Croÿ arrived at Versailles and took stock of the situation. Madame de Pompadour was "at the pinnacle, since the greatest affairs were dealt with *chez elle;* that was where the principal affairs of the day, of the interior, everything concerning *parlement*, were discussed." (Croÿ also relayed, without irony, the conversation he had had with Madame du Hausset, as the two of them waited for the marquise to return from Mass: "She astonished me by telling me of the boredom of this terrible place [Versailles], her own amazement at seeing seigneurs who could be Kings of their estates acting as valets in the antechamber, of her desire to live in the country away from this chaos. I was surprised to find her so sensible.")

At Versailles, Croÿ detected no echo of the tension in Paris. But Barbier, on the scene, recorded that "we are in very critical circumstances, fanaticism is rampant in Paris against the sovereign authority . . . the general will is to make the King give way in everything."

And so, at the end of 1756, Louis XV faced a mutinous Paris *parlement,* supported by other regional *parlements* in what was ominously called a "*union des classes*"; he faced a recalcitrant archbishop, determined to circumvent royal authority; and he faced war on land and on sea. The king seemed unaffected by these critical circumstances; but he had not failed to register the charged and hostile atmosphere.

Madame de Pompadour, tired and irritable, blamed Machault for the king's embarrassment. Frustrated at the turn of events, she lashed out at her confessor, the mild and accommodating Jesuit priest, père de Sacy. She had done everything he asked — given up the stage, written to her husband, prayed, read religious books; in return, she reasoned, the Church should have given its blessing to her remaining at court, where she would be able to further their cause. But the Church had remained unmoved; she had not been accepted as a reformed and pious woman.

She asked Sacy to leave court, and retained a lingering rancor toward him, and to all other overzealous clergymen, particularly Jesuits. She continued to conform to the Church's rules on such things as not eating meat on certain days and she continued to attend Mass every day, but with noticeably less fervor.

At the end of 1756 Louis XV—overwhelmed by a confluence of events he had not foreseen, deeply alarmed about the stability of the kingdom and the potential for civil strife, prompted by Madame de Pompadour—finally decided to break with his cousin, the prince de Conti. The occasion for the rupture devolved around the command of the French army destined to operate in Germany. Louis XV had formally promised it to Conti; he reneged. Possibly he was convinced that Conti in command of a large number of French troops might constitute a real military threat to the throne. "Because I have not given him the command of the army which, in all likelihood, will assemble on the lower Rhine, he says he is dishonored. This is a word one puts forward constantly nowadays, and which shocks me infinitely," the king wrote nonchalantly. "Perhaps he will put some water in his wine . . ." Conti returned his dossiers to Fontainebleau and moved out of his rooms at Versailles in early December.

During that month, musing on these ominous events, perhaps Louis XV took some consolation in his new, enlarged council chamber at Versailles, where superb wall panelling, the work of Jules-Antoine Rousseau had been installed. It was in these splendid and harmonious surroundings that Louis XV and his ministers would debate and discuss the dire events of the next seven years.

Chapter 17

*"Do not believe that these events can weaken my courage.
Only the loss of the King could cause that.
He lives, all the rest is the same to me."*

On Wednesday January 5, 1757, Louis XV went to Versailles from Trianon to visit his daughter, Madame Victoire, who was suffering from a fever. It was about six o'clock, dark and cold, when the king and his entourage went down from his room to the carriage waiting to take them back to Trianon. As they came into the courtyard, a man pushed forward, there was a moment of confusion, and then the king called out: "Someone has stabbed me!" and gestured to the stranger. "It is that man who has stabbed me," Louis cried. "Arrest him, do not kill him." Guards dragged away a man who would be identified as Robert François Damiens, a native of Artois, an unemployed lackey, about forty years of age. He was removed to the jail for questioning.

The king was taken upstairs to his bedroom. As he went up the staircase, he felt faint, and was heard to murmur, "I shall not recover." He called for his confessor and a surgeon. There were no sheets on his bed, no nightshirt, no valets de chambre, for the king was to have slept at Trianon. In the pandemonium, the dauphine's surgeon arrived to bleed him, all those present helped to undress him, and an almoner heard his confession. Shortly, Louis's own doctor, La Martinière, rushed back from Trianon and pronounced the wound not dangerous. He went so far as to say that, if the king were an ordinary individual, he could be in a dressing gown the next day and would recover in two or three days. But there remained the fear that the knife might have been poisoned.

Mesdames arrived in tears. The dauphin also wept, but remained calm. The queen was greeted by her husband with the words, "Madame,

I have been assassinated." The comte d'Argenson hovered in the bedroom, the other ministers next door. Another priest, the abbé de Soldini,
recommended by Madame Adélaïde, arrived and heard the king's second confession. The abbé was called back several times during the night.
When the official confessor, père Desmarets, arrived, Louis confessed
for the third time, this time for almost half an hour.

Meanwhile, Madame de Pompadour had arrived in haste from
Trianon. She found her rooms thronged with people, among them Bernis,
awash with self-importance: "She threw herself into my arms with cries
and sobs which would have softened even the hearts of her enemies."
Bernis claimed that he advised her to remain calm, and remain at her
post, "that, being the recipient of State secrets, letters from His Majesty,
she could be harmed herself." The abbé had been named to the Council
of State on January 1, 1757 together with the maréchal de Belle-Isle,
and he felt himself to be an important personage, able to speak to his
patroness as an equal. For the moment, she was grateful for his solicitude. But her moments of weakness were short-lived.

The marquise had no intention of leaving the court. By the next
evening, she was writing to Stainville in Rome: "Thursday, five o'clock
in the evening (January 6, 1757): The King is well, very well, he scarcely
has any fever. What abominable monster did Hell vomit up yesterday
evening . . . to give the best of all Kings a big blow from a knife in his
back, as he was going to mount his carriage to return to Trianon! It is
only a flesh wound. You cannot imagine the courage and calm of the King.
He has had the criminal arrested and ordered that he not be ill-treated.
He [the king] went back up without help to his rooms, asked for a surgeon and a priest, believing himself mortally wounded, consoling his
family, his subjects, reduced as they are to the depths of despair. The
day before yesterday, *parlement* said horrible things about him. Today,
there are only cries, prayers, in the city, at the Court. Everyone adores
him. I do not speak of myself. You can judge of my feelings, for you know
my attachment for the King. I am doing well, Bonsoir."

Dufort de Cheverny rushed to Versailles early in the morning of
Thursday, January 6, finding an "endless swarm of doctors; all the
rooms were full of them. The King was in bed, shut up behind four
curtains, and only opened his mouth to ask for one thing or the other;

he was given over to his reflections, for a strike directed against one is indeed a thing to consider . . ."

Lost to shock and depression, Louis XV stayed in his bed. The royal family made sure that he was surrounded at every moment and that no messages were sent downstairs to Madame de Pompadour. Life at Versailles was suspended while the king succumbed to melancholy and the marquise remained secluded. It was impossible not to recall the scenes of Metz, when Louis XV, from his sickbed, was persuaded to send away Madame de Châteauroux. Madame de Pompadour's fate was to be held in the balance.

Madame Adélaïde was the most decisive of the king's family. She encouraged the dauphin to send an intermediary to the marquise to per-suade her to leave. "They maneuvered vis-à-vis M. de Machault, they flattered him; they told him that, as he was the friend of Mme de Pom-padour, it would be better if he could advise her to retire; that would avoid the awkwardness of a dismissal. They made him see how pleased the dauphin and the royal family would be if he could help the King in this regard." Machault visited the marquise and gave her the impression that the king wished her to go without a scene. But she had made up her mind to stay, bolstered by Soubise, Gontaut, Bernis, and the maréchale de Mirepoix, her new confidante, who advised her that she who retired the ground lost the battle.

She requested that the comte d'Argenson pay her a visit. She asked him politely not to show the king any of the unpleasant and insulting pro-posals which he found in the mail. D'Argenson merely replied that his duty was to hide nothing from the king; when she begged him once again to protect the king from useless anxieties, he replied harshly that he gave explanations of his conduct only to His Majesty. As the minister got up to leave, the marquise cried: "Monsieur, you push me to the wall . . . I see very clearly that you hope that I shall soon leave the Court and the insult-ing advantage you are taking of the situation. I have not seen the King for five days, perhaps I shall never see him again; but be sure that, if I do see him, he will thenceforth see only one of us, either you or me." "Madame, have you anything more to say to me?" Then d'Argenson withdrew.

Upstairs at Versailles, the intrigues were played out in whispers around the king's bed. Downstairs, the marquise was abandoned by all except her intimate friends. One who did, however, cast his lot with Madame de Pompadour was the duc de Croÿ, who returned to Versailles and saw the marquise three days after Damiens's attempt. He found her "calm, strong, with great energy and strength of character, even though her position at court was at risk."

Finally, eight days after the attempt, in the afternoon of Thursday, January 13, there was a shift in the drama. The king was in his bedroom, in dressing gown and nightcap, leaning on a cane, surrounded by the dauphine and her ladies. A heavy silence reigned as Louis XV walked back and forth to the window, then stopped, lost in thought. Eventually he gave the dauphine a sign for her to leave. As she and her ladies withdrew, Louis asked the duchesse de Brancas to remain. Dufort recorded the scene which followed:

> The King said to Mme de Brancas: "Give me your cloak." He put it over his shoulders, walked into his bedroom in silence, then made his way to the cabinet next door. The dauphin, accustomed to follow him, advanced. He was not halfway down the room when the King turned and said: "Do not follow me!" . . . The King returned between three and four o'clock. He was not the same man: in place of his sad and severe look, his soul was calm, his expression agreeable, a smile on his lips; he spoke to us all, made jokes about the cloak which he wore, and left us saying he was going to have dinner, and urged us to do the same. . . . We had no trouble divining that he paid a visit to Madame de Pompadour. One single conversation with a friend who, more than anyone in his kingdom, was interested in his recovery, cured his mood.

Stainville, to whom the marquise described the details of the encounter, described its essence. "She was the god in the Opera who came down in the machine to calm all anxieties. She showed pleasure in seeing him, did not reproach him for his silence; she put him at his ease; he was most relieved to find peace instead of a storm of reproaches and from this moment he took up the same habit of going once a day to see her and telling her everything he knew."

In Paris, whatever shock there had been over the attempt on the king's life soon receded. At first, there was general consternation, many people going to church to pray for the king and to deplore the attempt on his life. But the mood did not last. On January 10 the theatres reopened and the populace went about its business—or at least the majority did so. The magistrates remained adjourned and, as Luynes put it, "*la fermentation subsiste toujours dans les esprits du Parlement*" ("the *parlement* is still in a state of agitation").

At Versailles, the king and the marquise took up the old way of life. "All the Court and all the foreign ministers were with her yesterday; the King goes there often; he was there yesterday standing with several others while she lunched, tête-à-tête, with M. le duc de Chaulnes. He supped there yesterday."

"The King is wonderfully well," the marquise herself told Stainville on January 20:

> I shall not tell you a word about all the horrors which took place in his rooms. Imagine for yourself the second volume of the Metz business, with the exception that he did not need to receive the sacraments. Add to the indignity of the proceedings the fact that everyone there was a man who owes his existence to me. The first favor I asked the King was that they not be punished. I do not wish that such despicable people be made objects of pity. . . . Do not believe that these events can weaken my courage. Only the loss of the King could cause that. He lives, all the rest is the same to me—cabals, indignities, libels. I shall serve him, whatever may happen to me, as long as I am in a position to do so. I rely on those who have seen me during the first six days to prove to you that, once the King's life was assured, my tranquility never failed for a moment.

Her anger at Machault ("a man who owes everything to me") was clear; her claim that he should not be punished ("I do not wish to have such despicable people be made objects of pity") disingenuous. She had survived her worst threat yet; revenge would be hers. "One must agree," noted Bernis, "that if the marquise had been spoiled by good fortune, if she had become too familiar with absolute power and supreme grandeur, she had had several days to reflect on her return to obscurity. But the danger passed, her reflections faded; she resumed her place on the throne with as much assurance, and perhaps more, than before."

Chapter 18

*"I admit that I was astonished at the facility,
the eloquence, the clarity of her expressions . . . and that
I regarded her with as much admiration as attention
on hearing her speak so well."*

After Damiens's attack, Louis XV became even more morose and even less decisive than usual. The marquise, on the other hand, her position stronger than ever, bounded with energy. She felt she understood the factors which had produced a Damiens, and she knew she could make the king understand them and take action. In her view, the insubordination of the *parlements*, the subversive activities of the prince de Conti, the overzealousness of the archbishop of Paris, the incompetence of Machault, and the arrogance of d'Argenson had all contributed to an atmosphere in which such an attempt at regicide was possible. She patiently and tenaciously set about pursuing those she considered responsible.

On February 1, 1757, Louis XV sent Machault a regretful note exiling him, but allowing him to remain at his house near Paris; to d'Argenson he wrote with icy coldness, ordering him to an exile far away at his estate in Poitou. Machault, who was tired and had expected something of this nature, was philosophical; d'Argenson, taken completely by surprise, was overcome with a bitter anguish which would never leave him.

The difference in approach is revealing. The marquise certainly had a hand in both dismissals; but she had been much more active in assuring that of d'Argenson. With the help of Berryer, she persuaded Louis that d'Argenson, who was responsible for Paris as one of his ministerial duties, had neglected to monitor the volatile security situation there. Somehow, she managed to blame d'Argenson for Damiens. And she was supposed to have shown the king a letter, *vraie ou supposée*, in which d'Argenson referred to Louis as an imbecile. Whether Janel had secretly opened his superior's mail and carried it to the marquise, or whether the whole letter was manufactured, d'Argenson was lost.*

As for Machault, the pretext for his exile was that he had become an irritant to *parlement;* in fact, this body remained just as recalcitrant after his dismissal as before. It was a specious reason, and, in his heart, Louis knew it. The day before the exile he was in a noticeably bad humor; the day after he wrote sadly to his daughter: "They have done so much that they have forced me to dismiss Machault, the man I trusted the most. I shall never console myself." Thus the king of France, with absolute power to act as he wished, acquiesced in the disgrace of the man he "trusted the most."

These competent men were replaced by mediocrities. The marquis de Paulmy, nephew of the comte d'Argenson, took over the war department from his uncle, and Monsieur Peyrenc de Moras took over the navy department from Machault. Rouillé remained at foreign affairs and took over the *Postes.* The two strongest presences on the Council of State were the abbé de Bernis, summoned there on January 2, 1757, and the seventy-two-year-old maréchal de Belle-Isle.

It was Madame de Pompadour who had selected Paulmy (*"ma petite horreur"*) and Peyrenc de Moras (*"mon gros cochon"*). Stainville voiced the general dismay. "Never was a Council more ridiculous as that of the King's after the dismissal of Messieurs d'Argenson and Machault." Paulmy was "puny in body, spirit, appearance, and talent, made precisely to receive kicks at a parade," and Moras "looked exactly like a large piece of beef, and had as many ideas as one. . . . I often asked Madame de Pompadour who could have encouraged her to make such laughable choices. She replied very naturally that, in order that the expulsion of those whom she wished to remove should not drag on, she had proposed their replace-

---

*Five days before the dismissals, the marquis d'Argenson, brother of the comte d'Argenson, died, "his pen in his hand." He was thus spared knowledge of his brother's disgrace and exile. But the last words he wrote in his journal were melancholy comments on the survival of Madame de Pompadour. For ten years he had expected her imminent fall and had done his best to precipitate it. He recognized that he had failed.

ment by those who were already in the ministry. I told her that this reason might be good for her, but that, on this occasion, at the beginning of
a terrifying war, she had not done the State a favor."

Madame de Pompadour no doubt used all her influence to bring
about the fall of d'Argenson, whom she had always hated, and Machault,
who had let her down. But there were plausible reasons of state for the
dismissals—d'Argenson had neglected Paris, and Machault was responsible for the disastrous ultimatum to *parlement*—and there were others
besides herself who thought the endless division between the two men
weakened the king's council. What is clear is that to let able men go at a
time of acute crisis and replace them with those below average was an
imprudent and shortsighted act.

The replacement of the two ministers was not the only activity upon
which Madame de Pompadour embarked in the weeks following
Damiens's attack. She used the king's weakened state to have him strip
the "birdcage" of its furniture, arguing that he must not provide his subjects with such obvious reasons for complaint. The Parc-aux-Cerfs was
maintained, but the king became more discreet. Almost under surveillance in his own palaces, he spent day after day hunting. Only when out
in the fresh air, with a few familiar faces, could he find peace.

It was Madame de Pompadour, thus, who took up part of the
burden of governing. When, on January 26, the magistrate Durey de
Meinières had an audience with the marquise, she used the opportunity to blame him for *parlement*'s attitude. Meinières was a reputed
lawyer, one of those most vocal in their opposition to the king. He had
taken himself to Versailles to plead for his son, who had been refused
a magistrate's post in order to teach the father a lesson. He left a vivid
account of his encounter with the marquise:

> Alone, standing near the fire, she looked me up and down with a dis-
> dain which has remained engraved in my mind all my life. Her head
> erect, she made no curtsy. Measuring me in the most imposing way in
> the world, she said in a dry tone, as if to a valet: "Be seated"; then,

seating herself, she listened to my request. Madame la marquise had
her eyes fixed on me in such a way as to disconcert me; she sat as
upright as a plank in her armchair, and made only a slight inclination
of her body when I mentioned her natural disposition to be obliging.
When I had finished, she took up my reply in a very lively fashion and
said: "How is this, monsieur, are you ignorant of your crime? . . . The
King is the master, monsieur, he does not judge it appropriate to express his displeasure personally, he contents himself with having you
feel the weight of it by depriving your son of a post." [She went on to
suggest that de Meinières help bring the striking magistrates back to
work] "and then you could hope for some change in the King's disposition. But when I have nothing else to say to His Majesty than: "Sire,
I saw M. de Meinières today; he sends his respect to your person, and
so on," the King replies: "What has he done to prove it?"

Meinières left. "I admit that I was astonished at the facility, the eloquence,
the clarity of her expressions, which I am perhaps rendering imperfectly,
and that I regarded her with as much admiration as attention on hearing
her speak so well."

Madame de Pompadour had made a strong impression on Meinières,
but he was unable to persuade his collegues to return to work. The king
responded by exiling sixteen of the leading magistrates. The atmosphere
was sinister. "Public discontent is everywhere," wrote Starhemberg. "The
estrangement and bullheadedness of *parlement* has become stronger than
ever, those who were the most disposed to submit have retracted; one
talks only of murder and poisoning. Someone has put up in the gallery
at Versailles terrible posters threatening the life of the King. In short, there
are nothing but complaints, murmurs, and protests against the ministry.
It is about Mme de Pompadour they complain most."

The marquise saw the hidden hand of the prince de Conti behind
such sedition. She was not alone in her suspicions. Frederick II of Prussia
also heard rumors. He did not believe them, but Madame de Pompadour
believed Conti capable of anything, even of trying to assassinate the king.
On February 7, 1757, Luynes noted that the marquise was convinced
that the king now "feared and hated Conti."

She instructed Berryer and Janel to keep up their surveillance of
the prince, and, unable to move directly against a member of the royal
family, contented herself with punishing Conti's associates. When one
of these, the comte de Broglie, asked to be considered for the embassy
to Vienna, one of the most important foreign posts, the marquise did
everything she could to hinder him. Broglie was one of those whom the
marquise disliked: intelligent, energetic, and ambitious, a brave soldier
and capable diplomat, he was also opinionated, outspoken, and tactless.
Devoted to the king, he had made no attempt to cultivate the marquise's
good graces. In addition, as a key player in the *secret du roi,* the small team
of diplomats dedicated to Louis's private objectives of playing off Poland against Russia, and other adventures, Broglie was closely attached
to the prince de Conti, a man who was now Madame de Pompadour's
bête noire. Madame de Pompadour only suspected the existence of the
secret, and did not associate Broglie with it; but she did associate him with
Conti, and did everything in her power to hinder his advance.

Broglie begged the king to support him against the marquise's hostility. Louis XV refused to intervene. Broglie would soon realize that he
stood no chance of getting the post to Vienna. Madame de Pompadour
had her own candidate, her protégé Stainville, and would continue to tar-
nish Broglie's reputation with the king. Years later the comte de Broglie
would write in the following letter to Louis XVI about the monarch's grandfather: "His sagacity, which enabled him in every case to perceive the better
course of action, was not, unfortunately, if I dare say so, always accompanied by the strength of character to execute it."

The comte de Stainville had rushed back from Rome after the news of
Damiens. (In his memoirs the comte records that he broke down in sobs
when he heard of the attack on the king.) He arrived at Versailles in mid-
February, and found the court in a somber mood, the king sad, Madame
de Pompadour agitated, the ministers frantically preparing for a war in
Germany, all against a backdrop of hostility from Church and *parlement.*

Armies were assembling and commanders being chosen. The main
French army, 100,000 men, was to march against the forces of Hanover,
and was placed under the command of the experienced maréchal d'Estrées.

The marquise's intimate friend, the prince de Soubise, would command a smaller army, which would march south into Germany.

The choice of generals was always a matter of intense interest and intrigue at court. The marquise was determined to push Soubise and did so successfully, using her influence with the all-powerful Pâris-Duverney to have him given a command. But apart from Soubise, she let Duverney and Belle-Isle decide. That did not prevent disappointed candidates from importuning her for positions. To one such, the comte de Clermont, the King's uncle, she wrote: "I esteem the maréchal d'Estrées because I believe him a very honorable man; with regard to his military talents, I assuredly cannot be the judge, and the public cannot tax me with the choice (without the greatest injustice)." She had learned not to be regarded as directing the king's choices. In the case of Soubise, however, she made no secret of her partisanship.

The duc de Croÿ had hastened north after the attempt on the king's life, in order to investigate the background of Damiens, a native of Artois. On his return to court in March, he found the marquise consumed with affairs of the state and the king as taciturn as ever. Louis XV gave Croÿ no word of thanks for his endeavors, no gracious acknowledgment of his pains, nothing. "I received only a little nod of the head. I was more upset on his account than on mine." Madame de Pompadour, on the other hand, was receiving the court like a queen, giving audience to the new *cordons bleus*, summoning the ministers, attending Mass daily, the very image of dignity and majesty.

Croÿ also noted that, after every meeting of the Council of State, all the ministers came to her supper to make *un petit doigt de cour* (a little gesture of obeisance), and that she treated the new ministers, particularly Paulmy at the war office, in a deeply patronizing manner. "He is coming along well!" she remarked. "If his health is good enough, there is hope that he will succeed!" Croÿ thought her "at the pinnacle, stronger than ever. There were no ministers in a strong enough position to speak out at the Council. . . . Mme de Pompadour, Belle-Isle, and the abbé de Bernis principally took the tiller." As for the king, he "only wished to talk of gardening, and his passion for evergreens, his new hobby."

In the marquise's intimate circle, Madame d'Estrades had been replaced as friend and confidante by Anne-Marguerite-Gabrielle de

Beauvau-Craon, maréchale de Mirepoix. Madame de Mirepoix was very charming, and Madame de Pompadour was soon acting on her behalf, seeing to it that Madame de Mirepoix's husband and later her brother, the prince de Beauvau, received promotions to Captains of the King's Bodyguard, leapfrogging over more senior candidates, and causing consternation in the great noble families who were used to receiving these posts.*

Madame de Pompadour's other protégé, the comte de Stainville, was about to receive the coveted posting to Vienna. "Be silent, ambassador, do not say a word about that which you spoke of so much today and yesterday," she warned him. "I hope that all will go well, but do not boast about anything, neither to princes nor princesses [a reference to the princesse de Robecq, Stainville's mistress] . . . I am going to order a *grillade* for Your Excellency."

The marquise had nothing but admiration for her "pretty little monkey of an ambassador." She loved his high spirits, his wicked sense of humor, his swagger. She rejoiced in his lofty appointment, and in the fact that she had, once again, overcome the king's reluctance. "Never mind, my dear comte, you are named! Remember all I wanted for the good of our plan and for you. I am very happy that the King has told your friend that it was she who had changed his mind! That was honorable of him, and must be true . . ." And in a casual fashion, she went on to refer to the trial of Damiens, which was coming to a conclusion in Paris. "Damiens will really be executed next week. Bonjour, monsieur l'ambassadeur à Vienne."

Damiens's trial had begun on February 12 before a court consisting of magistrates and lawyers of the Paris *parlement*. Conti was one of the judges and spoke often at the trial; so often in fact that the duc de Luynes and others thought that he was deliberately prolonging and confusing the proceedings. Luynes hinted that Conti was trying to deny any suggestion that some members of *parlement* might have had connections to Damiens; but Conti's eagerness in this regard merely reinforced suspicion that he

---

*Madame de Mirepoix was revered by Montesquieu, who called her simple, natural, and shy without awkwardness. Louis XV liked her, and later persuaded her to become the confidante of Madame du Barry. She died in 1791.

himself might know more than he admitted. Madame de Pompadour certainly believed that he did. She told Bernis that Conti's reputation would never be repaired, due to the "violent suspicion" attached to him.

Damiens was found guilty of attempted regicide on March 26 and sentenced to be executed on March 28. He underwent a ghastly punishment unknown in France for 150 years. Tortured, then set on fire, his mangled body, still breathing, was torn apart by four horses. These grisly efforts took over two hours, watched by a huge crowd on a cold and raw evening outside the hôtel de Ville. A few raised their voices against the brutality. "I loved the King with a passion," wrote Dufort de Cheverny. "I felt all the extent of the infamy; if I had been present I would have massacred the guilty man myself. But at the end of three months, nature and humanity resumed their rights. I did not understand how what one calls good society could savor a pleasure which belongs only to the vilest *canaille* [rabble]." The court averted its eyes. The savagery inflicted upon Damiens was also in evidence in a grim edict of April 1757 which decreed death to "all those convicted of having written or printed any works intended to attack religion, to assail the royal authority, or to disturb the order and tranquility of the realm." This decree was an act of repression, going far beyond the restrictions already in place on publishers and writers. A chill went through the intellectual community. Madame de Pompadour would not allow herself to recall happier times, when she invited writers to court, when Voltaire was her friend. She now considered the *encyclopédistes* dangerous men, bent on undermining the foundations of France.

On May 1, 1757, the second Treaty of Versailles was signed between France and Austria. It is not surprising that it was advantageous to Austria; the French were negotiating from a position of weakness. The whole object of the treaty was to destroy Prussia; Louis XV promised to support the empress by maintaining, at his expense, 10,000 German soldiers, in addition to the 24,000 auxiliaries promised under the first treaty. Louis also engaged himself to send her, for the duration of the war, an annual subsidy of 12 million florins and to put into the line of battle 105,000 of his own troops. In return, Louis XV would receive some towns in the Austrian Netherlands, and his son-in-law, Don Felipe, now in Parma, would get the rest.

Louis XV recognized the burdens which this treaty imposed on France, but did not believe it would be a long and costly war. The Russians were providing 80,000 men, Sweden 30,000. Surely Prussia could not withstand such a coalition. Louis, who would not go to war (it was impossible for a French king to pass through other neutral countries to battle), was no doubt content to watch as his armies set forth.

Stainville heard of the treaty at Crécy before he left for Vienna:

> I never saw anyone as enthusiastic about his work as the abbé de Bernis; as he gave me the documents he seemed to say: "You will agree, when you have read them, that I am the greatest diplomat there ever was." Belle-Isle approved of all the compliments Bernis gave himself, knocking his cane on the floor and patting his stomach. The marquise indicated that I was very fortunate to be the instrument which such great ministers were employing, and I, with a humble and idiotic air, replied: "I shall tell you what I think when I have read the documents." I spent the night reading them. What an astonishment to see all the ways in which they had muddled up everything . . . the most telling point was how France had been sacrificed for an illusion. . . . I took the treaty back to Madame de Pompadour. At my arrival, she, as well as M. de Belle-Isle and the abbé de Bernis, came to me and with an overjoyed air asked how I had liked their work. "It is so immense that it would be rash of me after a simple reading to give my opinion. One must study it for a long time in order to understand all its ramifications. The project is ambitious, very ambitious: but the execution of it, I admit, frightens me." "We shall reassure you," said M. de Belle-Isle, and after several words of ecstasy on the benefits of his work, we spoke no more of the treaty.

Stainville was making great progress in convincing Madame de Pompadour of his devotion, his shrewdness, and his ruthlessness, all qualities which appealed to her. Preparing for his ambassadorship to Vienna, he told the marquise that it would be hard for him to follow the orders of M. Rouillé, the minister for foreign affairs, whom he found tiresome and incompetent. The marquise responded that the king also found Rouillé out of his depth and would be very happy to see him resign his post, but "Madame Rouillé likes the court too much to allow her husband to retire; she is, after all, a bourgeoise not designed to be here[!]." Stainville assured her that he could procure Rouillé's resignation within an hour, and, with Madame de Pompadour's amused consent, rushed off to do so.

Stainville succeeded in frightening Madame Rouillé out of her wits by making her see that her existence at court depended on her husband's health, and that that in turn depended upon his being released from the cares of office. If her husband resigned from the foreign ministry, Stainville asserted, he would keep his job as superintendant of the *Postes*, as well as his seat on the Council, and there would be no need for him or her to leave the court. "She resisted for some time; but at last she agreed with Stainville and convinced her husband to hand in his resignation, which the comte carried in triumph to the marquise; Madame de Pompadour was as surprised as she was delighted." The marquise saw no irony in the fact that she herself, as a mere bourgeoise, had grown intoxicated with court life, and, one feels sure, Stainville never permitted himself any reference to such a notion, except in solitude.

Thus, on June 28, 1757, the abbé de Bernis became minister for foreign affairs. Madame de Pompadour now had her old friend in this key position, and Stainville, her miracle-working protégé, about to leave for Vienna. She felt more confident about the progress of the war, and able to tell her friend Madame de Lutzelbourg, "I hate to the death your Lutherans for loving the King of Prussia." "If I were at Strasbourg," she added, "I would fight all day long."

As to the king's condition, however, he remained sunk in gloom and seemed profoundly bored and distant, never addressing a word to those he did not know, taciturn with those he did. Only Madame de Pompadour could prevail upon him to take an interest in anyone. When the comte de Saint-Priest returned to court from distinguished service abroad, the marquise, who was "all-powerful . . . treated me with a very particular distinction; that favor caused the king to look in my direction. At Marly one day he asked me several questions about myself, with so much kindness that I responded without embarrassment. . . . It is Madame de Pompadour, without contradiction, who plays the leading role at Versailles, not from authority but from influence: every favor came from the favorite:

she received not only the homage of the courtiers, but also those of the Princes themselves. One assisted at her toilette on certain days of the week, and I have often seen there M. le duc d'Orléans and M. le prince de Condé as well as foreign princes, making a circle on foot at a respectful distance."

By June, preparations for war were well advanced. In London, William Pitt and the Duke of Newcastle divided up the government between them. Pitt believed in preemptive strikes; he planned to send an expedition to the French coast and the port of Rochefort, where it was believed that a landing would also spark rebellion among the French Protestants. In the region, Herrenschwand reported that the Protestants were ready to revolt and could receive foreign help. Madame de Pompadour made sure the king was made aware of Conti's possible role in this treachery, although hard evidence was impossible to find. The prince remained under close watch.

As for Frederick of Prussia, he too believed in striking first. He had started an offensive campaign in April, conquering half of Bohemia, and by May was besieging the 40,000 Austrian soldiers bottled up in Prague. However, on June 18 he was defeated at Kollin, on the Elbe, losing nearly half his 30,000 troops in the battle. Versailles and Vienna were jubilant; Kollin was Frederick's first defeat. On the same date as the battle of Kollin, Bernis was made Minister of Foreign Affairs. He seemed to be a lucky mascot, bringing the king nothing but good news. "Well, well, look at him," observed Louis XV, "he has the air of one who won a battle." "The King has emerged victorious," the marquise told Stainville, "the future will be even more brilliant. The abbé is a skilled and honorable man. I want you to adore him."

The alliance with Austria seemed to be the only matter in which Louis XV took a sustained interest. "Keep in mind the intimate union with the court of Vienna," he told the comte de Broglie. "It is my work and I believe it good and I wish to maintain it . . ." He and the marquise were looking forward to the complete defeat of the King of Prussia, as the French armies moved against him from the west, the Swedes and Russians from the north and east.

Frederick was discouraged. He begged Pitt for help and railed against Madame de Pompadour, whom he believed had turned King Louis against him. While railing against her, he was not beneath attempting a bribe, having his agents "boldly suggest and promise to Madame de Pompadour on my behalf that, peace being made between France and myself, I would cede to her, as long as she lives, the principality of Neuchâtel and of Valangin with all appurtenances and revenues." The offer was probably never made; the marquise would certainly have scorned its falsity. When it came to the king's *gloire*, she was as avid for it as the most patriotic Frenchman. Frederick would never lose his conviction that because of her low birth the marquise had to be dishonorable. But then he never understood women at all.

In early July 1757 the king, feeling optimistic about the war, followed the marquise to Champs, a country house on the banks of the Marne which she had rented from the duc de La Vallière for 12,000 livres a year. (There would be no visits to Compiègne for the duration of the war.) Champs was an exquisite little house, famous for its *chinoiseries*, wall panels depicting imaginary Far Eastern landscapes, painted in soft greens, blues, and pinks.

But Louis XV did not take to Champs. He had still not recovered emotionally from Damiens's attack. The British government heard rumors that the king was considering abdicating the throne. Horace Walpole thought that "their King threw a damp on all operations; melancholy, apprehensive of assassination, desirous of resigning the crown, averse to the war from principles of humanity, and still resigned to the influence of his mistress, every measure was confirmed by him with reluctance or obtained by intrigue."

These observations of Walpole's might take Louis's discomfort too far. There is no evidence that he considered abdication. But neither is there any doubt that he was severely depressed, haunted by fear of another attempt on his life, unable to forget his brush with death. As Choiseul later put it: "To a weak mind the fear of an imaginary danger lasts as long as that of a real danger."

On the war front, the armies set forth. The main French troops, under the command of the maréchal d'Estrées, were in northern Germany, about to do battle with the Duke of Cumberland, son of King George II, who was defending Hanover. The prince de Soubise, with a smaller army, had been sent south to join the Austrians, who were preparing to attack Silesia.

As usual in the French army of the time, intrigues were constantly afoot. D'Estrées was forced to set out before his supply lines were organized so that he might dispose of Cumberland more quickly, and then lend support to Soubise; d'Estrées complained privately that if he failed to support Soubise, "Madame de Pompadour would be displeased." He had hardly set out when there were whispers that he had quarreled with Pâris-Duverney over a shortage of supplies and that Duverney wanted d'Estrées replaced by Richelieu, his old crony. Belle-Isle warned his friend d'Estrées: "My dear Maréchal, if you wish to continue to command the army of the King, hurry to pass the Weser, to do battle and to win it . . ."

Unfortunately for those plotting against him, d'Estrées had the temerity to win the battle of Hastenbeck at the end of July, driving Cumberland's army back toward the Elbe and cutting him off. Immediately after this feat, he was dismissed from command, and replaced by the duc de Richelieu. "All Europe was astonished that, after such a considerable gain, the successful Estrées was removed from command; but Europe was unaware of the intrigues of Versailles . . ."

The normally reticent duc de Luynes was beside himself. "The change of generals is one of those events which will baffle posterity; a battle won, a country conquered . . . is that the moment when the general is recalled? They claim that the new arrangement was made and prepared without the King's knowledge, and that Mme de Pompadour was also in the dark; but how can one think so?" How indeed.

Duverney advised Richelieu to occupy Hanover and the left bank of the Elbe. Richelieu succeeded in doing so and Cumberland retreated. Madame de Pompadour began a correspondence with Richelieu, a man whom she had never trusted, trying to win him over and also to let him know that she would be watching his progress with great attention. "I have always wished for and sought the means to win your friendship, Monsieur le Maréchal. That is to tell you how much it matters to me . . ." She also wished to hasten his advance, for, once he had defeated Cumberland, he could then send troops to Soubise.

❀   ❀   ❀

At the salon in August, Boucher's great painting of the marquise was exhibited on a dais. She reclines on a chaise longue, a pillow of patterned cotton under her arm, behind her an elaborate glass-fronted bookcase surmounted by a clock and her coat of arms. Her head is reflected in a large mirror with a curved gilded frame. By her hand, a rosewood writing table, its drawer open, a quill pen in an inkwell, a candle, sealing wax, seal, and letter. She holds a book; other books, stamped with her emblems, lie on the table; a rolled-up map, music, and a portfolio of drawings and engravings are at her feet; Mimi, her black King Charles spaniel, sits at her feet. It is, as the Goncourts later wrote, "the favorite in her coronation robes."

This moment of supremacy was, in a way, the last triumph. The events of late 1757 did not bode well either for the marquise or for France. A serious rival appeared at court, in the person of Marie-Anne-Louise-Adélaïde de Mailly, marquise de Coislin. A member of the Mailly family, from whom Louis XV's first favorites had come, she was a tall, rather imposing young woman, who possessed great charm and lively intelligence. Madame du Hausset relates how one evening Madame de Pompadour returned from the salon at Marly in a state of complete agitation, throwing down her cloak and muff and undressing with furious impatience. She had played cards with Madame de Coislin, watched attentively by all the court, and Madame de Coislin had said two or three times, with an insulting look, "I stake all," and then, "I have a Royal pair." Madame du Hausset asked if the king had observed this. "You do not know him, my dear; if he were going to move her into my rooms this evening, he would still treat her coldly in public, and treat me with the greatest friendship. This is the result of his upbringing, for he himself is honest and open."

Madame de Pompadour was further disturbed by the king's decision to back down in his conflicts with *parlement*. The government was in dire need of the war funds *parlement* could approve, and so the king could not afford to keep the magistrates in exile much longer. On September 1, 1757, the *parlement* of Paris returned to work, after almost a year in exile, to tumultuous public acclamations. The king had drawn back from his firm stand of the previous year; all Madame de Pompadour's eloquence with Durey de Meinières had failed to produce any result. It was the king who had given in.

This was a bitter blow to the marquise; she despised the magistrates and considered the king's attitude by far too conciliatory. "The story of *parlement* adds to the fermentation they have stirred up with so much ill-will," she told Richelieu. "God knows what will happen. I am sick to death. My head, my nerves are in such disorder. You shouldn't be surprised, since you know how susceptible I am, and my attachment to the King and his glory."

Madame de Pompadour felt that the *parlements* were a profound threat to royal authority. To see the king obliged to recall them without obtaining any guarantees of obedience affected her physically. "My health has not been too good for the last two weeks, *grand'femme*," she told Madame de Lutzelbourg. "The crisis we are in with the *parlement* has been a terrible shock to my nerves. All I see in France are madmen and bad citizens."

In the military arena, Madame de Pompadour was anxious about the progress of Richelieu's army. From Fontainebleau, where the court spent only three weeks for reasons of economy, she encouraged him, albeit somewhat ambiguously: "I do not think, Monsieur le Maréchal, that you march too slowly—you surely cannot be suspected of not wishing to see Monsieur de Cumberland close up . . ."

On August 21, 1757, Cumberland, trapped between the Aller and the Elbe, wrote to Richelieu proposing a suspension of arms preparatory to an accord. The convention of Kloster-Seven was signed on September 10. Cumberland tried to make the best of a desperate position by negotiating a surrender on terms that saved his army. Richelieu named only two conditions: that Cumberland send home those of his troops who were not from Hanover, and that he withdraw half of his Hanoverian battalions beyond the Elbe, leaving the remainder in internment camps near the port of Stade. None of Cumberland's troops were made to surrender their arms.

On September 17 news reached London of Cumberland's capitulation. "Come back at once by warship and explain," wrote a furious George II to his son. London thought Kloster-Seven a diplomatic humiliation; the French court, initially at least, thought it a triumph, al-

though Bernis was horrified that Richelieu had not consulted the ministry. Richelieu was now free to link up with Soubise, whose army was in
southern Germany. But he delayed again, allowing his army to pillage
and loot, earning for himself the nickname "little father Marauder." The
marquise was unhappy about this. "I clearly see [if you do not put an
end to the indiscipline in your army] that the King will have no triumph
at all, that he will be ruined and that all the world will order him around,
when it is for him to order the entire universe." And then she issued a
veiled threat—her speciality. "Do not like me only halfway, Monsieur le
Maréchal. My heart is not made for lukewarmness. One must like me a
great deal, convince me of it, and one is sure afterward of a most sincere
reward."

Madame de Pompadour told Richelieu that her nerves had been
tormenting her for two weeks. It was not merely Richelieu's annoying
hesitations which caused her migraines, palpitations, and fevers. She was
already attacked by tuberculosis, fatigued and agitated equally, using
stimulants to sustain her energy and soporifics to help her sleep. When
the king's daughter, Madame Infante, arrived at court from Parma, with
every intention of making a long visit, this meant, for the marquise, yet
another unwelcome presence at court. Madame de Pompadour found her
a tiresome young woman who, with very little reason, fancied herself an
authority on political affairs. And the marquise was also worried about
Madame de Coislin, for she well knew how easily a skillful rival could
manipulate the king.

In addition to anxieties over Soubise, Madame de Coislin, *parlement*,
Madame Infante, the king's mood, a threat of invasion was imminent. A
huge fleet of British ships had set sail from Portsmouth on September
8—eighteen warships, six frigates, two hospital ships, forty-four transports, and six cruisers. Eight thousand land troops were aboard. Early
in the evening of September 20 the British fleet was observed off the
coast of France, near the Ile-de-Ré. On September 24 the news came to
Fontainebleau. Troops were rushed to Brittany and the local inhabitants,
many of whom were Protestants, were ordered to give up their arms. But
the fleet merely bombarded the coastline, set some barracks on fire, and
then, on October 1, sailed away. A rendezvous with French Protestants

had not happened. (Pitt, the chief promoter of the expedition, believed it had been sabotaged in London because George II did not want to put Hanover further at risk.)

At the French court, suspicion again centered on the role Conti might have played; it was made clear to him that he had forfeited all hope of the king's favor, and that it would be prudent for him to retire. Conti withdrew into his Parisian base at the Temple, where, as Grand Prior of the Order of Malta, he was immune from prosecution. He never returned to the public stage.

Conti's eclipse saw the rise of Berryer, the Paris chief of police and spy for Madame de Pompadour. He was named to sit on the Council for the Interior, and replaced as lieutenant of the Paris police by Henri Bertin, who was the king's representative at Lyon. Berryer had for a long time played a significant role in Madame de Pompadour's affairs. He had been her eyes and ears in Paris, the loyal servant who had tracked down her enemies, spreading misinformation and doubt about those who might seek to dislodge her. His influence had weighed heavily in the dismissals of d'Argenson and Machault, and the persecution of Conti. Now established in Versailles, he could continue his espionage on the marquise's behalf, even better placed to uncover an intrigue, or start one. With Conti definitively outmaneuvered, and Berryer at her side, the marquise could turn her attention to Richelieu. It was imperative, in her view, that he act more quickly to go to the aid of Soubise.

Madame de Pompadour was sure that Soubise's chance for glory was at hand. With Richelieu's men at his disposal, he could vanquish the insolent king of Prussia. She insisted Pâris-Duverney do everything he could to ensure Soubise's success: "Although I am quite sure, dear Blockhead, of the friendship which monsieur de Soubise has for you and of that which you have for him, his position is so precarious at the moment that I cannot prevent myself from calling your attention to him. . . . The only thing that can prevent his success is a lack of supplies; I therefore ask you, in the name of the friendship you have for me, to lend your help to his army. If you promise me this, I shall have no more worries and shall look forward to a happy outcome. You are perceptive, my Blockhead, you know me, see how grateful I shall be; but I would not love you any the less, for that has been true for a long time."

Richelieu's delay in sending reinforcements to Soubise was causing the latter to think of going with his men into winter quarters and then, when his army and that of Richelieu's had come together, attacking Magdebourg in the spring. But the empress was impatient; she wanted to see Saxony liberated; Paulmy, the minister for war, was unclear in his directives, but seemed to favor an attack, sending Soubise the authorization to give battle "if he believed he could do so with advantage." Stainville was also pushing for action: "And so, *mon prince,* in the execution of the orders given by M. le marquis de Paulmy, if you believe you should follow them, arrange it so that you add to our political glory and try to ensure that the blame for the occupation of Saxony not fall entirely on us."

With no clear orders, therefore, Soubise joined up with the Austrian army near Rossbach, west of Leipzig. The Prussian army, and Frederick, were waiting. Soubise and the Austrian commander, von Hildburghausen, disagreed on tactics and, on the morning of November 5, both hesitated as to their next move, despite having a superior position and troops superior to the enemy. The Franco-Austrian army slowly began to break camp, a process which consumed about three hours. After eleven o'clock they were finally on the march, the plan being to proceed across Frederick's front to form a new line perpendicular to his left flank, and then attack. But as they were turning to deploy northward, putting them in an awkward state, the Prussian cavalry caught their vanguard, consisting mostly of cavalry units, in front and by the right flank. By the time the first melée had ended, the Prussian infantry were descending upon the French and Austrian infantry, already demoralized by the spectacle of the rout of their cavalry. The allied troops fell into confusion, broke ranks, and fled. The losses were not heavy, by the standards of the time (the allies lost more than 7,000 men, but only about 500 were killed; the Prussians had fewer than 200 killed and about 350 wounded), but the disgrace was great. "This was not a battle at all," wrote Voltaire. "This was an entire army presenting itself at combat, and then leaving. . . . This was the most unheard of and the most complete defeat ever spoken of in history. . . . The defeats at Agincourt, at Crécy, at Poitiers, were not as humiliating." When, as was the custom, Frederick welcomed to his table the captured French officers, he said: "But, *messieurs,* I did not expect you so soon, nor in such great numbers."

"The allied army has just been defeated," Soubise told Stainville despondently. "Think of the despair of the French . . . I only wish to save the army and to revitalize it following the misfortune it has just suffered. . . . There are no more tents; all the rest is a battlefield. . . . What a fate! And whom can one trust? Ardor, good will, bravery, I dare say it, were on our side. But in half an hour, the maneuvers of the King of Prussia made the cavalry and the infantry bend; they all retired without flight, without ever turning their heads. . . . I can picture to myself the court's reaction when they learn of this sad news; my heart is broken."

The news reached Versailles in the evening of November 12. In Paris came mockery and derision:

> Soubise said, lantern in hand:
> "I had better look. Where the Devil is my army?
> It was there this morning
> Have they taken it or am I going mad?
> Ah! I lose everything, I am an idiot.
> Heaven, what do I see? How my soul is relieved!
> Happy omen! Behold! Behold!
> And *sacre vert*! What then is this?
> I am mistaken; it is the enemy's army."

On November 15, distraught at the news of the defeat, the marquise decided to make her will; in a characteristically thorough and orderly manner, she made requests to her lawyer, Collin, her doctor, Quesnay, her serving women, her valets de chambre, cooks, and so on. She asked the king to accept "my house in Paris as a gift as a palace for one of his grandsons. I wish that it go to monseigneur le comte de Provence (the third son of the dauphin)." She left most of her possessions to her brother, with Soubise as executor. In the final paragraph of the document is a touching testimonial to her deep affection for the defeated general. "However afflicting my commission may be for M. de Soubise, he should regard it as a certain proof of the trust which his probity and virtues have inspired in me. I beg him to accept two of my rings, the one a large aquamarine-colored diamond, the other an engraving by Guay representing Friendship. I flatter myself that he will always keep them, and that they will remind him of the person who has for him the most tender of friendships."

In a bout of serious estate planning, exemplifying her melancholy mood, she sold Crécy to the duc de Penthièvre, a cousin of the king, and Bellevue to the king.

"Monsieur de Soubise is incalculably unfortunate," she told Madame de Lutzelbourg. "You know my friendship for him, imagine my grief at the enormous injustices done him in Paris, for among his army he is admired and loved as he deserves. . . . Why does Providence permit such misfortunes? I am in despair. Bonsoir, *ma grande comtesse,* I do not wish to burden you any longer with the miseries you share with me because of your friendship for me, and which I return."

Bernis was even more distraught than the marquise. "I suffer on the wheel, and my martyrdom is useless to the State," he lamented to Stainville, before discussing the plight of Madame de Pompadour. "Our friend is indeed to be pitied. The public would have pardoned M. de Soubise for getting the command if only he had won a victory; the public is unjust, but that it is how it is. . . . I pointed out to her that we had not yet lost anything in the naval war . . . but that in the long run it was impossible that the English, superior in naval strength, would not eventually take our colonies, the foundation of our external commerce, that our allies could not compensate us for this loss . . . in this situation, it was madness to continue an immense war. . . . These considerations did not persuade Madame de Pompadour, who looked at political affairs like a child; but she had no good reasons to oppose to mine."

Madame de Pompadour might despair at Soubise's defeat, but she did not despair of the alliance with Austria, knowing how much it meant to the king, and she did not accept Bernis's pessimistic assessment. From here on, his constant complaints and sad predictions would undermine their relationship. Almost as soon as she had placed him in power, the marquise decided he was out of his depth. It was a bitter realization for her.

Richelieu, aware that the defeat at Rossbach might be laid at his door, sprang into action in Brunswick, ready to move either left, against the Hanoverians, or right, to prevent the king of Prussia from pursuing Soubise. Then he learned that the Hanoverians, whom he had allowed to depart at Kloster-Seven, were being added to the enemy troops. The "truce" of Kloster-Seven was ended. Richelieu was in dire straits. He had displeased the marquise, Belle-Isle, and Duverney.

Madame de Pompadour did not hesitate to let him know her feelings: "I am upset in every way, Monsieur le Maréchal, at the campaign you have recommenced. I hope it will be short and successful, and that you will soon be able to come here to repair your nerves and your head, for I must admit my astonishment that the immense volumes you have received from here these last two months have not made themselves understood. Time will clarify everything, one must count on that. My health is extremely precarious. I do not sleep or digest my food and I am not surprised. I am very aware of your concern for me, and you know, Monsieur le Maréchal, the sentiments I have for you."

Frederick of Prussia followed Rossbach with another great victory at Leuthen, near Breslau, on December 5. This battle, the tactical masterpiece of his career, left one-third of the Austrian army dead, captured, or wounded. After the battle, the Prussian army sang the chorale which would be known as the *"Leuthen"* ever after: *"Nun danket alle Gott."* ["Now let us all give thanks to God."] In fifteen days, Frederick had recaptured all Silesia.

Bernis digested the bad news and came to the conclusion that France needed "a man of will power . . . I shall be his valet de chambre, if he wish, and most willingly." The observation must have startled Stainville, to whom it was addressed; at Versailles, according to the Minister for Foreign Affairs himself, there was no one available to lead the country.

Louis XV, according to Bernis, was upset, but "not too much so. He has not said a word which is not firm and decided; this is an important point, but it is not all one would wish." Bernis looked to the king for leadership; he found none. Everything was in chaos: "Belle-Isle writes briefs to the War Office, who takes no notice; Duverney writes briefs which his friend Richelieu ignores. We have neither generals nor ministers. I unfortunately find this phrase so appropriate and so apt that I believe this to be true of myself . . ."

There would be war at sea, in the colonies, and in Europe. Paulmy at the War Office and Peyrenc de Moras at the navy were not up to their jobs. Bernis was overwhelmed. In fact, of all the protagonists at the French court, it was Madame de Pompadour who showed the most fight.

"'Leuthen does not weaken my courage," she told Kaunitz. "Every noble soul rebels against misfortune and only becomes more animated in finding ways to recover. . . . I hate the victor more than I ever have; let us take firm measures, let us pulverize the Attila of the North and you will see me as content as I am now in a bad humor." But the coming year would do little to restore her mood.

Chapter 19

*"I can no longer console myself over the nation's shame,
and the cruel situation in which we find ourselves."*

At Versailles, after the battle at Rossbach, the mood was grim. Bernis was desperately searching for money, trying to find men and supplies for the next year of the war. New generals must be found to replace the defeated Soubise and the discredited Richelieu. The coast of France must be protected from British attacks. The Austrians must be supplied with their promised subsidies. The task ahead was daunting.

And yet in this very troubling year, possibly the blackest of Madame de Pompadour's life, three ravishing portraits of her were painted by Boucher. The artist depicted her at her toilette, *en déshabillé*, gracefully applying rouge, the king's portrait prominent in her pearl bracelet; he painted her reading in her garden, in repose in a silvery gray dress, the works of Bernis and Voltaire at her elbow; and he most famously depicted her in a rose-pink lacy dress standing near a statue of Friendship in the gardens of Bellevue. In each painting, her serene and confident pose was clearly at odds with the realities of life at court during these difficult times.

Bernis was quite demoralized. "My opinion would be to make peace," he told Stainville. "Try to make two things clear to M. de Kaunitz, that the King will never abandon the Empress [Maria-Theresa], but it is not necessary that he ruin himself along with her. The project which seemed in September so certain of success has come to a shambles and an assured disaster, due to our respective failings. It was a beautiful dream, but one dangerous to continue. . . . The King will do what he can to support his allies, but I shall never advise him to put his crown at risk."

And yet Louis XV himself seemed oblivious to the setbacks. "The King never spoke of matters which would give hope to or animate his subjects," noted Croÿ, "and this caused a great deal of disappointment. He gave the impression of being unfeeling and indecisive, choosing to take the course others suggested to him, rather than the one he himself preferred, which would often have been the wiser one."

While Louis XV immured himself in silence and passivity, the marquise involved herself in everything. "All the ministers came twice a day to consult with her. She did absolutely everything, never has credit been pushed so far. She treated important affairs seriously, and with good sense, and seemed well intentioned and wished for the good." And yet, one senses Croÿ's discomfort with the seeming role reversal of king and favorite.

But Madame de Pompadour was all the more energized, as she had had the pleasure of seeing the proud marquise de Coislin sent away. A combination of the lady's arrogance, the king's timidity, and Madame de Pompadour's skillful intrigues caused her fall.

Madame de Pompadour had seen to it that a pretty young girl was brought to the Parc-aux-Cerfs, a girl who would distract Louis from Madame de Coislin. And she also made use of the gullible Bernis, telling him, with tears in her eyes, that she had asked the king for permission to retire from the court and was awaiting his response. Bernis immediately rushed to write to Louis himself, declaring that "a new mistress would harm his reputation, his affairs of state, and irritate the court of Vienna, which had addressed itself to Mme de Pompadour," and asserting that he, Bernis, "would certainly not work with another woman." On receiving a reply from the king, Bernis carried it, still unsealed, to the marquise who, upon opening it, wept with admiration and gratitude. Louis XV humbly promised to renounce his affair with Madame de Coislin, "aware of the danger to his reputation and his affairs." Bernis had earned a smile from his patroness, and the marquise had another reason to congratulate herself on her dramatic abilities. (As a reward for his services, Bernis received the abbey of Trois-Fontaines, near Dijon, worth 50,000 livres a year, and he became a member of the order of the Holy Ghost.)

In fact, Marie-Anne de Coislin had herself contributed to her own downfall. "She could have succeeded," wrote the worldly Duclos, "but, instead of leading her lover by degrees to the final conquest, which would have meant the downfall of her rival, instead of inviting his desires by withholding herself, she surrendered so quickly that she extinguished the desires of the King; she gave herself like a whore, and was taken and abandoned like a whore."*

Free of her rival, confirmed in her supremacy, Madame de Pompadour turned to the business of choosing the generals for the forthcoming campaign. While Richelieu was still in Germany, the decision to replace him was made. "The King has named monsieur the comte de Clermont, Prince of the Blood, to command the army of the maréchal de Richelieu, who has asked to resign for reasons of health. They say that M. de Richelieu has a kind of leprosy . . ." Richelieu's leprosy was a fiction; his real sin was to have refused to put himself and his army at the disposal of Soubise. But, given the results, he might as well have had leprosy. His disgrace was certain.

Clermont was not a good choice; except for his royal heritage, he had few qualities to recommend him. A man of the cloth, he nonetheless lived publicly with the actress La Camargo, and had yet to accomplish anything of military significance. But he pressed his case, and the list of alternative nominees was short.

Unfortunately the most able general in France, the maréchal d'Estrées, had fallen victim to the intrigues of the court. Then the competent duc de Broglie was sidelined due to Madame de Pompadour's suspicion that he and his brother, the comte de Broglie, were too close to the prince de Conti. The marquise was not aware that the comte de Broglie was in close contact with the king, as head of the *secret du roi*, the team of diplomats who communicated with the king in codes, and pursued policies often at odds with official French policy; but she held both Broglies in suspicion and treated them with contempt. "I could not obtain, Sire, the audience I requested of Mme de Pompadour," wrote the comte de Broglie to the king. "She lost her temper, in the presence of the maréchale de Mirepoix,

*Madame de Coislin died at an advanced age in 1829 at her home at the corner of the rue Royale and the place de la Concorde in Paris. She had held a salon there for many years, and was never reluctant to discuss her affair with Louis XV, albeit in rather different terms from those of Duclos.

speaking of me in the most insulting manner, and using terms Your Majesty would not use against the least and most blameworthy of his subjects. I cannot imagine how I might have merited such treatment . . ." But Louis XV could not find the courage to stand up for the loyal and honest Broglie. "I shall do what is possible for you . . . the circumstances are very delicate," was all he could offer.

As soon as the comte de Clermont left for his campaign against the Prussians, Madame de Pompadour began to write to him, making herself the king's official messenger. "This courier brings to Monseigneur the list of general officers. . . . The abbé de Bernis asks me to let you know that he thinks it appropriate for you to take the trouble of writing to the Empress to assure Her Majesty of his good intentions about the alliance. . . . Would you please tell the marquis de Montbrun that I have sent his memoranda to the controller general . . ."

Clermont did not find his march an easy one, as he toiled toward Hanover. The marquise could not resist one of her jabs: " I am indeed unhappy that the bad roads make your journey so tiring and so long, and I fear that they will be even more dangerous after Strasbourg."

On February 20, 1758, Richelieu returned to court. He knew he was blamed for the defeat of Rossbach, however unjustly, and he felt his relationship with the court to be foundering. He felt it essential to meet with Madame de Pompadour before anyone else. But the marquise, although assuring him with apparent sincerity that she believed he had good reasons for his conduct, told him to report to Belle-Isle. After a stiff interview with the old maréchal, who had just been named minister for war, Richelieu realized that his star had fallen beyond recall. Shortly afterward, he "decided" he must spend more time in Bordeaux, where he resided as governor of the province of Guyenne. From now on, he came to court only for his year of duty as First Gentleman of the Chamber. Thus, another of the marquise's enemies had been eliminated.

When the defeated Soubise returned, it was a different story. Madame de Pompadour was so excited at the prospect of seeing him again that she seemed to recover some of her former sparkle, if only for a brief period. "Gaiety has suddenly got the upper hand, to the point that she is once more as beautiful as the day. She has become plumper, talks only of '*choses galantes*,' and seems enchanted with everything." Soubise was received with the utmost warmth. "As badly as he was greeted by the people of Paris, who were furious with him, he was all the more warmly greeted within the court. Far from criticizing him, the marquise applied herself to consoling him. He seems, naturally, extremely unhappy, and so the King and the marquise overwhelmed him with goodwill."

And so Richelieu was disgraced, Soubise consoled, Clermont still communicating discouraging news from Germany. Madame de Pompadour deluged him with reproachful letters. "The details you send, Monseigneur, of the state of your army make us tremble ..." "Oh! Monseigneur, what despair your letter of the [February] 18th has inspired in my soul ..." "I could not be more displeased, Monseigneur, with the story of Werden [which the French had just abandoned] and I fear that it may be followed by other stories. The maréchal de Belle-Isle has purged himself in order to be able to work ..."

Belle-Isle had been reluctantly persuaded to take over the ministry of war from the ineffectual Paulmy. Old and in poor health, he began working closely with Pâris-Duverney to try to secure provisions for the war, while Bernis endeavored to raise money wherever he could, and the marquise fretted. Only the king seemed unconcerned. "He is marvelously well, and not at all worried about our misfortunes, nor upset at our embarrassments," noted Bernis.

The discouraged Clermont, having arrived in Germany, decided almost at once to retreat, claiming that his troops were not ready for combat. "It is impossible for me to paint, Monseigneur, the extent of my despair, and the disbelief at the court of Vienna when they learned of our retreat. They believe themselves abandoned or betrayed, they see themselves lost, the presence of King of Prussia in their capital, in short their consternation is extreme."

The next day, she wrote, "What can I say, Monseigneur, I am desperate at the necessity you find in crossing the Weser, and still more at the huge number of the sick you have been obliged to abandon. It seems to me that the Lorraine regiment has done wonders, what a shame that such brave men should have perished."

Clermont was stung: "One must allow me to act, Madame, and not overwhelm me with suggestions from so far away ... Madame, be calm; an army does not move as one moves one's finger over a map."

Then Clermont abandoned Minden, and returned to the banks of the Rhine. His retreat was turning into a debacle. "Only a miracle can save us from the swamp into which we have fallen," wrote Bernis to Stainville. "I pass terrible nights and sad days. My health is deranged. . . . Here they love the King of Prussia madly, because one always loves those whose affairs go well." Bernis seemed to have lost his perspective as a government minister and become a spectator of his own administration. His nerve had failed him, and he could not recover it.

The next predicament had Clermont talking of retreating further and refusing to detach troops for the empress. Louis XV roused himself to write a long dispatch which included this: "It would be shameful to abandon Dusseldorf and Wesl and I wish you to defend them. Honor is preferable to everything, and I do not separate yours from mine, nor that of the whole nation." This dispatch was accompanied by a letter from the marquise: "You are aware, Monseigneur, of the extreme grief which these unhappy times have caused me. . . . If we do not send the Empress the promised help, she is in very great danger of losing her throne. We would then be alone, having abandoned our friends and seen them perish, and where would we ever find nations so stupid as to wish to be our friend?"

In this, Madame de Pompadour was displaying all the ardor which Bernis had lost. The two were finding themselves increasingly at odds. Bernis had come a long way from his poverty-stricken days in Paris, when he lived in an attic at the Louvre and made his living on his slight poetic ability. He had developed so much *amour-propre* that he ignored the warning signals from his patroness and allowed himself to refer to the king with such condescension that the more prudent Stainville must have shuddered. "I like the King," wrote Bernis, "and I pity him with all my heart, for he is a decent man, capable of friendship and desiring only good. Yet he lets evil continue and spoil the glory of a reign which could have been glorious and tranquil . . ."

One feels for Bernis, trying to do his best at such unlikely odds, overwhelmed and out of his depth, and now losing the favor of the marquise. More and more desperately, he complained to Stainville about the lack of money, the lack of coordinated policy, the poor generalship. He began to mention the idea of a "central power" in the government, a "*débrouilleur général*" (chief executive), with the implicit notion that he himself was the man for the job. In May he aired the idea that the Council of State function as a "*comité*," rather like the British cabinet, decisions being made by majority vote and submitted to the king for approval. Even though he was careful to assign the marquise a role in the new arrangement ("Madame de Pompadour will remit to the King each decision of the Council"), and even though he was careful to name Belle-Isle, and not himself, as the minister "who will run the machine of government at home and abroad," his plan caused the marquise some chagrin. She saw her supremacy threatened, her role reduced, and she became petulant.

The more Bernis talked of a "central point" in the government, the more he was suspected of harboring ambitions for the job himself, of seeking to displace the marquise, his benefactress. In fact, Bernis did share with Stainville the thought that France would be better run by a powerful minister rather than an ineffectual Council of State. It is also clear that he thought of himself as the only man capable of doing the job, a measure of his self-delusion at the time. As he poured out his heart to Stainville, he did not realize that his friend was stabbing him in the back. Stainville told the marquise of Bernis's nervous condition, his defeatism and desperation. He began to suggest that he himself could do a better job. Poor Bernis, betrayed by Stainville, distrusted by the marquise, soldiered on with his enormous workload, exhausted and demoralized, but unable to give up the fruits of power.

Meanwhile, France's reverses continued. A French convoy bound for the relief of Louisbourg, on Cape Breton Island, was intercepted in the Bay of Biscay by a British fleet under Admiral Hawke; eighteen French warships, seven frigates, and more than forty storeships and troop transports were prevented from crossing the Atlantic. Louisbourg itself capitulated at the end of July after a six-week siege; the civilian population, more than 8,000 men, women, and children, were deported to France, while men who had borne arms were transported to England as prisoners.

The British not only were succeeding in blockading the French coast, but were also attacking it with impunity, launching raids on Cancale in June, Cherbourg in August. France lay open to invasion from the Channel.

As for the unlucky comte de Clermont, having abandoned Hanover, Brunswick, Hesse, and Westphalia, he and his army were defeated at Krefeld, near Dusseldorf, on June 23 and forced to retreat to Cologne. The only son of the maréchal de Belle-Isle, the comte de Gisors, was killed at Krefeld and the death of this promising young man seemed to symbolize all the disasters befalling France. "I weep for M. de Gisors," wrote the marquise, "and for his unhappy father, who will surely die soon, despite the incredible courage he shows before the world."

Madame du Hausset relates how Madame de Pompadour forced the king to pay a visit of condolence to the brokenhearted old man by declaiming the lines:

> Barbarian, whose pride
> Believes a subject's blood repaid merely by a glance.

"Who wrote those verses?" the king is said to have asked. "Voltaire," replied the marquise. "And so I am a barbarian, I who gave him the post of Gentleman in Ordinary and a pension." Grumpily, Louis XV went off to see the bereaved maréchal.

The marquise could not restrain her grief and anger. "What humiliation, Monseigneur!" she wrote to Clermont. "To let six thousand enemy troops disembark and establish a bridge over the Rhine! I cannot describe my enormous grief; it is proportionate to the low state into which we have fallen . . . I am in despair." Clermont returned to court, prepared for disgrace. But Louis XV could not bring himself to be severe with his own uncle. He talked of Clermont's loss of weight, the city of Cologne, and the new pope. Clermont was allowed to retire to his luxurious abbey and retain all the privileges of his royal birth.

As for Bernis, the defeats were too much for him. By August, he was entreating Stainville to return to France and come to his aid. He heard the whispered accusations that he was ungrateful to the marquise, attempting to oust her, forgetting what he owed her. Naively, he believed that his old friend Stainville would help him — not replace him: "Understand how much I suffer at seeing myself continually represented as a man who wishes to destroy his benefactress . . . the union of the three of us will be stronger, sweeter, and more solid." The poor man could not conceive that his two dearest friends might laugh at this thought.

❖ ❖ ❖

Even in these dark days, Louis XV and Madame de Pompadour could not restrain themselves from more building and more expenditure. The king was now so consumed by his passion for hunting that he was having hunting lodges built in all the royal forests. A very grand example of such a lodge was being finished at Saint-Hubert, near Rambouillet. In one of the last entries in his memoirs, the duc de Luynes (who died later in 1758) noted that "they are still working on the Salon, which will be decorated in white and yellow stucco." Even at the height of a war that was going from bad to worse, Louis XV did not hesitate to place his priorities on his own pleasures. As the ministers discussed retrenchments in the royal household, the best they could do was to propose not to redecorate the queen's bedroom every other year, and not to offer coffee to members of the household.

Madame de Pompadour also tried to economize. "I thank you for the fabric," she told Madame de Lutzelbourg. "I am a reformed creature, and so sensible that I surprise even myself. I have sold my knot of diamonds to settle my debts. Is that not a fine thing? You will say that I am like Cicero, who had no need of others to praise himself, but, to be honest, I do not deserve praise, for the sacrifice is very slight. Bonsoir, *grand'femme*, I embrace you with all my heart."

And to demonstrate her new virtues, she had Pigalle's statue of herself as the Goddess of Friendship more prominently displayed in the gardens at Bellevue. When the queen walked on the grounds there in May, she saw lilacs in bloom and, in a grove, the new statue. "This used to be the Grove of Love, presently it is the Grove of Friendship," the guide informed her. The queen nodded sagely, and continued on.

But reality would creep in. Bernis was growing desperate. "No more commerce, thus no more money, no more trade. No more Navy, thus no resources with which to resist England. The Navy has no more sailors, and the fact that there is no more money removes the means of procuring any . . ."

Then, on September 5, 1758, the British fleet made a serious assault on Saint-Malo, landing 7,000 men on the French mainland. The weather was so bad, however, and supplies so scarce, that the British troops were marched overland to Saint-Cast to reembark for home. As they set off, the governor of Brittany, the duc d'Aiguillon, attacked with a hastily gathered party of local militia, causing the British to lose almost a thousand men, killed, wounded, or captured. This was welcome news for the beleaguered French court, and d'Aiguillon was the hero of the hour.

D'Aiguillon was an ambitious young man who had been wise enough to maintain a dutiful correspondence with Madame de Pompadour. Now she, thrilled with her protégé's success, urged him on to greater things: "I regret, monsieur, that I could not tell you the day before yesterday all that I felt about the glory with which you have covered yourself, but my headache was so painful that I had not the strength to write a word. We have sung your Te Deum today, and I assure you that it was sung with the greatest satisfaction; I had predicted your success, and, in fact, how, with so much zeal and intelligence, with such a cool head, and with troops who burned as much as their leader to avenge the King, could you not be victorious?"*

But the success in Brittany could not compensate for defeats elsewhere. By the middle of September, Bernis was close to a breakdown. "I must let you know, madame, and I beg you to tell the King, that I can no longer answer for my work. My head is perpetually confused. For a year I have suffered as a martyr. If the King wishes to console me, he must comfort me. . . . If I can rest for a time, my health will reestablish itself; but it is sadly deranged today. I was ill all night. I no longer sleep . . ."

Bernis meant that he needed more support, more help to do his job. He wanted Stainville by his side. But Madame de Pompadour considered this *cri de coeur* as a sign of weakness. Yes, Stainville would return, but it would be to replace Bernis, not to help him. The marquise and Stainville began to lay their plans.

It was not only the return of Stainville for which Bernis was hoping. He was also longing to be elevated to cardinal, the highest honor his church could bestow. Louis XV had already requested the help of Pope Benedict XIV earlier in 1758, but Benedict had died before any progress

---

*Emmanuel-Armand de Vignerot du Plessis de Richelieu, duc d'Aiguillon, had been the lover of Madame de Châteauroux, and Louis XV always rather held that against him. But in 1770 he succeeded Choiseul as War Minister and Minister for Foreign Affairs.

could be made. Louis did not press the case; he had begun to think that the little abbé might be made too powerful by such an accolade. But Bernis pressed his own case with the new pope, Clement XIII, believing that, as a cardinal, he would be guaranteed security in the event of a fall from grace. The wheels were set in motion in Rome; as was usual at the time, neither Bernis's character nor his morals were an issue. Politics were everything.

Bernis badly wanted to become a cardinal. But he also realized that, once bestowed, the honor would be seen as further evidence of his inordinate ambition. He was well aware that Louis XV would not look kindly on a minister who would, by virtue of his exalted rank as a prince of the church, take precedence over all others. The honor would be a two-edged sword.

Meanwhile, the comte de Stainville was being prepared for greater things. Created duc de Choiseul in August, he was equipped for his move to Versailles. Bernis urged him on, seeing the triumvirate of himself, Choiseul, and the marquise as bringing new abilities to government. But behind Bernis's back Madame de Pompadour increased her complaints against him, having Berryer and Janel show the king letters taken from the diplomatic bag in which references were made to Bernis's future role as head of state. And, if one believes Michelet, they went further, accusing Bernis of flaunting his affair with the king's eldest daughter, Madame Infante, who had returned to the French court from Parma. Every weapon was employed to discredit the victim before he was sacrificed.

On October 6, 1758, Bernis resigned from the foreign ministry with the assurance that he would remain on the Council of State. Louis XV wrote to him the following day: "I am distressed, monsieur l'abbé comte, that the affairs with which I have charged you have affected your health to the point of making you unable to continue. . . . I agree, with regret, that you hand over your work at the foreign ministry to the duc de Choiseul, whom I think the only man suitable at present, as I am absolutely unwilling to change the position I have adopted with regard to Austria, nor do I even wish it to be discussed . . ."

The king then left for Fontainebleau, but only for a week and with only three ladies, in addition to Madame de Pompadour. The glorious autumn outings of the past were no longer practicable. At Fontainebleau the marquise would make sure that Louis did not brood over the unfortunate events that were to come about.

When the pope's letter confirming his elevation to cardinal arrived on October 10, Bernis wrote a touching letter to the marquise: "I owe it to you, as I owe everything to you." But he worried that he had not been told officially that his place on the Council of State was secure, that he could keep his rooms at Versailles, that his debts would be paid, all as he had been led to believe. He had not seen Madame de Pompadour since early October. Clearly she was avoiding him. He wrote to her in some desperation: "To depart at the right time, nothing is easier, but why push the thing to extremes? Why a *coup de poignard* [a stab in the back]?" The marquise was soothing; everything would be taken care of. In fact, she was only waiting for Bernis to finish his negotiations with the *parlement* and the clergy, negotiations which would bring much-needed revenue to the treasury to finance the war. Once that was accomplished, and Choiseul was in place, the game could run its course.

By November 30, when the king presented Bernis with his "hat" after Mass in the chapel at Versailles, the new cardinal knew things were not what they seemed. At the ceremony at Versailles, the king was gracious. "I have never made such a handsome Cardinal," he smiled. "What a fine day for you, Monsieur le Cardinal!" someone called from the crowd. "Say rather a fine safety net," responded Bernis. "I knew my disgrace to be very near," he later wrote. "The dignity of the title of cardinal increased the number of my enemies and the anxieties of the marquise; she promoted the jealousy of the other ministers, and I saw clearly that she would not come to my aid; but after my exile, I reflected that, considering the harshness with which I had been treated, and the ill will she has shown me, if I had not become a Cardinal, worse might have happened to me."

On November 27 Choiseul arrived in Paris. He sent no word to Bernis who, although now convinced that he was the victim of an ugly intrigue, preferred not to implicate his old friend in it. "I could come and see you on Thursday," wrote Bernis. "Despite the lies they spread about me, I wish only to be your friend . . ." There was no response.

On December 11 Bernis concluded the agreement with *parlement* for the allocation of monies, and the edict was registered the next day.

Two days later he met with Starhemberg in Paris when he received a letter from the king. "The repeated suggestions you have made to leave the Foreign Ministry have persuaded me that you are unable to fulfill your functions in the future, as much as you would like to . . . It is after reflecting on this that I have decided to accept your resignation of the post as Secretary of State. At the same time I have come to the conclusion that you will not respond to the trust I have placed in you, nor to the singular favors I have bestowed on you. Thus, I order you to depart for one of your abbeys in forty-eight hours, without seeing anyone."

Bernis concluded his meeting with Starhemberg calmly, giving no hint of what had befallen him. He then wrote a respectful letter to the king, and left for exile at Vic-sur-Aisne, near Soissons. Deeply hurt by the veiled reference to his ingratitude, he blamed Madame de Pompadour: "Partly from thoughtlessness, partly from *amour-propre*, partly from jealousy at my influence on affairs, she sought my disgrace with an importunity to which the King finally gave in. . . . The marquise had none of the great vices of ambitious women; but she had all the pettiness and unreliability of women intoxicated with their looks and their self-proclaimed intelligence; she did harm without being wicked, and she did good through infatuation; her friendship was as jealous as love, unreliable, inconstant, and never guaranteed."

As for the marquise herself, she told Madame du Hausset that she had seen by the end of Bernis's first week as a minister that he was not up to the job, "but I reflect on the humiliation he has endured, and the ambition which eats at him; and I also reflect that I could have enjoyed his company, and grown old with an aged and amiable friend, if he had not been a minister."

She was incapable of blaming herself for raising her friend up and then casting him down. In her view, she had had to act for the good of the state and expel a minister who did not wholeheartedly share her and the king's enthusiasm for the Austrian alliance and war "*à outrance*" (to the death). Having devoted some passing regrets to Bernis, she moved on. It would be up to Choiseul to bring about the king's glory and she her vindication.

PART FIVE
1759–1764

"What miseries are attached to ambition."

Chapter 20

"I would have preferred the top position, and am displeased that I must content myself with a lesser one; it does not suit my temperament at all."

In Etienne-François de Stainville, duc de Choiseul, Madame de Pompadour had found a man with exactly the qualities France needed. At thirty-nine years of age, he was already experienced at war and in diplomacy, at home in the highest circles of Rome, Vienna, and Versailles, a skillful negotiator and a *grand seigneur*. He was a man of contradictions. His friends praised his generosity, his kindness, his frankness, but he was also known for his malicious wit, his caustic words, his lack of scruples. Very sure of himself, he mastered issues easily and quickly, and was able to present them to the king in terms easy to understand. He always maintained a positive outlook, worked tirelessly, and played as hard. Having attained the summit of power, he gave no backward glances to the departed Bernis, nor dwelled on his own treachery. He was ready, willing, and able to take on the job of winning the war and restoring the glory of France.

Baron von Gleichen, the Danish minister in Paris, described him as "rather short, more robust than svelte, of a most agreeable ugliness. His little eyes sparkled with wit, his upturned nose gave him a pleasing air, and his fat, laughing lips preceded the gaiety of his proposals. . . . I never knew a man who could spread as much joy and happiness amongst his familiars. When he entered a room, he rustled in his pockets, and seemed to draw from them an inexhaustible abundance of jokes and gaiety."

At the age of thirty-one, he had married fifteen-year-old Louise-Honorine Crozat du Châtel, an extremely wealthy heiress who brought to the marriage a splendid mansion on the rue de Richelieu in Paris, as well as a sweet and submissive nature. Her husband never hesitated to spend her money, doing so to such an extent that he, and she, would both die financially ruined. He loved luxury; his house was one of the most magnificent in Paris, his way of life was that of the grandest aristocrats. He loved women; he told Voltaire that *"le cul de ma maîtresse me fait oublier tous ces objets"* ("my mistress's behind makes me forget all my cares"). But most of all, he loved power.

Upon arriving at Versailles, Choiseul took the measure of his fellow ministers—Berryer at the office of the navy, Belle-Isle at war, Boullongne as controller of finances. In his opinion, Berryer was too untrustworthy, Belle-Isle too old, Boullongne too incompetent. Choiseul knew that he outclassed them all. Only Madame de Pompadour, to whom he was now bound by ties of obligation and intrigue, was his equal in willpower and resolution. For Choiseul, anything was now possible. For Madame de Pompadour, help was at hand.

The marquise was, according to Croÿ, "more in command than ever, her hand in everything, all the ministers working with her, and the example she has just made of the cardinal (who had really shown great ingratitude, he above all) would have increased her power still more, if it were possible." Croÿ also noted the growing influence of Berryer, at the office of the navy, who was "on very good terms with the Marquise who was pleased with his work as lieutenant of police." As for the king, he was usually seen departing for the hunt, or for one of his lodges, in pursuit of game and girls. It would be up to Choiseul to put the French house of state in order.

He immediately acted to reassure Maria-Theresa of French support. Louis XV would continue to maintain an army of 100,000 men on the Rhine, but would no longer subsidize an army in Bohemia. The king's son-in-law, Don Felipe, would not be given a duchy in the Low Countries, but would keep Parma. The subsidies due to Austria would be continued, but the French obtained a delay in auditing the sums remaining from the preceding treaty; these sums owed would not be paid until the end of the current war, an appreciable help for French finances. The agreement was dated December 30, 1758 and, although not signed until March 1759, the conditions went into effect immediately.

Choiseul agreed with Bernis that an offensive war on the continent against Hanover and Frederick II, as well as a naval war against the British, was too much for France; but, whereas Bernis had thought of making peace, Choiseul's policy was to invade England and Scotland. He believed that a landing in England would force Pitt to make peace.

William Pitt was every bit Choiseul's equal in aggressiveness. His plans for 1759 were to conquer Canada (the principal effort); send troops to Germany; maintain operations in the English Channel, the Bay of Biscay, the North Sea, and the Mediterranean; oppose the French in India; and attack Martinique. He was bent on ending French colonial empire while keeping French troops fully occupied in Europe. The stage was set for major confrontation.

The court of Vienna, relieved at Bernis's fall, and aware of Madame de Pompadour's passionate advocacy of their cause, thought they should thank her for her efforts. In January Kaunitz sent her, on behalf of the empress, a present as token of the Austrians' gratitude for her unwaver-ing support. The present was a lacquer writing case in which a portrait of the empress was set, decorated with precious stones. It cost nearly 90,000 livres. Starhemberg took the desk to Versailles, where it was graciously received. "Mme de Pompadour asked me if it was permitted that she write to Her Majesty her very humble thanks. . . . The King, who was with Mme de Pompadour . . . let me know how much he was personally aware of this mark of distinction which Her Majesty had seen fit to give her."

The marquise expressed her thanks in the manner of the times. "If one must, madame, in order to deserve this precious gift, be filled to the bottom of one's soul with admiration for the seductive graces and heroic virtues of Your Imperial Majesty, no one without exception would be worthier than myself . . ."

This letter became known outside Vienna, and Frederick of Prussia, always eager to mock "Petticoat III," immediately circulated a parody: "I would be too happy, my beautiful Queen, if I can reconcile you as easily with my Goddess, with Venus, as I have reconciled you with my nation!" The parody was clandestinely printed at The Hague, where the king of Prussia's envoy received a note from his master asking that copies "enter France in good number and that the operation be so well executed that a copy reaches Madame de Pompadour herself."

The marquise may well have seen the parody. Every morning Janel showed her extracts from the post and pamphlets. She was well aware that part of public opinion held her responsible for the unpopular war, and she was only too aware of the derision with which Frederick delighted to treat her. About this time, Voltaire, now living at Ferney near Geneva, received a packet of letters from Frederick which included this:

> Your feeble monarch,
> Plaything of the Pompadour,
> Withered by more than one mark
> Of the injuries of love . . .
> This slave speaks as master,
> This Celadon beneath a beech tree
> Thinks to dictate the lot of kings!

Voltaire was alarmed enough to send this material on to Choiseul, making it clear that he had no part in it. The two men began a friendly correspondence in which the marquise occasionally took part. Voltaire, emboldened by the resumption of their relationship, asked if he might dedicate to her his new play *Tancrède*. "When I wish to oblige the dormouse of the Jura mountain," she replied, "I think only of Voltaire the Frenchman, and I forget that he has been Prussian; I still forget, even now, when I agree that he send me the manuscript of his tragedy, I shall not delay in giving him my opinion, it is likely that it will share the fate of (almost) all his works, and that would please me."

The marquise, her nerves somewhat calmer with the disappearance of Bernis and the arrival of Choiseul, rearranged her living quarters once again. At Bellevue, she moved into new rooms facing the courtyard, and the king moved downstairs into her former rooms next door. Then, just over a year after she had leased Champs for life, the marquise wrote to the duc de La Vallière and told him that it was too expensive and too far away, so she gave it up and requested reimbursement for the furniture she had bought and could not use. She and the duke agreed that she should pay the rent for three years. She had spent 200,000 livres there.

The marquise looked for a house where, in the future, she could perhaps take refuge from her fatiguing existence at court. She set her sights on the château of Saint-Ouen, just north of Paris, which was close to Soubise's country house and had a pleasant prospect. She took a lifelong lease from the family of the duc de Gesvres and undertook to restore the château at her own expense, paying 175,000 livres, but retaining 70,000 for these renovations. (Five years later the family received the château back, completely redone at great expense. There were new wings and a new long gallery leading to an orangery and a chapel.) Even before the sale was completed, she ordered Soufflot to build a relay station in the bois de Boulogne, with stables for ten horses to equip her for her journeys there.

In the meantime the war continued on the European continent. Clermont was replaced in Germany by the maréchal de Contades; Soubise kept his army, in which the duc de Broglie was second-in-command. On April 13, Soubise was still at Versailles when his army, under Broglie, met a large enemy force at Bergen, near Frankfurt-am-Main, and sent it reeling northward in defeat. "This victory is all the more important," wrote Barbier, "inasmuch as it puts in confusion all the allies' projects for the campaign, which were to carry Frankfurt and drive us back across the Rhine." There was a Te Deum at Notre-Dame and fireworks at the hôtel de Ville celebrating Broglie, "*le vainqueur de Bergen.*"

News of the battle was not so well received at Versailles, where Soubise's friends, particularly Madame de Pompadour, were irritated at Broglie's temerity in winning a battle and depriving Soubise of glory. Rumors began to spread that Broglie's disgrace was imminent. "This can only come from ill-intentioned people," noted Barbier, and he was right. Belle-Isle did not award the customary decorations and promotions requested by Broglie, nor was Broglie offered the supreme command of the French army. He went off in a fury to take the waters at Ober-Ingelheim. The discord between the French generals, and between the ministers and their generals, was clear for all to see.

Madame de Pompadour decided that the real victor at Bergen had been dear Soubise, who had been a hundred leagues away at court. "The battle has given me a great deal of pleasure," she told Madame de

Lutzelbourg. "Monsieur de Soubise had so well-placed his quarters and chosen such a good field of battle at Bergen that we could not be defeated. My only regret is that he was not there and that the King kept him at court." The marquise, blithely indulging her hatred for Broglie and her admiration for Soubise, was in this instance completely unfair and ridiculous.

But the debacles continued. On August 1, 1759, Contades lost the battle of Minden, on the Weser; the French lost nearly 5,000 men, killed or wounded, and several thousand captured. Prince Ferdinand of Brunswick regained control over most of Hesse, pushing Contades's army slowly back over nearly seventy miles to the River Lahn, a tributary of the Rhine. There in September the two armies dug in. Contades accused Broglie of having knowingly delayed his attack.

In spite of these distressing circumstances, superb new buildings for the war ministry were begun at Versailles in July 1759. Choiseul meant to demonstrate that he had not lost confidence, and that the French would rise again to military glory. But it would not be soon.

And then news came of the fall of Guadeloupe to the British. This Caribbean island and its neighbor, Marie-Galante, had a population of over 50,000, 80 percent consisting of slaves, and more than 300 plantations producing sugar, coffee, cocoa, and cotton. All these commodities would henceforth be shipped to Britain, not France, in exchange for goods and slaves. This was a tremendous blow for French sugar refiners, not to mention French pride. Losses in Senegal, India, and Canada were regularly reported. Pitt's policy was working; his only problem was the extraordinary costs of his expeditions, and the resistance they were facing in the City of London. But for the moment, French arms seemed at the nadir.

The mood in France itself was disturbing. In 1758 Starhemberg signaled a radical change in the spirit of the nation, reporting to Vienna that the once deep affection and respect for the King had been transformed into a dangerous hostility. Pâris-Duverney, when asked how to cure the army's woes, had remarked that it was important to regulate the spirit of the nation as a whole. The public was utterly tired of the war, its costs, and purpose. In September, Silhouette, the recently appointed controller of finances, asked, in effect, for a third *vingtième*. He requested taxes on "lackeys, horses, carriages, gold braid, velvets, silks, cloth of gold and silver, printed fabrics, boutiques, and shop signs." "The hour had sounded to ask for taxes to be imposed on the rich, which had up until now only been asked of the poor," as a later historian wrote. There was, of course, a predictable outcry from *parlement,* and a *lit-de-justice,* the ceremony in which the king imposed his will, was necessary at Versailles on September 20 in order to uphold the edict. It was a spendid occasion, held in the queen's Guardroom, which was hung with a tapestry depicting the Acts of the Apostles, brought especially from the Gobelins' factories. Madame de Pompadour sat with the other *dames du palais* in a gallery hung with crimson damask and silver fleurs-de-lys.

But unimpressed by all this grandeur, the *parlement* of Paris delayed any discussion of the new taxes until November 28. The magistrates had adopted the radical position that they had a right to resist the king's authority if they considered that the fiscal laws of the nation were being violated. This was a new and dangerous precedent. In this embarrassing situation, the king announced he was sending his silver plate to be minted, and invited his subjects to do the same.

After the French defeat at Minden on August 1, Choiseul accelerated preparations for an invasion of England. He ordered the French fleet based at Toulon in the Mediterranean to sail north to the port of Brest in Brittany. There they would link up with the invasion army. But on their way north, the French fleet ran into a British detachment near Gibraltar, lost five ships in the ensuing battle, and were forced to take refuge in Cadiz, where they were blockaded. The only hope for an invasion now lay with the transport vessels waiting in Brittany; these ships managed to slip out to sea, but were pursued by a British squadron to Quiberon Bay, on the south coast of Brittany, where they too were compelled to take refuge and blockaded in their turn. Choiseul's sole consolation was that there, at least, they were not far from the potential army of invasion, now assembled at nearby Vannes, under the command of the duc d'Aiguillon. "The villains will not wait for you, monsieur," the marquise wrote in haste to d'Aiguillon, "I am dying of fear, but I am sure that you will defeat them decisively. Your letters are a pleasure to read, one recognizes the citizen, the zealous and enlightened subject . . ."

Entirely caught up in her enthusiasm for a French retaliation, the marquise was suffering more and more from the effects of the sleepless nights and the constant strain under which she lived. She complained regularly about night fevers, sore eyes, coughs and colds, weariness. In one remarkable letter to d'Aiguillon, Madame de Pompadour expressed her innermost feelings: "You are right, Monsieur, it is very true that my mind and my heart are continually occupied with the King's affairs; but without the inexpressible attachment I have for his glory and for his person, I would often be discouraged by the difficulty of trying to be of use. I would have preferred the top position, and am displeased at being obliged to content myself with a lesser one; it does not suit my temperament at all. . . . I still have a fever that began last week and recover very slowly." Her frustration and anguish are evident.

Nowhere does one hear that Louis XV shared the marquise's anxieties, nor even that he interrupted his hunts or changed his way of life in any way in the face of these mounting difficulties. After a period of self-restraint following Damiens's attempt on his life, a period in which he was too depressed and afraid for his mortal soul to flaunt his vices, Louis turned once again to his "young birds" with renewed vigor; in the fall of 1759 a girl called Marguerite Hainault was pregnant by the king. Her daughter would be born in May 1760. The king was also sleeping with seventeen-year-old Lucie d'Estaing, who would also become pregnant in the summer of 1760.

The whole degrading situation was not only tolerated by Madame de Pompadour, but, according to Madame du Hausset, she took a lively interest in the girls, particularly in their pregnancies. Now a childless woman, she became sentimental when it was a question of the king's sons and daughters—not sentimental enough, of course, to have the children remain near their father. Louis XV never saw his children by the girls of the Parc-aux-Cerfs; he never legitimized them but merely had his lawyer arrange for their upbringing in religious institutions. The Parc-aux-Cerfs was far from the brothel of later fantasy; it was a rather modest establishment for girls who maintained a relatively stable relationship with the king. Many of the great nobles of his court had far more unsavory and extravagant ménages. But there was no doubt that its presence contributed greatly to the king's unpopularity, and to the tarnishing of the royal image.

The king's escapades were interrupted by the latest, and possibly worst, of the French disasters of 1759. On November 7 Admiral Hawke was forced to lift his blockade of the French transports in Quiberon Bay because of bad weather. As he returned to Torbay, a westerly gale blew a French squadron into Brest as it was returning from the West Indies. Finding the main British fleet gone, they put into harbor and reported Hawkes's absence to the comte de Conflans, admiral of the French fleet. Conflans immediately put to sea with twenty-one ships, sailing for a junction with the army of invasion assembling at Vannes. If he could collect the transports and troops and get back to sea before the British could return, he would have at his disposal a force powerful enough to strike anywhere he chose along the coasts of Ireland or Scotland.

But Hawke, with twenty-three warships, was already heading back down the Channel, so that at dawn on November 20 both squadrons were closing in on Quiberon Bay from opposite directions. The battle took place "in gathering darkness, among rocks, under gale-force winds and against a lee shore." The British won a decisive victory, sinking and stranding ten French ships, including the flagship *Soleil Royal*, the *Formidable*, the *Superbe*, and the *Juste*. The French lost more than 2,000 men, and all chance of invading Britain. Pitt believed that he was now in a position to dismantle the French colonial empire.

To d'Aiguillon, Madame de Pompadour reacted with anger, grief, and despair. "What can I tell you, monsieur le duc? I am miserable. . . . Is it possible to suffer more? Being defeated is only a misfortune; not fighting is a shame. What has become of our nation?" She answered her own question in terms which betrayed her deep frustration. "*Parlement*, the *encyclopédistes*, and so on, have changed [France] absolutely. When one is so unprincipled as not to recognize either divinity or master, one soon becomes the dregs of nature, and that is what has happened to us. I am a thousand times more frightened of our humiliation than I would have been by the loss of the whole fleet. It is indeed very fortunate that your troops were not there, you all would have perished. . . . Do not be as discouraged as I, monsieur, your zeal and your attachment for the King can be useful to him. I wish that they could be put to the test."

Madame de Pompadour was no longer, it seemed, the champion of the *Encyclopédie*, the admirer of the *philosophes*. Even as she resumed contacts with Voltaire, even as the French authorities relaxed their repression of Diderot's great work, she could not help blaming these intellectuals for the ills of the nation. But one senses that she was lashing out at convenient targets. From the perspective of the court, all those who derided royal authority were dangerous. Unfortunately for the marquise, the list was long and growing. As the military and naval setbacks continued, the government was ridiculed, the king himself scorned, and Madame de Pompadour subjected to hateful polemics. The insulting pamphlets and songs which rained down upon her were a foretaste of the wave of "philosophical pornography" that would later overwhelm Marie-Antoinette.*

Faced with disaster on land and on sea, the need for money to sustain future French military campaigns again loomed large. On October 29 Choiseul complained that no group of financiers was willing to make an advance on tax revenues to pay the troops. A shortage of funds compelled the treasury to suspend "for a year the payment of orders upon the general receipts of the finances, the bills of the general farms, and the reimbursement of capital," a virtual admission of bankruptcy.

In the face of such failure, Silhouette was dismissed as controller of finance, after such a short term in office that his name came to mean a fleeting impression. He was replaced by Henri Bertin, the chief of the Paris police, and former intendant of Lyon. Bertin was a pragmatist. He had a taste for economics, but would need all his skills to find the money the French army and navy were so desperately lacking.

The duc de Croÿ was back at Versailles in December. He found the marquise "unable to do without the duc de Choiseul. He and his family were of the most cheerful disposition, so much so that the Marquise, who was often bored, found those whom she trusted the most also the most diverting." She ceased entertaining forty or more people at her *petits soupers*, going instead to eat with the Choiseuls three times a week, limiting her own suppers to her most intimate friends, rarely more than eight guests. She even joked about the duchesse de Gramont (Choiseul's sis-

---

*In 1759 Diderot signed a new contract to prepare nine additional volumes of the *Encyclopédie;* d'Alembert offered to resume contributions on mathematics. Voltaire too rejoined the fold. The enterprise, which had been in peril for two years, was on its way once more.

ter) supplanting her at court. "All the Choiseuls were the most *à la mode*, and it seemed the duke was galloping toward supreme power, as long as he didn't overturn on the road."

Choiseul, on arriving at the pinnacle, had not hesitated to bring to court his favorite sister, Beatrix, who had been languishing in a convent. He found her a husband, the dissolute duc de Gramont, and he established her so closely by his side that inevitable rumors of incest were spread. One does not have to believe this to understand that Choiseul found his sister much more spirited and amusing than his wife; Louise-Honorine was a good and dutiful young woman, but she lacked confidence and did not shine in company. Madame de Gramont, on the other hand, positively sparkled with wit. She became as indispensable at the king's suppers as Madame d'Estrades had been.

In December 1759 an offer of mediation to end the war was made by Spain. Pitt was not ready to end his run of victories, but, facing financial pressure from the City of London, he entered upon preliminary negotiations at The Hague. These talks would go on for five months, until April 1760, before ending inconclusively. But for his part, Choiseul, even while engaged in preliminary talks, had concluded that peace was not within his reach, meaning that the war must be continued through new fiscal efforts, and ensuring new difficulties with the *parlements*.

At the end of the year, the young prince de Ligne, a great noble from the Austrian Netherlands, arrived at Versailles and was received by the king in the Council Chamber, with Choiseul present. He was then taken to be presented to the queen, the dauphin, and then, to his surprise, to Madame de Pompadour, in her red lacquer room *à la chinoise*. He thought the marquise "a kind of second Queen, who certainly had more of a regal air than the first one . . . she told me a hundred absurdities *'politico-ministérielles,'* and *'politico-militaires'*; she gave me two or three plans of campaign, then said with emphasis: 'You see, monsieur, what we are doing for you. Are you not satisfied? We are selling our silver plate in order to maintain your war.'"

"Your war"! The dire events of the past year had made Madame de Pompadour less enthusiastic about the Austrians; she could plainly see the financial, military, and naval morass into which France had fallen, and she was inclined to blame the allies for having dragged them into the mess. If it occurred to her that Bernis had been right in predicting such a disaster a year ago, that reflection no doubt caused her even more irritation.

The dreadful year of 1759 ended with the sudden death of the king's eldest daughter, Madame Infante, on December 6. Having contracted smallpox, she was dead in four days, at the age of thirty-two. She had been at court for the last two years, much preferring to live luxuriously with her brother and sisters at Versailles than with her husband and children in Parma. One of the objects of the war had been to establish her in a duchy in the Low Countries, on a rather grander footing than the one she enjoyed in Italy. This objective was now moot.

In the waning days of 1759 it seemed not surprising that even Jean-François Marmontel, protégé of the marquise and editor of the *Mercure de France*, should suddenly find himself in the Bastille. Marmontel had enjoyed his privileged position in the orbit of Madame de Pompadour, often dining at Versailles with Dr. Quesnay in the doctor's rooms above those of the marquise. "Downstairs they deliberated on war and peace, the choice of generals, the dismissal of ministers, and we, in the entresol, talked of agriculture, calculated the national product, or sometimes held convivial suppers with d'Alembert, Duclos, Helvétius, Turgot, and Buffon: and Mme de Pompadour, not being able to engage this troop of philosophers to go down to her salon, came up herself to see them at table and chat with them."

Quesnay did indeed hold such suppers in his rooms, but there is no evidence that all those mentioned by Marmontel ever attended, and it is very hard to imagine that the marquise would so casually condescend. It would have been imprudent. In addition, her sympathy for "enlightened" thinkers had undergone a sharp change. She regarded Diderot and his friends as a threat to the stability of France rather than as a hope for the future.

Marmontel's cheerful evenings came to an abrupt end in December when he was arrested and sent to the Bastille for having insulted the duc d'Aumont in one of his plays. In the fortress, he was accompanied by his servant, had the run of the library, good food, and passable wine. He settled down to translate Lucan. "Only one thing sometimes plunged me into melancholy: the walls of my room were covered with inscriptions which all carried the character of sad and somber reflections of the unfortunates who had been there. I thought I saw them still, wandering and groaning, and their shades surrounded me." Marmontel stayed in the Bastille for only eleven days. But his gloom seemed an apt note on which to end this worst of years.

Chapter 21

*"What shame for a nation such as ours to
be led by the caprices of a flirt!"*

When the prince de Ligne visited Paris after his encounter with the court, he found everyone talking about the disorder of the army and the ministries, "where favor replaced merit," about the destruction of the navy and the ruin of the treasury, "while they always find money for Mme de Pompadour's building."

The marquise was now used to the hostility of Paris; tired and frustrated as she was, she had to face a new and serious threat closer to home. "Madame had serious concern about an attachment of the King's that strongly ressembled love," wrote Madame du Hausset. "This was with a demoiselle Romans, a young and pretty girl from the provinces with whom the King was as infatuated as he could be."

This young woman was born Anne Roman Couppier in Grenoble in 1737, and came to be known as Mademoiselle de Romans. Casanova, who had met her in Grenoble, described her as "young and beautiful, her dazzling white skin contrasted with a magnificent head of black hair. Her features were of a perfect regularity; her complexion was delicately colored, her almond-shaped black eyes had the liveliest sparkle and at the same time the greatest gentleness; she had well-arched eyebrows, a small mouth, regular, well-placed teeth with a pearly finish, and lips of a tender rose on which reposed the smile of grace and modesty." The actress Sophie Arnould described her as the nymph Calypso and remarked that the king himself "although a very handsome man, had the air of a mere schoolboy or a half-king beside her." At the beginning of 1760 Anne de Romans was installed in a little *hôtel particulier* with a fine garden in the village of Passy, between Paris and Versailles.

The marquise was extremely alarmed, and expressed her fears to her confidante, Madame de Mirepoix. The maréchale had good advice. "I shall not say that he loves you more than her; perhaps you might have reason to tremble if, by a magic wand, she could be transported and installed here. But princes are, above all, creatures of habit; the king's attachment to you is as much about your rooms, your entourage; you are made for his ways, his stories; with you, he is not awkward, not afraid of boring you. Do you think he would have the courage to uproot all this in a day, and to make himself a spectacle by so doing?"

Madame de Pompadour might have agreed with her friend; but she still felt wounded and abandoned. Her thoughts turned more and more to retreating; not immediately, not while the war was on, not while the king needed her . . . but perhaps at some time in the distant future. Having acquired the lease of Saint-Ouen, to the north of Paris, she now bought the château of Ménars, situated on the banks of the Loire, near Blois. She paid 900,000 livres in installments and sold some pearl bracelets to meet the first payment. The château was spacious and handsome, but nevertheless the marquise asked Gabriel for plans for two more wings.* She also acquired Auvilliers, a seventeenth-century château with two little towers and a magnificent tree-lined avenue, near Artenay, to be used as a staging post for Ménars.

These expenditures, although mostly funded by financial stratagems not involving public money, provoked more grumbling in Paris—particularly as, at the same time, Choiseul was asking the king to restrict many favors and restrain the expenses of the court. Louis XV's response to his minister was characteristic: "My dear friend, the thefts in my household are enormous, but it is impossible to prevent them, there are too many powerful interests involved. Calm yourself, and allow this incurable evil to persist." Choiseul could only shrug his shoulders and turn to other ways of economizing.

In February 1760 Bertin proposed a third *vingtième*. The *parlement* of Paris, in a particularly hostile mood, refused to cooperate unless the king gave an account of his personal and secret expenses, a demand which

---

*Gabriel executed no less than fourteen plans for Ménars, the last dated April 10, 1764, five days before her death.

caused Berryer to exclaim that the magistrates wished to be like the English parliament—master of the king. "The Court was furious; the King seemed very changed. He had grown weary. The Marquise was anxious." She wrote testily to Bertin: "Oh! As for the little proposition of the King's rendering account of his personal expenses, I do not countenance it and I cannot conceive how you have had the patience not to spit in their face."

After long negotiations, Bertin persuaded *parlement* to agree that the king's affairs should be kept private. But the affair left the marquise embittered. "Everything you tell me of the souls of the Bretons," she told d'Aiguillon, "is nothing in comparison with those of this monstrous place [Versailles], and I think absolutely about Ménars as you do about Veretz. May God grant that my château there will soon be a reality, and that, although I do not propose to mix with my neighbors, you will be an exception to the rule. You see that I cede nothing to you in horror of this world."*

In May, Marmontel, freed from the Bastille, but dismissed from his job at the *Mercure,* arrived at Ferney to visit Voltaire. The two men fell to talking about the marquise. "She still likes you," said Marmontel, "she has told me so many times. But she is powerless and dares not or cannot do all she wishes; for the unhappy woman is no longer loved, and perhaps she envies the lot of Mme Denis [Voltaire's niece] and would like to be at Les Délices." "Let her come," exclaimed Voltaire, "she could play tragedy with us. I shall write parts for her, the roles of a queen. She is beautiful, she has learned to play the game of the passions." "She has also learned profound sadness and bitter tears," Marmontel added. "So much the better! That is what we need," Voltaire exclaimed as if enchanted at the arrival of a new actress.

In Paris, *parlement* was rebellious, generals were incompetent, bankers uncooperative, and at court a little nucleus of opposition was beginning to form. The dauphin, previously too intimidated to interfere in politics and risk his father's disapproval, began to speak up against Choiseul, whom he considered impious and immoral. Encouraged by the duc de La Vauguyon, the governor of the royal children, he went to the

---

*Veretz was a property of d'Aiguillon's near Ménars.

king to accuse Choiseul of plotting against the Jesuits. It is quite possible that there was something to the dauphin's accusation; Choiseul, in desperate need of money, and therefore wishing to appease *parlement*, might well have attempted some action against the Jesuits, cordially hated by the Jansenist magistrates as they were. A year later, exactly such an action would be taken. But Choiseul was much cleverer than the dauphin. He easily persuaded Louis XV and the marquise that he was the victim of an intrigue, and, in his memoirs, recorded a furious scene with the dauphin, in which he claims he told the prince, "I might have the misfortune to be your subject one day, but I shall never be your servant." As Choiseul left, the dauphin angrily slammed the door behind him.

The coterie around the dauphin was also, of course, hostile to Madame de Pompadour. Included in the group were the duc de Broglie and his brother, the comte. The duc, despite his difficulties with the court the previous year, had received the supreme command of the army in Germany for 1760 and on July 1, crossed the Main, then the Lahn, and defeated Prince Ferdinand of Brunswick at Corbach near Cassel on July 12. But then, inexplicably, he halted the troops. Instead of advancing into Hanover, he stayed encamped for six weeks. He quarrelled with his second-in-command, the comte de Saint-Germain, and replaced him with the chevalier du Muy, a protégé of the dauphin. Du Muy was promptly caught in an ambush and lost 6,000 of his 18,000 men.

Broglie had insisted on the enlistment of du Muy; the court had wanted Monsieur Dumesnil, protégé of the marquise. Now they hoped Broglie would be forced to resign over this issue. At Versailles, the marquise waited grimly for Broglie's return, ready to bring about his inevitable disgrace. Between the quarreling generals and the backbiting at court, the French war campaigns had become embarrassing disasters; more energy was spent plotting against one another than in fighting the enemy. The point of the war had long been forgotten.

Morale was low in all branches of the armed forces. In Brittany, the duc d'Aiguillon told the marquise he wished to leave his post. She — tired, ill, overwhelmed with worries — tried to raise his spirits: "You will probably agree at once, Monseigneur, that I am indeed insufferable in always being right. . . . You wish to leave Brittany, a fine notion to pass through your head; I shall not allow you indulge it any more than the

first time you had it. Remember that if you had followed your first inclination, you would not be "Cavendish."* . . . I blush at seeing you with
less courage than I. You have the cares of your small command, and I
those of all administration, since there is no minister who does not come
and tell me his troubles."

Amid all the cares, the marquise could take some pleasure in her
newly restored contacts with Voltaire. The great man was once again her
devoted admirer. He asked Madame de Lutzelbourg "to have a copy
made for me of the portrait of Mme de Pompadour. Would there not be
in Strasbourg some painter who would make a passable copy?"

Perhaps this was the portait of the marquise *en jardinière,* painted
by Carle Van Loo. In it, she wears a straw hat and holds a little sprig of
hyacinth; the basket hanging from her arm is full of flowers—pinks, vio-
lets, marigolds, sunflowers, lilies of the valley. She looks older than in
the paintings by Boucher, heavier and with a double chin, but still charming, still with a strong, direct gaze.

Voltaire took the opportunity of his new favor to ask the marquise
to read the manuscript of his play *Tancrède.* She did so, liked it, and even
agreed to the author's wish to dedicated to her; she told Malesherbes,
the official censor, that she had allowed this "because I have known the
author for twenty-five years, and I find nothing suspicious in his request."

However, the dedication had to go through several drafts owing to
Madame de Pompadour's concerns about its tone. Finally it read: "Madame, I have observed your graces and talents develop since your childhood; I have always received from you evidence of a kindness without
equal. . . . I dare to thank you publicly for the good you have done for so
many writers, artists, men of worth in more than one genre. . . . You
brought goodness to many, and with discernment, because you were your
own judge. . . . Believe me, madame, that it is important to have won the
approval of those who know how to think."

This was most gratifying. So, also, was the fact that Louis finally
acknowledged the *Ecole Militaire.* The king had never shown much enthusiasm for the project, and over the years Madame de Pompadour had

---

*Cavendish was the British general defeated by d'Aiguillon at St. Cast. The
marquise used it as a nickname.

also lost interest in it; she was bitter that her role in its establishment had never been properly recognized. It was Pâris-Duverney, the original sponsor, who had had to rescue the project many times from neglect, and in 1760, at the age of seventy-six, Duverney made one last effort. He asked his young protégé, Beaumarchais, music teacher to Mesdames, to persuade them to visit the *Ecole*. They did so, inspected a parade, and partake of a collation; on their return to Versailles, the four princesses, overcome with excitement, begged their father to do the same, and on August 12 Louis XV graciously put in an appearance, and watched a fireworks display and a carousel.*

The fact that it took such a great deal of energy to get the king to take an interest in a project universally admired was significant. "Everyone is convinced that the King spends so little time over the affairs of the Kingdom," wrote a leading magistrate from Rouen, "that he is ignorant of everything that is happening, in short, that he doesn't even know we are paying two *vingtièmes*. His ignorance is so widely known and they have taken so much trouble to spread it to the public, that there is hardly anyone who is not strongly convinced of the truth of it. I see with grief that the King seems somehow to give credence to this error, because he hardly appears in public at all, he never speaks, in short, he does not seem to take enough interest in the affairs of France."

At the beginning of 1761 there were discreet efforts toward peace. Despite impressive British successes in Canada and India, the City of London had begun to feel that the enormous costs of the war could not be justified. The death of George II on October 25, 1760 hastened this development, since the new king, the young George III, did not feel so strongly about fighting for Hanover. As for the French, their dearest wish was to take up preliminary negotiations again, but without offending their Russian and Austrian allies.

At the end of March Louis XV made a formal appeal for a peace treaty to be drawn up on the basis of the current status quo at a general conference of all the warring parties. Simultaneously, Pitt received a letter

---

*For his efforts, Beaumarchais received from Duverney a payment of 60,000 livres and an annual annuity of 6,000. He was now set up for life, and ready to pursue his passion, to write for the stage.

from Choiseul proposing that Britain and France exchange envoys to discuss issues; this was, implicitly, an offer to begin negotiations for a separate peace. Pitt agreed to send a diplomat to Paris and to receive a French representative in return.

But in the meantime, Pitt's long-planned expedition against Belle-Ile, an island off the coast of Brittany, had been launched; Pitt thought that if he could establish a British naval base and army garrison on the island, France would be obliged to divert thousands of troops from Germany to coastal defense. And so, the British landed on Belle-Ile on April 8, 1761. By the time the envoys were beginning to state their governments' respective positions in Paris and London, the island was in British hands.

The maréchal de Belle-Isle had not lived to see the island's fall. He died in January at the age of seventy-six. Choiseul seamlessly combined the ministry of war and the office of foreign affairs. A more poignant loss came in March, when the little duc de Bourgogne, eldest son of the dauphin, died at the age of ten. He had been the heir to his grandfather's throne; now the heir became his brother, the six-year-old Louis-Auguste, duc de Berry, the future Louis XVI. Bourgogne had been an intelligent child; everyone knew that his brother was not his equal.

As for Madame de Pompadour, at the end of March, in a gloomy frame of mind, she added a codicil to her will of 1757: "I leave to Abel-François Poisson, my brother, marquis de Marigny, my land of Ménars and its dependencies. In case of the death of my brother without posterity, I put in his place M. Poisson de Malvoisin." She was exhausted, worn out by the endless war, by her myriad self-imposed responsibilities, by Louis XV's detachment. As her health began to give way, she retired more and more from public view.

In the spring of 1761, the *parlement* of Paris began its assault on the Jesuits, and it was the Jesuits themselves who gave it the opportunity. The French Jesuits, who were heavily involved in trading ventures in the Caribbean, had lost five ships full of merchandise to the British, and the loss had led to a bankruptcy of almost two million livres. Being uninsured, the Company of Jesus should have taken the loss and indemnified the creditors. Unwisely, they preferred to go to court and took their case to the Paris *parlement*, whose hostility to the Jesuits was well-known.

On April 27, 1761, the abbé Chauvelin, one of the most radical members of *parlement*, denounced the Jesuits as the opponents of good order, ecclesiastical discipline, and the maxims of the kingdom. "As a Christian, a citizen, a Frenchman, a subject of the King and a magistrate," the abbé cried, "is it not necessary to examine the institution and the régime of the Jesuits? That is what I ask you, Messieurs, to consider." The Jesuits were already unpopular, unjustly suspected of complicity with the would-be assassin Damiens, of foreign intrigue, a fifth column, out of the state's control. When *parlement*, in its verdict on May 8, demanded that the society pay one-and-a-half million livres to their creditors, there was wild enthusiasm in the streets of Paris. Next, *parlement* appointed a commission to review the whole question of the Jesuits' position in French society.

The queen, the dauphin, and Mesdames were sympathetic to the Jesuits and begged the king to help. But he was having great difficulty in raising money from the magistrates and could not afford to alienate them further. When, later in the year, *parlement* ordered that recruitment to Jesuit colleges be ended, their congregations dissolved, and their final closure ordered for the end of 1761, the best the king could do to halt such sweeping actions was to delay them until April 1762. This delay, painfully acquired over *parlement's* furious objections, was to gain time for a negotiation with Rome, for Louis XV, influenced by his family, would have liked to preserve the Jesuits' presence, if they agreed to reform their constitution. But Rome would prove rigid. Madame de Pompadour's only recorded comment on this affair was that she believed the Jesuits "honorable men; but the King will not sacrifice his *parlement* to them, at a moment when it is so necessary to him."

The marquise has often been accused of turning on the Jesuits because they refused to approve of her position at court. But she took no part in the campaign against them. Indeed, she resented much more the *parlementaires*, men she had long considered dangerously radical, though absolutely necessary for the king's finances. She exhorted Bertin to stand up to them, giving him the benefit of her advice in a tone of weary experience:

'"Honest men are often duped," she told him, "and that is what is happening to you now, monsieur. I had predicted it, because sixteen years at court is worth one hundred of experience. They will string you along in this affair of the Jesuits, and if you do not do their bidding, they will refuse you everything. . . . If there is no peace, or if it is a bad one, it is *parlement* alone one should blame, and I would like the whole universe to know this truth . . ." She believed, not without reason, that the magistrates were more interested in their own conflicts with the Jesuits and others than they were in seeing France victorious at war. She despised them.

Her mood was further darkened by word that Anne de Romans was pregnant by the king. "The gossip of the public, even at Court, alarmed Madame infinitely," according to Madame du Hausset. "They claimed that if this lady had a son, the King would legitimize him and give his mother a rank." Once again Madame de Mirepoix had sound advice: "All this is very Louis XIV, these are the grand manners which are not those of our master." But Madame de Pompadour recognized in the black-eyed beauty a willpower as strong as her own, and she worried.

She added to her anxieties over Mademoiselle de Romans, seditious magistrates, and failing health, alarm over the British landing on Belle-Ile. She burned to defend the honor of France by driving out the invaders, urging d'Aiguillon to attack: "There is not a moment to lose, the minister of the Navy has done everything he could. I deign to believe that the victor of Saint-Cast will again be that of Belle-Ile. What glory for him and for the nation!" But d'Aiguillon abandoned the project due to lack of resources, and the French had to suffer the humiliation of seeing the enemy on their own soil.

On another front, Soubise and the duc de Broglie were uneasily joined in command in Germany. Miscommunications and misunderstandings were rife. Facing battle, the generals decided that, at dawn on July 16, Broglie should attack the enemies' right, and Soubise their left. The prince de Condé would be in the center. But during the previous night of July 15, Soubise heard the sound of cannon from Broglie's army and sent to find out what was going on; Broglie had jumped the gun, attacked, and now needed help. Soubise's men were roused and hastily marched off; but after a disorganized reunion, both French armies retreated. This was the battle of Fillingshausen.

Soubise, well versed in the ways of the court, was conciliatory to Broglie, and said that he would not send a courier to Versailles until after they had agreed on a version of what to send. But Broglie, impulsive as usual, had already sent off his own message, defending himself and obliquely blaming Soubise. Choiseul blamed both men, but most of the army blamed Broglie. Versailles certainly did. The court realized that Madame de Pompadour had been right about Broglie when she called him a hothead. Not only did he act unwisely, but he had tried to put Soubise, of all people, in the wrong. This would not be forgiven.

When the prince de Condé, the king's cousin, complained to the marquise about the duc de Broglie, she was quick to reassure him. "We are well aware of the kind of character with whom you have had to deal, and we realize what a great misfortune it is to be forced to serve such a man. In truth, Monseigneur, allow me to say that you have rendered too little justice to the Court, and to me personally, who am inviolably attached to you for all my life." It was very telling of the poisonous atmosphere which reigned in court and army circles that the king's confidante felt able to attack one of the king's commanders to another.

It never seemed to have occurred to anyone in these times that the king should be the one to encourage or criticize his commanders. Madame de Pompadour was the only reliable channel through which to reach him; Louis XV had more pressing matters on his mind. "The continual hunts of His Majesty have prevented him, Monseigneur, from replying sooner to your letter," she told Condé.

Rifts in French morale were occurring everywhere. In Brittany, the duc d'Aiguillon was discouraged. He saw no possibility of a French retaliation against the British navy, and was eager to move on. Hearing that the governorship of Languedoc was vacant, he wrote at once to the marquise. But he was too late. "Monsieur de Fitz-James had already accepted the command in Languedoc, monsieur le duc, when I received your letter. But we must indeed get you out of Brittany, if it displeases you so much, for, assuredly, we do not wish you harm."

Peace, so much desired and so difficult to obtain, seemed to recede again. Choiseul had never pursued the nascent negotiations with Great Britain with great urgency. Instead, he had concentrated on bringing the new king of Spain, Charles III, into alliance with France. On August 15

Choiseul and a representative of the court of Madrid signed two documents: the first, the "family pact," was a series of reciprocal guarantees
between the Bourbon monarchies of France and Spain; the second, a
secret convention by which, if peace was not concluded by May 1, 1762,
Spain would declare war on Great Britain. Pitt reacted to this news with
fury. Negotiations were broken off.

Once again, the French had to prepare for a new campaign. To ensure that his hold on events was strengthened, Choiseul named his cousin,
the duc de Praslin, as minister of foreign affairs, while he himself took
over the navy from Berryer, who became Keeper of the Seals. Thus, at
the end of 1761, the duc de Choiseul was minister for war and the navy
with his cousin seconding him at foreign affairs. He was as close to a
prime minister as he had ever been.

When Croÿ returned for his Christmas visit, he noted that "Mme de
Pompadour, tired of working so hard, spends her time entirely with M. le
duc de Choiseul, who amuses her, he finds time for everything, even for
his pleasures, being very decisive and having a great capacity for work.
The Marquise is always shut up with Mme la duchesse de Gramont, a very
intelligent and strong-willed woman, so much so that one hardly ever sees
Mme de Pompadour any more, which makes everything rather difficult.
The King amuses himself as usual at the hunt, supping once a week with
his children. People say he also amuses himself in his *petits cabinets* with
pretty young girls, who sometimes make the Marquise anxious."

There was a sense of staleness in the air. The war had gone on too long,
was becoming even more pointless. The king was invisible, the marquise exhausted. Choiseul still exuded confidence as he continued to
amass power, but the populace was cynical and restless. At the Salon
of 1761, as a symbol of the changes taking place in the artistic world,
Jean-Baptiste Greuze again took the audience by storm. His paintings
The Village Bride and *The Laundress* were phenomenal successes. "This
is moral painting," wrote Diderot approvingly in his review. In contrast, Nattier's portrait of the late Madame Infante *en habit de chasse* was
found "detestable." "Doesn't this man have any friends who tell him
the truth?" asked Diderot rhetorically. Louis-Michel Van Loo's por-

trait of Louis XV wearing an ermine robe had, said the critic satirically, "something of the dignity of the president of Parlement." As for Boucher: "This man has everything except the truth." And a bust of Pompadour by Lemoyne was simply "nothing."*

With court taste so repudiated at the Salon, it is ironic that, at the same moment at Versailles, the king's architect, Gabriel, was showing Louis XV and the marquise his first plans for the Petit Trianon, the building which became the perfect realization of Madame de Pompadour's taste, a building which would be not only supremely elegant, but forward-looking in style. The marquise would not see it completed, it would be taken over by Madame du Barry, and then by Marie-Antoinette, but its spirit is that of its creator, and it is her most lasting and most pleasing legacy.

*Diderot may have been particularly exuberant at the Salon, for he had finished his revision of the seventeenth and final volume of the *Encyclopédie*. Volumes VIII to XVII were printed in Paris in quick succession, the last volume appearing in 1765. The great endeavor was finished.

Chapter 22

"The peace we have just made is neither good nor glorious."

Britain declared war on Spain at the beginning of 1762. The British looked greedily at the opportunity of capturing Spanish possessions in the Caribbean, Cuba in particular. The royal navy, after capturing the French islands of Martinique, St. Lucia, Grenada, and St. Vincent in February, would soon take Havana. But there were signs that the British public was tiring of the war. As for the French, their armies, with Soubise back in command, marched drearily off to Germany, all illusions vanished, hoping only to escape another debâcle.

As expected, after the disastrous battle of Fillingshausen, the duc de Broglie, along with his brother, had been disgraced and exiled to the family estate in Normandy. Their own stubbornness, along with their refusal to play the court's game of intrigue, had cost them their careers: "Behold them lost forever, for the King never changes his mind," remarked the venerable maréchal de Noailles, and Croÿ noted that "following appearances, they are finished, and so young too."

Voltaire's tragedy *Tancrède* was being performed at the Paris Opera when the news of the Broglies exile came out. As the words "They rob Tancrède, they exile him, they insult him," the audience broke into wild applause. "The assembled public respects nothing," tut-tutted Barbier, "and that is indeed flattering for the duc de Broglie. The play has been banned." (But the comte de Broglie, brother of the duc, although seemingly in deepest disgrace and in exile, maintained unparalleled access to the king, continuing to direct Louis XV's secret correspondence with French representatives in Stockholm, Constantinople, and Saint Petersburg. Louis XV reveled in this duplicity and confusion.)

Madame de Pompadour was widely blamed for pursuing a vendetta against the Broglies, and indeed she was delighted to see them go. She had never trusted them, suspicious of their association with Conti and then with the dauphin's coterie. Now, dear Soubise had another chance to shine.

But there was to be no glory for the marquise's friend. At the end of March, peace talks got under way again. All parties were ready to end the war. By the end of July 1762 the Duke of Bedford and the duc de Nivernais were named plenipotentiaries, and prepared to travel to each other's courts.

Madame de Pompadour was as weary of the war as anyone was. But a humiliating outcome could not be tolerated. She hoped that Nivernais, her "little husband" of years before, would find a way to negotiate an honorable peace. As for Maria-Theresa and the court of Vienna, they too had tired of chasing the king of Prussia all over Europe. The time for peace was at hand.

Through these demoralizing days, Louis XV was occupying himself with Anne de Romans and her soon-to-be delivered baby. "I saw very clearly, *ma grande*, that you had something in your head as you left here," he wrote, "but I could not guess what it could be exactly. I have no wish that our child be under my name in the baptismal records, but neither do I have any wish not to be able to recognize him in some years' time, if that pleased me to do so. Thus I wish that he or she be named Louis-Aimé or Louise-Aimée, son or daughter of Louis le Roy or of Louis de Bourbon, as you wish. . . . I also wish that the godfather and the godmother be poor people, or servants, excluding all others. I kiss you, and embrace you very tenderly, *ma grande*."

A boy was born on January 13 at Passy and baptized the next day at the chuch of Chaillot. Madame du Hausset tells the story of Madame de Pompadour going in disguise to the bois de Boulogne to observe Mademoiselle de Romans and her baby. "One must agree that the mother and child are beautiful creatures," the marquise said sadly, "and let us not forget the father, the child has his eyes." When Madame de Pompadour told the maréchale de Mirepoix how worried she was that the king would legitimize the boy and make Anne de Romans his *maîtresse déclarée*, her friend reassured her. "You can be sure that he cares very little about children; he has enough, and would not wish to embarrass himself with the mother and the son. See how he cares about the comte du Luc who looks just like him. He never talks of him, and I am sure that he will do nothing for him. I repeat, we are no longer under Louis XIV."*

It was true that Louis XV never showed any interest in his illegitimate children, of whom he would have at least eight. But he showed a certain fidelity to his *petites maîtresses*; Louise Tiercelin, Marguerite Hainault, and Lucie d'Estaing each gave him two children. (Some years after the death of Madame de Pompadour, his conscience disturbed, grieving over the death of his wife and son, he saw to it that all three, and Mademoiselle de Romans, were respectably married.)

The marquise was used to the young girls, but much more concerned about Anne de Romans, who was intelligent, ambitious, and interested in politics. Increasingly unwell, suffering from failing sight, migraines, palpitations, and fevers, she gradually detached herself from the political arena, leaving to Choiseul the strategies and grand plans. But she continued to give audience to the ministers, ambassadors, and numerous other individuals who had requests to make. She could not bring herself to leave court; but she seemed to be engulfed in a mist of sadness.

Her protégé and spy, Berryer, the recipient of so much and the betrayer of so many, succumbed to madness. Quesnay, the marquise's doctor, told her that he had seen Berryer "in the chapel where he was sitting on one of the little chairs which are very low, and which served him to kneel; his knees were touching his chin and his eyes were wild. I am very worried about him." Four days later, Berryer died in delirium. Cardinal de Bernis, who thought him a profoundly dangerous man, recorded that "a premature death saved France."

Another protégé, the duc d'Aiguillon, insisted on leaving his post. "The zeal and the talents with which you have served the King in Brittany, monsieur," wrote the marquise, "have made me take serious interest in you, and I have given you evidence of it with pleasure when the occasion presented itself. That same interest demands of me that I strongly criticize you for the letter you have written me. What has become of the zeal of which you have given proof only three months ago? How is it pos-

---

*Louis-Aimé de Bourbon was destined for the church and became the abbé de Bourbon. He died in Naples in 1787 at the age of twenty-five.

sible that a moment of distaste makes you forget it? . . . I do not know when I shall pardon you, you deserve that I take no more interest in you. Bonsoir, monsieur, I am most provoked, and rightly so." D'Aiguillon reluctantly stayed at his post.

The marquise was determined to exert all her influence to keep the king's sujects mindful of their duty. When the duc de Nivernais, in London to negotiate peace, complained to her of the bad effects London rain and fog were having on his health, and of his fatigue, she chided him thus: "You talk of your fatigue, you can rest later, but God! finish now. This ugly courier displeases me to death. I am trembling with fear, and all our eloquence could not reassure Monsieur de Bredford [the Duke of Bedford, George III's envoy in Paris]."

Finally, on November 3, 1762, a preliminary peace signed at Fontainebleau put an end to hostilities between the king of England and the kings of France and Spain. The definitive Treaty of Paris was signed on February 10, 1763. France recovered Martinique and Guadeloupe but gave up Canada, the Ohio valley, India, and Senegal, keeping only the port of Gorée, essential for the slave trade. Minorca was given back to the British. To recover Havana and Cuba, Spain ceded Florida to Great Britain. Louis XV, who felt responsible for this loss, ceded Louisiana to Spain. France also renounced all claims to compensation for ships seized by British privateers and naval vessels since 1754; agreed to level its fortifications at Dunkirk; restored all territories still under its army's control in Hanover, Hesse, and Brunswick; and evacuated the Rhineland possessions of the king of Prussia. The continental war came to a close with the Treaty of Hubertsburg of February 15, 1763. Maria-Theresa again gave up Silesia to the king of Prussia. Seven years of bloody battles were over. The British and their empire were the great victors.

Louis XV, who had never seemed to take much interest in the war — except for insisting that it go on — acknowledged to his son-in-law that "the peace we have just made is neither good nor glorious; no one feels that more strongly than I. But even under these unhappy circumstances, it could not have been better, and I tell you that if we had continued the war, we would have made an even worse peace next year. . . . Let us adapt ourselves to what we have, so as not to be swallowed up by our enemies. For that, we must not start another war."

The king tried to put the best face on the losses. Choiseul made it clear that the loss of Canada was less important than the recovery of the sugar islands of the Caribbean. And it was true that in the first half of the eighteenth century the West Indies were far more important to France than Canada; 20 percent of France's total trade was with the West Indies. But everyone knew that the French armies, as Lee Kennett said, "entered the conflict without enthusiasm, fought without distinction and emerged from it without victory."

Madame de Pompadour was also making the best of the unsatisfactory peace. She congratulated the duc de Nivernais in London on his negotiation — "It is at last finished, let us embrace so that we can congratulate each other" — and professed admiration for King George III — "I like the King of England as much as you do, he seems to me full of candor, humanity, and all the virtues which make a great King." But she knew that the outcome was bleak. The war, "her" war, had caused nothing but grief; French arms were disgraced, French society fractured. Her melancholy mood deepened. More and more she let herself indulge in bouts of irritation and anger.

The marquise might have been unwell, discouraged, but she would not give up her old hatreds, and she continued to keep a vigilant watch over the king. In March 1763 the dauphin approached his father on behalf of the exiled Broglie brothers. Louis XV, taken by surprise, responded merely with "It is too soon to ask!" Then, a day later, his nerve stiffened by the marquise, he wrote his son a note: "I was surprised, my dear son, that you have asked so soon for the return of the maréchal de Broglie. . . . You must wait for a long time still, perhaps even several years."

At court Madame de Pompadour was "little seen, continuing to run everything." To celebrate the return of peace, she orchestrated an elaborate winter season of balls, ballets, and operas in the Versailles theatre, deciding on every production and its every detail. But the ambitious plans only highlighted the inadequacies of the cramped space in the Aile des Princes; there was no proper stage, and not enough room for all those who wished to attend. The marquise prevailed on the king to ask his architect Gabriel to dust off his existing plans for a new and splendid

theatre at Versailles. Within months, work had started on the sumptuous Opera we see today.

The king also began major transformations of his *petits appartements*,
the rooms on the upper floors above his bedroom at Versailles. In March
1763 a new bathroom with two tubs and a stove appeared, a new library
was constructed above the Council Chamber, the king's staircase was
extended up to this level, and a rôtisserie-pâtisserie was added to the huge
kitchen upstairs. (This kitchen, which served only the king's private dining room, comprised a game pantry, grills, ovens, and hot plates. All the
kitchen supplies came up service staircases and the food was sent down
by dumbwaiters.) Louis XV's taste for private life was made manifest in
these lovely little rooms, where he could entertain his girls or dine with
his hunting companions. Madame de Pompadour rarely went there; she
found the stairs difficult, and, in addition, she recognized that she was
no longer a part of the life which went on there.

In April the painter Drouais drew a likeness of Mme de Pompadour's
head for a portrait which would not be finished until May 1764. Sitting
at her embroidery, her little spaniel by her side, she wears a dress of
painted silk with wide skirts and extravagant lace sleeves. Her double
chin, gray powdered hair, and matronly lace cap bespeak her age, but
one recognizes her indomitable self-possession.

The marquise traveled more and more frequently to Ménars, which
had been greatly enlarged and embellished. She employed a young man
called Honoré Guibert to carve the wall paneling with allegories of Painting and Sculpture. Her private rooms included a boudoir where she kept
her Sèvres porcelain, particularly the small *biscuit* figurines of children,
which she loved; her windows overlooked flowered terraces extending
down to the Loire.

But she could not break the chains which held her to the court.
Convincing herself that Louis XV could not manage without her, she
maintained her debilitating vigil over his affairs. She watched with fury
as Bertin's attempts to establish a more equitable tax system ran into
organized opposition from the *parlements*. Bertin was trying to set up a
land registry of all real estate, without exception, including the domains

of the Church and the nobility, so that a proportional tax might be fairly imposed. A *lit-de-justice* was held on May 31, 1763 to impose its acceptance, but there were the usual *remonstrances*, and riots in Rouen, Grenoble, and Toulouse. The *parlements* by now claimed to believe that they represented the lawful rights of the people, and that they had the right to invoke them, even against the king, even though they themselves were in fact bastions of privilege, representing no one but themselves.

When peace was officially proclaimed on June 3, 1763, Louis XV dispensed with the traditional honorary visits from the *parlements*, who had wanted to remonstrate at the same time about the land registry. The king had heard more than enough on the subject. He tried to lose himself more than ever with his girls. In May 1763 the king impregnated both Louise Tiercelin and Lucie d'Estaing.

On June 20, Louis XV, together with the royal family and Madame de Pompadour, went to Paris for the inauguration of the king's statue in the new "place Louis XV" (now the place de la Concorde). The sculptor Bouchardon had portrayed the king in Roman dress crowned with laurels; at the four corners of the pedestal were bronze statues by Pigalle representing the Virtues "which make the King reign in the hearts of the people," Strength, Justice, Wisdom, and Peace.

For the inauguration, there were parades around the square and a salute to the statue; the king and his family watched from across the river, seated in loges covered with crimson damask set up in the gardens of the Palais-Bourbon. (There was, as yet, no pont de la Concorde across the Seine, and no colonnade of the National Assembly.)

Madame de Pompadour sat in her own box and, at the end of the spectacle, entertained Parisian society at her house, the hôtel d'Evreux (now the palais de l' Elysée), where the guests could admire the portraits of the marquise and Louis XV hung side by side in the grand salon. The fireworks display in her garden was even more splendid than that of the city. There was a confusion of carriages in the Champs-Elysées which lasted until dawn. But the populace was not enthusiastic, the atmosphere sullen. Louis XV had not visited the capital for over five years, and he was not particularly welcome. A few days after the ceremonies, a placard was hung around the neck of Bouchardon's horse, with the words:

OH! THE FINE STATUE! OH! THE FINE PEDESTAL!
THE VIRTUES ARE BENEATH, VICE IS ON THE HORSE.

And another ominous placard read STATUA STATUAE, the statue of a statue.*

Madame de Pompadour, frustrated by the lack of the crowd's acclaim and their obvious hostility, irritably "told the provost of merchants that she was furious that this ceremony, the most august, she said, of its kind, had not been more successful."

The marquise was indeed furiously irritable. It was said that she had insulted the popular artist Carle Van Loo when she visited the exhibition of paintings, the Salon, held every August at the Louvre. "The illustrious protectress of the Arts was at the Salon. Van Loo was escorting her. Someone said to Madame de Pompadour, who appeared to neglect Van Loo's painting: 'Madame, you are not paying attention to these Graces.' 'You call those Graces!' said the virtuoso scornfully, 'You call those Graces!' and at the same time made a pirouette to go and see the lemons of Javotte. The humiliated artist approached humbly and said to her: 'Madame, I shall repaint them.'" (According to a contemporary, Van Loo was so devastated by this cruelty that he attacked his painting with a palette knife.)

At the Salon, Madame de Pompadour preferred to inspect Bachelier's large paintings for the new foreign ministry at Versailles, in which *The Family Pact, The Alliances of France and Europe,* and *L'Europe Savante* were celebrated; in the latter, a portrait *en grisaille* of Marigny can be seen.**

On the return to Versailles, the marquise and Choiseul had to address a new problem. Louis XV had apparently decided to pursue a for-

*The statue was overturned and melted down in August 1792, replaced on the pedestal by a colossal statue of Liberty wearing a red bonnet. The guillotine was set up between this statue and the entrance to the Tuileries gardens in October 1792. It was here that Louis XVI was executed the following January, and where, between May 1793 and June 1794, more than a thousand people would perish during the days of the Terror, including the duchesse de Gramont, who was present at the inauguration in 1762.

**These paintings are still in place at the former ministry, today the Versailles library.

eign venture on his own initiative, an initiative to be kept from his own ministers. Even before the official proclamation of peace, Louis XV had been persuaded that he must find a way to take his revenge on Great Britain, that he could not allow the indignities of the past years to go unpunished. Even though he was well aware that yet another war would ruin France, he had rashly adopted the ideas of the comte de Broglie and the men in his "*secret,*" that an undercover mission be sent to reconnoiter the English coast for a possible invasion. (Louis XV still kept in close touch with Broglie, even though he had exiled him from court. It was characteristic of his desire to preserve a little independence of action, an area which was not under surveillance by Madame de Pompadour and Choiseul.) At the end of March the chevalier d'Eon—the same d'Eon whose transvestite dramatics would later cause such a stir in Europe— left for London to join the French embassy, initiated into the *secret du roi* and this reconnaissance mission.

On June 3, 1763, the King wrote to d'Eon in his own hand: "The sieur d'Eon will receive my orders by way of the comte de Broglie as to the reconnaissances to make in England, whether on the coasts, or in the interior of the country, and will conform himself in every regard to what will be prescribed as though I were telling him directly. My intention is that he keep the most profound secret of this affair, and that he give no knowledge of it to anyone who lives, not even to my ministers." If anyone knew of d'Eon's unstable character and love of intrigue, they would never have trusted him with such a potentially compromising document.

Prudent d'Eon was not. He caused such a commotion in London, barricading himself in a house in Soho, claiming to have been poisoned by the British government, that he was recalled in haste. Unfortunately, he refused to obey, and threatened to use the king's letter as blackmail. What a disaster! Louis XV would be exposed as not only plotting against his new British friends, but as keeping his own ministers in ignorance and undermining their work.

Louis XV wrote frantic letters, even during a performance of the opera *Scanderberg* at Fontainebleau, "produced with the greatest magnificence." His anxiety over d'Eon would be constantly with him for months. Madame de Pompadour watched him with wary suspicion. She and

Choiseul knew something, but not enough to confront the King with what they knew. Everyone at court was watching everyone else.

In his gloom, Louis XV decided to back down before his *parlements* and give up on the land registry, affirming his wish to rule "not by the imposition of his authority, which he held from God and would never allow to weaken in his hands, but by love, justice, and the observation of the rules and forms wisely established in his kingdom." He invited his *parlements* to explain their views on the means of "perfecting and simplifying" the fiscal system. "A new order of things commences!" proclaimed the *parlement* of Dijon on January 19, 1764. But in fact, the old order had triumphed.

Bertin, his attempts at modernization of monetary policy a failure, resigned as controller of finances. But he remained on the Council of State, and in December Louis created for him the position of fifth secretary of state "*le département de Monsieur Bertin.*" He was succeeded by Monsieur de L'Averdy, a man of *parlement* and noted Jansenist. Here was more cause for bitterness for Madame de Pompadour. The king had been forced to concede not only to his enemies abroad, but also, and even more humiliatingly, to his enemies within.

At the end of 1763 the long process of destroying all the Jesuit institutions in France—a process ordained by the Jansenist *parlements* to rid the country of an alleged "fifth column"—was almost at an end. "In general," wrote Voltaire, "all persecution is odious and the *parlement* of Paris is overstepping its powers, compromising its honor and its fairness, letting itself be led to fanaticism by its passion to govern. I and many others attended the college of Louis-le-Grand [a Jesuit school in Paris]. . . . They never taught us a single murderous doctrine, nor any dangerous principle, which are the reasons for their elimination imagined by the Jansenists, who will destroy themselves when they have no more enemies to conquer."

Madame de Pompadour might have agreed. Despite her occasional criticisms of the *philosophes*, despite her disappointment with the Jesuits, she hated the *parlements* more. To her, they were disloyal subjects, bent on destroying the nation, and the king was shamefully weak in not standing up to them. As 1763 drew to a close, Madame de Pompadour's mood was dark. And her health continued to decline.

One hopes she found some consolation in the visit to Versailles of the eight-year-old Wolfgang Amadeus Mozart, who, on New Year's Day 1764, played the organ in the chapel and in the evening attended the king and queen's supper. The queen spoke to him in German and translated his replies for the king. Wolfgang's father Leopold was given a tour of the château and marveled at the luxury of Madame de Pompadour's rooms. Before returning to Paris, little Wolfgang played the harpsichord for Mesdames and composed two pairs of sonatas for violin and harpsichord, one of them dedicated to Madame Victoire, who gave him fifty louis. It is a poignant image: the frail marquise, who had grown up with the music of Lully, had sung the arias of Rameau, and played the harpsichord with verve, listening to the first notes of the young virtuoso.

Chapter 23

"One moment, monsieur le curé, *we shall go together."*

In December 1763 the marquise fell seriously ill. Although she rallied, she remained frail, suffering from violent headaches, fevers, and colds. Her breathing was labored, her eyesight failing. She seemed distraught, restless, always exasperated or sad.

In January, after five years of exile, Bernis was permitted to return to court for a visit; he told Voltaire that the king had "given me as a present the first of all blessings: freedom, and the permission to pay him my respects." After visiting the royal family, he saw the marquise sitting at her embroidery, wearing a flowered silk dress, in reflective mood. "This peace is neither happy nor good," she told the cardinal, "but one had to make it; the King said that if it were made a year later, things would have been worse. Indeed, our frontier is not enlarged, and the Infant is not in Brussels as one had hoped, but that interested us less after the death of Madame Infante. To recover Belle-Ile, we had to give up Minorca. Canada, the isles of the St. Lawrence, behold fine spoils for the English; but we keep our rich Antilles, Bourbon, l'Ile de France and, in Africa as in the Indies, trading posts sufficient for commerce. That is still a fine colonial empire. The King is persuaded, moreover, that the possessions of the King of England in America will not remain his for long; we shall have our revenge, and we have already taken measures to acquire the maritime power we have lacked." This was the official line, and she delivered it nobly.

She and the cardinal spoke of the new financial controller, L'Averdy, who the marquise hoped would succeed where so many others had failed, of Pâris de Montmartel, with whom she had quarreled for being, she claimed, "too greedy for profit," of the Jesuits, of the archbishop of Paris,

with whom the king was still unhappy. She asked if the archbishopric of
Albi might suit the cardinal. Choiseul's brother, who was there, wished to
be nearer Versailles. . . . The conversation was affectionate, collected. They
parted as friends. But Bernis was certain he would never see her again.

A short time later, Madame de la Ferté-Imbault came to thank the
marquise for her intervention in favor of Bernis. "I found her beautiful
and grave, seeming in good health, even though she complained of in-
somnia, indigestion, and palpitations. She started to tell me, with all the
warmth and expression of a fine actress, how affected she was at the
deplorable state of the kingdom, the rebellion in *parlement*, and what went
on up there (indicating, with tears in her eyes, the King's rooms). She
assured me that she was giving the King a great token of her attachment
by staying at his side, that she would be a thousand times happier living
alone and tranquil at Ménars, but that the King would no longer know
what to do if she left him. . . . In short, she seemed to me mad and en-
raged, and I have never needed a finer sermon to prove the miseries attached to ambition; and, at the same time, I saw her, so miserable, so
insolent, so violently agitated, so overwhelmed by her supreme power,
that I left her after an hour of this conversation, my imagination struck
with the thought that there remained for her no other refuge than death."

One cannot help but share Madame de la Ferté-Imbault's view that
the marquise was once more putting her acting abilities on display. She
might well have thought of retirement occasionally — she was certainly
weary of court life, physically worn out, profoundly discouraged by the
results of the war and the attitude of the *parlements*. But while she had
relinquished much of her political activities to Choiseul, and remained
much of the time in seclusion, she still maintained her influence over the
king's private life, her control of appointments and preferment, her involvement in every aspect of court life. As the Goncourts wrote, "her
hands, although already cold, still held tight to power."

At the end of February the king and Madame de Pompadour were at
Choisy. The weather was bitterly cold and wet. On the evening of February 29, as she was sitting in the salon, the marquise was struck with
such a violent headache that she stood up trembling and a valet had to

take her to her room. That night she slept badly with a high fever; then, as pneumonia set in, she retired to the *petit château* at Choisy. She remained there throughout March, surrounded by her beloved porcelain, her flower paintings, her furniture with its marquetry of birds, flowers, and fruit, writing short notes to her friends from her sickbed, embroidering and reading, trying to overcome her failing eyesight, trying to recover her strength. Louis XV, who had returned to Versailles, came to see her nearly every day.

The marquise's decline greatly alarmed Choiseul and his friends; in this circle, Madame de Pompadour was regarded as the guarantor of the duke's continuing favor. Madame du Deffand, a close friend of the duchesse de Choiseul, told Voltaire, "We are in a great state of alarm. Mme de Pompadour is very ill; I will not close this letter until I have had news of her." The news was not good. On March 8 the marquise's state deteriorated. "The anxiety has increased. The King was almost always there. On March 10 she was at death's door." She sent for the abbé Cathelin, a priest from her parish church in Paris, the Madeleine de la Ville-L'Evêque, and solemnly confessed. All the court and all of Paris sent word or went to Choisy. "There was commotion. Everyone agreed that she was a good person, and the public seemed to really care about her."

A few days later Madame du Deffand had better news. "Mme de Pompadour is much improved, but her illness is not yet over, and I dare not hope too much. I think that her loss would be a very great misfortune: I myself would be greatly afflicted by it, not for any personal reason, but for the sake of some people I love." The duchesse de Choiseul, of whom Madame du Deffand was thinking, was also temporarily relieved, although still anxious: "Mme de Pompadour has coughed a great deal and had a slight fever tonight. However, they assure us that she is in no danger; but I am worried, because I love her." When Madame de Choiseul finally went to Choisy, she found the marquise "asleep in her armchair, calm, her breathing free . . . I am overwhelmed with joy, for Mme de Pompadour has recovered."

On March 24 the weather was good enough for the marquise to go out in her carriage in the park at Choisy, and a few days later her doctor, Quesnay, allowed her return to Versailles. The weather was atrocious, windy, cold, dark, and rainy. She developed another fever, then bronchial pneumonia. Croÿ, who had been shocked at how fat and bloated she seemed, thought her state was very bad. He was not alone. "My anxieties have not lessened at all," wrote Louis XV to his son-in-law on Monday, April 9, "and I admit to you that I have very little hope of a perfect recovery for her, and a great deal of fear that an end is perhaps too near. A relationship of almost twenty years and a solid friendship! But God is the master and one must cede to everything he wishes. M. de Rochechouart has learnt of the death of his wife after much suffering; I pity him, if he loved her."

Sensing that her end was near, the marquise asked to be moved to her nearby hôtel des Réservoirs. Etiquette required that only members of the royal family die in the château of Versailles. But the king insisted she remain.

On Wednesday, April 11 the court knew the marquise was lost. Louis XV recognized that it was his duty to request her to receive the last rites, and that, after she had done so, he would not be allowed to see her again. He delayed as long as he could. On Friday, April 13 she sat in her armchair, unable to breathe. The king, Gontaut, Soubise, Marigny, and the Choiseuls came and went. In the evening the doctors abandoned hope.

The next day, Saturday, April 14, 1764, abbé Cathelin was called back to Versailles from Paris. The king went down again to see her in the evening; these were their last moments together. She received extreme unction during the night of April 14 to 15, and sent a message to her husband asking his pardon. "She showed much courage and resignation," wrote Croÿ, who most likely heard the details from Soubise.

'She is dying with a courage rare in either sex," the dauphin told the bishop of Verdun. "Every time she breathes, she believes it to be for the last time. It is one of the most painful ways to die and one of the cruelest one can imagine. . . . The King has not seen her since yesterday. The curé of the Madeleine does not leave her. And so these are reasons to hope for pity for her."

During the day of the 15th she reread the will she had made in 1757, made no changes, but dictated a codicil to her lawyer, Collin:

"My wish is to give, as a mark of friendship, so that they will remember me, the following persons:

To madame du Roure, my daughter's portrait set in a box with
   diamonds.
To madame la maréchale de Mirepoix, my new diamond watch.
To madame de Châteaurenard, a box with a portrait of the King,
   with diamonds, which they were going to give me any day.
To madame de Choiseul, a silver box with diamonds.
To madame la duchesse de Gramont, a box with a butterfly of
   diamonds.
To monsieur le duc de Gontaut, a rose and white alliance of diamonds, tied with a green knot; and a carnelian box he has always
   liked.
To monsieur le duc de Choiseul, a diamond the color of aquama-
   rine and a black box and a goblet.
To monsieur le maréchal de Soubise, a ring of Guay's signifying
   friendship; it is my portrait and his the twenty years I have
   known him.
To madame d'Amblimont, my parure of emeralds.

If I have forgotten any of my people in my will, I beg my brother to provide for them, and I confirm my will; I hope that he will find good the
codicil which friendship dictates to me and which I am having monsieur
Collin write, not having the strength to write it myself.
—At Versailles 15 April 1764."
     Collin was weeping, today we see that the document is stained, and
clumsily written; he handed it to her for revision, she signed: "La marquise
de Pompadour." She asked for Soubise, the executor of her will, and gave
him her various keys; she told Collin which carriage should take her to
her hôtel des Réservoirs. "In general, she arranged all the details, with that
methodical spirit she had to the highest degree." And then she murmured,
"It is coming, leave me to my soul, my confessor, and my women."
     But she refused the services of her women when they wished to
change her: "I know that you are very careful; but I am so weak that you
could not prevent yourselves from hurting me, and it is not worth the
trouble for the little time I have left to live." Then, turning toward the curé,
who was about to leave discreetly: "A moment, *monsieur le curé*, we will
go together." Several instants later, at seven-thirty, on the evening of

April 15, 1764, Palm Sunday, she died at the age of forty-two years and four months.

Without waiting for the carriage, her servants took her body, covered with a sheet, to the hôtel des Réservoirs. The rule that only those of royal birth might die at Versailles had already been broken. Now she must be transported as quickly as possible to her hôtel, where a funerary chapel had been set up. The duchesse de Praslin observed the procession: "I saw two men carrying a stretcher; when they approached (they passed beneath my windows), I saw that it was the body of a woman, covered only with a sheet so short that the shape of the head, the breasts, the stomach, and the legs were clearly distinct. . . . It was the body of that poor woman, who, according to the strict law that no one dead could remain in the château, was being taken *chez elle* . . ." And she burst into tears as she told Dufort de Cheverny. At the hôtel des Réservoirs, the marquise was placed on a bed in a room hung with black, lit by hundreds of candles. All night two priests prayed at the bedside.

Louis XV had been in the chapel at Versailles for Palm Sunday services. His doctor, Sénac, broke the news. "Only I, Sénac, know the extent of my loss," he murmured. There was no public supper; Louis ate in private with the duc d'Ayen, the duc de Gontaut, and the duc de La Vallière. The next day he wrote to his son-in-law in Parma: "My preceding letter will have told you why I did not reply today to your letters. All my anxieties are over, in the saddest way, you will easily guess it . . ."

Madame de Pompadour was to be buried in the crypt of the Capucine convent in the place Vendôme in Paris, next to her mother and her daughter. After a Mass at the church of Notre-Dame-de-Versailles, her body would be taken to the capital in a funeral procession, with all the honors of a duchesse.

On April 17, at six o'clock on a rainy, stormy night, Louis XV went to the balcony of his study, from where he could see the funeral procession go down the avenue de Paris. Laborde, his premier valet de chambre, had hoped to close the shutters and spare his master the sad spectacle. But the king was already on the balcony with his other valet, Champlost.

"He maintained a religious silence, watched the procession move along the avenue and, despite the bad weather and the cold air to which he seemed insensible, followed it with his eyes until it was entirely lost to view. He went back into his study; two large tears were running down his cheeks, and he said only a few words to Champlost: '*Voilà les seul devoirs que j'aie pu rendre!*' ('Behold the only respects I can pay her!'), the most eloquent words he could pronounce at that instant."

The hearse was drawn by twelve horses bedecked in black and silver silk, followed by one hundred priests, twenty-four children with candles, forty-two servants in livery, and seventy-two beggars. These latter had been lent decent clothes and hats (which they were expected to return). But the weather was so bad that two men lost their hats to the wind and could not retrieve them from the rain-swollen ditches. The battered cortège arrived at the convent of the Capucines in the middle of the night. In the presence of fifty monks, Père Gardien pronounced the funeral eulogy, solving the problem of how to refer to the marquise by devoting his eulogy to the queen: "I receive the body of the very great lady, Madame la marquise de Pompadour, *dame du palais* de la Reine. She was at the school of all the virtues, for the Queen is a model of kindness, of piety, of modesty and indulgence . . ." The coffin descended into the crypt.*

Madame de Pompadour's body had not reached Paris when reactions to her death and appraisals of her role and character began. The court was eager to observe how Louis XV conducted himself without her. But the king was too experienced at hiding his feelings to display much emotion. Croÿ thought him "very affected at first, but then he seemed to collect himself and not be too distressed at having to act on his own." Louis XV turned to Anne de Romans for consolation, and to Choiseul for advice. The *petits soupers* continued with the same familiar faces, but it would be the duchesse de Gramont, Choiseul's sister, who took over the role of hostess.

Marigny (Abel Poisson) told a friend of the overwhelming affliction into which his sister's death had plunged him. But his brutal comment, "Now the bows will be for me," was also widely reported. He

---

*In 1806 the land belonging to the Capucines was sold and divided into lots. The cloister and the chapel were demolished to make room for the rue de la Paix. The tomb of the marquise carried no inscription, so it is reasonable to suppose that her remains still repose in the heart of Paris, some steps from the place Vendôme.

offered to resign his post at the *Bâtiments* and give up the valuable per-
quisites his sister had obtained for him, but the king refused to let him
go. He had proved himself an able administrator and Louis XV had become used to him. Marigny stayed on at the *Bâtiments* until 1773.

At Versailles, the queen discreetly expressed her contempt for the
court. "No one talks anymore of the person who has just died," she wrote
cautiously, "as though she had never existed. So much for the world, it is
indeed hard to love it." The dauphin took a pious view. "We have lost the
poor marquise. The mercy of Our Lord is infinite, and we must hope that
it be bestowed on her. . . . Our greatest wish is that the King be mindful of
his children as those he loves the most in the world, that he be pleased with
us and that God touches his heart, draws him in and blesses him."

Those in the king's inner circle missed the marquise. "She had the
grand gift of amusing the man who was the most difficult in the kingdom to amuse because he was satiated with everything. He liked private
life by inclination, but felt that his position demanded the contrary; so
that, when he could escape his ceremonial duties, he went down his hidden staircase to her, where he often found his special friends, and at once
put aside the trappings of King," wrote Dufort.

Croÿ agreed: "In general she was missed, being a good person and
doing only good to most who came to her . . . and she had never done
any harm, except when forced, but so many misfortunes had befallen
France during her life, and so many extravagances!"

In Paris, the tributes were predictably satiric:

> Here lies one who was twenty years a virgin,
> Seven years a whore and eight years a pimp.

Diderot was only slightly more charitable. "Mme de Pompadour
died at a time when they thought her out of danger. And so, what remains of that woman who exhausted us of men and money, left us without honor and without energy and who has overturned the political
system of Europe? The Treaty of Versailles, which will last while it is
possible. The Cupid of Bouchardon which one will admire forever, some
stones engraved by Guay which will astonish the antique dealers to come,
a good little painting by Van Loo which one will regard from time to time,
and a handful of ashes."

In Geneva, Voltaire was taken by surprise. "It is indeed ridiculous that an old scribbler is still alive, and that a beautiful woman should die at forty while in the midst of the most dazzling career in the world." He devoted many letters to the death of Madame de Pompadour, the tone varying to suit his audience. He told his Parisian friend, d'Argental, "I loved her, for I have a good soul; she even rendered me some little services, I had some attachment to her and gratitude, and I grieve for her. . . . I imagine that her death will bring about some new scene in the theatre of the court . . ."

More seriously, to Bernis: "I believe, Monseigneur, that you have suffered a real loss. Mme de Pompadour was your sincere friend; and if I may go further, I believe, in my Swiss retreat, that the King is experiencing a great loss; he was loved for himself by a soul born sincere who had *justesse dans son esprit et de la justice dans son coeur* (sound judgement and sure instinct). One does not meet with this every day . . ."

And, as one philosopher to another, to d'Alembert Voltaire wrote: "Have you grieved for Mme de Pompadour? Yes, no doubt, as she was at the bottom of her heart one of us; she was a patron of letters as much as she could be: behold the end of a beautiful dream. They say that she died with a courage worthy of your praises; at court such courage is rare, for there they cling more to life, I don't exactly know why. . . . Believe that Mme de Pompadour never persecuted anyone. I am very affected by her death."

After her death, her possessions were removed from the royal palaces and put into storage in Paris. It was necessary to rent three large town houses to hold everything, and it took over a year to finish the inventory. Marigny sold most of her furniture, paintings, and porcelain, taking the pieces he retained to Ménars.

Today, traces of Madame de Pompadour's houses and gardens are to be found at Versailles, where her first set of rooms are preserved, and where her Hermitage and the hôtel des Réservoirs stand, albeit in mutilated form; at Champs, where the boiseries survive; at her Hermitage at Fontainebleau; and, perhaps most poignantly, at the Petit Trianon, which she did not live to see, but which was executed according to her wishes. Of Choisy, Bellevue, Crécy, nothing remains.

AFTERWORD

How does one assess the personality and measure the influence of Madame de Pompadour?

Endowed with intelligence, charm, and beauty, Jeanne-Antoinette Poisson was brought up to be the finest flower of the financial élite of Paris. Her talents burnished, her appetite whetted, she was put on view by her mentors to attract the favor of a powerful man—perhaps, if it were to be so, of the king himself. When it did indeed come to pass, she moved smoothly into the position for which she had been trained. In her wake, her mentors and their associates were propelled to power. She set about establishing herself so closely by the side of the king that she would become indispensable, and the "clan Pompadour" also.

From the beginning, Madame de Pompadour understood that Louis XV needed a warm and comfortable setting for his private life, and she set out to create it. She and a small group of intimates entertained the king at supper parties and theatricals, establishing an exclusive little society in which he could throw off his ceremonial self. Louis quickly became dependent on this way of life and on the woman who inspired it. As for the marquise, having gained the king's adoration, she concentrated the creation of an image, a persona intended for the public. For this public persona, she chose that of an educated woman with interests in art, music, and architecture. Surrounded by books, music, and all the attributes of a cultivated mind, she wished to be acknowledged as the supreme patron of the arts, the ultimate arbiter of taste.

In the privacy of the *petits appartements*, she presented herself as the seductive nymph, the irresistible Diana, the incomparable Venus. She made Bellevue into a temple dedicated to her own divinity. But reality was, of course, not so simple, nor so serene. Louis XV was a morose, mean-spirited, and moody man. Even in the early years of their relationship, he often showed himself callous and insensitive. As he became more and more dependent on sexual escapades with young girls, he became even more furtive and withdrawn, glumly bearing the burden of his guilt.

He could not escape the psychological domination of the woman who had provided him with an agreeable *cadre de vie*, and on whom he relied for help and support; but he could and did escape her in his sexual escapades, and in the machinations of the *secret du roi*.

From the beginning, Madame de Pompadour exerted her influence over appointments, promotions, honors, and preferments of all kinds. As her sexual relationship with Louis faded, she gradually informed and insinuated herself into foreign affairs, military matters, and high policy. She saw her role as that of confidential secretary to the king, and felt herself perfectly qualified to perform it. For his part Louis XV found her unfailingly trustworthy, helpful, and discreet. And, being a lazy man, he was gratified at her eagerness to take on the time-consuming and laborious task of communicating with his generals and ministers. The marquise adopted this role out of a conviction that she would thus maintain her place at Versailles. For, despite all her protestations, she was too wedded to the luxury and stimulants of court life to give it up. Then, as Duclos remarked, "Kaunitz made her mistress of the state."

When the Austrian chancellor decided to approach her as intermediary between the Empress Maria-Theresa and Louis XV, he had already observed her qualities. He knew of her eagerness to take part in affairs of state, to be the adviser and confidante of the king. Kaunitz knew how flattering to her his approach would be and how much she would invest in helping his cause. He was not disappointed. When Louis XV decided to break with his former ally, Prussia, and make an alliance with France's hereditary enemy, Austria, Madame de Pompadour became a passionate proponent of the new policy, and then a staunch adherent of the war it brought about. She faced the defeats of the French military with courage and fortitude, worked at finding financial support for the war, and shouldered the burden of acting on behalf of the increasingly absent king. She convinced herself that her presence was necessary for the king's wellbeing, that without her, he would succumb to melancholy, that affairs of state would suffer.

The marquise's influence on the choice of ministers and generals became of paramount importance. And today her choices leave her open to the charge of incompetence and shortsightedness. The replacement of Machault and d'Argenson by Paulmy and Moras was foolish; the persecution of the Broglie brothers wrong; the favor shown to Soubise blind. On the other hand, those who pandered to the marquise's paranoia and spied on her behalf received rewards; Berryer and Janel were her evil geniuses, the use she made of them distasteful.

She was a cold woman, physically and in her soul. Firmly at the center of her own life, she measured everyone in relation to their devotion to her, their loyalty, their sense of obligation. Men and women had to profess their love for her, and only her, and then she would be generous and indulgent. Soubise, Choiseul, and Berryer understood this. Bernis did not. Once he, her protégé, had failed her, she became a tenacious and vindictive hater, as Madame d'Estrades and Machault would discover. As for those who never played along—Richelieu, Broglie, Conti—all would be disgraced and made to pay the price for underestimating her. Although these men greatly contributed to their own downfall, it was Madame de Pompadour who made sure that their shortcomings were noticed, their faults illuminated. "It was the patience she brought to her hatred which made her almost always victorious."

She believed she acted for the good of the state. But in reality, she was unable to rise above games of intrigue and struggles for power. It was fortunate for France that one of her protégés, Choiseul, had the qualities necessary to govern France, when so many others had failed, politically and militarily.

Madame de Pompadour's narcissism drove her. She was always acutely conscious of how history would judge her. To that end, she commissioned artists, writers, and sculptors to fashion her image, first as Venus, the Goddess of Love, and then as Venus transformed into the Goddess of Friendship. Under this last guise she was represented as the noble and disinterested friend and helpmate of the king, the wise and judicious colleague, her closeness to him sanctified by their former intimacy. Desire was replaced by devotion, passion by respect. Eventually, this woman, who at the beginning of her affair with Louis XV had preferred the bourgeois terms of fidelity and respectability to define their relationship, in spite of its fundamental illicitness, became the embodiment of those same bourgeois virtues, as she sat placidly at her needlework, wearing her respectable lace cap, the irreproachable and beneficent matron. She saw herself as a latter-day Madame de

Maintenon, whose influential position as Louis XIV's mistress she
wished to emulate.

It was also with an eye to posterity that she labored to persuade
Louis XV to establish the *Ecole Militaire,* supported the building of the
Sèvres porcelain factory, gave encouragement to artists and writers, and
acted as a showcase for the fine arts of the day. She herself was not as much
of a leader of taste, as has often been said; she followed the advice of others,
particularly her brother Abel, as to which artists she should be seen to be
encouraging. Her own taste ran more to the decorative and the pretty—to
Bachelier's paintings of dogs and flowers, Boucher's nymphs, and
Falconet's figurines of children. But she wished to be seen as the supreme
patron of the arts, and, in the context of the times, she could be accepted
as such. This was an area in which women were allowed to have influence,
whereas any idea of a woman as minister, general, or financier would have
been laughable (unless one was born a queen or empress). It was the perception of Madame de Pompadour, as a woman attempting to play these
roles, to step out of her designated position, which caused her male contemporaries to fume.

She herself complained that she would have liked the *"grande niche"*
and found it displeasing to make do with the *"petite."* She had seen
enough of how the state operated at the highest levels to believe that
she had the necessary toughness and acumen to match any of the ministers with whom she had worked. But it could not be. The irony is that
she was ridiculed and insulted for exercizing the very power she felt
herself unable to attain.

Frederick of Prussia observed of Louis XV that "he had all the qualities, except that of being a King," and perhaps one could say of Madame
de Pompadour that she had all the qualifications, without being queen.
Over the years, she added to her innate intelligence, grace, and tact, an air
of dignity, graciousness, and authority. She ruled Versailles, gave audience to ambassadors, decided on all matters of preferment as absolutely
as any monarch. But she was not queen, and her presumption of such a
queenly role caused offense. It also damaged the respect in which the king
was held. The erosion of royal authority was not caused by the presence
of Madame de Pompadour; religious conflict and financial quarrels did
that—not to mention Louis XV's indecisiveness and timidity. But the

marquise came to represent the extravagance and arrogance of the court, and this impression, once created, would prove to be insidious.

Madame de Pompadour was her own greatest creation. It was Louis XV who turned Jeanne-Antoinette Poisson into madame la marquise de Pompadour; but it was Jeanne Poisson who made Madame de Pompadour the dazzling personage known to history. She was, after all, an actress, and she assumed the role of mistress to the king with aplomb, as she did its subsequent evolutions. Whatever the heartache and disillusionment, the exhaustion and disgust, she stayed in character. She died convinced of the purity of her intentions, with a clear conscience, and with a control of iron over her life's last act.

One must admire that last act. Madame de Pompadour had little faith in an afterlife; her piety, like so much else, had been a useful pretext, a political weapon. At her death, her courage was exemplary, her touch light. This woman, so often vindictive, imperious, and cruel, died a stoic and gentle death. This, together with the testimony of Voltaire, "In her heart, she was one of us," and the luminous portrait by La Tour earn her our liking and respect. Exactly as she intended.

EPILOGUE

LOUIS XV (1710–1774). The king managed without an official mistress until 1768 when he became enamored of Jeanne Beçu, who was presented at Versailles in April 1769 as the comtesse du Barry. Madame du Barry remained the *maîtresse déclarée* until the king's death five years later.

Louis worked with Choiseul until 1770, pursuing a policy of peace and stability, cultivating good relations with the *parlements*. But then Choiseul was abruptly dismissed, and the duc d'Aiguillon, together with the abbé Terray and René-Nicolas de Maupeou, took power. The *parlement*s were attacked and emasculated. Louis XV hoped that, by doing so, he would provide a more solid political environment for his grandson.

The king died at Versailles on May 10, 1774, after being taken ill on April 26 at Petit Trianon; he did not realize he had contracted small-pox, having always thought he had already had the disease. It took him two weeks of torment to die, his bedchamber the scene of unseemly in-trigue and ghastly suffering; Croÿ saw him on his deathbed, his face "a mask of bronze," all swollen with boils . . . he looked like a Moor, a Negro, the color of copper."

The new king, twenty-year-old Louis XVI, and his nineteen-year-old wife, Marie-Antoinette, were spirited away to Choisy to escape infec-tion. From Choisy, Louis XVI summoned to the government the seventy-four-year-old-comte de Maurepas, after an exile of a quarter of a century.

LOUIS, THE DAUPHIN (1729–1765). The only son of Louis XV died of tuberculosis at the age of thirty-six, having left little mark, but three of his sons became kings of France: Louis XVI, Louis XVIII, and Charles X.

MARIE-JOSÈPHE DE SAXE, THE DAUPHINE (1731–1767). At the death of the dauphin, Louis XV offered Marie-Josèphe the former rooms of Madame de Pompadour at Versailles. She lived there briefly but died in March 1767 at the age of thirty-six.

MARIE LECZINSKA (1703–1768). The queen survived her son and daughter-in-law, dying piously at the age of sixty-five.

MESDAMES DE FRANCE: ADÉLAÏDE (1732–1800), VICTOIRE (1733–1799), SOPHIE (1734–1782), AND LOUISE (1737–1787). The younger princesses, Sophie and Louise, died before the Revolution, Louise having become a Carmelite nun. Adélaïde and Victoire fled France in February 1791, enduring a long and uncomfortable journey to Turin. They made their way to Rome where they joined the French émigrée society which gravitated around the cardinal de Bernis.

THE CARDINAL DE BERNIS (1715–1794). In disgrace for six years after his dismissal in 1758, Bernis was then named archbishop of Albi. He went to Rome in 1768 as French *chargé d'affaires* at the Vatican. He held that post until 1791, observing the Revolution from afar, writing his memoirs, and entertaining French émigrés at the Palazzo Carolis (now the Palazzo Simonetti) on the Corso. He died there, in poverty, in 1794.

THE PRINCE DE CONTI (1717–1776). Conti never played a part in public life after his break with Louis XV in 1756. He lived in Paris with his mistress, the comtesse de Boufflers, dabbling in politics and literature, and outliving Louis XV by two years.

THE MARQUIS DE MARIGNY (ABEL POISSON) (1727–1781). He remained as director general of the *Bâtiments du Roi* until 1773, when he resigned after disagreements with Madame du Barry. In 1767 he married Marie-Françoise Filleul, the natural daughter of the financier Bouret; it was not a happy marriage, as Madame de Marigny was abundantly unfaithful to her husband, notably with the cardinal de Rohan, with whom she carried on an affair, meeting him in his carriage, dressed as a man. Marigny retired to Ménars, left to him by his sister, where he lived in great elegance. He left no descendants.

THE DUC DE CHOISEUL (1719–1785). He governed France until 1770, pursuing a policy of accommodation with the *parlements*, keeping the peace, and stimulating trade. Louis XV dismissed him on a false pretext, determined on an aggressive policy of confrontation with the magistrates. Choiseul, together with his loyal wife, his sister, the duchesse de Gramont, and his mistress, the comtesse de Brionne, went to live in splendor at his estate of Chanteloup, near Amboise. When Louis XVI came to the throne in 1774 he summoned Choiseul to court, at the urging of Marie-Antoinette, but said only: "You have put on weight, Monsieur de Choiseul, and you are losing your hair." Insulted, Choiseul returned immediately to Chanteloup, where he, as Claude Mancelon wrote, "used the intoxication of his debts to drug his despair." In 1781 his palatial house on the rue de Richelieu in Paris had to be sold. He died in rented rooms in Paris in May 1785, "as though giving an audience."

The duchesse de Choiseul and the duchesse de Gramont suffered greatly in the Terror, and Madame de Gramont was guillotined in April 1794. Madame de Choiseul lived on in poverty, until 1801, having managed to pay all her husband's debts.

VOLTAIRE (1694–1778). After living outside Geneva for more than twenty years, the eighty-four-year-old sage was persuaded to travel to Paris in February 1778 for the opening of his play *Irène*. On arrival, after five days on the road, he lodged with the marquis de Villette at his house on the corner of the rue de Beaune and the quai des Théâtins (now the quai Voltaire). He was visited by all Paris, including Benjamin Franklin, Diderot, d'Alembert, Beaumarchais, and Marmontel. On February 15, five days after his arrival, he fell ill, but rallied. On March 30 he was cheered by two thousand people when he arrived at the Louvre to be eulogised by the *académie Française*, and was mobbed when he attended a performance of *Irène*. A bust of the author, garlanded with laurel, was unveiled on stage before his eyes. The emotion was intense. And then he collapsed and took to his bed. After much suffering, alone and in torment, having been mercilessly harassed by priests and neglected by his niece, Madame Denis, the great man expired on the night of May 30. Jean-Jacques Rousseau followed him to the grave a month later.

MACHAULT D'ARNOUVILLE (1701–1794). His peaceful retirement after the storms of 1757 ended when he was arrested and guillotined at the age of ninety-three.

THE COMTE D'ARGENSON (1696–1764). Devastated by his exile, d'Argenson lived sadly at his estate of Les Ormes near Poitiers, prey to gout and depression. Marmontel painted a pathetic portrait of him there. As they walked in the gardens, they approached a statue of Louis XV, which d'Argenson could not bring himself to look at. "If you knew how zealously I served him! If you knew how many times he assured me that we would spend our lives together, and I that I had no better friend on earth than he! So much for the promises of Kings! So much for their friendship!" And he dissolved in tears. In 1764, after the death of Madame de Pompadour, d'Argenson returned to Paris to attempt to find a cure for his gout. He died there on August 22.

The comtesse d'Estrades shared the exile of her lover, the comte d'Argenson. After his death, she married a man twenty years younger than she, Nicolas Seguier de Saint-Brisson. She died in 1784.

THE DUC D'AIGUILLON (1720–1788) played an important part in the government after the fall of Choiseul, as minister of war and minister of foreign affairs. Having been a great friend to Madame du Barry, he was dismissed by Louis XVI in 1774 and exiled the following year to the château d'Aiguillon, near Agen in the southwest of France.

ANNE COUPPIER DE ROMANS (1737–1808) remained in favor with Louis XV after the death of Madame de Pompadour, but in August 1765 she was banished to a convent in Blois and forced to give up her son, having been associated with an obscure intrigue against Choiseul. In 1771 Louis XV consented to her marriage to the marquis de Cavanac.

CHARLES-GUILLAUME LENORMAND D'ETIOLES (1717–1800) married his mistress Marie-Anne Raime in 1764 and legitimized their children. Having made a great deal of money from the office of tax farms, he lived comfortably in Paris and survived the Revolution, dying in 1800 at the age of eighty-three. In 1794, in an odd twist of fate, one of his sons married a daughter of Marie-Louise O'Murphy.

MARIE-LOUISE O'MURPHY (1737–1815) survived the Revolution. She died in 1815 at the age of seventy-eight. Her first husband, Beaufranchet, was killed in 1757 at the battle of Rossbach, leaving her with two small children. She then married a wealthy businessman, returned to Paris, and made herself very comfortable with the help of other influential men. Her daughter by Louis XV died at the age of twenty in 1774.

ACKNOWLEDGMENTS

I would like to thank, once again, Joan Bingham for her wisdom and encouragement. Also, and particularly, Zelimir Galjanic; his suggestions, made with tact and sensitivity, have vastly improved the book. Wayne Furman and Elie Weitsman of the Office of Special Collections at the New York Public Library Center for the Humanities have been models of helpfulness, as has Rebecca Pine of Art Resource. Katharine Brannig, Marie-Thérèse Casseus and Ronda Murdock of the library of the Alliance Française in New York have been unfailingly cheerful in answering my persistent questions. And Paulette Zabriskie has greatly improved my knowledge of the fine points of French grammar.

SOURCE NOTES

Chapter 1

"One of the most beautiful women . . ." Barbier, *Journal d'un Bourgeois . . .*, Paris, 1963, p. 188.

"She was as clever as four devils . . ." Ibid., p. 191.

"Black holes . . ." Giles Perrault, *Le Secret du Roi*, Paris, 1992–6, vol. I, p. 205.

"The *ton du monde . . .*" Bernis, *Mémoires et Lettres*, edited by Masson, Paris, 1878, vol. I, p. 110.

"Your amiable daughter . . ." Fromageot, *Revue de l' Histoire de Versailles* (August, 1902), p. 198.

"They have told us . . ." Ibid., p. 204.

"Six hundred livres . . ." J. A. Leroi, *Curiosités historiques*, Paris, 1864, p. 222.

"Madame Poisson . . ." Barbier, op. cit., p. 190.

Chapter 2

"Neither holy . . ." Voltaire, *Essai sur les Moeurs et l'Esprit des Nations*, 1769.

"Every spring . . ." Perrault, op. cit., vol. I, p. 201.

"Women are not . . ." Duclos, *Romanciers du XVIII Siècle*, vol. II, p. 205.

"Presided over . . ." Voltaire to M. Lefèvre, 1732, in Cravieri, *Madame du Deffand*, Boston, 1994, pp. 62–3.

"Un lieu de brassage . . ." Rouart, *Bernis, le Cardinal des Plaisirs*, Paris, 1998, p. 37.

"It is not surprising . . ." Duclos, op. cit., vol. II, p. 253.

"My very dear father . . ." Sept. 3, 1741, in Poulet-Malassis, p. 2.

"I have just met . . ." Mme du Deffand, *Correspondance Complète avec ses Amis*, edited by Aide Lescure, Paris, 1885, vol. I, p. 70.

"How lucky you are . . ." P. de Ségur, *Le Royaume de la rue Saint-Honoré*, Paris, 1925, p. 159.

"Had always had . . ." Voltaire, *Mémoires*, Paris, 1998, p. 105.

Chapter 3

"Toujours coucher . . ." D'Argenson, ed., *Journal et Mémoires*, vol. I, p. 232.

"Well-made, young . . ." Ibid., vol. I, p. 233.

"Having had the misfortune . . ." Michel Antoine, *Louis XV*, Paris, 1989, p. 308.

"Do you not know . . ." Ségur, op. cit., appendix III, p. 411.

"The King's temperament . . ." Gaxotte, Le Siècle de Louis XV, Paris 1998,
    pp. 177–8.
"And her sister too!" Richelieu, *Mémoires,* edited by M. F. Barrière, Paris, 1869,
    vol. II, p. 61.
"When he returns . . ." Hubert Cole, *First Gentleman . . .* , New York, 1965, p. 129.

Chapter 4

"They even say . . ." Luynes, *Mémoires,* edited by L. Dussieux & E. Soulié, Paris,
    1860–65, vol. VI, p. 288.
"Long, boring and bad . . ." Voltaire, *Correspondance,* vol. II, p. 1586, n. 1.
"In a black cloak . . ." Valfons, *Souvenirs,* edited by Barante, Paris, 1929, p. 132.
"All these masked balls . . ." Luynes, op. cit., vol. VI, p. 354.
"They are talking . . ." Barbier, op. cit., p. 188.
"The King hunted . . ." Luynes, op. cit., vol. VI, p. 375.
"In a box . . ." Ibid., vol. VI, p. 382.
"That which seemed . . ." Ibid., vol. VI, p. 382.
"This Madame d'Etioles . . ." Barbier, op. cit., p. 190.
"He could no longer count . . ." Luynes, op. cit., vol. VI, p. 423.
"Belle Babet . . ." Voltaire, *Correspondance,* op. cit., vol. II, p. 1202.
"No one at the time . . ." Rouart, op. cit., p. 71.
"Madame d'Etioles . . ." Bernis, *Mémoires,* op. cit., vol. I, pp. 109–10.
"This hero . . ." Voltaire, *Correspondance,* op. cit., vol. II, p. 965.
"It is the King . . ." Ibid., vol. II, p. 1596.
"Ah, what fine work . . ." Ibid., vol. II, p. 963.
"I do not know . . ." Pomeau, *Voltaire et Son Temps,* Oxford, 1985–1995, vol. II,
    p. 224.
"Sincere and tender . . ." Voltaire, *Correspondance,* op. cit., vol. II, p. 960.
"Just like Hebe . . ." Michel, *Prestigieuse marquise de Pompadour,* pp. 133–4.
"She was well brought up . . ." Voltaire, *Mémoires,* op. cit., p. 105.
"I was talking . . ." Voltaire, *Correspondance,* op. cit., vol. II, p. 1016.
"I advised her . . ." Bernis, *Mémoires,* op. cit., vol. I, p. 114.
"With the exception . . ." Ibid., vol. I, p. 114.
"An excellent piece . . ." du Hausset, *Mémoires,* Paris, 1985, p. 175.
"Rather plump . . ." Luynes, vol. VII, p. 59.
"Very well-made . . ." Dufort de Cheverny, *Mémoires,* Paris, 1990, *1st Epoque,*
    p. 97.
"She seemed to mark . . ." Leroy, Charles-G., *Portraits Historiques,* Paris, 1802.
"All Paris . . ." Luynes, op. cit., vol. VII, p. 60.
"At the time . . ." Choiseul, *Mémoires,* ed. Mercure de France, Paris, 1982,
    p. 63.
"She is excessively common . . ." Castries, *La Pompadour,* Paris, 1983, pp. 97–
    98.

Chapter 5

"They have made . . ." Verlet, *Le Château de Versailles*, Paris, 1985, p. 482.
"As soon as dressed . . ." Luynes, op. cit., vol. VII, p. 110.
"Is it possible . . ." Voltaire, *Correspondance*, op. cit., vol. II, p. 1037.
"Madame d'Etioles . . ." Valfons, *Souvenirs*, op. cit., p. 127.
"It seems everyone . . ." Luynes, op. cit., vol. VII, p. 110.
"Here lies . . ." Feydeau de Marville, *Lettres au ministre Maurepas*, Paris, 1896,
    vol. II, p. 216.
"Un petit club . . ." Rouart, op. cit., p. 84.
"A little bourgeoise . . ." *Recueil Clairambault Maurepas*, vol. VII, p. 142.
"I found Mme de Pompadour . . ." Choiseul, *Mémoires*, op. cit., p. 63.

Chapter 6

"Very handsome . . ." Luynes, op. cit., vol. VII, p. 303.
"Madame la Dauphine . . ." July 8, Michel, op. cit., p. 29.
"I was very coldly . . ." Choiseul, *Mémoires*, op. cit., p. 69.
"People are always . . ." D'Argenson, op. cit., vol. III, p. 140.
"One has difficulty . . ." Luynes, op. cit., vol. VIII, p. 13.
"Between ourselves . . ." Michel, op. cit., p. 31.
"She asks me . . ." Valfons, op. cit., p. 185.
"The same man . . ." Choiseul, *Mémoires*, op. cit., p. 71.
"Madame de Pompadour has been . . ." Butler, p. 669.

Chapter 7

"Of commonplace ideas . . ." D'Argenson, op. cit., vol. III, p. 314.
"Was abandoning himself . . ." Croÿ, *Journal*, vol. I, p. 56.
"After I had worked . . ." Ibid., vol. I, p. 71.
"One entered . . ." Ibid., vol. I, p. 71.
"You have rather forgotten . . ." Luynes, op. cit., vol. VIII, p. 105.
"M. le Dauphin . . ." D'Argenson, op. cit., vol. III, p. 175.
"I can be counted . . ." Luynes, op. cit., vol. VIII, p. 105.
"Masked, at the feet . . ." Croÿ, op. cit., vol. I, p. 78.
"Madame de Pompadour . . ." Butler, *Choiseul*, Oxford, 1980, vol. 1, p. 669.
"Graceful and charming . . ." Croÿ, vol. I, p. 81.
"Four desperate hours . . ." Butler, op. cit., p. 690.
"It is not printed cotton . . ." July 28, Poulet-Malassis, p. 99.
"I am bored to tears . . ." August 25, Michel, op. cit., p. 42.
"She received her courier . . ." Kaunitz, *Mémoire*, 1752, p. 448.
"Charnelhouse of pillage . . ." Butler, op. cit., p. 707.
"On Monday . . ." Michel, op. cit., pp. 44–5.
"It is the Pâris . . ." D'Argenson, op. cit., vol. III, p. 179.

"A kind of ceremony . . ." D'Argenson, op. cit., vol. III, p. 219.
"In the most base manner . . ." Croÿ, op. cit., vol. I, p. 69.
"There was almost no favour . . ." Ibid., vol. I, p. 92.
"Here I am . . ." Voltaire, *Correspondance*, op. cit., vol. II, p. 1135.
"Cara, siamo . . ." Ibid., vol. II, p. 1192.

Chapter 8

"It is not possible . . ." Luynes, op. cit., vol. VIII, p. 404.
"Low cut bodice . . ." Campardon, *Madame de Pompadour . . .*, Paris, 1867,
    p. 105–6.
"As ladies are . . ." Luynes, op. cit., vol. IX, p. 461.
"The court . . ." D'Argenson, op. cit., vol. III, p. 193.
"Raising myself . . ." Voltaire, *Correspondance*, op. cit., vol. II, p. 1195.
"Pompadour, you . . ." Barbier, op. cit., p. 196.
"These verses . . ." Ibid., p. 196.
"Between ourselves . . ." Orieux, *Voltaire*, Paris, 1966, p. 435.
"A warm cell . . ." Voltaire, *Correspondance*, op. ed., vol. II, p. 1203.
"One can add nothing . . ." Luynes, op. cit., vol. IX, p. 2.
"She cannot stand up to . . ." D'Argenson, op. cit., vol. III, p. 205.
"The misfortune . . ." Poulet-Malassis, p. 100.
"A fine brown complexion . . ." Luynes, vol. VIII, p. 482.
"She besieges the King . . ." D'Argenson, op. cit., vol. III, p. 250.

Chapter 9

"The restitutions . . ." Antoine, p. 402.
 "People once so proud . . ." Perrault, vol. I, p. 192.
"I believe it essential . . ." D'Argenson, *Autour d'un Ministre*, p. 299.
"Carnage on the quai . . ." Ibid., *Mémoires*, vol. III, p. 243.
"You are as stupid . . ." Barbier, op. cit., p. 203.
"You say we shall have . . ." Fonds Richelieu, Biblio. Victor Cousin, folio 173,
    cited Lever, *Madame de Pompadour*, Paris, 2000, p. 349.
"The maréchal de Richelieu . . ." D'Argenson, *Mémoires*, vol. III, p. 237.
"I hope and flatter myself . . ." Poulet-Malassis, op. cit., p. 103.
"I spend half my life there . . ." Ibid., p. 102.
"The King supped yesterday . . ." Luynes, op. cit., vol. IX, p. 254.
"They will not say . . ." D'Argenson, op. cit., vol. III, p. 263.
"This will bring her . . ." Ibid., vol. III, p. 268.
"By your manners . . ." D'Argenson, vol. III, p. 262.
"What sadness . . ." Barbier, op. cit., p. 208.
"The great lords . . ." Du Hausset, p. 177.
"A rock of diamonds . . ." Augustus Hervey's *Journal*, p. 87.

"Unfortunate predilection . . ." Croÿ, op. cit., vol. I, p. 148.

"We have had news . . ." D'Argenson, op. cit., Vol. III, pp. 286–7.

"You cannot imagine . . ." Gallet et al., *Mme de Pompadour: La Floraison des Arts*, p. 64.

"You did well . . ." December 28, Poulet-Malassis, op. cit., p. 29.

Chapter 10

"My brother is killing himself . . ." D'Argenson, op. cit., vol. III, p. 305.

"One does not know . . ." Barbier, op. cit., p. 219.

"Man is by nature good . . ." J.-J. Rousseau, *Correspondance complète*, vol. X, pp. 24–9.

"The more I advance in age . . ." Poulet-Malassis, op. cit., p. 54.

"He thinks me very cold . . ." Du Hausset, op. cit., p. 59.

"To have seen her die . . ." Voltaire, *Correspondance*, vol. III, p. 105.

"If you wish to perfect . . ." Ibid., vol. III, p. 44.

"I see that you are afflicted . . ." 5 September 1749, Pomeau, vol. II, p. 389.

"At least as in love . . ." Croÿ, op. cit., vol. I, p. 135.

"Women are not made . . ." Fonds Richelieu, Biblio. Victor Cousin, Paris, folio 154, cited Lever, p. 350.

"You can easily imagine . . ." Poulet-Malassis, op. cit., p. 32.

"You have done well . . ." Ibid., p. 34.

"Find out what clothes . . ." Ibid., p. 37.

"As for courtiers . . ." Ibid., p. 40.

"I am still in charge . . ." Bailey, *The Loves of the Gods*, p. 410.

"Great favor . . ." D'Argenson, *Autour d'un Ministre*, p. 287.

"I defy the King . . ." Castries, op. cit., p. 122.

"I believe I have already . . ." Poulet-Malassis, op. cit., p. 12.

"Your sister . . ." Michel, op. cit., p. 150.

"She is in good health . . ." Poulet-Malassis, op. cit., p. 17.

"Dear Papa . . ." Castries, op. cit., p. 124.

"I have been to see M. de Tournehem . . ." Poulet-Malassis, op. cit., p. 55.

"A propos of folly . . ." Ibid., p. 55.

"I have asked the little Saint . . ." Ibid., p. 121.

"Not conducive to the love . . ." Michel, op. cit., p. 106.

"All this has an air of flight . . ." D'Argenson, op. cit., vol. III, p. 379.

"Insolent for subjects . . ." Barbier, op. cit., p. 230.

"One cannot give . . ." Voltaire, *Correspondance*, vol. III, p. 213.

"Bad news . . ." D'Argenson, op. cit., vol. III, p. 349.

"Real misfortune . . ." Poulet-Malassis, op. cit., p. 64.

"Keep in their cupboards . . ." D'Argenson, op. cit., vol. III, p. 379.

"In truth, nothing is more touching . . ." Poulet-Malassis, op. cit., pp. 72–3.

"Her eyes are blue . . ." Kaunitz, *Mémoire*, op. cit., p. 447.

"Which surpasses . . ." Ibid., p. 449.

"My bon mot . . ." Casanova, *Mémoires*, vol. I, p. 587.

"The best stew . . ." Ibid., p. 588.

"Which could incommode her . . ." Gallet, Danielle, *Gazette des Beaux-Arts* (October 1991), p. 137.

"Think that Friday . . ." Ibid., p. 136.

"I have been in the enchantment . . ." Poulet-Malassis, op. cit., p. 129.

"I believe that this affair . . ." Ibid., p. 69.

"The most beautiful thing . . ." Castries, op. cit., p. 109.

"Daughter of a leech . . ." Barbier, op. cit., p. 235.

"In good faith . . ." Ibid., p. 235.

"They say on all sides . . ." D'Argenson, op. cit., vol. III, p. 377.

Chapter 11

"Mme de Pompadour has had . . ." D'Argenson, op. cit., vol. IV, p. 20.

"It is not very large . . ." January 3, 1751, Poulet-Malassis, op. cit., pp. 105–6.

"It is the prettiest place . . ." February 10, 1751, Ibid., p. 75.

"The Parisians tell such lies . . ." Ibid., p. 74.

"This establishment . . ." Barbier, op. cit., p. 237.

"*Le chagrin affreux* . . ." D'Argenson, *Autour d'un Ministre*, p. 300.

"M. de Tournehem . . ." February 17, 1751. Poulet-Malassis, op. cit., p. 76.

"All this is arranged in good taste . . ." Ibid., vol. I, p. 148.

"This has cost a good deal . . ." Ibid., vol. I, p. 148.

"One talks only . . ." D'Argenson, op. cit., vol. IV, p. 10.

"The marquise de Pompadour is all powerful . . ." Nolhac, *Madame de Pompadour et la Politique*, p. 31.

"The marquise must be delighted . . ." Ibid., p. 32.

"One has never seen such devotion . . ." Barbier, op. cit., p. 244.

"Poor madame de Mailly . . ." April 1, 1751, Poulet-Malassis, op. cit., p. 82.

"It is true . . ." April 1, 1751, Poulet-Malassis, op. cit., p. 107.

"Regretted by all . . ." D'Argenson, op. cit., vol. IV, p. 23.

"She was fairly well-made . . ." Choiseul, *Mémoires*, p. 91.

"She is young and pretty . . ." D'Argenson, op. cit., vol. IV, p. 27.

"A man who has read . . ." Durant, *The Age of Voltaire*, p. 638.

"We find this work . . ." Ibid., p. 359.

"I have a bad cold . . ." Poulet-Malassis, op. cit., p. 85.

"M. de Tournehem awaits . . ." Ibid., p. 85.

"I do not know when . . ." Ibid., p. 87.

"One after the other . . ." Croÿ, op. cit., vol. I, p. 192.

"Mme de Pompadour has had a fever . . ." Luynes, op. cit., vol, X1, p. 135.

"Madame your daughter . . ." Michel, op. cit., p. 129.

"M. de T. is rather ill . . ." Poulet-Malassis, op. cit., p. 90.

"Fairly pretty . . ." Croÿ, op. cit., vol. I. p. 167.

"As beautiful as an angel . . ." Dufort de Cheverny, 1 Epoque, ch. XI, p. 155.

"You can judge of my joy . . ." September 29, 1751, Poulet-Malassis, op. cit., p. 108.

"Perhaps he was not content . . ." Antoine, op. cit., p. 667.

"A sad silence . . ." Croÿ, op. cit., vol. I, p. 166.

"M. de Richelieu . . ." D'Argenson, op. cit., vol. IV, p. 52.

"The comte du Luc . . ." Du Hausset, op. cit., p. 66.

"I feel only too much . . ." December 5, 1751, Poulet-Malassis, op. cit., p. 110.

"Nothing is more dangerous . . ." D'Argenson, op. cit., vol. IV, p. 10.

"A priest . . ." *Autour d'un Ministre*, p. 277.

"I believe it essential . . ." Ibid., p. 299.

"Not yet been able . . ." Michel, op. cit., p. 109.

"I do not wish . . ." *L'Amateur d'autographe*, 1906.

"This *bel esprit* . . ." D'Argenson, vol. IV, p. 56.

"Behold a good idea . . ." Antoine, p. 642.

"What a triumph . . ." D'Argenson, op. cit., vol. IV, p. 59.

"She is more beautiful . . ." Ibid., vol. IV, p. 60.

"What are remarked . . ." Ibid., vol. IV, p. 62.

Chapter 12

"His natural tenderness . . ." Croÿ, op. cit., vol. I, p. 169.

"Madame la marquise went to Trianon . . ." Ibid., vol. I, p. 170.

"Since she shows great courage . . ." D'Argenson, ed. (Rathery), vol. VII, p. 117.

"And so they are beginning . . ." Croÿ, op. cit., vol. I, p. 171.

"They are completely destroying . . ." Luynes, op. cit., vol. XI, p. 448.

"As these rooms . . ." Ibid., vol. XI, p. 449.

"The court has been much afflicted . . ." Croÿ, op. cit., vol. I, p. 171.

"This is serious . . ." Barbier, op. cit., p. 252.

"A necessary reserve . . ." Durant, *The Age of Voltaire*, p. 639.

"Mme de Pompadour who was . . ." Butler, op. cit., p. 929.

"There is no sign that . . ." Croÿ, op. cit., vol. I, p. January 25, 1752.

"Mlle. Poisson . . ." Dufort de Cheverny, Epoque 1, Chapter VI, p. 97.

"A little poem . . ." Marmontel, Part 1, Book IV, p. 145.

"She told me I was born to be . . ." Marmontel, Part 1, Book IV, p. 146.

"Very frightened . . ." Croÿ, op. cit., vol. I, p. 178.

"It is done . . ." Marmontel, op. cit., Part 1, Book V, p. 172.

"But, whether it was . . ." J.-J. Rousseau, *Les Confessions*, vol. VIII, p. 369 ff.

"You were wrong . . ." Cranston, op. cit., p. 266.

"I felt uneasy . . ." Choiseul, *Mémoires*, op. cit., p. 104.

"It is not nice of you . . ." Poulet-Malassis, op. cit., p. 14.

"I have had your Alexandrine . . ." Ibid., pp. 17–18.
"Mme de Pompadour has chased . . ." D'Argenson, op. cit., vol. IV, p. 121.
"I have been paid back . . ." To Choiseul, de Piépape, p. 12.
"The mistress is . . ." D'Argenson, op. cit., vol. IV, p. 100.
"She believes herself . . ." Ibid., vol. IV, p. 100.
"A perpetual combat . . ." Du Hausset, op. cit., p. 82.

Chapter 13

"If Mme de Pompadour . . ." August 22, 1751, Michel, op. cit., p. 121.
"Is killing herself . . ." Kaunitz, *Mémoire*, op. cit., p. 846.
"*Quel vieux conte* . . ." Ibid., p. 449.
"It requires more skill . . ." Ibid., p. 447.
"I found the marquise . . ." Croÿ, op. cit., vol. I, p. 189.
"I have had your *Fanfan* . . ." Poulet-Malassis, op. cit., p. 19.
"There has never been . . ." Ibid., p. 25.
"I wrote at once . . ." Marmontel, op. cit., Part 1, Book IV, p. 147.
"Had an uncertain self-esteem . . ." Ibid., Part 1, Book IV, p. 163.
"It is his heart . . ." Du Hausset, op. cit., p. 69.
"Mme de Pompadour has consented . . ." D'Argenson, op. cit., vol. IV, p. 123.
"With the knowledge . . ." Ibid., vol. IV, p. 124.
"We saw the King . . ." Croÿ, op. cit., vol. I, p. 197.
"The most knowledgeable . . ." Luynes, op. cit., vol. X, p. 438.
"Well-made, quite tall . . ." Michel, op. cit., p. 151.
"To shop for . . ." D'Argenson, op. cit. (Rathery) vol. VII, p. 440.
"It was through the copy . . ." Fleury, op. cit., *Louis XV*, p. 116.
"With very little, if any . . ." *Correspondance des Directeurs*, vol. X, ed. Montaiglon et Guiffrey pp. 438–9.
"Her system . . ." Croÿ, op. cit., vol. I, p. 200.
"Given the impossibility . . ." Antoine, op. cit., p. 658.
"The Dauphin jumped . . ." D'Argenson, op. cit., vol. IV, p. 136.
"Place me under . . ." Du Hausset, op. cit., p. 61.
"As soon as he . . ." Choiseul, *Mémoires*, op. cit., p. 106.
"I received a note . . ." Ibid., p. 109.
"If he had lived . . ." Ibid., p. 110.
"Stab us to the heart . . ." Butler, op. cit., p. 1006.
"All the symptoms . . ." Durant, vol. IX, *The Age of Voltaire*, pp. 86–7.
"The reign of Mme de Pompadour . . ." Levron, *Madame de Pompadour*, pp. 176–7.
"One must admit . . ." Voltaire, *Oeuvres Historiques*, p. 1654.
"With some complacency . . ." Duclos, *Mémoires secrets*, vol. X, p. 113.
"At the King's supper . . ." D'Argenson, op. cit., vol. IV, p. 165.
"The porcelain . . ." Luynes, op. cit., vol. XIII, p. 129.
"They will be seen . . ." *Correspondance des Directeurs*, Nov. 28, 1756.

Chapter 14
"Like an apparition . . ." Croÿ, op. cit., vol. I, p. 208.
"How few people . . ." Ibid., vol. I, p. 209.
"For a salon in the forest . . ." Ibid., vol. I, p. 213.
"There is nothing so pretty . . ." Ibid., vol. I, p. 214.
"He develops a yellow color . . ." Ibid., vol. I, p. 218.
"I do not know . . ." Ibid., vol. I, p. 217.
"The new buildings . . ." Ibid., vol. I, p. 253.
"It was most agreeable . . ." Ibid., vol. I, p. 227.
"The meeting . . ." Barbier, op. cit., p. 260.
"The better one knows . . ." Luynes, op. cit., vol. XIII, p. 430.
"The King is plunged . . ." D'Argenson, op. cit., vol. IV, p. 178.
"I have seen several . . ." Saint-Priest, *Mémoires*, p. 7.
"Very afflicted and unwell . . ." Luynes, op. cit., vol. XIII, p. 283.
"More recherche . . ." Croÿ, op. cit.,vol. I, p. 280.
"I saw her for the first time . . ." Ibid., vol. I, p. 282.
"I have told you . . ." Butler, p. 1063.
"He was seventy years old . . ." Choiseul, *Mémoires*, op. cit., p. 112.
"She had the courage . . ." Butler, p. 1067.
"With excellent qualities . . ." Kaunitz, *Mémoire*, op. cit., p. 447.
"Her rooms will be furnished . . ." Luynes, op. cit., vol. XIII, p. 442.
"The King cannot make . . ." D'Argenson, op. cit., vol. IV, p. 196.
"The King has given me . . ." Marmontel, Part 1, Book V, p. 164.
"Du Barailh . . ." Luynes, op. cit., vol. XIV, p. 372.
"The King felt no gratitude . . ." Butler, op. cit., p. 1067.
"I often fall back . . ." To Choiseul, de Piépape, p. 13.
"To hold its hand . . ." Antoine, op. cit., p. 663.
"My nerves . . ." Fonds Richelieu, Biblio. Victor Cousin, op. cit., fol. 130. Cited
    Lever, p. 351.
"Close and inevitable . . ." Croÿ, op. cit., vol. I, p. 296.

Chapter 15
"Do not lose courage . . ." February 1, 1755, To Choiseul, de Piépape, pp. 13–14.
"The marquise still had . . ." Croÿ, op. cit., vol. I, p. 297.
"Being a woman . . ." Besenval, *Mémoires*, p. 102.
"Once we have shown our teeth . . ." Croÿ, op. cit., vol. I, p. 303.
"If anything were to . . ." April 21, 1755, To Choiseul, de Piépape, p. 17.
"I fear war only . . ." May 12, 1755, To Choiseul, de Piépape, p. 19.
"Bernis liked to caress . . ." Levron, *Choiseul*, p. 91.
"I found her . . ." Bernis, *Mémoires*, op. cit., vol. I, p. 206.
"You know that it is at court . . ." Luynes, op. cit., vol. XIV, p. 201.
"Occasion and motive . . ." Anderson, p. 124.

"Never talk to me . . ." June 21, 1755, To Choiseul, de Piépape, p. 20.
"Well-made . . ." D'Argenson, op. cit., vol. IV, p. 251.
"It is certain . . ." Ibid., vol. IV, p. 225.
"His Majesty proposes . . ." August 3, 1755, To Choiseul, de Piépape, p. 21.
"The marquise pushed the King . . ." D'Argenson, op. cit., vol. V, p. 228.
"They behaved to her . . ." Croÿ, op. cit., vol. I, p. 309.
"No, assuredly . . ." August 15, 1755, Poulet-Malassis, op. cit., p. 130.
"Mme de Pompadour does not want . . ." Nolhac, op. cit., p. 128.
"She herself . . ." Sainte-Beuve, *Causeries du lundi,* vol. II, p. 506.
"If you should seek . . ." Goncourt, E. and J. de, *French Eighteenth-Century Painters,*
    1948, p. 190.
"Moral art . . ." Diderot, *Salons,* vol. I, p. 243.
"Madame, I have often . . ." Nolhac, op. cit., p. 130.
"A trap set . . ." Bernis, *Mémoires,* op. cit., vol. I, p. 223.
"She was not insensible . . ." Duclos, *Mémoires secrets,* vol. VII, p. 268.
"The arbitress . . ." Butler, op. cit., p. 1067.
"I received . . ." Nolhac, op. cit., p. 88.
"Ask him in payment . . ." To Choiseul, de Piépape, p. 15.
"What the Pope has written . . ." To Choiseul, de Piépape, p. 19.
"Will feel the necessity . . ." Ibid., p. 20.
"They talk a great deal . . ." Ibid., vol. IV, p. 250.
"My brother has named . . ." Ibid., vol. IV, p. 250.
"For he hid from her . . ." Choiseul, *Mémoires,* p. 138.
"Whatever difficulty . . ." December 1, 1755, To Choiseul, de Piépape, p. 22.

Chapter 16
"The marquise told . . ." Luynes, op. cit., vol. XV, p. 322.
"She has stopped . . ." Croÿ, op. cit., vol. I, p. 335.
"One goes no longer . . ." Pomeau, *Voltaire et son Temps,* vol. III, p. 310.
"I have made myself . . ." To Choiseul, de Piépape, pp. 22–23.
"Judge at present . . ." Ibid., p. 23.
"She has not the interest . . ." Luynes, op. cit., vol. XV, p. 324.
"Paints very well . . ." Ibid., vol. XV, p. 325.
"The most satisfied . . ." Du Hausset, op. cit., p. 89.
"Glittering with diamonds . . ." Croÿ, op. cit., vol. I, p. 341.
"I have to tell you . . ." Cole, op. cit., p. 196.
"As sparkling as usual . . ." Croÿ, op. cit., vol. I, p. 344.
"She spoke with much force . . ." Ibid., vol. I, p. 354.
"His desk . . ." Ibid., vol. I, p. 345.
"I did not wish . . ." Bernis, *Mémoires,* op. cit., vol. I, p. 206.
"She very often comes . . ." Luynes, op. cit., vol. XV, pp. 337–8.

"Mlle Poisson . . ." Voltaire, *Mémoires*, p. 141.

"The principles . . ." Luynes, op. cit., vol. XV, p. 340.

"Regarded the treaty . . ." Bernis, *Mémoires*, op. cit., vol. I, p. 274.

"You did not expect . . ." Voltaire, *Correspondance*, vol. IV, p. 804.

"Let us spill . . ." Michel, op. cit., pp. 211–12.

"Enchanted at the conclusion . . ." Nolhac, op. cit., p. 154.

"One owes absolutely . . ." Kaunitz, op. cit., p. 154.

"I have not hidden . . ." To Choiseul, de Piépape, p. 25.

"I believe that you are sure . . ." Fonds Richelieu, Biblio. Victor Cousin, folio 182. Cited Lever, p. 356.

"Mme de Pompadour . . ." Cole, op. cit., p. 207.

"What ought to be said . . ." Luynes, op. cit., vol. XV, p. 339.

"I am innocent . . ." McDonogh, *Frederick the Great*, p. 274.

"You cannot doubt . . ." October 10, 1756, Michel, op. cit., p. 208.

"What do you call . . ." September 18, 1756, Poulet-Malassis, op. cit., p. 111.

"You will know about . . ." To Choiseul, de Piépape, p. 174.

"Your sermon . . ." To Choiseul, de Piépape, p. 173.

"I have the greatest . . ." To Choiseul, de Piépape, p. 174.

"Messieurs, you have heard . . ." D'Argenson, op. cit., vol. IV, p. 298.

"You know me well enough . . ." To Choiseul, de Piépape, p. 178.

"It was totally impossible . . ." Antoine, op. cit., p. 709.

"Silent wrath . . ." D'Argenson. op. cit., vol. IV, p. 315.

"At the pinnacle . . ." Croÿ, op. cit., vol. I, pp. 358–9.

"We are in very critical . . ." Antoine, op. cit., p. 711.

"Because I have not . . ." Perrault, *Le Secret*, vol. I, p. 371.

Chapter 17

"Someone has struck me . . ." The accounts of Luynes, Croÿ, and Dufort de Cheverny are consistent.

"She threw herself . . ." Bernis, *Mémoires*, op. cit., vol. I, p. 354.

"Thursday, five o'clock . . ." To Choiseul, de Piépape, op. cit., pp. 179–80.

"There was an endless . . ." Dufort de Cheverny, *Mémoire* 11 Epoque, chapter XV, p. 201.

"They manoeuvred . . ." Ibid., 11 Epoque, chapter XV, p. 205.

"Monsieur, you push me . . ." Choiseul, *Mémoires*, op. cit., p. 140.

"Calm, strong . . ." Croÿ, op. cit., vol. I, p. 366.

"The King said to Mme de Brancas . . ." Dufort de Cheverny, *Mémoires*, 11 Epoque, ch. XV, pp. 206–7.

"She was the god . . ." Choiseul, *Mémoires*, op. cit., p. 140.

"*La fermentation* . . ." Luynes, op. cit., vol. XVI, p. 371.

"All the court . . ." Ibid., vol. XVI, p. 282.

"The King is wonderfully well . . ." To Choiseul, de Piépape, op. cit., pp. 181–2.
"One must agree . . ." Bernis, *Mémoires,* op. cit., vol. I, p. 356.

Chapter 18

"*Vraie ou supposée* . . ." Choiseul, *Mémoires,* p. 140.
"They have done so much . . ." Antoine, op. cit., p. 723.
"Never was a council . . ." Choiseul, *Mémoires,* op. cit., p. 147.
"Alone, standing near the fire . . ." Poulet-Malassis, op. cit., pp. 173–214.
"Public discontent is general . . ." Antoine, op. cit., p. 722.
"Feared and hated . . ." Luynes, vol. XVI, op. cit., pp. 288–9.
"His sagacity . . ." Perrault, op. cit., vol. I, p. 557.
"I esteem the maréchal . . ." Michel, op. cit., p. 240.
"I received only . . ." Croÿ, op. cit., vol. I, p. 387.
"Be silent . . ." To Choiseul, de Piépape, p. 182.
"Pretty little monkey . . ." To Choiseul, de Piépape, p. 182.
"A violent suspicion . . ." Bernis, *Mémoires,* op. cit., vol. I, p. 225.
"Never mind, my dear comte . . ." Michel, op. cit., p. 233.
"I felt all the extent . . ." Dufort de Cheverny, op. cit., 11 Epoque, chapter XV,
    p. 210.
"All those . . ." Durant, *The Age of Voltaire,* op. cit., p. 496.
"I never saw anyone . . ." Choiseul, op. cit., *Mémoires,* op. cit., p. 150.
"Madame Rouillé . . ." Bernis, *Mémoires,* op. cit., vol. I, p. 387.
"I hate to the death . . ." May 29, 1755, Poulet-Malassis, op. cit., p. 112.
"All-powerful . . ." Saint-Priest, op. cit., p. 4.
"Well, well . . ." Bernis, *Mémoires,* op. cit., vol. I, p. 389.
"The King has come out . . ." To Choiseul, de Piépape, op. cit., p. 180.
"Keep in mind the intimate union . . ." Perrault, op. cit., vol. I, p. 389.
"Boldly insinuate . . ." Michel, op. cit., p. 245.
"Their King . . ." Horace Walpole, *Memoirs of King George II,* edited by J. Brooke,
    vol. II, p. 272.
"The fear of an imaginary danger . . ." Choiseul, *Mémoires,* op. cit., p. 134.
"Madame de Pompadour . . ." Valfons, op. cit., pp. 256–7.
"My dear marechal . . ." Bernis, *Mémoires,* op. cit., vol. I, p. 397.
"All Europe was . . ." Ibid., vol. I, p. 398.
"The change of general . . ." Luynes, vol. XVI, p. 297.
"I have always desired . . ." Fonds Richelieu, Biblio. Victor Cousin, folio 149.
    Cited in Lever, p. 358.
"It is the favorite . . ." Goncourt, E. and J. de, *French Eighteenth-Century Painters,*
    p. 80.
"You do not know him . . ." Du Hausset, op. cit., p. 78.
"The story of parlement . . ." Fonds Richelieu, op. cit., folio 164, p. 368.
"My health . . ." September 1, 1757, Poulet-Malassis, op. cit., p. 113.

"I do not think . . ." Fonds Richelieu, Biblio. Victor Cousin, folio 158, p. 360.
"Come back at once . . ." Trench, *George II*, p. 284
"I clearly see . . ." Fonds Richelieu, Biblio. Victor Cousin, folio 161, p. 366.
"Do not like me . . ." Ibid., folio 163, cited in Lever, p. 368.
"I shall tell you a little . . ." Ibid., folio 153, cited in Lever, p. 370.
"Although I am very sure . . ." Michel, op. cit., p. 247.
"If he believed . . ." Bernis, *Mémoires*, op. cit., vol. II, p. 37.
"And so, mon prince . . ." Ibid., op. cit., vol. I, pp. 354–6.
"This was not a battle . . ." Voltaire, *Mémoires*, op. cit., p. 73.
"But, messieurs . . ." Michelet, op. cit., vol. V, p. 402.
"The combined army . . ." Michel, op. cit., p. 250.
"Soubise dit . . ." Bachaumont, op. cit., vol. I, p. 20.
"The gift of my house . . ." Poulet-Malassis, pp. 217–22.
"M. de Soubise . . ." November 28, 1757, Ibid., p. 114.
"I am dying . . ." November 22, 1757, Bernis, *Mémoires*, op. cit., vol. II, p. 141.
"I am upset . . ." Fonds Richelieu, Biblio. Victor Cousin, folio 161, cited in Lever,
    p. 374.
"A man of will-power . . ." Dec. 13, 1757, Bernis, *Mémoires*, op. cit., vol. II, p. 153.
"Not in consternation . . ." Dec. 18, 1757, Bernis, *Mémoires*, op. cit., vol. II, p. 155.
"Leuthen does not . . ." Nolhac, op. cit., p. 241.

Chapter 19

"My opinion . . ." Jan. 6, 1758, Bernis, *Mémoires*, op. cit., vol. II, p. 161.
"The King never spoke . . ." Croÿ, op. cit., vol. I, p. 417.
"All the ministers . . ." Barbier, pp. 275–6.
"A charming young Sultana . . ." Du Hausset, op. cit., p. 79.
"It is right that . . ." Du Hausset, op. cit., p. 79.
"A new mistress . . ." Bernis, *Mémoires*, op. cit., vol. II, p. 72.
"She could have succeeded . . ." Duclos, *Mémoires secrets*, op. cit., vol. VII,
    p. 277.
"The King has named . . ." Michel, op. cit., p. 260.
"I could not obtain . . ." Perrault, op. cit., vol. I, p. 437.
"This courier . . ." Michel, p. 261.
"I received today . . ." Ibid., p. 261.
"Gaiety has got . . ." Croÿ, vol. I, p. 420.
"As badly as . . ." Ibid., vol. I, p. 420.
"The details you send . . ." Michel, op. cit., p. 262.
"He is marvellously well . . ." May 13, 1758, Bernis, *Mémoires*, op. cit., vol. II, p. 228.
"It is impossible . . ." Michel, op. cit., p. 264.
"What can I say . . ." Michel, op. cit., p. 265.
"One must let me . . ." Ibid., p. 265.
"Only a miracle . . ." June 6, 1758, Bernis, *Mémoires*, op. cit., vol. II, p. 238.

"It would be shameful . . ." Michel, op. cit., p. 268.
"I like the King . . ." March 31, 1758, Bernis, *Mémoires,* op. cit., vol. II, p. 198.
"I weep for . . ." Michel, op. cit., p. 274.
"Barbarian . . ." Du Hausset, op. cit., p. 140.
"What humiliation . . ." Michel, op. cit., p. 272.
"Understand how . . ." August 1, 1758, Bernis, *Mémoires,* op. cit., vol. II, p. 256.
"They are still working . . ." Luynes, op. cit., vol. XVI, p. 470.
"I thank you . . ." Poulet-Malassis, op. cit., p. 115.
"This used to be the grove of Friendship . . ." Luynes, op. cit., vol. XVII, p. 113.
"No more commerce . . ."August 20, 1758, Bernis, *Mémoires,* op. cit., vol. II,
        pp. 258–9.
"It is with great regret . . ." Poulet-Malassis, op. cit., p. 140.
"I let you know . . ." Sept. 19, 1758, Bernis, *Mémoires,* op. cit., vol. II, p. 274.
"I am distressed . . ." Michel, op. cit., p. 282.
"I owe it to you . . ." October 10, 1758, Bernis, *Mémoires,* op. cit., vol. II, p. 300.
"To separate at the proper time . . ." Ibid., p. 441.
"Handsome cardinal . . ." Ibid., vol. I, p. 94.
"The repeated instances . . ." Dec. 13, 1758, Ibid., vol. II, pp. 346–7.
"Partly from thoughtlessness . . ." Ibid., vol. I, p. 75.
"But I reflect . . ." Du Hausset, op. cit., p. 79.

Chapter 20

"Rather short . . ." Von Gleichen, *Souvenirs,* pp. 61–2.
"Le cul . . ." Choiseul to Voltaire, December 20, 1759. Perrault, op. cit., vol. I,
        p. 394.
"More in command . . ." Croÿ, op. cit., vol. I, p. 434.
"Berryer was on very good terms . . ." Ibid., vol. I, pp. 434–5.
"Mme de Pompadour asked me . . ." Michel, op. cit., p. 300.
"You would be mistaken . . ." Ibid., p. 347.
"If one must . . ." Ibid., p. 301.
"My beautiful Queen . . ." Ibid., pp. 303–4.
"Enter France . . ." Ibid., p. 304.
"Your feeble monarch . . ." Voltaire, op. cit., vol. V, p. 1347, letter 5494, no. 3.
"When I was determined . . ." Ibid., vol. V, p. 1375, no. 4.
"You are in truth . . ." February 6, 1759, Poulet-Malassis, op. cit., p. 142.
"Do not worry about anything . . ." Croÿ, op. cit., vol. I, p. 450.
"Be patient . . ." Ibid., vol. I, p. 452.
"This victory . . ." Perrault, op. cit., vol. I, p. 473.
"This can only come . . ." Ibid., vol. I, p. 473.
"The battle has given me . . ." May 6, 1759, Poulet-Malassis, op. cit., p. 116.
"Radical change . . ." Antoine, op. cit., p. 610.
"Lackeys, horse . . ." Durant, op. cit., vol. X, p. 56.

"The hour has sounded . . ." Antoine, op. cit., p. 791.
"The villains will not wait . . ." Poulet-Malassis, op. cit., p. 138.
"You are right . . ." Ibid., p. 137.
"In gathering dark . . ." Weigley, *The Age of Battles*, p. 228.
"What can I tell you . . ." Michel, op. cit., p. 310.
"Philosophical pornography . . . Darnton, *The Forbidden Bestsellers of Prerevolution-ary France*, New York, 1996, passim.
"For a year . . ." Antoine, op. cit., p. 791.
"Unable to do without . . ." Croÿ, op. cit., vol. I, p. 479.
"A second Queen . . ." Dumont-Wilden, *La Vie* . . . pp. 72–73.
"Downstairs . . ." Marmontel, Part 1, Book V, p. 219.
"Only one thing . . ." Ibid., Part 1, Book VI, p. 219.

Chapter 21
"Where favor replaced merit . . ." Dumont-Wilden, op. cit., p. 85.
"Madame had serious concerns . . ." Du Hausset, op. cit., p. 168.
"She was young . . ." Casanova, op. cit., vol. II, p. 474.
"Although a very handsome man . . ." Castries, pp. 299–300.
"I shall not say . . ." Du Hausset, op. cit., p. 167.
"My dear friend . . ." Michel, op. cit., p. 318.
"The court was furious . . ." Croÿ, op. cit., vol. I, p. 492.
"Oh! As for the little . . ." Michel, op. cit., p. 330.
"Everything you tell me . . ." Poulet-Malassis, op. cit., p. 148.
"She still likes you . . ." Marmontel, Part 1, Book VII, p. 243.
"He might have the misfortune . . ." Choiseul, *Mémoires*, op. cit., p. 176.
"You are going to agree at once . . ." Poulet-Malassis, op. cit., p. 146.
"To have a copy . . ." Voltaire, *Correspondance,* vol. V, p. 1097.
"Because I have known . . ." Ibid., vol. V, p. 1097.
"Madame, I have observed . . ." Michel, op. cit., p. 305.
"Everyone is persuaded . . ." Antoine, op. cit., p. 608.
"I leave to . . ." Poulet-Malassis, op. cit., p. 222.
"As a Christian . . ." Antoine, op. cit., p. 783.
"Honorable men . . ." Michel, op. cit., p. 330.
"Probity is often . . ." Ibid., pp. 330–1.
"The gossip in the public . . ." Du Hausset, op. cit., p. 167.
"There has not been . . ." Michel, op. cit., p. 331.
"We are well aware . . ." Ibid., p. 334.
"The continual hunts . . ." Ibid., p. 334.
"M. de Fitzjames . . ." Poulet-Malassis, op. cit., p. 153.
"Honorable men . . ." Michel, op. cit., p. 334.
"Mme de Pompadour abandons . . ." Croÿ, vol. I, p. 514.
"This is moral painting . . ." Diderot, *Salons,* vol. II, p. 1761.

Chapter 22

"Behold them lost . . ." Perrault, op. cit., vol. I, p. 539.
"Following appearances . . ." Croÿ, op. cit., vol. II, p. 28.
"The public respects . . ." Perrault, op. cit., vol. I, p. 540.
"I saw very clearly . . ." Michel, op. cit., p. 313.
"One must agree . . ." Du Hausset, op. cit., p. 169.
"In the chapel . . ." Ibid., p. 139.
"A premature death . . ." Bernis, *Mémoires*, op. cit., vol. II, p. 79.
"The zeal and talents . . ." August 20, 1762, Poulet-Malassis, op. cit., p. 154.
"You talk of fatigue . . ." Michel, op. cit., pp. 335–6.
"The peace we have made . . ." Nolhac, op. cit., p. 333.
"Entered the war . . ." Kennett, *The French Armies* . . . p. 1X.
"It is at last finished . . ." Michel, op. cit., pp. 344–5.
"It is very soon . . ." Perrault, op. cit., vol. I, p. 561.
"Little seen . . .", Croÿ, op. cit., vol. II, p. 96.
"Oh! The fine statue . . ." Bachaumont, op. cit., vol. I, p. 70.
"Told the provost . . ." Croÿ, op. cit., vol. II, p. 93.
"Illustrious protectress . . ." Bachaumont, op. cit., vol. I, p. 81.
"The sieur d'Eon . . ." Perrault, op. cit., vol. II, p. 23.
"Produced . . ." Bachaumont, op. cit., vol. I, p. 82.
"Not by the imposition . . ." Antoine, op. cit., pp. 798–9.
"A new order . . ." Ibid., p. 799.
"She had the goodness . . ." Marmontel, Part 1, Book VII, p. 251.
"I owe witness . . ." Ibid., Part 1, Book VII, pp. 252–3.
"In general all persecution is odious . . ." Antoine, op. cit., p. 790.

Chapter 23

"Given me as a present . . ." Rouart, *Le Cardinal* . . . pp. 189–90.
"This peace . . ." Michel, op. cit., p. 349.
"Too greedy for profit . . ." Ibid., p. 351.
"I found her beautiful . . ." Ségur, *Le Royaume* . . . p. 164.
"Her hands . . ." Goncourt, E. and J. de, op. cit., p. 406.
"We are in a state . . ." Mme du Deffand to Voltaire, March 7, 1764. Lettres, op. cit., pp. 57–8.
"The anxiety redoubled . . ." Croÿ, op. cit., vol. II, p. 133.
"There was the greatest commotion . . ." Ibid.
"Mme de Pompadour is much better . . ." Mme du Deffand to Voltaire, March 14. op. cit., p. 60.
"Mme de Pompadour has coughed . . ." Nolhac, op. cit., p. 337.
"My anxieties do not lessen . . ." Antoine, op. cit., p. 823.
"She showed much courage . . ." Croÿ, op. cit., vol. II, p. 137.

"She is dying . . ." Michel, op. cit., p. 395.

"My wish is to give . . ." Poulet-Malassis, op. cit., pp. 223–4.

"In general she arranged . . ." Croÿ, vol. II, p. 138.

"It is coming . . ." Bachaumont, op. cit., vol. I, p. 122.

"I know you are careful . . ." Michel, op. cit., p. 356.

"A moment . . ." Bachaumont, op. cit., vol. I, p. 122.

"I saw two men . . ." Dufort de Cheverny, 11 Epoque, chapter XXII, pp. 333–4.

"Only I, Sénac . . ." Michel, op. cit., p. 357.

"My preceding letter . . ." Michel, op. cit., p. 357.

"It is not possible . . ." Perrault, op. cit., vol. II, p. 81.

"He maintained a silence . . ." Dufort de Cheverny, 11 Epoque, chapter XXII, pp. 334–5.

"I receive the body . . ." Michel, op. cit., p. 359.

"Very affected . . ." Croÿ, op. cit., vol. II, p. 149.

"Now the bows . . ." Dufort de Cheverny, 11 Epoque, chapter XXII, p. 334.

"There is no more question . . ." Autour d'un Ministre, op. cit., p. 256.

"We have lost . . ." Michel, op. cit., p. 357.

"She had the great art . . ." Dufort de Cheverny, 11 Epoque, chapter XXII, p. 331.

"In general she was regretted . . ." Croÿ, op. cit., vol. II, p. 138.

"Here lies one . . ." Bachaumont, op. cit., vol. I, pp. 114–5.

"Mme de Pompadour . . ." Diderot, Salons, op. cit., vol. II, p. 67.

"It is indeed ridiculous . . ." Voltaire, op. cit., vol. VII, p. 695.

"Although Mme de Pompadour . . ." Ibid., vol. VII, p. 669.

"I believe, Monsieur . . ." Ibid., vol. VII, p. 670.

"Have you grieved . . ." Ibid., vol. VII, p. 690.

Afterword

"Kaunitz made her mistress . . ." Duclos, op. cit., vol. VII, p. 277.

"It was the patience . . ." Besenval, op. cit., p. 102.

"He had all the qualities . . ." Frederick II, Oeuvres, vol. XXIII, p. 281.

"In her heart . . ." Voltaire, Correspondence, vol. VII, p. 690.

What happened to:

"A mask of bronze . . ." Croÿ, op. cit., vol. III, p. 104.

"You have put on weight . . ." Perrault, op. cit., vol. III, p. 46.

"Used the intoxication . . ." Manceron, The French Revolution, vol. IV, p. 54.

"As though giving an audience . . ." Ibid., vol. IV, p. 58.

"If you knew how zealously . . ." Marmontel, op. cit., Book VIII, p. 275.

BIBLIOGRAPHY

N.B.: The letters of Madame de Pompadour (of which several hundred are known) are scattered in various collections. In 1878 J.-A. Poulet-Malassis published forty-three letters to her father and brother, five to Pâris-Duverney, eighteen to the duc d'Aiguillon, and fifteen to the comtesse de Lutzelbourg. In 1917 Général de Piépape published, in the *Revue de l'Histoire de Versailles*, extracts from her letters to the duc de Choiseul. Twenty letters to Bertin reside in the Cabinet des Manuscrits de la Bibliothèque Nationale, Département des Manuscrits (Nouvelles Acquisitions Françaises, 6498, fol. 224–271). Pierre de Nolhac also published one letter to Bertin, hitherto unpublished, in *Madame de Pompadour et la Politique*, as well as notes to the duc de Nivernais and the duc de Mirepoix, which reside in the former Morrison Collection at the British Museum, and letters to the comte de Clermont, sixteen of which are in the Archives de la Guerre. Eighty-five letters or notes from the marquise to the comte d'Argenson can be found in *Autour d'un Ministre de Louis XV*, edited by the marquis d'Argenson in 1923. Letters to Pâris-Duverney concerning the *Ecole Militaire* are in the Archives Nationales in Paris (carton K149). Evelyne Lever has reclassified letters to the duc de Richelieu, deposited in the Fonds Richelieu at the Bibliothèque Victor-Cousin at the Sorbonne. Ludovic Michel published many of the letters mentioned above and other material in *Prestigieuse Marquise de Pompadour*, published in 1972. (The chapter dedicated to "sources et orientation bibliographique" found in Danielle Gallet's biography, *Madame de Pompadour ou le Pouvoir Féminin*, published in 1985, is a model of erudition and clarity.)

Contemporary Sources

Argenson, le marquis d'., ed. *Autour d'un Ministre de Louis XV: Lettres Intimes Inédites*. Paris, 1923.

Argenson, René-Louis de Voyer de Paulmy, marquis d'. *Mémoires et Journal Inédit*. Edited by M. le marquis d'Argenson. Paris, 1857–8.

Bachaumont, Louis P. de. *Mémoires Secrets*. Paris, 1809.

Barbier, E. J. F. *Journal d'un Bourgeois sous le Règne de Louis XV.* Edited by Ph. Bernard. Paris, Union Générale d'Editions, 1963.

Bernis, F.-J. Pierre de. *Mémoires.* Edition *Mercure de France.* Preface by J.-M. Rouart. Notes by P. Bonnet. Paris, 1980 and 1986.

Bernis, F.-J. Pierre de. *Mémoires et Lettres.* Edited by F. Masson. 2 vols. Paris, 1878.

Besenval, baron de. *Mémoires sur la Cour de France.* Edited by G. de Diesbach. Paris, 1987.

Casanova, Giovanni Giacomo, *Histoire de Ma Vie.* Edited by F. Lacassin. 3 vols., Bouquins dirigés G. Schoeller, Paris, 1960.

Choiseul, Etienne-François de Stainville, duc de. *Mémoires 1719–1785.* Edition *Mercure de France.* Preface by J.-P. Guicciardi. Notes by P. Bonnet. Paris, 1982.

Correspondance des Directeurs de l'Académie de France à Rome avec les Surintendants des Bâtiments, ed. M. A. Montaiglon et J. Guiffrey 18 vols. Paris 1887–1912.

Croÿ, Emmanuel, duc de. *Journal Inédit.* Edited by Vicomte de Grouchy and P. Cottin. 4 vols. Paris, 1906–7.

Diderot, Denis. *Salons.* Edited by Séznec et Adhémar. 3 vols. Oxford, 1975.

Deffand, marquise du. *Correspondance Complète avec Ses Amis.* Edited by A. de Lescure. 2 vols. Paris, 1865.

Duclos, C.-P. *Mémoires Secrets sur les Règnes de Louis XV et de Louis XIV.* Edited by Petitot et Monmerqué. 2 vols. Paris, 1829.

Dufort de Cheverny, Jean-Nicolas. *Mémoires sur les Règnes de Louis XV et Louis XVI et sur la Révolution.* Edited by J. P. Guicciardi. Paris, 1990.

Flammermont, Jules. *Correspondance des Agents Diplomatiques Etrangers en France avant la Révolution.* Paris, 1896.

Frederick II *Oeuvres,* ed. J. D. Preuss, Berlin, 1846–57.

Gleichen, Baron von. *Denkwürdigkeiten des Barons.* Leipzig, 1847.

Grimm, Frédéric Melchior. *Correspondance littéraire.* Edited by M. Tourneux. Paris, 1877–82.

Hausset, Mme du. *Mémoires sur Louis XV et Madame de Pompadour.* Edition *Mercure de France.* Notes by J.-P. Guicciardi. Paris, 1985.

Hénault, President, *Mémoires.* Edited by Baron de Vigan. Paris, 1855.

Kaunitz-Rietburg, count von. *Mémoire sur la Cour de France.* 1752. ed. de Dresnay. Paris, 1960.

Kaunitz-Rietburg, count von. *Correspondance Secrète avec le Baron Ignaz Koch.* Paris, 1899.

Leroy, Ch.-Georges. *Portraits de Louis XV et Mme de Pompadour.* Paris, 1802.

Luynes, Charles Philippe d'Albert, duc de. *Mémoires sur la Cour de Louis XV.* Edited by L. Dussieux et E. Soulié. 17 vols. Paris, 1860–65.

Marmontel, Jean-François. *Mémoires.* Edition *Mercure de France.* Edited by J.-P. Guicciardi. Paris, 1999.

Marville, Feydeau de. *Lettres au Ministre Maurepas.* Edited by A. de Boislisle. 3 vols. Paris, 1896.

Pompadour, marquise de. *Correspondance avec Son Père, Son Frère...*, ed. by J.-A. Poulet-Malassis. Paris, 1878.

Pompadour, marquise de. *Lettres à Choiseul.* Edited by de Piépape *Revue de l'Histoire de Versailles.* Versailles, 1917.

Recueil Clairambault, ed. E. Raunié, 10 vols. Paris, 1879–84.

Richelieu, maréchal-duc de. *Mémoires.* Edited by M. F. Barrière. Paris, 1869.

Romanciers du XVIII Siècle. Editors of La Pléiàde. Paris 1965.

Rousseau, J.-J. *Correspondance Complète.* Edited by R. A. Leigh. Geneva, 1965.

Saint-Priest, comte de. *Mémoires.* Edited by de Barante. Paris, 1929.

Valfons, marquis de. *Souvenirs.* Edited by A. de Sebourg. Paris, 1906.

Voltaire. *Correspondance.* Edited by T. Bestermann. 13 vols. Editors of La Pléiade. Paris, 1977–1992.

Voltaire. *Mémoires pour Servir à la Vie.* Introduction by Jacqueline Hellegouarc'h. Paris, 1998.

Voltaire. *Oeuvres historiques.* Edited by R. Pomeau. Editors of La Pléiade, Paris, 1959.

Walpole, Horace. *Memoirs of the last ten years of the reign of George II.* Edited by John Brooke. New Haven, 1985.

Other Works

Anderson, Fred. *The Crucible of War.* New York, 2000.

Antoine, Michel. *Louis XV.* Paris, 1989.

Bailey, Colin B. *The Loves of the Gods.* Fort Worth, TX, 1992.

Braham, Alan. *The Architecture of the French Enlightenment.* California, 1980.

Butler, Rohan. *Choiseul.* vol. 1, *Father and Son,* Oxford, 1980.

Campardon, Emile. *Madame de Pompadour et la Cour de Louis XV.* Paris, 1867.

Castries, duc de. *La Pompadour.* Paris, 1983.

Cole, Hubert. *First Gentleman of the Bedchamber.* New York, 1965.

Cordey, Jean. *Inventaire des Biens de Mme de Pompadour Rédigé après son Décès.* Paris, 1939.

Cranston, Maurice, Jean-Jacques. *The Early Life of Jean-Jacques Rousseau, 1712–54.* New York, 1983.

Cravieri, Benedetta. *Madame du Deffand and Her World.* Boston, 1994.

Crow, Thomas E. *Painters and Public Life in Eighteenth-Century Paris.* Yale, 1985.

Darnton, Robert. *The Forbidden Best-Sellers of Pre-Revolutionary France.* New York, 1996.

Delorme, Eleanor P. *Garden Pavillions and the 18th Century French Court.* Woodbridge, 1996.

Desprat, J.-P. *Le Cardinal de Bernis.* Paris, 2000.

Dumont-Wilden, L. *La Vie de Charles-Joseph de Ligne.* Paris, 1927.

Durand, Yves. *Les Fermiers Généraux au XVIIIème siècle.* Paris, 1996.

Durant, Will and Ariel. *The Story of Civilization.* vol. IX and vol. X. New York, 1967.

Egret, Jean, *Louis XV et l'Opposition Parlementaire.* Paris, 1970.

Fleury, comte M. *Louis XV Intime.* Paris, 1899.

Fromageot, P. "L'Enfance de Mme de Pompadour" and "La Mort et les Obsèques de Mme de Pompadour," in *Revue de l'Histoire de Versailles,* 1902.

Gallet, Danielle. *Madame de Pompadour ou le Pouvoir Féminin.* Paris, 1985.

Gallet, Danielle, et al. *Madame de Pompadour et la Floraison des Arts.* Montreal, 1988.

Gallet, Danielle. *"Madame de Pompadour et l'Appartement d'en bas au Château de Versailles."* *Gazette des Beaux-Arts.* Paris, 1991.

Gaxotte, Pierre. *Le Siècle de Louis XV,* Paris, 1998.

Goncourt, Edmond and Jules de. *French Eighteenth-Century Painters.* Ithaca, NY, 1948.

———. *Les maîtresses de Louis XV.* Paris, 1860.

Goodman, Elise. *The Portraits of Madame de Pompadour.* Berkeley, CA, 2000.

Hervey, Augustus. *The Journal.* Edited by D. Erskine. London, 1953.

Kaiser, Thomas E. "Madame de Pompadour and the Theatres of Power." *French Historical Studies,* Fall 1996, vol. 19, no. 4.

Kalnein, Wend von. *Architecture in France in the Eighteenth Century.* New Haven: Yale University Press, 1995.

Kennett, Lee B. *The French Armies in the Seven Years' War.* Durham, NC, 1967.

Leroi, J.-A. *Curiosités Historiques.* Paris, 1864.

Lever, Evelyne. *Madame de Pompadour.* Paris, 2000.

Levey, Michael. *Painting and Sculpture in France, 1700–89.* New Haven: Yale University Press, 1993.

Levron, J. *Choiseul, un Sceptique au Pouvoir.* Paris, 1976.

———. *Madame de Pompadour: L'Amour et la Politique.* Paris, 1977.

Manceron, Claude. *The French Revolution.* vol. IV. New York, 1983.

Marquiset, A. *Le Marquis de Marigny.* Paris, 1918.

Maurepas, Arnaud de, and Brayard Florent. *Les Français Vus par Eux-mêmes.* Paris, 1996.

McDonogh, Giles. *Frederick the Great.* New York, 2000.

Merrick, Jeffrey W., *The Desacralization of the French Monarchy in the Eighteenth Century.* Baton Rouge, LA, 1990.

Michel, Ludovic. *Prestigieuse Marquise de Pompadour.* Paris, 1972.

Mitford, Nancy. *Madame de Pompadour.* London, 1954.

Nicolle, Jean. *Madame de Pompadour et la Société de Son Temps.* Paris, 1980.

Nolhac, Pierre de. *Louis XV et Madame de Pompadour.* Paris, 1903.

———. *Madame de Pompadour et la Politique.* Paris, 1928.

Orieux, Jean. *Voltaire.* Paris, 1966.

Perrault, Giles. *Le Secret du Roi.* 3 vols. Paris, 1992, 1993, 1996.

Pichon, Baron Jérôme. *Mélanges des Bibliophiles français.* 1856.

Pomeau, René, ed. *Voltaire et Son Temps.* 3 vols., Oxford, 1985–1995.

Posner, Donald, "Madame de Pompadour as a Patron of the Visual Arts," *Arts Bulletin.* (March 1990.)

Rouart, Jean-Marie. *Bernis, le Cardinal des Plaisirs.* Paris, 1998.

Sainte-Beuve, A. *Causeries du Lundi.* Paris, 1852–62.

Salmon, Xavier, et al. *Madame de Pompadour et les arts.* Paris, 2002.

Ségur, P. de. *Le Royaume de la Rue Saint-Honoré,* Paris, 1925.

Solnon, Jean-François. *La Cour de France.* Paris, 1987.

Stein, Perrin. "The Harem Imagery at Bellevue," *Gazette des Beaux-Arts* (Jan. 1994).

Stryienski, Casimir. *Mesdames de France, Filles de Louis XV.* Paris, 1911.

Toth, K. *Woman and Rococo in France.* London, 1931.

Trench, C. Chevenix. *George II.* London, 1973.

Verlet, Pierre. *Le Château de Versailles.* Paris, 1985.

Walker, K. K. "Madame de Pompadour and the Iconography of Friendship." *Arts Bulletin* (September, 1968).

Weigley, Russell F. *The Age of Battles: The Quest for Decisive Warfare from Breitenfeld to Waterloo.* Indiana, 1991.

Woodbridge, John D. *Revolt in Prerevolutionary France: The Prince de Conti's Conspiracy Against Louis XV.* Baltimore, 1995.

Index